INSIGHT AND
ILLUSION

Anthem Studies in Wittgenstein

Anthem Studies in Wittgenstein publishes new and classic works on Wittgenstein and Wittgensteinian philosophy. This book series aims to bring Wittgenstein's thought into the mainstream by highlighting its relevance to 21st-century concerns. Titles include original monographs, themed edited volumes, forgotten classics, biographical works and books intended to introduce Wittgenstein to the general public. The series is published in association with the British Wittgenstein Society.

Anthem Studies in Wittgenstein sets out to put in place whatever measures may emerge as necessary in order to carry out the editorial selection process purely on merit and to counter bias on the basis of gender, race, ethnicity, religion, sexual orientation and other characteristics protected by law. These measures include subscribing to the British Philosophical Association/Society for Women in Philosophy (UK) Good Practice Scheme.

Series Editor

Constantine Sandis – University of Hertfordshire, UK

Insight and Illusion

Themes in the Philosophy of Wittgenstein

Third Edition

P. M. S. HACKER

With a new foreword by Constantine Sandis

ANTHEM PRESS

Anthem Press
An imprint of Wimbledon Publishing Company
www.anthempress.com

This edition first published in UK and USA 2021
by ANTHEM PRESS
75–76 Blackfriars Road, London SE1 8HA, UK
or PO Box 9779, London SW19 7ZG, UK
and
244 Madison Ave #116, New York, NY 10016, USA

The first edition of the book was published in 1989

This is a reprint of the revised and corrected 1997 edition

Copyright © P.M.S. Hacker 2021

Foreword copyright © Constantine Sandis 2021

The author asserts the moral right to be identified as the author of this work.

All rights reserved. Without limiting the rights under copyright reserved above,
no part of this publication may be reproduced, stored or introduced into
a retrieval system, or transmitted, in any form or by any means
(electronic, mechanical, photocopying, recording or otherwise),
without the prior written permission of both the copyright
owner and the above publisher of this book.

British Library Cataloguing-in-Publication Data
A catalogue record for this book is available from the British Library.

ISBN-13: 978-1-78527-683-5 (Hbk)
ISBN-10: 1-78527-683-2 (Hbk)
ISBN-13: 978-1-78527-686-6 (Pbk)
ISBN-10: 1-78527-686-7 (Pbk)

This title is also available as an e-book.

FOR MY PARENTS

CONTENTS

FOREWORD	xi
PREFACE TO THE REVISED EDITION	xv
PREFACE TO THE FIRST EDITION	xix
LIST OF ABBREVIATIONS	xxiii

I. WITTGENSTEIN'S EARLY CONCEPTION OF PHILOSOPHY

1. Background	1
2. The 'Preliminary' on Philosophy	12
3. Philosophy and Illusion	15
4. Philosophy as Critique and as Analysis	22

II. THE DIALOGUE WITH FREGE AND RUSSELL

1. Agreements and Disagreements	28
2. The *Grundgedanke* of the *Tractatus*	34
3. The Laws of Logic	42
4. A Prelude to Conventionalism	50

III. MEANING, METAPHYSICS, AND THE MIND

1. The Picture Theory of Meaning	56
2. The Metaphysics of the *Tractatus*	65
3. Connecting Language with Reality: the role of the mind	73

IV. EMPIRICAL REALISM AND TRANSCENDENTAL SOLIPSISM

1. The Self of Solipsism	81
2. 'I am my World'	90
3. 'The limits of language means the limits of my world'	100
4. Later Years	104

V. DISINTEGRATION AND RECONSTRUCTION

1. The Colour-Exclusion Problem	108
2. Dismantling the *Tractatus*	113
3. The Brouwer Lecture	120

	4. Moving off in Fresh Directions	128
	5. The Vienna Circle and Wittgenstein's Principle of Verification	134
VI.	**WITTGENSTEIN'S LATER CONCEPTION OF PHILOSOPHY**	
	1. A Kink in the Evolution of Philosophy	146
	2. A Cure for the Sickness of the Understanding	151
	3. Philosophy, Science, and Description	156
	4. Philosophy and Ordinary Language	161
	5. The Phenomenology and Sources of Philosophical Illusion	165
	6. Systematic Philosophy	175
VII.	**METAPHYSICS AS THE SHADOW OF GRAMMAR**	
	1. Grammar	179
	2. The Autonomy of Grammar	185
	3. Grammar and Metaphysics	193
	4. A Note on Kant and Wittgenstein	206
VIII.	**THE REFUTATION OF SOLIPSISM**	
	1. Introduction	215
	2. From Transcendental Solipsism to Methodological Solipsism	218
	3. The Solipsist's Predicament: a restatement and second diagnosis	226
	4. The Refutation	229
IX.	**PRIVATE LINGUISTS AND PUBLIC SPEAKERS**	
	1. A Disease of the Intellect	245
	2. Following Rules	247
	3. Philosophical Investigations, §243	251
	4. The Private Language	255
	5. The Epistemology of the Private Linguist	261
	6. Wittgenstein's Criticism of the Private Language	264
	7. 'Only I Know' and 'Only I have'	272
X.	**'A CLOUD OF PHILOSOPHY CONDENSED INTO A DROP OF GRAMMAR'**	
	1. Can one know that one is in pain?	276
	2. Self-consciousness: the overthrow of the Cartesian picture	278
	3. The 'Inner' and the 'Outer'	284
	4. Experience and its Natural Expression	291
	5. Avowals and Descriptions	297
	6. Objections and Deflections	302

XI. CRITERIA, REALISM AND ANTI-REALISM

1. The Origins of the Idea 307
2. Plotting the Contour-lines 310
3. Further Complications 318
4. Red Herrings: realism and anti-realism 322

INDEX 337

FOREWORD

Hacker's Guide to Wittgenstein's Treasure

Constantine Sandis

> Philosophers hunt for the map of Treasure Island in order to find the treasure, and they do not realise that the treasure is the map!
> – P. M. S. Hacker, *Insight and Illusion*, p. 149

I first got my undergraduate hands on *Insight and Illusion* in its 1997 Thoemmes Press reprint of the revised second edition, subtitled *Themes in the Philosophy of Wittgenstein*. While, at the time, I was a finalist at St Anne's College, Oxford, it was owing to sheer providence that I had been farmed out to Peter Hacker at St John's for my Philosophy of Mind tutorials. These sessions constituted not only my introduction to Wittgenstein, but also to the work of Elizabeth Anscombe, J. L. Austin, Arthur W. Collins, Anthony Kenny, Norman Malcolm, Gilbert Ryle, G. H. von Wright and A. R. White. Just as my degree (and, with it, also my interest in philosophy) was coming to an end, Peter opened up a whole new world to me. The door to that world was Wittgenstein's philosophy and the key to it was *Insight and Illusion*.

It is customary to say of books one adored as a student that they got one through college but, such was the hostility towards Wittgenstein's philosophy at the time within UK academia, that it would be closer to the truth to say that *Insight and Illusion* almost stood in the way of my degree. Undaunted, I returned to it several times over the years to explore philosophy until I arrived where I had begun, knowing the place for the first time.[1]

Insight and Illusion was the first single-authored book to cover all phases of Wittgenstein's life and thought.[2] The portable guide takes the

---

[1] See T. S. Eliot, 'Little Gidding', Four Quartets, IV, lines 239–43, quoted by Hacker on p. 244 of this volume.

[2] Its 1972 edition, entitled Insight and Illusion: Wittgenstein on Philosophy and the Metaphysics of Experience, offers an interpretation of Wittgenstein that is considerably more Kantian than the one Hacker replaced it with in its second edition in 1986, and which has remained constant throughout his work ever since. Readers curious about the differences between the two editions will want to read Hacker's introduction to the second edition, reprinted at the beginning of this volume.

reader through the major themes and concepts in Wittgenstein's works. In the name of exhaustiveness, these include the so-called picture theory of meaning; the say/show distinction; the principle of verification; antimetaphysics; anti-scientism; tautologies; the nature of mathematical propositions; ordinary language and nonsense; the law of the excluded middle; the Augustinian picture of language; knowledge and certainty; explanation and understanding; volition and the will; the relation of meaning to use; ostensive definition; ownership of experience; the first-person pronoun; the inner/outer; philosophical psychology; antisolipsism; forms of life; the so-called private language argument; the autonomy of grammar; language games; and rule-following.

In so doing, Hacker gives us a picture of Wittgenstein's intellectual development: from his early conception of philosophy (influenced by thinkers as varied as the likes of Schopenhauer, Hertz, Boltzmann, Frege and Russell), through the 'middle period', which began with his return to philosophy in 1929, to his later work—of which Hacker takes the *Philosophical Investigations* to be his masterpiece—thereby devoting far less attention to Wittgenstein's very final writings (published as *On Certainty* and *Remarks on Colour*).

The final decades of the twentieth century have seen the emergence of several other single-volume introductions to Wittgenstein's body of work. Those in English included Kenny (1973), Ayer (1980) and Grayling (1988). The past half-century has seen the rise of new ideas, interpretations and debates, many of them benefitting from the electronic availability of his entire *Nachlass*, in addition to the 2005 publication of *The Big Typescript*, as well as various editions of Wittgenstein's Cambridge lectures from 1930 onwards. These diverse (and sometimes *competing*) interpretations of Wittgenstein include Hacker's own (now also in revised edition) monumental four-volume analytical commentary on the *Philosophical Investigations* (the first two volumes of which were co-written with Gordon Baker), as well as the resolute 'New Wittgenstein' readings of the *Tractatus* (largely inspired by the Austrian's reception in the United States),[3] and the 'Third Wittgenstein' of the post-*Investigations* years, whose focus on *On Certainty* has breathed new life into Wittgenstein studies in the form of 'hinge epistemology'.[4]

---

[3] For Hacker's response to alternative conceptions of the Tractatus, see 'Was he Trying to Whistle It?', published as the sole 'dissenting voice' in Crary and Read (2000: 353–88).

[4] See Moyal-Sharrock (2004) and Colliva and Moyal-Sharrock (2017).

Recent introductions that capture some of these aspects include Schroeder (2006), Kanterian (2007), Tejedor (2011) and Child (2011). While Wittgenstein studies have come a long way since 1972, *Insight and Illusion* remains the cornerstone of all subsequent commentary, anticipating numerous contemporary exegetical concerns and offering a clear, coherent and robust reading of Wittgenstein, which stands the test of time. J. L. Austin famously said of ordinary language that 'it is not the last word: in principle it can everywhere be supplemented and improved upon and superseded. Only remember, it is the first word' (Austin 1961: 133), Likewise, *Insight and Illusion* may not be the last word on Wittgenstein's œuvre, but it is the first. As Wittgenstein once again returns to mainstream philosophy, I cannot imagine a better time for the reissue of Peter Hacker's first masterpiece.

Constantine Sandis
Ely, August 2020

References

Austin, J. L. (1961), *Philosophical Papers*. Oxford: Oxford University Press.
Ayer, A. J. (1980), *Wittgenstein*. London: Penguin.
Child, W. (2011), *Wittgenstein*. London: Routledge.
Colliva, A., and Moyal-Sharrock, D. (2017), *Hinge Epistemology*. Leiden: Brill.
Crary, A., and Read, R. (2000), *The New Wittgenstein*. London: Routledge.
Grayling, A. C. (1988), *Wittgenstein*, Oxford: Oxford University Press.
Hacker, P. M. S. (1972), *Insight and Illusion: Wittgenstein on Philosophy and the Metaphysics of Experience*. Oxford: Oxford University Press.
———. (1986), *Insight and Illusion: Themes in the Philosophy of Wittgenstein*. Oxford: Clarendon Press.
Kanterian, E. (2007), *Ludwig Wittgenstein*. London: Reaktion Books.
Kenny, A. J. P. (1973), *Wittgenstein*. London: Penguin.
Moyal-Sharrock, D.-M. (ed.) (2004), *The Third Wittgenstein: The Post Investigations Works*. London: Ashgate.
Schroeder, S. (2006), *Wittgenstein*. Bristol: Polity Press.
Tejedor, C. (2011), *Starting with Wittgenstein*. London: Bloomsbury.
Wittgenstein, L. (1921), Wittgenstein, L. ([1921] 1961), *Tractatus Logico-Philosophicus*, revised trans. D. F. Pears and B. F. McGuiness. London: Routledge.

———. Wittgenstein, L. ([1953] 2009), *Philosophical Investigations*, 4th edn, trans. G .E. M. Anscombe, P. M. S. Hacker and J. Schulte. Oxford: Wiley-Blackwell.
———. (1959), *On Certainty*, trans. G. E. M. Anscombe. Oxford: Blackwell.
———. (2005), *The Big Typescript: TS 213*, ed. and trans. C. G. Luckhardt and M. A. E. Aue. Oxford: Blackwell.

PREFACE TO THE REVISED EDITION

In the course of the fifteen years since I wrote *Insight and Illusion* I have continued to study and write about the philosophy of Wittgenstein. During this period many further volumes culled from his voluminous *Nachlass*, as well as lecture notes taken by his students, have been published and, indeed, the whole of the *Nachlass* has been made available in xerox. This extensive material illuminates countless aspects of his better known works, in particular the *Tractatus* and *Philosophical Investigations*, and the results of researches into it were incorporated in two volumes I wrote together with Dr G. P. Baker on the *Philosophical Investigations*, viz. *Wittgenstein: Understanding and Meaning* (1980) and *Wittgenstein: Rules, Grammar and Necessity* (1985). As I struggled to understand the thoughts of 'the first philosopher of the age' I came to recognize that on many issues I had previously misunderstood him, sometimes as a result of reading his works through the spectacles of Oxford philosophy and its preoccupations in the 1960s. When I was offered the opportunity to produce a revised second edition of *Insight and Illusion*, I welcomed the chance to correct, in the light of this subsequent research, the distorted picture I had earlier sketched. For not all struck me as hopeless, and it seemed worthwhile to set the record as straight as I could. This did, however, mean that I was committed to very extensive rewriting.

In the Preface to the first edition I compared the structure of the book to the elements of a theatrical production, with a central drama, a set, and a back-cloth. Surveying the production afresh, it did not seem as flawed as *Hamlet* without the Prince, but the back-cloth, which consisted of a sketchy presentation of Wittgenstein's conception of meaning, looked more like Piccadilly Circus in the rush-hour than Elsinore Castle. I had been much impressed with the idea that it is illuminating to view the *Tractatus* as a paradigm of realism or truth-conditional semantics, and the *Investigations* as informed by a wholly different approach to meaning inspired by constructivism or intuitionism in mathematics, namely anti-realism or assertion-conditions semantics.

This now seems to me altogether misguided as well as anachronistic. The *Tractatus* does not propound anything that can justly be called truth-conditional semantics or realism as these terms are now understood, and the *Investigations* does not propound anything that can rightly be called anti-realism, let alone a theory of meaning based on the notion of assertion-conditions. It was a mistake to present Wittgenstein's remarks about criteria as the foundations of a novel semantic theory, for he would have viewed the whole enterprise of constructing philosophical theories of meaning as yet another house of cards—something to be demolished, not fostered. Accordingly I have had to repaint the back-cloth from scratch, and in more detail than before. In Chapters II and III, 'The Dialogue with Frege and Russell' and 'The Metaphysics of the *Tractatus*', which are both new, I have tried to give a better picture of Wittgenstein's reactions to his predecessors, of his account of meaning in the *Tractatus*, and of the reasons why it is not to be thought of in terms of the questionable contemporary dichotomy of realism versus anti-realism. In particular, I have tried to make clear the main achievement of the *Tractatus*, namely the first remarkable steps towards clarification of the nature of logic and logical necessity. In Chapter V, which is almost wholly rewritten, I have explained Wittgenstein's reasons for faulting the *Tractatus* and his diagnosis of the ineradicable flaws in the picture theory of meaning. Here too I have re-examined his relation to Brouwer's 1928 lecture with its intuitionist philosophy of logic and mathematics. The suggestion that these inspired Wittgenstein's changed perspective is wholly wrong. I have also paid more attention to Wittgenstein's short-lived verificationism, and tried to sketch the trajectory of his post-1929 work. In Chapter XI I have adumbrated the reasons why the concept of a criterion is not part of a new semantic theory, and why his later philosophy is not to be viewed as a version of anti-realism.

The set for the drama which I had tried to rehearse consisted of Wittgenstein's conception of philosophy, early and late. Here I have found less to fault, although I have in Chapters I and VI eliminated elements that now seem to me wrong or unnecessary, and have added items that I had previously not seen clearly or at all.

The drama that I tried to rehearse on this set I referred to, alas, as 'Wittgenstein's metaphysics of experience'. It consisted of his great discussion of the impossibility of a private language, his account of self-consciousness and knowledge of other minds, and (to a lesser extent) his account of knowledge of objects. I have left my description

Preface to the Revised Edition

of the *Tractatus* remarks on solipsism (Chapter IV) more or less intact, and the discussion of the later refutation of solipsism (Chapter VIII) I have modified only in a limited, though important way. I have tried to improve my presentation of the private language argument (Chapter IX), rewriting half of it. Where, however, the first edition was sorely wrong was the discussion of first-person psychological utterances. In the grip of a neo-Kantian picture of the relation between experience and the objects of experience and obsessed with *forms* of propositions to the point of being blind to the diversity of their uses, I misconstrued Wittgenstein's argument. Having done so, I then tried to demolish the argument thus distorted. I have now attempted to rectify this in Chapter X, which is completely rewritten, and have replied to those of my earlier counter-arguments to Wittgenstein's case that seemed worthy of rebuttal.

A leitmotif of the first production was the affinity between Kant and Wittgenstein. It was boldly trumpeted by my use of the phrase 'metaphysics of experience'. One cannot deny affinities between the two philosophers. Nevertheless, I exaggerated and distorted them, thinking wrongly that Wittgenstein's demonstration of the impossibility of a private language was, in a loose sense, a transcendental argument. To put this and related matters aright, I have rewritten Chapter VII, 'Metaphysics as the Shadow of Grammar', clarifying Wittgenstein's critique of metaphysics, adding a section on Kant and Wittgenstein, and virtually expunging the misleading phrase 'Wittgenstein's metaphysics of experience'.

Because of this, and also to mark the fact that this edition of the book does differ significantly from its predecessor (six chapters being written *de novo* and others significantly reworked), I have changed the subtitle from 'Wittgenstein on Philosophy and the Metaphysics of Experience' to 'Themes in the Philosophy of Wittgenstein'. I have not attempted in this book to survey the whole of Wittgenstein's work, but restricted myself, as in the first edition, to a limited (though wider) range of central themes. If these are better discussed than they were previously, this book may serve to help others to find their way around the numerous topics I have not examined.

I have been fortunate over the years to incur intellectual debts to colleagues, friends, and pupils. I have learnt much from the writings of Professor Norman Malcolm, from the indispensable bibliographical researches on the Wittgenstein papers conducted by Professor G. H. von Wright, and I have continued to profit greatly from the work of Dr

Anthony Kenny and from the generous advice of Dr Joachim Schulte and Professor Herman Philipse. Frequent discussions with Dr Joseph Raz and Bede Rundle have taught me much, and Saturday teas with Dr Ray Frey illuminated problems and never failed to lift my spirits. Among my pupils, past and present, I must mention Dr John Dupré, Dr Stuart Shanker (instigator of this revised edition), Hanjo Glock, John Hyman, and Stephen Mulhall, who made teaching not only delightful but also instructive for the instructor. My greatest debt is to my colleague Dr Gordon Baker. Over the past decade we have worked together on the Wittgenstein *Nachlass* and written five books on different topics in a partnership that has been immensely exciting and rewarding. Swimming against the current in pursuit of Wittgenstein's ideas would have been an even more difficult task without his skill, aid, and companionship. If, in this second edition, I have managed to give a better account than before, it is largely because of what I have learnt from our joint labours.

St John's College, Oxford   P. M. S. HACKER
1985

PREFACE TO THE FIRST EDITION

The structure of this book can best be captured by means of a theatrical metaphor. The book has, as it were a central drama, a set, and a back-cloth. The subject with which I am primarily concerned, the drama which is enacted throughout the book, is Wittgenstein's metaphysics of experience. This Kantian term of art is chosen advisedly, for one of the leitmotifs consists in exploring the Kantian affinities of Wittgenstein's philosophy in general, both in the *Tractatus* and in the post-1929 works. Wittgenstein's metaphysics of experience can be seen as consisting of a triad of problems, two of which are examined comprehensively. These are: self-consciousness, our knowledge of other minds, and our knowledge of objects. The secondary concern of the book, the set upon which the main drama takes place, is Wittgenstein's general conception of philosophy. This theme is intended to illuminate, and be illuminated by, the examination of Wittgenstein's metaphysics of experience. For the latter, particularly in Wittgenstein's later work, is an exemplification of his conception of the task, process, and result of philosophical investigation. As my work progressed, it became increasingly clear that the back-cloth against which the two main subjects had to be seen could not be wholly neglected. The back-cloth consists of the development of his semantic theories from the strict realism of the *Tractatus* to the constructivist-inspired conventionalism of the *Philosophical Investigations*. I have explored this most difficult subject only so far as seemed to me necessary in order to grasp the nature of Wittgenstein's metaphysics of experience, his general contribution to epistemology, and his conception of philosophy. So the back-cloth is, as is customary in stage design, uneven. In parts it is filled in with colourful detail, at other points it is rough and ready.

Wittgenstein is almost unique among philosophers in having produced two complete philosophies, the later containing substantial criticism and repudiation of the earlier. The controversy over the degree of change and the degree of constancy will doubtless rage for many years to come. With respect to the subjects with which I am concerned in this book I have tried to plot both transformation and continuity. It is certainly impossible to understand Wittgenstein's later concern with and refutation of solipsism and idealism without seeing its roots in his fascination with Schopenhauer in the *Notebooks 1914–16* and the 'methodological solipsism' of the *Philosophische Bemerkungen*. Equally one can only obtain a proper grasp of his later conception of philosophy and metaphysics by comparing and contrasting it with his earlier views. And doubtless his later semantics must be seen against the background of his repudiation of his earlier realism. Accordingly the first four chapters of this book are concerned with Wittgenstein's first philosophy, tracing the development of his views upon the themes I have chosen, from the early 'Notes on Logic' through the high point of the *Tractatus* to the transitional period of the late nineteen-twenties and early thirties. The last six chapters are concerned with much the same aspects of his later philosophy in which they loom so much larger.

I am grateful to Mr Ray Frey, Dr Kit Fine, and Dr Joseph Raz for their criticisms of earlier drafts of this book, for their encouragement and for the many illuminating discussions with them upon the topics on which I was working. My greatest debts are to Dr Anthony Kenny and Dr Gordon Baker. To Dr Kenny I owe the original inspiration to pursue my interest in Wittgenstein seriously; what grasp I have of the private language argument I owe largely to the many conversations I have had with him. His detailed comments upon my first drafts of Chapters IV, VII, VIII, IX were of very great help to me. To my colleague at St John's, Dr Baker, I owe the opportunity to sound out practically every idea I have had upon my subjects with a sympathetic and erudite listener. His criticisms, suggestions, and advice, as well as his comments upon my manuscripts, were of inestimable value to me. The privilege of reading his own unpublished work upon Wittgenstein's semantics gave me insights into the constructivist tenor of Wittgenstein's later philosophy which I would not have achieved unaided. I should also like to acknowledge my debt to Mrs Pearl Hawtin and to my wife for their generous secretarial aid.

All quotations from *Ludwig Wittgenstein und der Wiener Kreis*, *Philsophische Bemerkungen*, and *Philosophische Grammatik*, have been translated. Where the translators of Wittgenstein's other works have seemed to me to err I have provided my own translation. I am grateful to Mr T. J. Reed and to my mother Mrs Thea Hacker for their assistance with the German. I am indebted to the publishers Basil Blackwell & Mott Ltd., Routledge & Kegan Paul Ltd. and the Humanities Press Inc., for kind permission to quote from works of Wittgenstein for which they own the copyright.

St John's College, Oxford　　　　　　　　　　　　　　　　P.M.S.H.
1971

LIST OF ABBREVIATIONS

Abbreviations used to refer to Wittgenstein's writings listed in chronological order:

NB   *Notebooks 1914–16*, ed. G. H. von Wright and G. E. M. Anscombe, trans. G. E. M. Anscombe (Blackwell, Oxford, 1961).
PT   *ProtoTractatus—An Early Version of Tractatus Logico-Philosophicus*, ed. B. F. McGuinness, T. Nyberg, G. H. von Wright, trans. D. F. Pears and B. F. McGuinness (Routledge & Kegan Paul, London, 1971).
TLP   *Tractatus Logico-Philosophicus*, trans. D. F. Pears and B. F. McGuinness (Routledge & Kegan Paul, London, 1961).
LLW   *Letters from Ludwig Wittgenstein with a Memoir*, Paul Engelmann, ed. B. F. McGuinness, trans. L. Furtmüller (Blackwell, Oxford, 1967).
RLF   'Some Remarks on Logical Form', *Proceedings of the Aristotelian Society*, supp. vol. ix (1929).
WWK   *Ludwig Wittgenstein und der Wiener Kreis*, shorthand notes recorded by F. Waismann, ed. B. F. McGuinness (Blackwell, Oxford, 1967). The English edition *Wittgenstein and the Vienna Circle*, trans. J. Schulte and B. F. McGuinness (Blackwell, Oxford, 1979) preserves the original pagination.
PR   *Philosophical Remarks*, ed. R. Rhees, trans. R. Hargreaves and R. White (Blackwell, Oxford, 1975).
M   'Wittgenstein's Lectures in 1930–33', in G. E. Moore, *Philosophical Papers* (Allen & Unwin, London, 1959).
PG   *Philosophical Grammar*, ed. R. Rhees, trans. A. J. P. Kenny (Blackwell, Oxford, 1974).
AWL   *Wittgenstein's Lectures, Cambridge 1932–5, from the notes of Alice Ambrose and Margaret MacDonald*, ed. Alice Ambrose (Blackwell, Oxford, 1979).
BB   *The Blue and Brown Books* (Blackwell, Oxford, 1958).
NFL   'Wittgenstein's Notes for Lectures on "Private Experience" and "Sense Data"', ed. R. Rhees, *Philosophical Review, lxxvii (1968)*.
LSD   'The Language of Sense Data and Private Experience', notes taken by R. Rhees of Wittgenstein's lectures, 1936, *Philosophical Investigations* 7 (1984) pp. 1–45, 101–40.
RFM   *Remarks on the Foundations of Mathematics*, ed. G. H. von Wright, R. Rhees, G. E. M. Anscombe, trans. G. E. M. Anscombe 3rd edn. (Blackwell, Oxford, 1978).

PI	*Philosophical Investigations*, ed. G. E. M. Anscombe, R. Rhees, trans. G. E. M. Anscombe (Blackwell, Oxford, 1953).
Z	*Zettel*, ed. G. E. M. Anscombe and G. H. von Wright, trans. G. E. M. Anscombe (Blackwell, Oxford, 1967).
RPP I	*Remarks on the Philosophy of Psychology*, Volume I, ed. G. E. M. Anscombe and G. H. von Wright, trans. G. E. M. Anscombe (Blackwell, Oxford, 1980).
RPP II	*Remarks on the Philosophy of Psychology*, Volume II, ed. G. H. von Wright and H. Nyman, trans. C. G. Luckhardt and M. A. E. Aue (Blackwell, Oxford, 1980).
LW	*Last Writings on the Philosophy of Psychology*, Volume I, ed. G. H. von Wright and H. Nyman, trans. C. G. Luckhardt and M. A. E. Aue (Blackwell, Oxford, 1982).
OC	*On Certainty*, ed. G. E. M. Anscombe and G. H. von Wright, trans. D. Paul and G. E. M. Anscombe (Blackwell, Oxford, 1969).

References to the *Nachlass* are by MS or TS number followed by page number, cf. the von Wright catalogue (G. H. von Wright, *Wittgenstein* (Blackwell, Oxford, 1982), pp. 35 ff.).

I

WITTGENSTEIN'S EARLY CONCEPTION OF PHILOSOPHY

1. *Background*

Ludwig Wittgenstein came to Cambridge in 1912 in order to study under the supervision of Bertrand Russell. It was the beginning of seven years of intensive and single-minded research in logic and philosophy which resulted in the only book Wittgenstein published in his lifetime, the *Tractatus Logico-Philosophicus*. It is not to the present purpose to investigate the wide range of philosophical views embodied in that work, but rather to examine the conception of philosophy propounded in it. In order to do so, some appreciation of Wittgenstein's intellectual background and the problem-setting context of his work is necessary. For a twenty-three-year-old research student of philosophy, Wittgenstein in 1912 was remarkably ill-read in the history of the subject. His intellectual milieu was that of a highly cultured and sophisticated member of the Viennese intelligentsia. His training was, however, scientific. In 1906 he had begun studying engineering in the Technische Hochschule in Berlin-Charlottenburg, and in 1908 he came to Manchester to pursue research in aeronautics. In the course of research into the design of a jet-reaction propeller he was led from dynamics to pure mathematics, and from there to logical and philosophical investigations into the foundations of mathematics. He apparently read Russell's *Principles of Mathematics* and was greatly impressed by this imposing work which had, significantly, germinated in theoretical problems in dynamics.[1] It was probably the appendix to the *Principles of Mathematics* which led Wittgenstein first to read the works of Frege, and then to visit him. On Frege's advice he returned to England to study under Russell.

Wittgenstein, like any well-educated Viennese at the turn of the

---

[1] For the origin of Russell's investigations into the foundations of mathematics, see *The Principles of Mathematics*, Preface, pp.vi f. (Cambridge University Press, Cambridge, 1903).

century, had read Schopenhauer in his teens. He is reported to have been greatly impressed, and he told von Wright[2] that his first philosophy was a Schopenhauerian epistemological idealism. It was not, however, a Schopenhauerian interest which brought him to philosophical investigation. Although Schopenhauer's influence upon the later sections of the *Tractatus* is profound, it is clear from Wittgenstein's correspondence with Russell,[3] from the 1913 and 1914 notes on logic[4] and from the three remaining philosophical notebooks covering the periods from 22 August 1914 to 22 June 1915, and from 15 April 1916 to 10 January 1917, that the driving force behind his investigations was logic and its metaphysical implications. It was only in May 1915 that there emerged, amidst the logical speculations, a slight hint of the Schopenhauerian pre-occupation which dominates the third and final surviving notebook. This belated Schopenhauerian impact upon his logico-metaphysical researches did not influence his fundamental thoughts upon the nature of philosophy, although it moulded his conception of the metaphysical self and his notion of the mystical.[5] To find the dominant influences upon the *Tractatus* in general, and its conception of philosophy in particular, one must look in a quite different direction from either classical or popular contemporary philosophy.

The end of the nineteenth century and first decade of the twentieth was a period of great philosophical ferment amongst some of the most distinguished physicists of the day. The problems of the nature of scientific explanation, of the structure of scientific theories, of the attainability of truth in science, were discussed in detail by such eminent figures as Duhem, Poincaré, and Mach. From the point of view of Wittgenstein's intellectual development, however, the most significant philosopher-scientists were Hertz and Boltzmann.

Hertz's *The Principles of Mechanics*[6] undertook a philosophical examination of the logical nature of scientific explanation. The point of science, he argued, is the anticipation of nature. Its data are our knowledge of past events, its method is theory-construction, its mode of reasoning is deductive. The possibility of describing reality by an

[2] G. H. von Wright, 'A Biographical Sketch', in N. Malcolm, *Ludwig Wittgenstein: A Memoir* (OUP, London, 1966), p. 5.
[3] L. Wittgenstein, *Letters to Russell, Keynes, and Moore*, ed. G. H. von Wright (Blackwell, Oxford, 1974). A selection is printed in *NB*, Appendix III.
[4] Published in *NB*, Appendices I and II.   [5] See below Ch. IV.
[6] H. Hertz, *The Principles of Mechanics*, trans. D. E. Jones and J. T. Walley (Macmillan, London, 1899).

axiomatic mechanics is explained by reference to the nature of symbolization. We form pictures (*Scheinbilder*) to ourselves of external objects. These symbolic or pictorial conceptions of ours must satisfy one essential condition: their deductive consequences must match the facts: 'the necessary consequents of the images in thought are always the images of the necessary consequents in nature of the things pictured.'[7] It is necessary to distinguish sharply in our pictures between what arises from necessity in thought, what from experience and what from arbitrary choice. Any acceptable scientific theory must satisfy three requirements. It must be logically permissible or consistent. This requirement arises from necessities of thought. It must be correct, i.e. the relations between elements of the picture must, when given an interpretation, correspond to the relations between external things. Thus experience confirms the theory. Finally, it must be appropriate, i.e. the notation in which we chose to represent the theory must be as simple and economic as it can be, consistently with the other requirements. The bare structure of a theory thus conceived may be illuminated and supplemented by giving models or concrete representations of the various conceptions of the nature of the elements of the theory. This may aid our power of imagination but one must remember that the colourful clothing in which we dress the theory is heuristic and optional, and must not be allowed to obscure the underlying structure of the theory. Thus Hertz argued in *Electric Waves*[8] that three distinct models or interpretations of Maxwell's electromagnetic theory all have the same testable consequences, are all expressible by the same equations, and hence are the same theory.[9] With these considerations in mind, especially the requirement of appropriateness, Hertz undertook the rational reconstruction of Newtonian dynamics. The point of this endeavour was neither pedagogic nor practical. Hertz stressed that, from the point of view of the needs of mankind, the usual methods of representing mechanics cannot be bettered in as much as they were devised for these purposes. Hertz's aim was to display the logical structure of the theory. His representation stood to the normal one, so he claimed, as the systematic grammar of a language stands to a learner's grammar.

[7] H. Hertz, op. cit., Introduction p. 1.
[8] H. Hertz, *Electric Waves*, trans. D. E. Jones (Macmillan, London, 1893).
[9] For a criticism of Hertz's dismissal of the theoretical significance of model-building in science and his excessive deductivism, see M. B. Hesse, *Forces and Fields* (Nelson, London, 1961), p. 215.

Following the path laid out by Mach and Kirchhoff, Hertz intended to eliminate the concept of force from mechanics as anything other than an abbreviating convenience. The only primitive notions he employed were space, time, and mass. By displaying the logical structure of the theory, he dispelled the illusion that physicists had not yet been able to discover the true nature of force. In a brief passage Hertz outlined his conception of the analytic dissolution of conceptual confusion. This became for Wittgenstein a classical, concise, and beautiful statement of the philosophical elimination of pseudo-problems.

> We have accumulated around the terms 'force' and 'electricity' more relations than can be completely reconciled amongst themselves. We have an obscure feeling of this and want to have things cleared up. Our confused wish finds expression in the confused question as to the nature of force and electricity. But the answer which we want is not really an answer to this question. It is not by finding out more and fresh relations and connections that it can be answered; but by removing the contradictions existing between those already known, and thus perhaps by reducing their number. When these painful contradictions are removed, the question as to the nature of force will not have been answered; but our minds, no longer vexed, will cease to ask illegitimate questions.[10]

These are the fundamental Hertzian themes which influenced the young Wittgenstein. They were reinforced and supplemented by reading the works of Ludwig Boltzmann. Prior to studying at the Technische Hochschule, Wittgenstein had intended to study physics under Boltzmann in Vienna, a wish that was frustrated by Boltzmann's suicide in 1906, the same year that Wittgenstein finished school. As late as 1931, Wittgenstein cited Boltzmann (together with Hertz and others[11]) as a seminal influence upon his thought.

Unlike Hertz, Boltzmann emphasized the importance of model-building in science. A fruitful model is not an explanatory hypothesis, nor is it, as Hertz had suggested, a mere colourful wrapping for bare equations. Rather is it an *analogy*, which unlike a hypothesis, need not be rejected if it fails perfectly to fit the facts. Maxwell's discovery of the great formulae in the theory of electricity were a consequence of the ingenuity and insight involved in creating fruitful mechanical models

---

[10] Hertz, *Principles of Mechanics*, Introduction, pp. 7 f; at one stage Wittgenstein intended to use the last lines of this quotation as a motto for the *Philosophical Investigations*.

[11] See L. Wittgenstein, *Culture and Value*, ed. G. H. von Wright in collaboration with H. Nyman. trans. P. Winch (Blackwell, Oxford, 1980), p. 19. Others cited are Schopenhauer, Frege, Russell, Kraus, Loos, Weininger, Spengler, and Sraffa.

which constitute analogies, rather than explanatory hypotheses, for the behaviour of electrical current. Like Hertz, however, Boltzmann emphasized that apparent contradictions involved in philosophical puzzlement can be *dissolved*. The elemental preconditions of experience and the laws of thought cannot be explained, only *described*, but their proper description will reveal the nonsensicality of the questions that give rise to philosophical puzzlement.

> If ... philosophy were to succeed in creating a system such that in all cases mentioned it stood out clearly when a question is not justified so that the drive towards asking it would gradually die away, we should at one stroke have resolved the most obscure riddles and philosophy would become worthy of the name of queen of the sciences.[12]

This thought is echoed in the *Tractatus* at 4.003:

> Most of the propositions and questions to be found in philosophical works are not false but nonsensical. Consequently we cannot give any answer to questions of this kind, but can only establish that they are nonsensical. Most of the propositions and questions of philosophers arise from our failure to understand the logic of our language.
>
> (They belong to the same class as the question whether the good is more or less identical than the beautiful.)
>
> And it is not surprising that the deepest problems are in fact *not* problems at all.

The *Tractatus* was, *inter alia*, an attempt to give substance to Hertz's and Boltzmann's insights by laying bare the underlying logical structure of any possible language, and showing that philosophical questions are strictly nonsensical.

By far the most important, specifically philosophical, influences upon Wittgenstein were Frege and Russell. Their work constituted the primary context for Wittgenstein's reflections. Frege's professional life was a single-minded pursuit of a demonstration that arithmetic had its foundations in pure logic alone, that it involved no forms of inference peculiar to it, and that its fundamental concepts were derivable from purely logical ones. Noting that subject/predicate logic was wholly incapable of representing inferences involving multiple generality that are characteristic of mathematical induction, Frege was induced to

---

[12] L. Boltzmann, 'On Statistical Mechanics', in B. McGuinness ed., *Ludwig Boltzmann: Theoretical Physics and Philosophical Problems*, trans. P. Foulkes (Reidel, Dordrecht, 1974), p. 167. Boltzmann's influence upon the *Tractatus* is particularly evident in the discussion of natural science at 6.3 ff.

harbour the deepest suspicions about the logical propriety of natural languages with their typical subject-predicate grammar. Eschewing traditional logic, Frege invented modern function-theoretic logic, conceiving of his creation not as an analysis of natural languages but as a logically perfect language that, for the purposes of deductive sciences, would replace them. His new concept-script (*Begriffsschrift*) represented not the sentences of German, but the judgements (or, more accurately, the *contents* of judgements) expressed thereby. His innovation was to conceive of the content of judgement not as synthesized from subject and predicate, but as decomposable into function and argument. This involved generalizing mathematicians' conception of a function by admitting any entities whatever as arguments and values of functions. Hence he (initially) viewed judgements (conceived as objects) as the values of concepts for arguments and concepts as functions mapping arguments on to judgements. The function-theoretic apparatus enabled him to construct a formal logic of generality, for he construed expressions of generality ('all', 'some', 'there is') as variable-binding, variable-indexed, second-level functions. These quantifiers he then represented as second-level concepts taking first level concepts as arguments and mapping them on to judgements (judgeable-contents). He gave the first complete formalization of the predicate calculus with identity, and mastered the formal presentation of inferences involving multiple generality (e.g., if every number has a successor, then there is no number such that it is larger than every other number).

Ab initio Frege viewed his well-formed formulae as standing for judgements, and of judgements (the values of appropriate functions for arguments) as objects. Hence a well-formed formula was, from a logical point of view, a singular referring expression. Later he distinguished within an expression for a judgement between a sense, the thought expressed, and a reference, the truth-value denoted. He applied this distinction also to the constituents of a well-formed formula, so that the argument-expression and function-name (concept-word) are likewise said to express senses and denote referents. Every proper name expressed a sense, a mode of presentation of a referent, and, in a properly constructed language, denoted an object. Concepts were now conceived as functions mapping objects on to truth-values. A sentence or well-formed formula of his logical calculus was held to express its sense, a thought, and to refer to its referent, a truth-value. It was a *proper name* of The True or The False, the latter being conceived as peculiar logical objects. Negation and conditionality were the two primitive logical connectives of Frege's system. He conceived of both as literal functions, initially as mapping judgements on to a judgement, later as mapping objects (typically, but not only, truth-values) on to a truth-value.

One will search Frege's works in vain for a systematic discussion of the nature of philosophy. He was a mathematical logician whose primary interest was to 'set mathematics upon secure logical foundations'. But in so far as he conceived of his work on the foundations of mathematics and on logic as philosophical, three points stand forth clearly from his practice. First, he thought that philosophical theses (if logicism is a philosophical thesis) could be *proved* by a priori argument. Secondly, he thought that philosophy could make ontological *discoveries*, for example that concepts are really a species of function and that truth and falsehood are special kinds of objects, namely the values of such functions for arguments.[13] Thirdly, he thought, as many before him had, that ordinary language stands in the way of philosophical insight. Thought is enslaved by the tyranny of words.[14] Conventional grammatical forms (e.g. subject/predicate structure) conceal the logical forms underlying them (viz. the true function/argument structure). Second-level concepts can appear in linguistic guise as pronouns, behaving like proper names of objects (e.g. 'somebody' or 'nobody', giving rise to such exercises of literary wit as Odysseus' exchange with Polyphemus or the White King's with Alice) or as names of first-level concepts (e.g. 'exists'). Ordinary language is rife with ambiguity, the same word being used now to stand for an object, now for a concept; it contains hosts of vague predicates allowing the formulation of sentences to which no determinate truth-value can be assigned; it permits the construction of vacuous singular referring expressions, hence the formation of sentences expressing propositions with *no* truth-values; and it is even *incoherent*, for it permits such expressions as 'the concept of a horse' which are meant to stand for concepts, but inadvertently, as it were, stand for objects. These defects of natural languages can be overcome, he thought, by the invention of an improved language, namely his own concept-script, which is logically rigorous and lays bare the true logical nature of what it represents.

[13] He compared his discovery of The True and The False to the discovery of two chemical elements (cf. G. Frege, *Posthumous Writings* (Blackwell, Oxford, 1979), p. 194).
[14] G. Frege, *Begriffsschrift, eine der arithmetischen nachgebildete Formelsprache des reinen Denkens* (Halle, 1897), Preface p. vi.

Russell pursued a similar logicist goal to Frege, but with much wider philosophical interests. Three issues alone need concern us briefly here, his Theory of Descriptions, his Theory of Types, and his general conception of philosophy. Frege had distinguished simple proper names from complex ones such as 'the father of Plato', which are decomposable into function- and argument-expressions. But he thought that ordinary (simple) proper names and definite descriptions alike were, in natural languages, sometimes lacking in reference (e.g. 'Zeus', 'the golden mountain'). Accordingly sentences formed from them would express a proposition but lack any truth-value. Russell, in his Theory of Descriptions argued that a definite description is not a complex proper name or singular referring expression at all but what he called 'an incomplete symbol'. He treated it, in effect, as a second-level concept-word taking first-level concept-words as argument-expressions to form a sentence. A sentence of the form 'The ϕer ψs' is analysable into a conjunction of the form 'For some x, x ϕs; and for all y if y ϕs, y is identical with x; and x ψs'. According to this account, the non-existence of the ϕer does not render such a proposition truth-valueless, but false. So whereas Frege thought that natural languages contained sentences expressing propositions without a truth-value, Russell held to the principle of bivalence for natural languages, and not just for artificial or 'logically perfect' languages. Every proposition must have a truth-value. The Theory of Descriptions seemed to reveal the true logical form of certain kinds of proposition, and to highlight the gulf between deceptive grammatical form and logical form. In Russell's philosophy this analysis was rich in epistemological and ontological implications. It was an essential part of his distinction between knowledge by description and knowledge by acquaintance, and of his thesis that 'wherever possible, logical constructions are to be substituted for inferred entities'. It not only enabled Russell to thin out the luxuriant Meinongian jungle of entities (such as the square circle) which, it had appeared, must *in some sense* subsist in order to be talked about, but also it put Russell on the highroad of empiricist reductionism in the novel form of *logical*, as opposed to merely psychological, analysis.

Like Frege, Russell aimed to establish arithmetic 'on secure logical foundations' by demonstrating that the purely logical notions of identity, class, class-membership, and class-equivalence suffice for constructing the series of natural numbers. Notoriously he discovered the famous paradox (concerning the class of classes that are not members of themselves) in Frege's system. To cordon off the possibility of generating such paradoxes, Russell erected his Theory of Types limiting the range of significance of propositional functions according to the general principle that a function must always be of a higher type than its argument. Violating this principle, as in 'The class of men is a man', results not in falsehood but in meaninglessness. The price of this *cordon sanitaire*, however, was the need to postulate that the number of objects in the universe is not finite (the axiom of infinity). Arguably the price was excessive; the adamantine logical foundations upon which arithmetic was to be safely erected turned out to contain at their heart an apparently soft empirical hypothesis which is not even known to be true.

Unlike Frege, Russell had an explicit and elaborate conception of philosophy and its methods. He conceived of philosophy as the most general of the sciences, variously characterizing it as the science of the general (since logic, the core of philosophy, consists of perfectly general propositions), as abstracting from all particularity (since logical propositions contain only 'logical constants' which are obtained by a process of abstraction), as an investigation into what is a priori possible, as concerned only with logical form. These different formulations he took to be (roughly) equivalent. He advocated the emulation in philosophy of scientific method, in particular of its piecemeal probabilistic advances ensuring the possibility of successive approximations to the truth. The route to philosophical knowledge is the logical analysis of propositions. 'Every philosophical problem when it is subjected to the necessary analysis and purification, is found to be not really philosophical at all, or else to be, in the sense in which we are using the word, logical'.[15] It aims at a theoretical understanding of the world. Its hypotheses systematize facts about the world, and, Russell was frequently tempted to argue, are more or less probable according to the weight of their inductive support. One of its tasks is the construction of catalogues of logical forms of propositions and of logical possibilities. This is necessary for the identification of errors in traditional ontology, metaphysics, and epistemology. Logical analysis, coupled with the principle of acquaintance, viz. 'that every proposition which we can understand must be composed wholly of constituents with which we are acquainted', would reveal the foundations of knowledge. To this extent logical analysis, in Russell's work, is

[15] B. Russell, *Our Knowledge of the External World as a Field for Scientific Method in Philosophy* (Open Court, Chicago, 1914), p. 33.

subordinate to epistemology. Empiricist reductionism by means of the new logical techniques aims to establish whatever bastions of certainty we can achieve against the seas of Cartesian doubt.

The setting of the stage at the time of Wittgenstein's entry upon the scene, first as Russell's pupil and very quickly as his equal, was far from final. To be sure, the main props seemed to be in place. The advances in logic pioneered by Frege and Russell were considerable. Logic, after twenty-five centuries, had undergone a profound revolution. Its problem-setting impact upon philosophy was, and has remained throughout the twentieth century, comparable to the impact of the advances made by seventeenth-century physics upon philosophy from Descartes to Kant. Forms of reasoning previously resistant to formalization had at last yielded their secrets. That there was a disparity between grammatical form and logical form was an old doctrine, but the new logic seemed, by means of its function-theoretic structure, to have penetrated for the first time to the true underlying logical forms of propositions. The Theory of Descriptions appeared to set the venerable notion of analysis of ideas on to firm logical foundations. The central challenge to philosophy was to explore the philosophical implications of the discovery (or invention?) of this unprecedentedly powerful logical calculus. What did it show us about the nature of human thought and reasoning? Did it bring with it revelations about the ultimate nature of the world? Or was it a description of objects in a timeless Platonic world of abstract entities? Did it show that natural languages were logically defective, and so pave the way for, or even constitute, *better*, logically perfect, languages?

Much remained unclear, and much was contentious. The logicist reduction of mathematics stood, rather shakily propped up against the Russellian paradoxes by the Theory of Types. Its soft core, in particular the axiom of infinity, seemed patently unsatisfactory. The very status of logic was unclear. Were the propositions of logic truths *about* propositions or *about* what Russell termed 'logical constants'? To what did they owe their necessitarian status? Or were the necessary truths of logic as brutish as brute empirical facts, as it were brute facts about non-empirical objects? If logic was, as Frege and Russell suggested, an axiomatic science, what was the status of its basic axioms? Do we know these by a special faculty of logical knowledge? Are the basic laws of logic ultimate self-evident truths? Equally problematic was the relation of logic to natural languages. Did the revelations of the new logical calculus show that our ordinary language is, in certain respects, illogical? If so, how is it that we manage to express and communicate our thoughts by using it? Is it only, so to speak, a *little bit* illogical? But what is illogical, what contravenes the laws of logic is surely nonsense, not an approximation to some truth, nor even a falsehood, but meaningless or (in the case of an argument) invalid. If any language, natural or ideal, is to depict reality, what kinds of relationships must obtain between its expressions and the reality depicted? And what do the logical forms of propositions, as revealed by logical analysis, tell us about the essential nature of what those propositions represent? It was to these great sweeping questions that Wittgenstein, starting from a fairly narrow range of logical problems, was drawn.

The specific problems with which he was first concerned were what Russell had called 'the chief part of philosophical logic',[16] namely the discussion of 'indefinables'. His interest focused upon the nature of the symbolism of the new logic and what corresponds to it in natural languages on the one hand and in the world on the other. His first great insight, which he was later to call the *Grundgedanke* of the *Tractatus* (TLP 4.0312), was that there are, in Russell's sense of the term, no 'logical constants',[17] i.e. the logical connectives, the signs of generality, the *summa genera* of logic such as 'relation', 'property', are not names of entities (neither of special logical objects nor of special kinds of functions). These are not 'constituents' of the propositions of logic, nor are they the special subject-matter of the science of logic, as it were, the most general features of reality as Russell thought or denizens of a Platonic 'third-world' as Frege suggested. Their role, or rather their various roles, are quite different from that of names signifying entities, and a misunderstanding of their roles was the primary source of the philosophical confusions in Frege and Russell. From this early insight sprang, in due course, the most important achievement of the *Tractatus*, viz. the account of the nature of logical necessity. (This theme will be examined in the next chapter.) It also led him to the conclusion that a Theory of Types is neither necessary nor possible. What it attempts to say (e.g. that Socrates is a different type of thing from mortality and *hence* that what can intelligibly be said of the one type of thing cannot be intelligibly said of another) is shown by the nature of any symbolism which can express the proposition that

---

[16] B. Russell, *The Principles of Mathematics*, Preface, p. xv.
[17] Cf. second letter to Russell, dated 22.6.1912, *Letters to Russell, Keynes, and Moore*, p. 10. This question will be discussed in detail in Ch. II.

Socrates is mortal. The details need not concern us here.[18] What is important for present purposes is that his repudiation of the Theory of Types played a major role in moulding his conception of the nature and limits of philosophy, from the 'Notes on Logic' of 1913 to the *Tractatus*.

2. *The 'Preliminary' on Philosophy*

To understand Wittgenstein's brief remarks about philosophy in the *Tractatus* it is essential to realize that its practice and its theory are at odds with each other. The official *de jure* account of philosophy is wholly different from the *de facto* practice of philosophy in the book. The practice conforms to the account of philosophy which Wittgenstein had given in the brief 'Preliminary' of the 1913 'Notes on Logic'.[19] The extent to which his conception of philosophy changed can be gauged by comparing the 'Notes on Logic' with the *Tractatus*. The cause of the change can be attributed to the emergence of the distinction between showing and saying.

The 'Preliminary' of the 'Notes on Logic' contains three theses jointly demarcating the domain of philosophy, and characterizing its nature. The first thesis claims that philosophy is purely descriptive and contains no deductions. Thus there are no privileged propositions in philosophy which enjoy logical or epistemological priority over other propositions deduced from them. Philosophy is 'flat'. This distinguishes philosophy from axiomatic a priori sciences such as geometry, and also, bearing in mind the Hertzian deductivist conception of scientific theories, from natural sciences thus conceived. Accordingly the second thesis states that philosophy is above or below, but not beside the natural sciences. Philosophy may be the queen of the sciences or their underlabourer; but either way the philosopher is not an ordinary enfranchized citizen of a republic of ideas.[20] The reason given for this line of demarcation is couched in Hertzian terms. The natural sciences give us *pictures* of reality, i.e. theoretical models. Philosophy does not; hence it is not in competition with the natural sciences, and can neither confirm nor confute scientific propositions. Together with the

---

[18] For a detailed discussion, see H. Ishiguro, 'Wittgenstein and the Theory of Types', in I. Block. ed., *Perspectives on the Philosophy of Wittgenstein* (Blackwell, Oxford, 1981), and A. J. P. Kenny, *Wittgenstein* (Allen Lane, London, 1973), pp. 43 ff.

[19] The 'Preliminary', it is now evident (*NB*, second edition, preface and Appendix I) is an arrangement by Russell of a cluster of remarks in the fourth MS of the 'Notes on Logic'. This does not affect the above argument.

[20] This is a paraphrase of *Z*, §455, but is equally applicable here.

Wittgenstein's Early Conception of Philosophy

previous thesis, the second thesis yields the claim that philosophy is *sui generis*. The third thesis describes the domain of philosophy. It is the doctrine of the logical form of scientific, i.e. empirical, propositions. Thus the forms of proposition, and so of thought in general, provide philosophy with its subject-matter. On this issue, incidentally, there was initial agreement between Wittgenstein and Russell. In his Herbert Spencer lecture in 1914 'On Scientific Method in Philosophy',[21] and likewise in the Lowell Lectures of 1914, *Our Knowledge of the External World*, Russell emphasized that philosophy properly speaking is indistinguishable from logic, and is concerned above all with the study of logical forms. Russell, however, as we shall see in the next chapter, did not grasp the full implications of this demarcation of subject-matter. For, as Wittgenstein came to realize, Russell's conception of logical form was defective. Furthermore, his grasp of the character of philosophical investigation was methodologically unsound. Russell argued in 'On Scientific Method in Philosophy' that it was by concentrating attention upon the investigation of logical form that the new style analytic philosophy could avoid the holistic methods and consequent errors of past philosophy, and emulate the progressive methods of the sciences.

A scientific philosophy such as I wish to recommend will be piecemeal and tentative like other sciences; above all, it will be able to invent hypotheses which, even if they are not wholly true, will yet remain fruitful after the necessary corrections have been made. This possibility of successive approximations to the truth is, more than anything else, the source of the triumphs of science, and to transfer this possibility to philosophy is to ensure a progress in method whose importance it would be almost impossible to exaggerate.[22]

It is not surprising that in his philosophical notebook Wittgenstein remarked in 1915: 'Russell's method in his "Scientific Method in Philosophy" is simply a retrogression from the method of physics' (*NB*, p. 44).[23] For, as Hertz had shown, the method of physics is the construction of pictures of reality. These are indeed optional and tentative, enabling greater or lesser approximations in their hypothetico-

---

[21] Russell, 'On Scientific Method in Philosophy', in *Mysticism and Logic* (Penguin, Harmondsworth, 1953), Ch. VI, pp. 95–119.
[22] Ibid., Ch. VI, p. 109.
[23] It is clear from the adjacent comments in the *Notebooks* that this remark and others accompanying it are directed against the Lowell Lectures, Chapter 3. 'Scientific Method in Philosophy' was part of the full title of the Lowell Lectures.

deductive consequences to the facts. But logic, in so far as it is a condition of sense, can allow no hypotheses. If philosophy is a description of logical form, there can be nothing piecemeal or merely probably correct about it. For what would be a mere approximation in science would be nonsense in philosophy. It is inconceivable that philosophy should share in the methods of the natural sciences.

The 'Preliminary' adds a programmatic demand: the correct explanation of logical propositions must give them a unique position as against all other propositions. This programme was fulfilled in the *Tractatus*. There is also a claim concerning the structure of philosophy itself—it consists of logic and metaphysics, the former its basis. It is, however, unclear how a purely descriptive account can have one part as a basis for another. Presumably Wittgenstein meant that logical investigations reveal metaphysical truths, that the logical forms of expressions show something about the essential, metaphysical structure of the world. Finally there is a methodological requirement in conformity with Fregean and Russellian doctrines: distrust of grammar is the first requisite for philosophizing.

By the time he wrote the *Tractatus*, Wittgenstein had changed his mind upon some of the salient claims about the nature of philosophy which he had made earlier. The *de jure* status of philosophy had changed dramatically. The thesis that philosophy is the description of logical form, which both he and Russell had previously propounded, was now rejected. Logical form is indescribable, hence philosophy's concern with logical form cannot be aimed at its description. Everything, however, was not repudiated. The earlier demarcation of philosophy distinguished it sharply from the natural sciences. To this Wittgenstein continued to adhere. In the *Tractatus*, 4.111, he declared 'Philosophy is not one of the natural sciences', and in parentheses added a remark taken from the 'Notes on Logic': 'The word "philosophy" must mean something whose place is above or below the natural sciences not beside them.' He emphasized this negative thesis in 4.1121: 'Psychology is no more closely related to philosophy than any other science.' In the following remark he added 'Darwin's theory has no more to do with philosophy than any other hypothesis in natural science' (*TLP*, 4.1122). This apparent *non sequitur* is another barb aimed at the views expressed in Russell's Lowell Lectures. Russell[24] distinguished three kinds of philosophy—the classical tradition

---

[24] Russell, *Our Knowledge of the External World* (Open Court, Chicago, 1914), Ch. 1; see also 'On Scientific Method in Philosophy', in *Mysticism and Logic*.

derived ultimately from the Greeks, Evolutionism derived from Darwin, and logical atomism which represents the same kind of advance in philosophy as Galileo introduced in physics. Although Russell rejected Evolutionism, as he did the classical philosophical tradition, because it was not a 'truly scientific philosophy', he conceived of it as a type of philosophy. Wittgenstein thought this involved a mis-classification based on an unclear grasp of the nature of philosophy.

Although the first and third theses of the 'Preliminary' were rejected, the view that philosophy is *sui generis* was nevertheless adhered to. However, Wittgenstein ceased to believe that the uniqueness of philosophy is expressible in philosophical propositions describing a special a priori subject-matter. Its singularity lies in the activity of philosophy, not in its product. Wittgenstein had come to believe that there are no philosophical propositions. Hence philosophy is not a doctrine, either of logical form, or of anything else.

3. *Philosophy and Illusion*

In his preface to the *Tractatus*, Wittgenstein specified the subject-matter of the book as 'the problems of philosophy'. The outcome of the book, he continued, shows that 'the reason why these problems are posed is that the logic of our language is misunderstood'. A corollary of this, as we shall see, is that once the logic of our language is grasped, these problems will no longer be posed, for they are not genuine problems, but the product of illusion. As befits such a view of philosophy as *Scheinprobleme*, Wittgenstein provided a brief sketch of the sources of error and illusion. The doctrine that there exists a gulf between the ordinary grammar of a language and its logical form, implicit in the methodological requirement of the 'Preliminary', is reiterated in the *Tractatus* in a metaphor reminiscent of Hertz.[25]

Language disguises thought. So much so, that from the outward form of the clothing it is impossible to infer the form of the thought beneath it, because the outward form of the clothing is not designed to reveal the form of the body, but for entirely different purposes. (*TLP*, 4.002.)

Ordinary language does not show its logical structure, and it is not humanly possible to gather *immediately* from everyday language what its underlying logic is. Despite our ability to speak correctly, we may be blind to the logical structure of our language, and its outward aspect

[25] Hertz, *Electric Waves*, p. 28.

makes every kind of illusion and confusion possible (*PT*, 4.0015). Wittgenstein gave a few illustrations of the way in which the conventional grammatical structure and the ordinary modes of speech conceal the logical structure. On the one hand, the same word has different modes of signification. The word 'is' does service for three logically distinct symbols, the copula, the sign of identity, and the existential quantifier. This kind of homonymity is deceptive. Russell stressed, in *Our Knowledge of the External World*, how Hegelian logic came to grief through taking the 'is' of predication as the 'is' of identity.[26] On the other hand, two words that do have different modes of signifying are sometimes used in such a way that the formal similarity of their surface grammar deceptively suggests a similarity in their mode of signification. Thus the existential quantifier 'exist' and the predicate 'go' both appear in ordinary language as intransitive verbs. Similarly 'identical' appears as an adjective, erroneously suggesting that it is a predicate. We use one and the same word as a name variable ("There is something on the floor') and as a propositional variable ('Something happened yesterday'). In 'Green is green', where the first occurrence of 'green' is a proper name, the expressions not only have different meanings (*Bedeutungen*), they are different kinds of symbols. The apparent logical form of a proposition that is represented in ordinary grammar, as Russell showed in his Theory of Descriptions, need not be its real form. Moreover ordinary language gives the appearance of being vague and imprecise. The complicated tacit conventions of languages make this possible, but what is said, by itself, does not reveal the form of the underlying thought that is meant.

It is this gulf between the appearance and the reality of language that produces fundamental confusions characteristic of philosophy (*TLP*, 3.324). Clarity can be achieved by the use of an adequate sign language or conceptual notation which is perspicuously governed by logical syntax (*TLP*, 3.325). The Fregean or Russellian notations, though not adequate, are such sign languages. Notoriously, this passage in the *Tractatus* led to Russell's misinterpretation of the fundamental contentions of the book.[27] Russell took Wittgenstein to be concerned with the conditions which would have to be fulfilled by a logically perfect language,

---

[26] Russell, op. cit., p. 39.
[27] Already pointed out by F. P. Ramsey in his review of the book in 1923 (reprinted in his *Foundations of Mathematics* (Routledge & Kegan Paul, London, 1931), pp. 270–86).

not that any language is logically perfect, or that we believe ourselves capable, here and now, of constructing a logically perfect language, but that the whole function of language is to have meaning, and it only fulfils this function in proportion as it approaches to the ideal language which we postulate. (*TLP*, Introd. p. x)

Wittgenstein, in Russell's opinion, was describing the conditions for accurate symbolism, since 'In practice, language is always more or less vague, so that what we assert is never quite precise'. In fact what Wittgenstein was doing was specifying the conditions which must be fulfilled by any language, for any language is and must be logically perfect. Russell overlooked Wittgenstein's comments on the adequacy of ordinary language. Natural languages which mankind constructs, Wittgenstein stressed (*TLP*, 4.002), are capable of expressing every sense. All the propositions of everyday language, he wrote, in direct opposition to Russell's interpretation, are in perfect logical order just as they are (*TLP*, 5.5563). Were this not so, language would not be capable of picturing, and so representing, reality at all. It is not, as Frege and Russell thought, that we have a handmade but imperfect instrument which is to be replaced by a precision tool which is perfect. The very possibility of propositional signs, i.e. certain kinds of facts expressing propositions in virtue of a method of projection, requires that the 'logical pictures' thus expressed be logically in perfect order. Certainly we want a perspicuous conceptual notation *for philosophical purposes*, and the *Tractatus* is intended to clarify the fundamental principles of such a notation. But again, analogously to Hertz's rational reconstruction of mechanics, this is not in order to put into language something which is not yet there, but to reveal the underlying logical structure of any possible language.

It is still not clear what specific *philosophical* errors arise out of the misleading surface features of language and are to be eradicated by a proper conceptual notation. Almost all Wittgenstein's references to past philosophy are disparaging. Philosophy is full of fundamental confusion (*TLP*, 3.324). Most philosophers do not understand the distinction between internal and external relations and consequently produce nonsense (*TLP*, 4.122). In short, most of the questions asked in philosophy are nonsense, and the putative philosophical propositions purporting to answer them are nonsense too (*TLP*, 4.003). This is a result of failure to understand the logic of our language. These pseudo-questions are unobviously of the same class as 'Is the good more or less identical than the beautiful?' The task of philosophy is of course not to answer such nonsense, but to show that it is nonsense. 'For a long time now I have thought that philosophy will one day devour itself'—the words are Lichtenberg's,[28] but the sentiment is eminently Wittgensteinian.

The claim that all past philosophy is riddled with error is quite common in the philosophical world. But that it is all a subtle form of gibberish is not. To understand Wittgenstein's thought here we must look briefly at his notion of senselessness and nonsense. Genuine propositions have sense. They picture facts and say, truly or falsely, that the world is thus or otherwise. All genuine propositions are empirical and contingent. The limiting case of propositions with sense are tautologies and contradictions. They do not violate any principles of logical syntax, but they do not picture a possible state of affairs out of a range of possibilities. They do not *say* anything, and how things are in the world can neither confute nor confirm them. ('Either it is raining or it is not raining' tells us nothing.) Although they neither say, nor try to say anything, they show the logical structure of the world (see Ch. II). Such logical propositions lack sense but they are not nonsense. They are *sinnlos* but not *unsinnig*. Nonsense, on the other hand is a feature, not of degenerate propositions, but of pseudo-propositions. Nonsensical pseudo-propositions violate the rules of logical syntax. Like senseless propositions they say nothing. But unlike senseless propositions they show nothing about the world, neither about its form nor about its content. Within the domain of nonsense we may distinguish overt from covert nonsense. Overt nonsense can be seen to be nonsense immediately. Thus, for example, 'Is the good more or less identical than the beautiful?' falls into the class of overt nonsense. But most of philosophy does not obviously violate the bounds of sense. It is covert nonsense for, in a way that is not perspicuous in ordinary language to the untutored mind, it violates the principles of the logical syntax of language. Philosophers try to say what can only be shown, and what they say, being nonsense, does not even show what they try to say. Nevertheless, even within the range of philosophical, covert nonsense we can distinguish, as we shall see, between what might (somewhat confusingly) be called illuminating nonsense, and misleading nonsense. Illuminating nonsense will guide the attentive reader to apprehend what is shown by other propositions which do not purport to be philosophical; moreover it will intimate, to those who grasp what

---

[28] Quoted in J. P. Stern, *Lichtenberg, A Doctrine of Scattered Occasions* (Thames and Hudson, London, 1963), p. 322.

is meant, its own illegitimacy. The task of philosophy in this respect then is twofold, to bring one to see what shows itself, and to prevent one from the futile endeavour to say it by teaching one 'to pass from a piece of disguised nonsense to something that is patent nonsense'.[29]

The source of the error of past philosophy lies in its failure to understand the principles of the logical syntax of language which are obscured by grammatical forms. These principles reflect the essential nature of any possible symbolism, the conditions of the very possibility of representation. Failure to grasp them engenders the illusion that one can say things which can only be shown. This in turn leads to misleading nonsense. The cardinal problem of philosophy, and the main point of his own work, Wittgenstein wrote to Russell,[30] is the theory of what can be expressed [*gesagt*] by propositions and what cannot be expressed by propositions but only shown [*gezeigt*]. Wittgenstein's distinction between what can be said and what can only be shown is bound up with his repudiation of Russell's Theory of Types, as well as with his rejection of his own earlier view that the task of philosophy is the description of logical forms. It provides the rationale for the conception of philosophy propounded in the *Tractatus*, in particular for the view that there are no philosophical propositions, that philosophy does not aim at achieving new knowledge, that philosophy is not a kind of science. The distinction is held to be vindicated by a variety of strands interwoven in the argument of the book, namely the bipolarity of the proposition, the picture theory of meaning, the distinctions between a name and a variable, a material property and a formal property, a genuine concept and a formal concept. Most of these themes will be examined in later chapters. For the moment only what is necessary to illuminate the conception of philosophy will be sketched.

The world, according to the *Tractatus*, is composed of facts. Facts are conceived to be concatenations of simple objects. These objects constitute the sempiternal substance of reality. They have both form and content. The forms of an object are its internal or formal properties. A property is internal if it is unthinkable that its object should not possess it (*TLP*, 4.123). In addition to its formal properties an object has external or material properties. *The* form of an object is its *possibility* of occurring in the various states of affairs in which it can occur (*TLP*, 2.0141). Its form is thus determined by the sum of its

[29] *PI*, §464 and §524. This later comment is equally apt for *TLP*.
[30] Letter No. 37 to Russell, 19 Aug. 1919.

formal properties, for it is they that determine with what kinds of other objects it can combine to constitute a fact. This is what constitutes its ontological type. The contingent concatenations into which a specific object does as a matter of fact enter are the external properties of the object.

The names in a language are either definable or indefinable. The definable expressions are analysable into their characteristic marks (*Merkmale*). The last residue of analysis consists of simple unanalysable names (logically proper names). It is they that 'pin' language to reality, for their meanings *are* the simple, sempiternal objects in reality for which they stand. To know the meaning of such a simple name is to know what object *is* its meaning. To know an object is to know all its possible occurrences in states of affairs, i.e. its internal properties (*TLP*, 2.0123 f.). The logical syntax of a name must mirror the form of the object which it names. For names too have both form and content. Their content is their meaning. Their form is their logico-syntactical combinatorial possibilities. This corresponds precisely to the metaphysical combinatorial possibilities of the object that is the content of the name. Just as the combinatorial possibilities of an object constitute its ontological type, so too the grammatical combinatorial possibilities of a name constitute its logico-syntactical category. The logical syntax of a name must be established independently of its specific content (meaning). Names of different objects of the same ontological type belong to the same logico-syntactical category; they differ only in their content, not in their licit combinatorial possibilities. The shared syntactical form that is common to different names of the same logico-syntactical category *is* the variable of which they are substitution-instances. The variable tacitly embodies the syntactical formation rules, the combinatorial possibilities, of the names that belong to the same category, i.e. of the names of all objects of a given ontological type. The variable is therefore the *formal concept* of the type. But a variable cannot occur in a well-formed proposition with a sense. (There are no 'real variables', only 'apparent variables'.) Hence the form of an object cannot be described; it is *shown* by the fact that the name of the object is a substitution instance of a given kind of variable. To put the same point slightly differently, the formal properties of an object can be neither named (since they are not themselves objects) nor described (since formal concepts cannot occur in well-formed propositions), but they are manifest in the logico-syntactical features (the combinatorial possibilities) of its name.

In subsequent chapters we shall try to fill out this highly abstract logico-metaphysical picture. To aid one's flagging imagination it may be helpful to think of spatio-temporal points, of unanalysable colours or notes as 'objects', of the concepts of space, time, and being coloured as formal concepts. It is of the essence of a colour that it can 'concatenate' with a spatio-temporal point, but not with a note. Parallel to this, it makes *sense* to characterize a point in the visual field as being scarlet, but not as being B-flat. The logical syntax of colour names *shows* that spatial objects, but not auditory ones, *can* be coloured. Of course, on this view, it makes no sense to say that red is a colour—that is something *shown* by the logical syntax of colour names. The general concept of colour is the common form of unanalysable colours, hence represented in a logically perspicuous notation by a variable.

A Theory of Types is intended to tell us what the range of significance of a propositional function is. It prohibits as ill-formed sentences which attempt to predicate of an entity properties that can only, in the nature of things, be predicated of an entity of a different logical type (Socrates may be mortal or immortal, but mortality cannot be!). On Wittgenstein's view, this is neither necessary nor possible. It is not necessary, for if we know the meaning of a symbol, we already know its combinatorial possibilities. For the formal concept is given immediately any substitution-instance of it is given. It is not possible, since in order to state the relevant prohibitions one would have to mention the meaning of a sign in order to lay down the rules for it (*TLP*, 3.331), but a sign cannot have a meaning without its logical syntax being fixed. Moreover, in order to justify the type-restrictions, formal concepts must be employed as if they were genuine concepts (e.g., Mortality is not an *individual*, therefore it cannot be said to be mortal or not mortal).

A venerable tradition in philosophy conceived of the goal of the subject as the attainment of knowledge about the essential, metaphysical, nature of the world. It would clarify the nature of mind, the essence of matter, the ontological status of number, and so on. This Wittgenstein held to be incoherent. An attempt to describe the essence of things will unavoidably violate the bounds of sense, misuse language, and produce nonsense. For essences would have to be expressed by the illegitimate use of formal concepts in the role of material (genuine) concepts. Thus, for example, that *A* is or is not an *object* cannot be said because 'object' is a formal concept. In a logically perspicuous notation it will be evident that formal concepts are expressed by variables not by predicates or function-names. It will be visible that expressions such as 'is an object', 'is a property', or 'is a number' cannot be used to form a genuine proposition.

The remedy for the confusions characteristic of past philosophy is to be found by devising an adequate conceptual notation. This will give us a correct logical point of view; we shall then apprehend what can and what cannot be said, and cease the futile attempt to say what can only be shown. To be sure, the correct notation will merely make explicit what is actually present in ordinary language. But what is obscured by the deceptive uniformity of grammatical forms will be laid bare to sight. And what philosophers misguidedly endeavour to say will be shown by features of the notation. That there are infinitely many objects (Russell's 'axiom of infinity') cannot be said, but it would be shown by the existence of infinitely many names with different meanings (*TLP*, 5.535). Philosophical confusions would be *visible*; for example, Frege's definition of nought as the number belonging to the concept 'not identical with itself' would be *evident* nonsense, since it would be perspicuous that identity is not a relation between objects (*TLP*, 5.5301). In a perspicuous conceptual notation it will be impossible to produce nonsensical philosophical propositions. However, it will also be impossible to produce any philosophical propositions at all!

4. *Philosophy as Critique and as Analysis*

'All philosophy', Wittgenstein wrote (*TLP*, 4.0031) in a remark that heralded the 'linguistic turn' characteristic of twentieth-century analytic philosophy, 'is a "critique of language".' Its task is not to describe the most general truths about the universe—that is the province of physics. It is not concerned with studying the workings of the human mind—that is the province of psychology. It does not investigate the metaphysical nature of things and report its findings in special philosophical, synthetic a priori, propositions, for there are no such propositions. Philosophy does not aim at new knowledge, but at a correct logical point of view upon existing non-philosophical knowledge.

A critique is an investigation into the limits of a faculty. Kant's *Critique of Pure Reason* had aimed to curb the pretensions óf philosophy by demonstrating that pure reason alone cannot arrive at transcendent metaphysical truths. All it can achieve is knowledge of synthetic a priori propositions describing the conditions of the possibility of experience. The *Tractatus* aimed to clarify the principles for a critique of language and its use.[31] Its task was:

> to set a limit to thought, or rather—not to thought, but to the expression of thoughts: for in order to be able to set a limit to thought, we should have to find both sides of the limit thinkable (i.e. we should have to be able to think what cannot be thought). (*TLP*, p. 3)

The limits of the thinkable are set in language, determined by the essential nature of representation. What lies beyond those limits cannot be said. The totality of genuine propositions constitutes the thinkable; the totality of true propositions constitutes the whole of 'natural science'. In specifying the limits of language, philosophy sets limits to the much disputed sphere of natural science, the sphere of possible knowledge. Can science thus broadly conceived tell us whether we possess an immortal soul or whether God exists? Only if the totality of propositions encompasses propositions about God and the soul. Is there any possible ethical or aesthetic knowledge? Only if there are ethical or aesthetic propositions. Kant's critique of speculative reason denied knowledge to make room for faith, for belief which is justified by practical reason. Wittgenstein's critique of language reached more radical conclusions. What we are not able, *in principle*, to know we cannot think either. The traditional metaphysical subjects of God and the soul lie beyond the boundaries of language. More radically, there can be no ethical or aesthetic propositions. Knowledge is denied to make room for silence. Finally, and here the contrast with Kant is deep, the critique itself, the description of the limits of language, lies beyond the realm of what can be said. Language can no more describe its own essence than it can describe the essence of the world.

Philosophy propounds no doctrines, constructs no theories, attains no knowledge. It is an activity of logical clarification. It eliminates misunderstandings, resolves unclarities, and dissolves philosophical

---

[31] Like the Critical philosophy of Kant, the *Tractatus* is concerned with clarifying the bounds of sense. Similarly, it identifies the roots of philosophical error in attempts to traverse them. Unlike Kant, however, Wittgenstein did not think that the bounds of sense are describable by means of synthetic a priori propositions, since these too are 'on the Index'. Far from holding that the forms of thought and language are imposed by the mind upon sensible intuitions to 'make nature', he held that they are determined by the mind-independent logical forms of reality and by the essential, objective, nature of the possibility of representation. Wittgenstein's 'Copernican Revolution' came later, with his conception of the autonomy of grammar (see Ch. VII). But this too is very different from Kant's Copernican Revolution.

problems that arise out of ordinary empirical propositions. This is to be done by analysis:

> The idea is to express in an appropriate symbolism what in ordinary language leads to endless misunderstandings. That is to say, where ordinary language disguises logical structure, where it allows the formation of pseudo-propositions, where it uses one term in an infinity of different meanings, we must replace it by a symbolism which gives a clear picture of the logical structure, excludes pseudo-propositions, and uses its terms unambiguously.[32]

The need for such analysis arises from unclarities about the sense of a given ordinary proposition. Whether the analysis will need to be pursued to the level of elementary (atomic) propositions and logically proper names or not will depend upon whether the difficulties that need to be resolved can be eliminated at a higher level than the ultimate 'atomic' structure.

In addition to its role as clarifier of good sense, philosophy has a more negative, dialectical task. Whenever someone wants to state metaphysical truths, the philosopher must show him that he has given no meaning to certain signs in his propositions (*TLP*, 6.53). If someone, trying to describe essences, endeavours to use 'is a number' or 'is an object' as predicate expressions, one must point out that *as* substitution–instances of predicate variables, these signs have been given no meanings. They are signs for variables, not names. This may seem unsatisfactory to the person whose puzzlement we are resolving and whose metaphysical pronouncements we are demolishing. For in doing philosophy this way, we say nothing metaphysical about the essence of the world and present no doctrine of logical form about the essence of language. But this method is the only strictly correct one. The metaphysician's hankering after the essence of the world cannot be satisfied in philosophical propositions, but only by apprehending the forms of non-philosophical propositions. For every genuine proposition, in addition to saying what it says, shows some logical property of the universe (*NB*, p. 107). When the forms of language are laid bare in a proper conceptual notation, then the essence of the world, which philosophy has always striven to describe, though unutterable, will be lying upon the surface in full view.

It follows that the philosophical method practised *in* the *Tractatus* (as

---

[32] This remark is from Wittgenstein's 1929 paper 'Some Remarks on Logical Form', *Proceedings of the Aristotelian Society*, supp. vol. ix (1929), p. 163. It was written before the fundamental change in his philosophical ideas and sheds important light upon his conception of analysis in the *Tractatus*.

opposed to the method preached *by* the *Tractatus*) is not strictly the correct one. The *Tractatus* does not set a limit to thought by a clear presentation of what can be said. The propositions of the *Tractatus* are not clarifications of ordinary empirical propositions. On the contrary, they are, as Wittgenstein pointed out in the penultimate remark of the book, nonsensical pseudo-propositions. A critique of the kind constituted by the *Tractatus* itself would have to stand, as it were, on both sides of the limits of the thinkable. Such a critique could not possibly make sense. What then is its rationale? What point can such nonsense have?

Wittgenstein's remark that whoever understands him will recognize that the propositions of the *Tractatus* are nonsense (*TLP*, 6.54) was greeted by philosophers with incredulous indignation. In his preface Russell observed that 'after all Mr. Wittgenstein manages to say a good deal about what cannot be said'.[33] Black, like Russell, cannot doubt that we understand the book and learn much from it, so there must be some way out of this paradox. He suggests[34] that we may concede that if communication is equated exclusively with 'saying' then the *Tractatus* communicates nothing. Nevertheless there is, according to the *Tractatus* itself, much that can be shown even if it cannot be said. Hence, surely, the *Tractatus* shows a great deal, and this is salvageable. Black proceeds to erect what he calls 'a line of defence'. According to this, all cases in which Wittgenstein is seeking the essence of something that results in a priori statements belonging to logical syntax or philosophical grammar (Black's example is 'A proposition is not a complex name') consist of formal statements showing something that can be shown. These, Black claims, are no worse than logical statements which involve no violation of the rules of logical syntax.

This is mistaken. Logical propositions are senseless but not nonsense. They say nothing, but they show the internal properties of compound propositions and represent the scaffolding of the world.[35] 'Formal statements', however, neither say nor show anything. They do violate the rules of logical syntax, for they wrongly employ formal

---

[33] *TLP*, p. xxi. Borrowing from F. P. Ramsey, *Foundations of Mathematics*, p. 268, one might indeed say that the *Tractatus* gives an impression of similarity to the child's remarks in the following dialogue: 'Say "breakfast".' 'Can't.' 'What can't you say?' 'Can't say "breakfast".'

[34] M. Black, *A Companion to Wittgenstein's Tractatus* (Cambridge University Press, Cambridge, 1964), pp. 378 ff.

[35] This will be clarified in Ch. II.

concepts. Thus, in Black's example, 'proposition', 'name', and 'complex' are all formal concepts. Hence the 'formal statements' that use them are nonsense. Wittgenstein was quite correct and consistent; the *Tractatus* does indeed consist largely of pseudo-propositions. Of course, what Wittgenstein meant by these remarks (like what the solipsist means (*TLP*, 5.62)) is, in his view, quite correct, only it cannot be said. Apparently what someone means or intends by a remark can be grasped even though the sentence uttered is strictly speaking nonsense. (Thus Wittgenstein claims to understand what the solipsist means.)

The uneasy distinction between illuminating nonsense and misleading nonsense has frequently been attacked by critics. Ramsey[36] argued that either philosophy must be of some use, or else it is a disposition which we have to check. If philosophy is nonsense, then it is useless and we should not pretend as Wittgenstein did that it is important nonsense. Later commentators[37] have followed Ramsey in finding this notion absurd, and it has been objected in defence[38] that Wittgenstein neither said nor intended any such absurdity. Certainly, Wittgenstein did not use the phrase 'illuminating nonsense'. What he said was that the propositions of the *Tractatus* elucidate by bringing whoever understands their author to recognize them as nonsensical. They are not elucidations in the sense of analyses of 'scientific' propositions into their constituents. Rather are they pseudo-propositions by means of which one can climb beyond them. They lead one to see the world aright, from a correct logical point of view. One will then realize that they are nonsensical, and throw away the ladder up which one has climbed.

Ramsey claimed that if philosophy is nonsense, it is a disposition which ought to be checked. Does this follow? In one sense it does. Philosophy of the kind practised in the *Tractatus* should no longer be written. If anyone tries to say anything metaphysical we should dialectically, bring him to see his errors. His metaphysical questions will not have been answered, but his mind, 'no longer vexed, will cease to ask illegitimate questions'. To this extent future philosophy, according to the *Tractatus*, ought to be purely analytical and

[36] F. P. Ramsey, 'Philosophy', in *Foundations of Mathematics*, p. 263.
[37] e.g. R. Carnap, *The Logical Syntax of Language* (Routledge & Kegan Paul, London, 1937), pp. 282 ff.; G. Pitcher, *The Philosophy of Wittgenstein* (Prentice Hall, New Jersey, 1964), p. 155.
[38] K. T. Fann, *Wittgenstein's Conception of Philosophy* (Blackwell, Oxford, 1969), p. 34.

therapeutic. The *Tractatus* itself, though a manifestation of our natural disposition to metaphysics, is a justifiable undertaking which has been fully and finally discharged. It is not a prolegomenon to any future metaphysics, but the swansong of metaphysics.

II

THE DIALOGUE WITH FREGE AND RUSSELL

1. *Agreements and Disagreements*

The *Tractatus* is, *inter alia*, a dialogue with Frege and Russell, a dialogue in which, to a large extent, the voices of the two initiators are supposed to be familiar to the reader. Difficult to understand at best, it is quite impossible to follow without a grasp of the positions against which Wittgenstein was, often implicitly, arguing. Problems are compounded by three further factors. First, one must identify Wittgenstein's specific targets. Sometimes they are to be found in Frege's *Begriffsschrift*, sometimes in *The Basic Laws of Arithmetic* or in his articles. In Russell's case Wittgenstein was not only criticizing the views propounded in *The Principles of Mathematics*, *Principia Mathematica*, and *Our Knowledge of the External World*, but often also views Russell never published and which only publicly came to light with the posthumous publication in 1984 of the suppressed 1913 manuscript entitled *Theory of Knowledge*.[1] Secondly, one must beware of reading modern conceptions into these works. Though familiar technical terms such as 'function', 'truth-function', 'truth-condition', 'logical constant', 'form' occur in the writings of Frege, Russell, and the *Tractatus*, it must not be presumed that they are used in the same way or understood in the same manner as they are now. Otherwise one will misconstrue Wittgenstein's targets and misunderstand his criticisms. Thirdly, it is not enough to clarify how Frege and Russell used and construed their terms of art; one must make clear, when necessary, whether Wittgenstein, in criticizing them, interpreted them as they intended. An exhaustive record of this dialogue would pay rich dividends in terms of

---

[1] B. Russell, *Theory of Knowledge, the 1913 Manuscript*, ed. E. R. Eames in collaboration with K. Blackwell, Vol. 7 of *The Collected Papers of Bertrand Russell* (Allen & Unwin, London, 1984). Russell, as a result of Wittgenstein's criticisms in 1913, never completed this work and published only a fragment of it in the form of six articles in *The Monist*.

understanding the roots of modern philosophical logic. Here, however, I shall merely sketch some of the main theories and outline some of the central arguments.

Wittgenstein sided with Frege against psychologism in logic. Logical analysis is wholly independent of introspective psychology. Analysis of mental processes of thought and association, investigation into the empirical nature of human understanding, explanations of our modes of acquisition of concepts in learning-theory all belong to psychology and are irrelevant to logic (*TLP*, 4.1121). Accordingly, like Frege,[2] Wittgenstein brushed aside as irrelevant to logic a host of questions concerning the nature of understanding. Only in the 1930s did he gradually realize the crucial relevance of a correct grasp of the *logical* character of understanding to a coherent account of meaning and language. The misguided picture he had of understanding when he wrote the *Tractatus*, his implicit commitment to a range of misconceptions, is visible only as the tip of an iceberg. We shall examine this in the next chapter. He agreed with Frege and Russell that ordinary language disguises logical form (an insight he attributed to Russell's Theory of Descriptions (cf. *TLP*, 4.0031)), but, as we noted, disagreed radically with them over their claim that natural languages are logically defective. Since logical order is a condition of sense, every sense that is expressed in ordinary language is perfectly expressed, any indeterminacy is determinately indeterminate. That is not to say that there are no nonsensical 'sentences' formed by users of natural languages; of course, *every* notation can be misused. Nor is it to say that there are no ambiguities. It is rather that there can be no halfway house between sense and nonsense. But the logical order of natural language is not perspicuous in its grammatical forms. The new function-theoretic logic goes some way to providing an instrument, a conceptual notation (*Begriffsschrift*) that can reveal the underlying logical structures of natural language. Hence, Wittgenstein argued against Frege and Russell, it aims to be an ideal *notation*, not an ideal *language*. There

---

[2] Frege conceived of propositions or 'thoughts in a non-psychological sense' as abstract Platonic entities. Understanding or 'grasping' these objects is, he thought, a mental process 'and this process is perhaps the most mysterious of all. But just because it is mental in character we do not need to concern ourself with it in logic. It is enough for us that we can grasp thoughts and recognize them to be true; how this takes place is an independent question'. (G. Frege, *Posthumous Writings*, ed. H. Hermes *et al.*, trans. P. Long, R. White (Blackwell, Oxford, 1979), p. 145.) Wittgenstein repudiated the Platonism, but like Frege held it to be unnecessary to subject the concept of understanding to philosophical scrutiny.

cannot *be* an *illogical language* (cf. *TLP*, 3.03-3.032), but a logically perspicuous notation can lay bare the hidden logical forms of thought and language that are revealed by logical analysis. Such a notation, however, had not yet been attained.

Complex concepts are analysable into their components, in the simplest case by displaying their characteristic marks (*Merkmale*) that are necessary and sufficient for their application. Names of complexes, viz. definite descriptions and proper names that abbreviate definite descriptions, are analysable along the lines Russell showed. But Russell had erred in retaining the sign of identity in his analysans (viz. in paraphrasing '$\psi(\imath x)(\phi x)$' as '$(\exists x) (y) ((\phi y) \equiv (y=x) \& (\psi x))$'). For 'to say of *two* things that they are identical is nonsense, and to say of *one* thing that it is identical with itself is to say nothing at all' (*TLP*, 5.5303). Accordingly, Wittgenstein showed how the identity sign could be eliminated from the paraphrase. Analysis breaks down logically complex propositions into simpler ones which are their constituents. Logical relations of implication or exclusion between propositions betoken hidden complexity that can be revealed by analysis. Entailments are always consequences of truth-functional combinations of propositions that are made explicit by analysis. The terminus of analysis consists in elementary propositions in which there is no hidden complexity and which have no (non-trivial) entailments. An elementary proposition consists of simple names that have a meaning or reference (*Bedeutung*) but no sense. Such a name stands for, or is a representative of, an 'object' or entity in reality (a matter we shall explore further in Chapter III). Every proposition has a *unique* analysis (*TLP*, 3.25), contrary to what Frege thought.[3]

[3] This is a contentious matter. An interpretation of Frege as licensing alternative analyses is in G. P. Baker and P. M. S. Hacker, *Frege: Logical Excavations* (Blackwell, Oxford, 1984), pp. 154 ff. and *passim*. In correspondence Frege wrote 'I do not believe that for any judgeable-content there is only one way in which it can be decomposed, or that one of these possible ways can always claim objective pre-eminence' (Frege, *Philosophical and Mathematical Correspondence*, ed. G. Gabriel *et al.*, trans. H. Kaal (Blackwell, Oxford, 1980), p. 101). In *Begriffsschrift* §10 Frege makes it clear that the content Φ A is just as much the value of a second-level concept for the concept Φ (*x*) as argument as it is the value of the first-level concept Φ (*x*) for the object A as argument. This principle of parity, i.e. viewing the manner of function/argument decomposition as (at least in some cases) relative to our *Auffassungsweise*, is apparently retained in later writings, despite the introduction of the sense/reference distinction (cf. Frege, *The Basic Laws of Arithmetic* §22). If so, the symbols of *Begriffsschrift* are type-ambiguous, and analysis is *not* unique. It is not clear whether Wittgenstein had Frege in mind at this point. What is clear is that his conception of uniqueness of analysis wars with alternative function/argument decomposition. It is further noteworthy that uniqueness of analysis is a corollary of Russell's principle of acquaintance.

The Dialogue with Frege and Russell

As regards the philosophical task of analysing the nature of the proposition, Wittgenstein argued that logic is concerned only with the *unasserted* proposition (*NB*, p. 96). Frege had held that a declarative sentence and a corresponding sentence-question express the same proposition (thought, *Gedanke*), but that a corresponding order or wish does not express a proposition at all. Wittgenstein, like Russell (at least in *Theory of Knowledge*[4]), went further. For the assertion that it is the case that *p*, the question of whether it is the case that *p* and the command to make it the case that *p* all seem to have in common the unasserted proposition *that p*.[5] And that is all that is of interest to logic. Consequently, Wittgenstein insisted against Frege *and* Russell (in the *Principles* and *Principia*), the assertion sign is logically irrelevant.

Frege had recurrently argued that one can draw inferences only from true assertions. In *Begriffsschrift* every premiss in the proof of a theorem *must* be flagged by an assertion-sign. A related confusion was evident in Russell. In *The Principles of Mathematics*[6] he held that true propositions have a quality not belonging to false ones, namely of being asserted 'in a non-psychological sense' (*PrM*, p. 35). Assertion 'in a logical sense' is a crucial logical feature, for 'when we say *therefore*, we state a relation which can only hold between asserted propositions'. In *Principia*[7] the assertion-sign is employed to flag assertions and can be read, the authors explain, as 'it is true that'. Wittgenstein thought that this was confused. The assertion-sign is *logically* quite meaningless and irrelevant (*TLP*, 4.442). It is only of psychological significance, indicating which propositions the authors hold to be true. But it is not a component part of a proposition or a proof. For, Wittgenstein

---

[4] On p. 107 Russell argued that 'Beggars are riders', 'Beggars would be riders', 'Are beggars riders?', and 'Beggars shall be riders!' all express a common proposition, which Russell formulates by means of a verbal noun, viz. 'beggars being riders'. The different sentences, he thought express different 'attitudes' to the same proposition.

[5] This was a move down the road to theories of 'semantic-mood' and 'sentence-radical' ('neustic'/'phrastic'; 'force'/'sense') that flourished in the second half of this century. By then, however, Wittgenstein had long since gone off in the opposite direction, having subjected the basic inspiration of such conceptions to brief but damning criticism (*PI*, §§22 ff.). For detailed elaboration of the matter, see G. P. Baker and P. M. S. Hacker, *Language, Sense and Nonsense*, Chs. 2–3 (Blackwell, Oxford, 1984). For analysis of Wittgenstein's arguments against such theories, see G. P. Baker and P. M. S. Hacker, *Wittgenstein: Understanding and Meaning* (Blackwell, Oxford, 1980), pp. 110 ff., 140 ff.

[6] B. Russell, *The Principles of Mathematics* (Cambridge University Press, Cambridge, 1903); subsequent references in the text will be abbreviated *PrM*.

[7] A. N. Whitehead and B. Russell, *Principia Mathematica to *56* (Cambridge University Press, Cambridge, 1967) p. 92; subsequent references are abbreviated *PM*.

insisted (as we would today), one can draw inferences from a *false* proposition (*TLP*, 4.023), 'one can actually see from the proposition how everything stands in logic *if* it is true'. In *Begriffsschrift* Frege had suggested that the assertion-sign or, more accurately, the 'judgement-stroke' in his concept-script corresponded to a verb-phrase 'is a fact' that is, as it were, the common (formal) predicate of every judgement, and is attached to a nominalized sentence (e.g. 'The death of Caesar in 44 BC *is a fact*'). This too, Wittgenstein responded, must be wrong. The verb of the proposition is not 'is true' or 'is false' as Frege had suggested[8], rather that which 'is true' must already contain the verb (*TLP*, 4.063).

Neither in the *Tractatus*, nor at any other time in his life, did Wittgenstein accept the 'realist' conception of a proposition that informed all Frege's work. A proposition is not an abstract entity that corresponds to a sentence which 'stands for' or 'expresses' it. It is rather a propositional-sign (a sentence) *in its projective relation to the world*. A propositional-sign is not a complex name, either of a truth-value (as Frege argued in his mature work) or of a complex object (as Russell thought and Frege had held in *Begriffsschrift*). It is essentially a description of a (possible) state of affairs. If the state of affairs described obtains, the proposition is true, otherwise it is false. Truth and falsity are not logical objects denoted by *some* propositions, as Frege thought, but are *essential* properties of any genuine proposition. There can be no such thing as a proposition which lacks a truth-value, for if a propositional-sign has a sense, it determines a possibility which the world either satisfies or does not. (The Law of Excluded Middle is not, as Russell suggested, like 'All roses are either yellow or red', which, even if true, is accidentally true (*TLP*, 6.111). It is of the *nature* of a proposition to be either true or false.) Wittgenstein, however, not only accepted bivalence (like Russell), but insisted that propositions other than tautologies and contradictions, are *bipolar*, i.e. capable of being true *and* capable of being false (so there are no necessary truths or necessary falsehoods among elementary propositions). This followed from the essential nature of representation (see Chapter III below).

[8] Wittgenstein's phrasing is odd and the *exact* target obscure. Frege argued in *Begriffsschrift* that the judgement-stroke corresponded to 'is a fact', not to 'is true', let alone 'is false'. Later he dropped this paraphrase and suggested that the thought (sense of a sentence) expressed is 'the circumstance that . . .' and that by asserting a declarative sentence one 'makes a transition' from sense to reference, from a thought to a truth-value. Both claims are undoubtedly confused, but it remains unclear (to me) what Wittgenstein had in mind here.

Wittgenstein agreed that a proposition is essentially composite, composed of function and argument. Like Frege and Russell, he wrote (*TLP*, 3.318), he construed the proposition (the propositional-sign in its projective relation) as a function of the expressions contained in it. Like Russell, he apparently conceived of a propositional function as mapping its arguments on to *propositions*. Frege, in *Begriffsschrift*, in effect conceived of propositional functions as mapping unjudgeable-contents (non-linguistic entities) on to judgeable-contents (propositions conceived as abstract entities). For Wittgenstein, it seems, the arguments of (first order) propositional-functions were not Russellian 'individuals' or Fregean 'unjudgeable-contents' but (arguably) names, i.e. symbols (not signs). The constituent names of a fully analysed proposition have meanings which are the 'objects' they stand for. Logically simple names have only meaning (reference), no *sense* (they do not represent *possibilities*, but stand for entities, and they do not *present* the entities they stand for as values of functions for arguments). Borrowing Frege's famous dictum (but using it for very different reasons and purposes) Wittgenstein claimed that names have a meaning only in the context of a proposition. Unlike Frege, however, he did not distinguish between kinds of names (proper names and names of concepts of various levels) according to 'completeness' or 'incompleteness', nor did he distinguish their referents according to whether they are 'saturated' or 'unsaturated'. *All* names are essentially 'incomplete' and can occur meaningfully only in logico-syntactical co-ordination, and correspondingly the objects they stand for can occur only in concatenation, as constituents of facts. But quantifiers, which Frege thought of as names of second-level functions, are not names at all. Names are of very varied logical categories, corresponding to the ontological character of the object they represent. Names belonging to the same category have the same logical form, are governed by the same rules of logical syntax stipulating their combinatorial possibilities. Their common form is shown by the fact that they are substitution instances of the same variable (which corresponds to a *formal concept*). Their difference in content consists in the different meanings that they have, the different objects of the same kind that the distinct names of a given category stand for (*TLP*, 2.0233).

Propositions, unlike simple names, have a sense. Contrary to Frege's view, they are not names of truth-values, nor do they have truth-values as their reference. They are not names at all, but facts that constitute descriptions or logical pictures of states of affairs. The co-ordination of simple names in accord with logical syntax produces a representation, a model or picture, of the co-ordination of objects in a (possible) state of affairs. The *fact* that the constituent names are thus co-ordinated represents the corresponding co-ordination of the objects they name in a state of affairs, given the appropriate method of projection. 'A proposition *shows* how things stand *if* it is true' (*TLP*, 4.022), that is its sense. Hence Wittgenstein's conception of sense is wholly different from Frege's. For Frege the sense of a sentence was 'a mode of presentation of a truth-value', viz. its presentation as the value of some particular function for a specific argument (e.g. the function ξ *is hot* for *the Sun* as argument). For him sense was not essentially connected with a *possibility*. For mathematical and logical sentences (formulae) express thoughts (have a sense), but being *necessary* do not describe a state of affairs that *could* be otherwise. Equally, he thought that sentences of fiction express a sense, but lack a truth-value. For Wittgenstein, by contrast, to have a sense is to present a *possible* arrangement of objects in a state of affairs, which arrangement may obtain (in which case the proposition is true) or not obtain (in which case it is false). Propositions of logic all have the same sense, viz. none, and propositions of mathematics are pseudo-propositions.

So far, then, some of the agreements and disagreements with his august predecessors. Their logical systems were pregnant with philosophical confusions which they had not understood. Wittgenstein's deepest objections, and his constructive ideas, stemmed from what he called his *Grundgedanke*. This in turn led to his explanation of logical necessity. I shall discuss these two themes in this chapter, deferring the picture theory of meaning to the next.

2. *The* Grundgedanke *of the* Tractatus

As noted in the previous chapter, the fundamental thought of the *Tractatus* was that 'the "logical constants" are not representatives; that there can be no representatives of the *logic* of facts' (*TLP*, 4.0312). In an importantly different context, this is repeated later in the book, 'there are no "logical objects" or "logical constants" (in Frege's and Russell's sense)' (*TLP*, 5.4; cf. 4.441). What was Wittgenstein's target?

Frege had held that expressions such as 'object, 'concept', 'function', were names. (Notoriously, he was dimly aware of having painted himself into a corner with 'concept' and 'function', for which he *blamed natural language*.) Object, concept, first-level function, second-level function, etc. were *super-categories*, as it were ultimate

The Dialogue with Frege and Russell

logical and ontological *summa genera*. These distinctions, he wrote, are 'founded deep in the nature of things'.[9] Numbers, he tried to prove, were kinds of logical objects—a view with which Wittgenstein always disagreed. More importantly for present purposes, Frege argued that truth and falsehood were special logical objects named by sentences. Finally, he treated the logical connectives as names of literal functions, viz. 'not' as the name of the concept of negation (a unary function), the binary connectives as names of relations, and the quantifiers as names of second-level functions.

Russell had more visibly enmeshed himself in confusions. In *The Principles of Mathematics* (1903) he had claimed that

> The discussion of indefinables—which forms the chief part of philosophical logic—is the endeavour to see clearly, and to make others see clearly, the entities concerned, in order that the mind may have that kind of acquaintance with them which it has with redness or the taste of a pineapple ... the indefinables are obtained primarily as the necessary residue in a process of analysis ...[10]

These indefinables are the fundamental logical concepts, which, in Russell's view, mathematics accepts *as* indefinable. Russell called these 'logical constants' (*PrM*, p. vii). When we replace all non-logical constants in a proposition by variables in a process of successive generalization, Russell argued, we obtain the formal essence of a proposition. Such a general proposition will contain only variables and indefinables—the logical constants. Thus a process of abstraction or generalization will lead us from 'If Socrates is a Greek, Socrates is a man' to 'if a and b are classes, and a is contained in b, then "x is an a" implies "x is a b" '. This proposition contains, according to Russell, three variables and the logical constants *class*, *contained in*, and those involved in the notion of formal implication with variables. The logical constants are to be defined only by enumeration, for they are so fundamental that all the properties by which the classes of them might be defined presuppose some terms of the class (*PrM*, pp. 8 f.). They are, he thought, implication, the relation of a term to a class of which it is a member, the notion of *such that*, the notion of relation, and truth (*PrM*, p. 11). Later in the book he enlarged the list to include propositional function, class, denoting, and *any* or *every term* (*PrM*, p.

---

[9] G. Frege, 'Function and Concept', p. 41, repr. in P. Geach and M. Black, ed., *Translations from the Philosophical Writings of Gottlob Frege* (Blackwell, Oxford, 1960).
[10] B. Russell, *The Principles of Mathematics*, Preface to the first edition, p. v.

106). With the exception of *truth*, these logical constants were, Russell thought, constituents of the general propositions in which they occur. And these perfectly general propositions are the propositions of (and subject-matter of) logic.

By 1913 Russell had pushed this line of thought further. In *Theory of Knowledge* he argued that we must, as a condition of understanding a proposition of logic and hence as a pre-condition of logical knowledge, have acquaintance with the pure forms with which logic is concerned. These pure forms are the *summa genera* of logic, the residue 'from a process of generalization which has been carried to its utmost limit'.[11] These Russell called 'logical objects' and also 'logical constants' (*TK*, p. 98). Acquaintance with these objects is by means of *logical experience*.

> There certainly is such a thing as 'logical experience', by which I mean that kind of immediate knowledge, other than judgment, which is what enables us to understand logical terms ... such terms ... for instance as particulars, universals, relations, dual complexes, predicates. Such words are no doubt, somewhat difficult, and are only understood by people who have reached a certain level of mental development. Still, they are understood, and this shows that those who understand them possess something which seems fitly described as 'acquaintance with logical objects'. (*TK*, p. 97.)

Prior to Russell's writing this, however, Wittgenstein, as we have noted, had already told him that 'there are no logical constants', since the propositions of logic contain only *apparent* variables, not real variables, and these signify the forms of propositions, not constituents of propositions of logic. Wittgenstein's ideas were still in flux, and there is no doubt that Russell did not clearly understand what he was driving at. He tried to budget for Wittgenstein's objections by remarking that it would seem that logical objects cannot be regarded as 'entities' (*TK*, p. 97). They 'might seem to be entities occurring in logical propositions, but are really concerned with pure *form*, and are not actually constituents of the propositions in the verbal expression of which their names occur' (*TK*, p. 98). Having made what appears to be a perfunctory gesture in Wittgenstein's direction, he continued to argue that his 'indefinables of logic' are *names of objects* (pure forms) with *which we must be acquainted by means of logical experience* or 'logical intuition' (*TK*, pp. 99, 101). For acquaintance with them is a prerequisite for understanding the propositions of logic and for the

---

[11] B. Russell, *Theory of Knowledge, the 1913 Manuscript*, p. 97. Subsequent references in the text are abbreviated to *TK*.

philosophical task of making inventories of logical forms. A form, he thought, must be a genuine object, such as an absolutely general fact like 'Something is somehow related to something' which has no constituents, is unanalysable, and therefore *simple*. The proposition 'Something is somehow related to something', he claimed, is much the same as the proposition 'There are dual complexes' and so belongs to the inventory of the most general features of reality. The pure form which such a proposition describes is always a constituent of the understanding-complex that occurs when we understand that proposition, so we must be acquainted with such an object by a logical experience (*TK*, p. 129).

Apart from logical experience of these objects, i.e. forms, Russell thought that we must also be acquainted with other kinds of logical objects:

Besides the forms of atomic complexes, there are many other logical objects which are involved in the formation of non-atomic complexes. Such words as *or*, *not*, *all*, *some*, plainly involve logical notions; and since we can use such words intelligently, we must be acquainted with the logical objects involved. (*TK*, p. 99.)

The matter of the logical connectives and quantifiers will be deferred for a moment.

The issue of Russell's 'indefinables of logic', the 'logical constants', preoccupied Wittgenstein throughout 1913 and 1914 (see 'Notes on Logic' and 'Notes dictated to G. E. Moore'). Russell was, he thought, enmeshed in deep confusions as regards the concepts of proposition, constituent of a proposition, and, most of all, *form*. Correspondingly, Russell was muddled about the notions of a complex, a fact, and the idea of a 'logical object' in reality, viz. a form with which we must be acquainted.

In the 'Notes on Logic' (*NB*, p. 104), Wittgenstein criticized Russell's confusions:

It is easy to suppose that only such symbols are complex as contain names of objects, and that accordingly '$(x,\phi) \phi x$' or '$(\exists x, y) xRy$' must be simple. It is then natural to call the first of these the name of a form, the second the name of a relation.[12] But in that case what is the meaning e.g. of '$\sim(\exists x,y)xRy$'? Can we put 'not' before a name?

---

[12] Not, I think, a specific relation (e.g. is older than), but a form of relation (in this case the 'dual relation' as Russell put it). In the next paragraph he writes 'The indefinables of logic must be independent of each other. If an indefinable is introduced,

This is arguably directed against Russell's view that abstraction yields general propositions that are names of logical objects or pure forms that are simple[13], such as a dual (triple, etc.) relation. Subsequently he goes to the heart of the matter:

> It is easy to suppose that 'individual', 'particular', 'complex' etc. are primitive ideas of logic. Russell, e.g., says 'individual' and 'matrix' are 'primitive ideas'. This error presumably is to be explained by the fact that by employment of variables instead of the generality-sign, it comes to seem as if logic dealt with things which have been deprived of all properties except thing-hood, and with propositions deprived of all properties except complexity. We forget that the indefinables of symbols [*Urbilder von Zeichen*] only occur under the generality sign, never outside it.[14]

These ideas evolved, via the 'Notes dictated to Moore' of 1914, into the *Tractatus* discussion of formal properties and formal concepts (which we mentioned in the previous chapter) and into Wittgenstein's repudiation of the need for, or even intelligibility of, any Theory of Types. They had profound implications not only for the nature of philosophy and metaphysics (which we have seen), but also for the status of the propositions of logic, the nature of logical necessity, and our knowledge of necessary truths of logic.

Russell's conception of logic as the science of the completely general, i.e. a science of the properties and relations of logical objects or constants that are constituents of logical (i.e. 'completely general') propositions, bargained away the necessity of such propositions (since completely general propositions may nevertheless be only accidentally valid), and distorted the *essential* validity of logic in the endeavour to obtain for it a subject-matter, viz. the most general features of the world (*TLP*, 6.1232). But 'All theories that make a proposition of logic appear to have content are false'. The properties of the propositions of logic are not *material* properties and if one treats them as if they were,

---

it must be introduced in all combinations in which it can occur ... e.g. if the form xRy has been introduced, it must henceforth be understood in propositions of the form aRb just in the same way as in propositions such as $(\exists y)xRy$ and others' (ibid.). The issue, however, is murky. The key to the matter lies in clarifying Russell's conception of relations and their forms at this period and seeing Wittgenstein's remarks as responses to Russell.

[13] 'Russell's "complexes"', Wittgenstein remarked acidly, 'were to have the useful property of being compounded, and were to combine with this the agreeable property that they could be treated like "simples"' (*NB*, p. 99).

[14] *NB*, Appendix I, p. 107, *second edition* (1979). The improved version of the 'Notes on Logic' differs here importantly from the Costelloe version in the first edition.

as Frege and Russell had, then 'the logical proposition acquires all the characteristics of a proposition of natural science and this is the sure sign that it has been construed wrongly' (*TLP*, 6.111). As Wittgenstein had already noted in his second letter to Russell in 1912, 'Logic must turn out to be of a TOTALLY different kind than any other science', not merely different in its subject-matter. Russell only multiplied confusion by arguing that the 'logical constants' are not *constituent entities* of logical propositions, but pure forms, and *then* proceeding to argue that they are *logical objects* of which we must have logical experience. 'The "experience" that we need in order to understand logic is not that something is thus and so [*dass sich etwas so und so verhält*] but that something *is*: That, however, is *not* an experience. Logic is prior to every experience—that something *is so*' (*TLP*, 5.552). The propositions of logic presuppose only that simple names have meanings, i.e. that the world has a sempiternal substance (*TLP*, 2.021 ff.) the objects of which are the meanings of the simple names in a fully analysed proposition, and that elementary propositions have sense (*TLP*, 6.124). Understanding them does not presuppose (as Russell thought) experience of pure forms, since there is no such thing. Russell (and Frege too) employed formal concepts as if they were names or genuine concepts. But these formal concepts cannot be represented by means of a function (*TLP*, 4.126). They are signified by a variable, hence they cannot occur in a well-formed proposition with a sense. So one cannot say, as Frege and Russell did, that 1 is a number, or that there are $\aleph_0$ objects (the axiom of infinity), or even that there are objects (*TLP*, 4.1272). Every variable represents a constant form that all its values possess. The formal properties that Frege and Russell thought to be signified by (formal) concepts are in fact expressed by the common logico-syntactical features of all symbols belonging to the same category which are substitution instances of a given kind of variable. Hence to 'understand a formal concept' one need not have (and cannot have) a 'logical experience' of a formal property (a 'logical object' it signifies). For 'a formal concept is given immediately any object falling under it is given' (*TLP*, 4.12721). So it is neither possible nor necessary to introduce as primitive ideas objects belonging to a formal concept *and* the formal concept itself, e.g. primitive indefinable functions *and* the general concept of the function in question, as Russell did. For 'if I know an object I also know all its possible occurrences in states of affairs . . . I must know all its internal properties' (*TLP*, 2.0123 f.) and thus to know an object is to understand the name of which it is the meaning and to grasp its logico-syntactical form. Russell's 'logical constants' therefore are not entities of any kinds, nor are they logical objects, but forms of genuine objects. These forms are not named by any kind of expression, but *shown* by logico-syntactical *features* of the names of the objects in question.[15] And *that* is what Wittgenstein was driving at in the remarks (*TLP*, 4.0312) with which we began, viz. 'My fundamental idea is that the "logical constants" are not representatives, that there can be no representatives of the *logic* of facts'.

A similar remark, as noted, occurs in the *Tractatus*, 5.4 (cf. 4.441). But there Wittgenstein is focusing specifically upon the idea that the logical connectives are names of functions (as Frege thought) or of logical objects (as Russell argued). While Frege never got entwined in Russell's confusion about logical experiences of the 'logical objects' signified by the connectives, he did think that connectives were names of functions. In *Begriffsschrift* he conceived of the conditional as signifying a relation between judgeable-contents; in his later work he conceived of the binary connectives as referring to relations between truth-values (or other objects). Similarly he conceived of the negation sign as standing for a concept (a unary function) mapping judgeable-contents on to judgeable-contents, and later as mapping a truth-value on to a truth-value. Thus if 'p' and 'q' are both names of the True then '$p \supset q$' says of the True that it stands in a certain relation to the True.

---

[15] Some of this rubbed off on Russell. The impact of discussions with Wittgenstein in 1913 led to the suppression of *Theory of Knowledge*, and the effect of the 'Notes on Logic' is, in this respect, evident in *Our Knowledge of the External World* (Chicago and London, 1914), which was delivered in place of *Theory of Knowledge* as the Lowell Lectures. On p. 208 Russell wrote:

Such words as *or, not, if, there is, identity, greater, plus, nothing, everything, function*, and so on are not names of definite objects, like 'John' or 'Jones', but are words which require a context in order to have meaning. All of them are *formal*, that is to say, their occurrence indicates a certain form of proposition, not a certain constituent. 'Logical constants' in short are not entities; the words expressing them are not names, and cannot significantly be made into logical subjects except when it is the words themselves, as opposed to their meanings, that are being discussed.

In a footnote he acknowledged Wittgenstein's unpublished work. But one may doubt how far he understood the matter. A further, post-*Tractatus* retraction of his earlier conception of logical constants is in the introduction to the second edition of *The Principles of Mathematics* (Allen & Unwin, London, 1937):

Logical constants, therefore, if we are to be able to say anything definite about them, must be treated as part of the language, not as part of what the language speaks about. In this way, logic becomes much more linguistic than I believed it to be at the time when I wrote the 'Principles'. It will still be true that no constants except logical constants occur in the verbal or symbolic expression of logical propositions, but it will not be true that these logical constants are names of objects, as 'Socrates' is intended to be. (*PrM*, 2nd edn. pp. xi f.)

Wittgenstein thought that both Frege and Russell had misconstrued the nature of these expressions and misunderstood their role.

Against Frege in particular he observed that if the True and the False were objects, and were the arguments of molecular propositions such as '$\sim p$' or '$p \supset q$', 'then Frege's method of determining the sense of [for example] '$\sim$' would leave it absolutely undetermined' (*TLP*, 4.431). For if '$\sim$' were a name of a genuine function the argument of which is one of the two truth-values, then provided that 'p' (e.g. 'The sun is cold') has the same truth-value as 'q' (e.g. 'The moon is hot'), '$\sim p$' would have the same sense as '$\sim q$'. The argument turns on the extensionality of functions. In such a case each compound proposition merely expresses the thought that the False falls under the concept of negation. For each such proposition determines the True as the value of the same function for the same argument. But this is absurd by Frege's own lights. For obviously '$\sim p$' is taken to have the same sense as '$\sim q$' if and only if 'p' has the same sense as 'q'. But if so, then Frege's explanation of the negation sign does *not* determine its sense.

In fact, Wittgenstein argued, these sentential operators are not function-names at all. He gave various reasons for this. (1) These 'primitive signs of logic are in fact inter-definable, and that suffices to show that they are not primitive signs (*TLP*, 5.42). (2) '$p \supset q$' is the same truth function of p and q as '$\sim pvq$', and that shows that the binary connectives are not names of relations (*TLP*, 5.41–2). (3) If '$\sim$' were a name, than '$\sim\sim p$' would say something different from 'p', since the former would then be about $\sim$ and the latter would not (*TLP*, 5.44). (4) A function cannot be its own argument (though its value may be identical with its argument, and its value for one argument may be its argument for the same or different value), but an operation can take one of its results as its base, e.g. '$\sim\sim p$' (*TLP*, 5.251). The result of an operation, however, is not the same as the value of a function. (5) Operations, unlike functions, can vanish, e.g. negation in '$\sim\sim p$': '$\sim\sim p = p$' (*TLP*, 5.254) or '$\sim (\exists x). \sim fx$', which says the same as '$(x).fx$' (*TLP*, 5.441). (6) If '$\sim$' were a function-name, then from one proposition p, infinitely many *different* propositions would follow, viz. $\sim\sim p$, $\sim\sim\sim\sim p$, etc. This would be as remarkable as the thought that from half a dozen 'primitive propositions' an infinite number of propositions of logic (and mathematics) follow (as Frege and Russell thought). In fact, all the propositions of logic say precisely the same thing, namely nothing (*infra*); and the members of the series of doubly reiterated negations of a proposition say precisely what its first member 'p' says (*TLP*, 5.43). For '*p*', '∼∼*p*', '∼∼∼∼*p*' are just different ways of writing the same symbol—a feature which ought to be evident in an ideal notation, but is not obvious in the concept-scripts of Frege and Russell. In the T/F notation of the *Tractatus* (*TLP*, 5.101), however, they would all be represented by the sign' (T,F) (*p*)'.

The logical constants, Wittgenstein stressed, signify *operations* not functions. They produce a *proposition* (the result of an operation) out of a proposition or propositions upon which they operate (the base of the operation). The truth-value of a proposition that is the result of such an operation on a proposition or propositions is a function of (is dependent on) the truth-value(s) of the proposition(s) that are its base. The *sense* of the result of such an operation is a function of (dependent upon) the *sense* of the base of the operation (*TLP*, 5.234 f.); thus, for example, negation *reverses* the sense of a proposition (*TLP*, 5.2341). All propositions are results of truth-operations on elementary propositions and are truth-functions of elementary propositions (*TLP*, 5.3 ff.).

3. *The Laws of Logic*

These insights, mostly arrived at very early, led Wittgenstein to disagree profoundly with Frege and Russell over the character of logic and the nature of the laws of logic. They also led to what is the most significant achievement of the *Tractatus*, namely its account of logical necessity. Frege and Russell both conceived of logic as an axiomatic science (akin, in this respect, to geometry). The theorems of logic are accordingly deduced from axioms by means of stipulated rules of inference. What then is the status of the axioms and how do we know them to be true?

Frege thought the axioms of logic (the 'basic laws') are certified directly by a 'logical source of knowledge'.[16] He did not conceive of these axioms as mere consequences of the definitions of symbols, any more than he conceived of the axioms of geometry as mere consequences of Euclidean definitions. Just as the latter are fundamental a priori truths about space, the former are indemonstrable necessary truths about logical entities, unfolding the essential nature of primitive logical concepts and relations. The axiomatic presentation of logic is not a pedagogic or stylistic convenience, but corresponds to the logical nature and order of things. Knowledge of the laws of logic rests ultimately on self-evident truths: 'The question why and with what

---

[16] Cf. Frege, *Posthumous Writings*, pp. 273, 278 f.

The Dialogue with Frege and Russell

right we acknowledge a law of logic to be true, logic can answer only by reducing it to another law of logic. Where that is not possible, logic can give no answer.'[17] In response to Russell's discovering the paradox in his system, Frege wrote of his Basic Law V, 'I have never concealed from myself its lack of self-evidence which the others possess, and which must properly be demanded of a law of logic.'[18]

This issue was a central preoccupation for Russell and a matter regarding which he seems to have wavered uncomfortably. In *Principia* (1910) he argued that the primitive propositions of his logical system must indeed be assumed without proof. 'They are obvious to the instructed mind, but then so are many propositions which cannot be quite true, as being disproved by their contradictory consequences.' (*PM*, p. 12.) Roughly speaking, the proof of the pudding is in the eating, in the adequacy and coherence of the system. (Russell was groping here for the notions of consistency and completeness proofs, but that metalogical gambit was yet to be invented.) He conceived of the axioms (in particular, for example, of the axiom of reducibility) as receiving inductive support from their consequences:

Self-evidence is never more than a part of the reason for accepting an axiom, and is never indispensable. The reason for accepting an axiom, as for accepting any other proposition, is always largely inductive, namely that many propositions which are nearly indubitable can be deduced from it, and that no equally plausible way is known by which these propositions could be true if the axiom were false, and nothing which is probably false can be deduced from it. If the axiom is apparently self-evident, that only means, practically, that it is nearly indubitable; for things have been thought to be self-evident and have yet turned out to be false. (*PM*, p. 59.)

This conception was repeated in 'The Philosophical Implications of Mathematical Logic'[19] (1911) where he argued that consequences may well be more self-evident than the premisses on which they rest, and that the question of the role of logical intuition in logical deduction is a psychological one. In *The Problems of Philosophy* (1912), however, he shifted ground. In the brief chapter entitled 'Intuitive Knowledge' he discussed different *kinds* of self-evidence (e.g. in logic, perception, memory, ethics) and different *degrees* of self-evidence. He concluded

---

[17] Frege, *The Basic Laws of Arithmetic*, Vol. I, Introduction, p. xvii.
[18] Ibid. Vol. II, Appendix.
[19] B. Russell, 'The Philosophical Implications of Mathematical Logic', repr. in B. Russell, *Essays in Analysis*, ed. D. Lackey (Allen & Unwin, London, 1973), see especially pp. 293 f.

very tentatively, that 'it seems, however, highly probable that... the highest degree of self-evidence is really an infallible guarantee of truth'.[20] The fundamental propositions of logic are self-evident and incapable of any proof (but the axiom of reducibility is not mentioned). We have intuitive knowledge of them, and they 'may be taken as quite certain'.[21] In the 1913 manuscript *Theory of Knowledge* he allocated a whole chapter to this issue (Chapter VI, 'Self Evidence' pp. 156–66). Here he seems to have abandoned the view held in *Principia*. Self-evidence is indispensable, not only in logic, but throughout the whole of epistemology. 'Inductive empiricism' that contends 'that the truth of the premises is only rendered probable by the conclusion to which they lead' does *not* in fact enable us to dispense with self-evidence at all, but merely relocates it. Hence, he contends in conformity with traditional wisdom:

> every series of definitions and propositions must have a beginning, and therefore there must be undefined terms and unproved propositions. The undefined terms are understood by means of acquaintance. The unproved propositions must be known by means of self-evidence. (*TK*, p. 158)

What exactly were these laws of logic, primitive or otherwise? Both Frege and Russell thought of them as general a priori truths about logical entities, laws of a kind of super-physics. Their apodeictic status was clear enough. As Frege put it, in a famous purple passage, 'they are boundary stones set in an eternal foundation, which our thought can overflow, but never displace.'[22] But what gives them this necessitarian status, why they are so, neither Frege nor Russell could coherently explain. On their relation to human thinking, however, both had clear views. Just because they are immutable laws about propositions, truth-values, relations of implication or exclusion, etc., these laws about logical entities have an authority for our thinking. Frege called them 'laws of truth', and held that just as laws of physics are the foundations for technical rules which prescribe what one ought to do to achieve a certain practical end (boil water, float something on water, etc.), so too the laws of logic are the foundations for laws of thinking, i.e. for norms which prescribe how one should think, judge, or infer if one wants to achieve the goal of truth and validity in

---

[20] B. Russell, *The Problems of Philosophy* (Oxford University Press, Oxford, 1967), p. 68.
[21] Ibid., p. 81.
[22] Frege, *The Basic Laws of Arithmetic*, Introduction, p. xvi.

reasoning. Russell argued that the traditional name 'Laws of Thought' (for the laws of Identity, Contradiction, and Excluded Middle, which have no special status in his or Frege's logic) was misleading 'for what is important is not the fact that we think in accordance with these laws, but the fact that things behave in accordance with them; in other words, the fact that when we think in accordance with them we think *truly*'.[23] Here, indeed, super-physics and physics seem to merge!

Wittgenstein thought this was utterly confused. Self-evidence is irrelevant to logic, 'If the truth of a proposition does not *follow* from the fact that it is self-evident to us, then its self-evidence in no way justifies our belief in its truth' (*TLP*, 5.1363). 'Self-evidence, which Russell talked about so much', Wittgenstein wrote (alluding perhaps to *Theory of Knowledge*),[24] 'can become dispensable in logic, only because language itself prevents every logical mistake. —What makes logic *a priori* is the *impossibility* of illogical thought' (*TLP*, 5.473; cf. *NB*, p. 4). Language prevents every logical mistake in the sense that the logical-syntax of language, coupled with assignments of meanings, determines what makes sense. 'Whatever is possible in logic is also permitted' (*TLP*, 5.473). Of course, we can violate these formation rules, and talk nonsense. Or we can form an apparent sentence with an expression to which we have given no meaning in such an occurrence, e.g. 'Socrates is identical'. But we cannot have in our language a false or incorrect logic, for the logic of a language is not a theory about something which, like a theory in physics, may actually be false, or not very accurate and hence capable of being improved. For 'logic must take care of itself' (*NB*, p. 2; *TLP*, 5.473); every sign that is *possible*, i.e. does not violate logical syntax, is capable of signifying. Whether it does or not is a matter of *our* arbitrary determinations (we could have given an adjectival meaning to 'identical' in the context of 'Socrates is identical', although, of course, it would then not mean what 'identical' now means (*TLP*, 5.4733)). Hence the idea, embraced by both Frege and Russell, that the logic of natural languages can be *improved upon* by logicians is absurd. For logic, the one and only logic of any possible language, is a condition of sense.

Furthermore, self-evidence is dispensable as regards the propositions of logic. For *all* the propositions of logic (laws of logic), Wittgenstein argued, are tautologies. They all have the same sense, viz. none or 'zero' sense. Hence to say that A knows that *p*, where '*p*' is a tautology,

[23] B. Russell, *The Problems of Philosophy*, pp. 40 f.
[24] Or to conversations in 1913 (cf. *NB*, pp. 2 f.) or both.

does not, even in the case of p's being a primitive proposition of Frege's or Russell's logic, require that p be self-evident to A. For in all cases of p's being a tautology, 'A knows that p' is itself senseless (*TLP*, 5.1362). For when A knows that either it is raining or it is not raining, or that if everything is F then a is F, he knows nothing.

In the special case of logical propositions of the propositional calculus, one may *recognize* that p is a tautology by means of a calculation, viz. by the truth-tabular decision-procedure.[25] Its philosophical implications and significance were first explored and explained by Wittgenstein in the *Tractatus*. Of course, no such decision procedure is available for logical truths of the predicate calculus. Yet such propositions are likewise vacuous tautologies, and we demonstrate that they are by a *proof* which consists in successively applying certain operations to initial tautologies (*TLP*, 6.126). A proof in logic is merely an expedient for recognizing tautologies in complicated cases, for only tautologies *follow* from a tautology (*TLP*, 6.1262). In order to recognize that a proposition *is* a proposition of logic no self-evidence is requisite. And to know that p is a tautology is not to know that p, for if p is a tautology, then there *is nothing to know*.

Wittgenstein contended that Frege and Russell had totally misunderstood the character of the propositions of logic. They are not propositions about special concepts or relations (e.g. $\sim$, v, $\supset$) for these signs do not signify concepts or relations. They are not about logical objects or forms, because there are no logical objects and the forms of objects or of facts can only be *shown* by features of a symbol signifying an object or describing a fact of a certain form. The Law of Excluded Middle, for example, if expressed (as it most commonly is) by the formula '$p \vee \sim p$', is not a generalization about propositions (viz. that all propositions are either true or false), since it is neither a generalization nor *about* anything at all. Like all the propositions of logic it is an empty tautology. That every proposition is either true or false (viz. '$(p)(p \vee \sim p)$'), however, is not a proposition of logic, but a pseudo-

---

[25] This now familiar decision procedure was simultaneously published by E. L. Post, 'Introduction to a general theory of elementary propositions', *American Journal of Mathematics* 43 (1921), pp. 163–85. The fundamental idea of using the truth-tabular explanation of the logical connectives (which is already to be found in G. Boole's *Mathematical Analysis of Logic* (1847)) in a mechanical decision procedure was mooted in C. S. Peirce in 1885 (cf. *Collected Papers*, iii, §387) and by E. Schröder in his *Vorlesungen über die Algebra der Logik* (1890–5). It came to technical fruition in Post and Wittgenstein. What mattered to Wittgenstein, however, was not primarily the decision procedure, but rather what the T/F *notation* (cf. *TLP*, 4.442 ff., 5.101) shows about the nature of the propositions of logic and the truth-functional operators.

proposition specifying a formal property of the formal concept of a proposition.

'The correct explanation of the propositions of logic', Wittgenstein wrote, repeating the insight of the 'Notes on Logic', 'must assign to them a unique status among all propositions' (*TLP*, 6.112). He was now in a position to cash that blank cheque. Logical propositions, contrary to what Russell thought, are not essentially general. 'Either it is raining or it is not raining' is no less a logical proposition than '$(x) fx \supset fa$'. The validity of the propositions of logic is not *general* validity, which may well be accidental, but *essential* validity (*TLP*, 6.1231 f.). What is distinctive of logical propositions is that they can be recognized to be true *from the symbol alone*. This differentiates them from empirical propositions. They are molecular propositions compounded from elementary (atomic) propositions by means of logical connectives. (Quantified propositions, Wittgenstein thought, were analysable into logical sums or products.) What is distinctive about them is that they are so co-ordinated that no matter what truth-value each constituent proposition may have, the resultant proposition is true. It is true, as it were, come what may, under all conditions. In this sense one may say that it has *no* truth-conditions (*TLP*, 4.461). In a tautology propositions are so combined by sentential connectives to yield a proposition *that says nothing at all*; their form ensures that all information conveyed by constituent propositions is cancelled out (*TLP*, 6.121). They are therefore limiting cases of propositions, degenerate propositions in the sense in which a point is a degenerate conic section. They are not nonsense, since they are not ill-formed, do not violate the rules of logical syntax. But, unlike propositions with a sense, they are not bipolar. They are *senseless*, have 'zero sense'. And this is crucial, both to grasping their status and to understanding what they show.

If a certain combination of propositions is a tautology, that fact shows something about their structural properties (internal relations). That '$\sim(p. \sim p)$' is a tautology shows that 'p' and '$\sim p$' contradict each other. That '$(p \supset q). (p): \supset : (q)$' is a tautology shows that 'q' follows from 'p' and '$p \supset q$'. That '$(x) . fx : \supset : fa$' is a tautology shows that 'fa' follows from '$(x) . fx$'. (*TLP*, 6.1201.) A tautology is not a rule of inference. But *that* a certain proposition *is* a tautology shows that a proposition may be inferred from other propositions (e.g. 'q' from '$p. (p \supset q)$'). Indeed, Wittgenstein emphasized, every proposition of logic is a *modus ponens* represented in signs (*TLP*, 6.1264), it is *a form of a proof*. ('$pv\sim p$' is equivalent to '$p \supset p$'; these two different signs are the same symbol, and in an ideal notation this would be evident. Hence in the T/F notation, both are represented by the single sign '(TT)(*p*)'.) It follows further that the laws of inference which Frege and Russell laid down to *justify* inferences are altogether superfluous (*TLP*, 5.132).

The very idea that one needs to *justify* an inference from one proposition to another which is deducible from it involves a failure to apprehend that any two such propositions are internally (structurally) related to each other. No rule of inference is necessary to mediate between the relata of an internal relation, nor is it intelligible that it should do so (*TLP*, 5.13 ff.). The internal relations between such propositions can be made perspicuous by making perspicuous the forms of the propositions thus related. For if '*q*' follows from '*p*', Wittgenstein thought, that can only be because '*p*' is a complex proposition the truth-conditions or truth-grounds of which contain the truth grounds of '*q*' (*TLP*, 5.12). Or, to put it differently, the sense of '*q*' is contained in the sense of '*p*'(*TLP*, 5.122). All entailment is a consequence of complexity of propositions. (Elementary propositions have no non-trivial entailments.) It follows further that we can actually do without logical propositions altogether (*TLP*, 6.122).

E.g. take φa, φa ⊃ ψa, ψa. By merely looking at these three, I can see that 3 follows from 1 and 2; i.e. I can see what is called the truth of a logical proposition, namely, of the proposition φa. φa ⊃ ψ a : ⊃ : ψ a. But this is *not* a proposition; but by seeing that it is a tautology I can see what I already saw by looking at the three propositions: the difference is that I *now* see THAT it is a tautology. (*NB*, pp. 107 f.)

In a suitable notation which displays the structure (truth-functional composition) of '*p*' and '*q*' where '*q*' follows from '*p*', one would be able to recognize their internal relations or structural properties by mere inspection of the symbols themselves (*TLP*, 5.13, 6.122). Thus, for example, that '*q*' follows from '*p*. (*p* ⊃ *q*)' is *visible* in the T/F notation of the *Tractatus* in as much as the symbols for '*p*' ((TFTF) (*p*, *q*)) and for '*p* ⊃ *q*' ((TTFT) (*p*, *q*)) both contain a T in a position in which it also occurs in the symbol for '*q*' ((TTFF) (*p*, *q*)) (cf. *TLP*, 5.101 ff.).

A further consequence of Wittgenstein's revolutionary conception is that the axiomatic method in logic is philosophically deeply misleading. The axioms of a logical system thus presented are not privileged by their special self-evidence, or by their indemonstrability. They are tautologies, like the theorems. They are not essentially 'primitive', nor are the theorems essentially 'derived' propositions (*TLP*, 6.127), for 'all the propositions of logic are of equal status', viz. tautologies. The *number* of the 'basic laws' in an axiomatic presentation is, in a sense, quite arbitrary. For one could derive the theorems from a *single* 'primitive proposition', e.g. the logical product of Frege's basic laws or Russell's primitive propositions. For the logical product of tautologies is another tautology. If Frege were to object that this single 'primitive proposition' would not be luminously self-evident, as his basic laws are supposed to be, that just shows how misguided he was in appealing 'to the degree of self-evidence as the criterion of a logical proposition' (*TLP*, 6.1271).

The proof procedure of an axiomatic system of logic, though perfectly licit, is also profoundly misleading. The '*old* Logic' (as Wittgenstein calls it (*NB*, p. 108)) specifies axioms (primitive propositions), rules of deduction, 'and then says that what you get by applying the rules to the propositions is a *logical* proposition that you have *proved*' (ibid.). This makes proof *in logic* look confusingly like proof *by logic* (*TLP*, 6.1263), for 'if we say one *logical* proposition *follows* logically from another, this means something quite different from saying that a *real* proposition follows logically from *another*'. The proof of a logical proposition does not so much prove its *truth* as prove *that it is a logical proposition, i.e. a tautology*. It tells one that by a series of transformations upon symbols in accord with certain rules of combination one can derive a further tautology. The proof tells one something about the *nature* of the proposition derived, not about its actually being true. For a logical proposition, a tautology, is itself *a form* of a proof, and a proof of such a proposition shows that it *is* a form of a proof (not a truth about something or other).

A fortiori, the laws of logic are not the *foundations* for the elaboration of technical norms of human thinking. Since the propositions of logic, unlike those of physics, are not descriptions of the properties and relations of objects in a certain domain, since they are senseless and say nothing at all, they cannot constitute (as Frege and Russell thought they did) a genuine anankastic foundation for prescriptive norms of thinking. But nor, in a sense, is any such thing necessary. For one cannot 'think illogically' (although one can err in one's thinking, of course). To 'think illogically' would be to traverse the bounds of sense, hence to talk nonsense, i.e. not to think or to express a thought. Nor, in a sense, can one systematically reason illogically (as opposed to making frequent *mistakes* in one's reasoning). For (logical) reasoning *is* simply a matter of transforming propositions in a manner that *corresponds* to a tautology. Any other transformations (not slips and errors) are not *logical inferences* and do not constitute reasoning.

4. A Prelude to Conventionalism

Wittgenstein's explanation of the nature of logical necessity is, in a sense, the high point of the *Tractatus*. The nature of necessity had bewildered and bedazzled philosophers for twenty-five centuries. Various explanations had been essayed. These fall, very crudely, into two main classes. Platonism conceived of necessary truths as descriptions of the properties and relations of special kinds of entities. Different versions of Platonism told different tales. Some thought of such entities as transcendent, non-spatio-temporal objects that exist in their own right, independent of all else. Others in the Augustinian Christian tradition conceived of eternal truths as archetypes in, and so part of the essence of, the divine mind. Later Descartes was, heretically, to take them to be voluntary creations of the will of God, not independent of God, but independent of the mind of God, for He could have created different necessary truths. Or, as super-physics merges with physics, one might, with Russell in some phases of his career, conceive of the propositions of logic as descriptions of the most general features of the world. The main alternative to Platonism was psychologism, itself typically a version of empiricism. This too came in many variants. On some, necessary truths are descriptions of relations of ideas (British empiricists), ideas being psychological objects whose features are accessible to the eye of the mind. On others, necessary truths, or more particularly logical truths, are laws about the ways in which we humans are constrained to think. This constraint might be conceived to be empirical (Erdmann) or transcendental (Kant). Both these large and diverse classes of explanation are patently unsatisfactory. A third alternative, later to be called 'conventionalism' or 'the linguistic theory of *a priori* truth' had been mooted (e.g. by Hobbes and Berkeley, and more recently, with respect to geometry, by Hilbert and Poincaré) but never developed.

The *Tractatus* eschewed both psychologism and Platonism. All necessity is logical necessity (*TLP*, 6.375), and logical necessity is a matter of tautologousness. Tautologies are neither about mental objects nor about abstract Platonic objects. They do not describe the laws of human thinking or the putative super-physical laws of abstract entities. Nor do they state what are the most general features of the universe. For tautologies describe nothing, state nothing, are about nothing.

In some ways this may seem very misleading. First, it is misleading of the *Tractatus* to say that all necessity is logical necessity, since after all most of the propositions of the *Tractatus* itself seem to state non-contingent truths, metaphysical necessities about the nature and essence of reality, of any possible world. Of course, Wittgenstein claimed that the propositions of the *Tractatus* are pseudo-propositions. Strictly speaking they are all literally nonsense. So all *expressible* necessity is logical. Metaphysical necessity is *ineffable*, but is *shown* by empirical propositions, namely by *features* (logico-syntactical forms) of their constituent symbols. But one might still remonstrate that metaphysical necessities have not been *explained*. For to be told that it is of the ineffable *nature* of such-and-such objects to concatenate thus-and-so, of the nature of a speck in the visual field to have some colour, of a note to have some pitch (*TLP*, 2.0131) is not to explain *why* that is so. It is to present metaphysical necessities (ineffably) as being every bit as brutish as brute empirical facts that lie at the limits of scientific explanation at a given epoch (e.g. Planck's constant).

Secondly, it will have been noticed that little has been said about logical propositions involving generalization (quantifiers), i.e. logical truths of the predicate calculus. Wittgenstein was perfectly aware that his truth-table decision procedure does not apply to them. But when he wrote the *Tractatus* he assumed that generalizations are always (in principle) reducible to logical sums or products (finite or infinite). The absence of a decision procedure is irrelevant to the insight that logical truths of the predicate calculus are tautologies. Thus the logical proposition that (*x*).f*x* : ⊃ : *fa* is, he thought, a tautology, namely *fa. fb. fc. . . : ⊃ : fa* (i.e. *p. q. r. . . . : ⊃ : p*). Similarly, it seemed we can infer (∃*x*) *fx* from *fa*, just because (∃*x*) (*fx*) is a disjunction of the form *fa* v *fb* v *fc* v . . . In short, he thought, as he later said,[26] that all 'following' was the same. This was a dogmatic commitment to a form of analysis. In the 1930s, when he abandoned the metaphysics of *symbolism* that is characteristic of the *Tractatus*, he rejected this dogmatism.

He came to realize that the conception of an elementary proposition was 'an idea, not an experience', a product of a preconceived requirement rather than the result of a careful description of our use of the term 'proposition'. The conception of a general propositional form

[26] See A. Ambrose, ed., *Wittgenstein's Lectures, Cambridge 1932–1935* (Blackwell, Oxford, 1979), p. 6.

was a metalogical myth which had prevented him from seeing that the concept of a proposition is a family-resemblance concept. There are indeed forms of logical implication that are *not* consequences of truth-functional composition, e.g. determinate exclusion (see Chapter V), and generality is not uniformly analysable into logical sum or product nor accountable for in terms of an operation upon a totality of elementary propositions. The *Tractatus* had misguidedly wrapped important insights into the nature of logical propositions in metaphysical claims about the essential nature of symbolism (e.g. that the proposition is a fact, that only facts can represent facts, that all representation is essentially a matter of isomorphism). Nevertheless, the core of his insights into logical necessity can and did survive the removal of these metaphysical trappings.

What was the *punctum saliens* of the *Tractatus* explanation? 'It is the peculiar mark of logical propositions', he wrote, 'that one can recognize that they are true from the symbol alone, and this fact contains in itself the whole philosophy of logic' (*TLP*, 6.113). For this distinguishes logical propositions from empirical ones, which must 'be compared with reality' to determine their truth. The propositions of logic are *made so as to be* true (*NB*, p. 55; *TLP*, 6.121). The essential modes of combining propositions by truth-operations permit, in the limiting cases of tautology and contradiction, such combinations as cancel out all content.

One can calculate whether a proposition belongs to logic, by calculating the logical properties of the *symbol*.
And this is what we do when we 'prove' a logical proposition. For without bothering about sense or meaning, we construct the logical proposition out of others using only *rules that deal with signs*. (*TLP*, 6.126)

This is no Platonism or psychologism. Nor did Wittgenstein argue that the propositions of logic are 'true by convention'. (How could a convention *make* a proposition true? What, if anything, makes the proposition that *p* true is the fact that *p*!) Rather he argued that the *degenerate truth* of propositions of logic was the result of a particular array of truth-operations (using conventional signs of such operations which represent *nothing at all*) upon elementary propositions. What is presupposed thereby, however, is that names have meanings and elementary propositions have sense (and so are bipolar). It was from the essential bipolarity of the elementary proposition and its internal relation to truth and falsity that the necessary propositions of logic flow. For if the elementary proposition is given, so are all the logical constants. The concept of a proposition and the concepts of truth and falsehood are inseparable, for it is of the nature of the proposition to be either true or false and capable of being either. Since 'p is false' = '$\sim p$', the concept of negation is given with the concept of a proposition. And if one proposition is assertible, a conjunction of propositions is assertible. But if negation and conjunction are given, so are all the logical constants. If so, then all the propositions of logic are given too. 'Logic is not a field in which *we* express what we wish with the help of signs, but rather one in which the nature of the natural and inevitable signs speaks for itself' (*TLP*, 6.124). The 'natural and inevitable signs' here are the propositional sign and signs for truth-operations upon propositional signs which can be reduced to one single sign, viz. of successive negation. The propositions of logic indicate something about the world. They represent 'the scaffolding of the world' (*TLP*, 6.124), *show* the formal, logical, features of language and the world (*TLP*, 6.12). The *Tractatus* conception of logical propositions is not a form of Platonism—on the contrary, it was propounded in critical reaction to Frege's Platonism. But it is not a form of conventionalism either. For Wittgenstein's arguments against the view that logical propositions are truths about logical objects, properties and relations committed him to the metaphysics of logical atomism (which we shall examine in the next chapter) and an essentialist conception of symbolism.

It is striking, however, that the most influential readers of the *Tractatus* took it to be propounding a 'linguistic theory of necessary truth'.[27] The forms of conventionalism propounded by members of the Vienna Circle were commonly prefaced by acknowledgements to 'Wittgenstein's linguistic explanation of necessary propositions'. In the manifesto of the Vienna Circle, written in 1929, Neurath, Hahn, and Carnap announced:

The ... basic error of metaphysics consists in the notion that *thinking* can either lead to knowledge out of its own resources without using any empirical material, or at least arrive at new contents by an inference from a given state of affairs. Logical investigation, however, leads to the result that all thought and inference consists of nothing but a transition from statements to other

---

[27] Cf. A. Pap, *Semantics and Necessary Truth*, Chs. 6–7 (Yale University Press, New Haven, 1958).

statements that contain nothing that was not already in the former (tautological transformation).[28]

'The most important insight I gained from Wittgenstein's work in the *Tractatus*', Carnap wrote later, 'was the conception that the truth of logical statements is based only on their logical structure and on the meanings of the terms.'[29] Schlick, who saw the *Tractatus* as 'the turning point in philosophy', an epoch-making achievement that finally clarified the nature of logic, necessity and philosophy itself, argued that 'Tautologies (or analytic judgements) are the only propositions a priori, they have absolute validity, but they owe it to their own form, not to a correspondence to facts, they tell us nothing about the world, they represent structures'.[30] Similar remarks, claiming that logically necessary truths are empty tautologies, vacuous consequences of linguistic conventions, hence not objects of genuine knowledge are to be found scattered throughout the writings of members of the Vienna Circle. This insight they attributed to Wittgenstein (and, to his annoyance,[31] used it as a stick with which to beat metaphysics). For 'the conception of the nature of logical truth, which was developed in the Vienna Circle on the basis of Wittgenstein's ideas'[32] made it possible, it seemed, to plug a loophole in empiricism. It gave a seemingly satisfactory account of logical (and, they thought) mathematical necessity without conceding anything to rationalism or opening the gate to the synthetic a priori.

It is ironic that the Circle misunderstood so much of the *Tractatus* and misread it so extensively. Wittgenstein did think, when he wrote the *Tractatus*, that there were ineffable metaphysical necessities. He did not think, as Carnap later did, that '*In logic there are no morals.*

---

[28] *The Scientific Conception of the World: The Vienna Circle* (Reidel, Holland, 1973), p. 10. The insight into the nature of 'tautological transformation' they attributed to Wittgenstein.

[29] R. Carnap, 'Intellectual Autobiography', in P. A. Schilpp, ed., *The Philosophy of Rudolf Carnap* (Open Court, Illinois, 1963), p. 25.

[30] M. Schlick, 'Form and Content, an Introduction to Philosophical Thinking' repr. in M. Schlick, *Gesammelte Aufsätze 1926–36* (Georg Olms Verlag, Hildesheim, 1969), p. 226.

[31] Cf. his letter to Waismann in which he comments on the Manifesto of the Circle 'Just because Schlick is no ordinary man, people owe it to him to take care not to let their "good intentions" make him and the Vienna school which he leads ridiculous by boastfulness. When I say "boastfulness" I mean any kind of self-satisfied posturing. "Renunciation of metaphysics!" As if *that* were something new!' (*WWK*, Editor's Preface, p. 18).

[32] R. Carnap, 'W. V. Quine on Logical Truth', in P. A. Schillp, ed., *The Philosophy of Rudolf Carnap*, p. 915.

The Dialogue with Frege and Russell   55

Everyone is at liberty to build up his own logic, i.e. his own form of language, as he wishes.'[33] On the contrary, in logic there are no options at all. He was not interested, as the Circle was, in the T/F method merely as a decision procedure for the propositional calculus, but as a *notation* which makes it perspicuous that seemingly different propositions (e.g. '$p \supset q$', '$\sim p \vee q$' and '$\sim q \supset \sim p$') are simply different ways of writing the same proposition (viz. '(TTFT) (p,q)'). He did not delude himself (as members of the Circle thought he had) into thinking that there was a decision procedure for the predicate calculus. His claim that logical truths of the predicate calculus were tautologies in exactly the same sense as logical truths of the propositional calculus was a claim about the *nature* of logical truth, not about a decision procedure for it. He did not assimilate mathematical propositions to tautologies, and his reasons for not doing so (which members of the Circle never understood) had nothing to do with the supposition of an essential difference between first- and higher-order logic.[34]

The irony is that when he returned to philosophy in 1929 and came into contact with some members of the Circle, he was indeed moving in a direction that might with justice be termed 'conventionalist'. But it differed deeply and importantly from the inadequate version of conventionalism propounded by members of the Circle. He retained the most fundamental insights of the *Tractatus* into logical necessity, but stripped them of their metaphysical wrappings, i.e. of the metaphysics of logical atomism on the one hand and of the essentialism about symbolism on the other.[35] Those insights can with justice be thought of as among the great achievements of modern philosophy.

---

[33] R. Carnap, *The Logical Syntax of Language* (Routledge & Kegan Paul, London, 1937), §17.

[34] This was what Carnap thought underlay Wittgenstein's view, cf. R. Carnap, 'Intellectual Autobiography', p. 47.

[35] For an account of Wittgenstein's later conception of necessity see G. P. Baker and P. M. S. Hacker, *Wittgenstein: Rules, Grammar and Necessity* (Blackwell, Oxford and New York, 1985), pp. 263–346.

III

MEANING, METAPHYSICS, AND THE MIND

1. *The Picture Theory of Meaning*

On 29 September 1914 Wittgenstein, in his notebook, referred to the fact that in law courts in Paris a motor car accident is represented by a model employing toy cars and figures. It struck him that there is not merely an analogy between the way such a model represents the facts of the accident and the way a proposition represents a situation, but rather that a model, a picture, a proposition are severally special cases of representation and must share certain common features in virtue of which they *can* represent whatever it is that they represent. In all such cases the representation must, in some way, be co-ordinated with what it represents. Yet, it may represent falsely, for things may *not* be related as it represents them as being. Rather, as in the model, 'a world is as it were put together experimentally' (*NB*, p. 7). The representation can be true or false, but it must have a *sense* independently of its truth or falsehood, it must represent a *possible* configuration of things even if not an actual one.

From this seed grew the famous picture theory of meaning for which the *Tractatus* is best known. It is important, however, not to exaggerate the importance of the new idea that a proposition is a picture, a *logical* picture, of a situation. A great many of the ingredients of the *Tractatus* conception of meaning and representation had occurred to Wittgenstein well before this idea crossed his mind. It enabled him to weld together into a unified whole the thoughts which he had been developing since 1912, as well as leading to what seemed to be fresh insights. I shall try to give a brief sketch of the central points of the picture theory.

First, bear in mind some of the antecedent commitments. The most fundamental was the idea of the bipolarity of the proposition. This had occurred to Wittgenstein very early. While he had never thought Frege right in saying that propositions refer to truth-values, he did originally think that a proposition refers to a fact (has a fact as its *Bedeutung* or meaning). What was crucial was the realization that the proposition 'is a standard with reference to which the facts behave [*sich verhalten*]' (*NB*, p. 97), that how things are in the world either matches the proposition or it does not. It is one and the same fact, which if it makes '*p*' true also makes '~*p*' false. This means that propositions, *pace* Frege, are radically unlike names. Names are like points, Wittgenstein wrote (*NB*, p. 97); to understand a name is to know what object it refers to, and this must be explained to us (*TLP*, 4.026). Propositions on the other hand are like arrows, they have a direction or sense, which can be reversed by the operation of negation. If nothing corresponds to a genuine name (as opposed to a definite description) it is meaningless; but if things in the world are not as a proposition says they are, it is false not meaningless. At this early stage Wittgenstein argued that '*p*' and '~*p*' have the same meaning (*Bedeutung*) but opposite *sense*. To understand a proposition is to know what must be the case if it is true (i.e. what state of affairs it depicts), hence also what must be the case if it is false. For to understand '*p*' one must not only know that '*p*' implies '*p* is true' but also that '~*p*' implies '*p* is false'. Every genuine proposition divides a logical space into two, depicts a possibility which the world either satisfies or does not. Wittgenstein was shortly afterwards to abandon the idea that propositions refer to facts (or to anything at all), but not what he called 'the bipolarity business'. For 'being true or false actually constitutes the relationship of the proposition to reality, which we mean by saying that it has meaning (*Sinn*), (*NB*, p. 112). Bipolarity seemed an essential feature of a proposition; the explanation of its possibility and of how it is possible for a proposition to be meaningful even though nothing corresponds to it in reality was given by the picture theory. Propositions are further unlike names in that in order to understand a proposition one does not have to have its sense explained to one (*NB*, p. 94; *TLP*, 4.02). If we know the meanings of its constituents and their form of combination we understand the proposition even if it is one we have never encountered before. 'It belongs to the essence of a proposition that it should be able to communicate a *new* sense to us' (*TLP*, 4.027).[1] This too Wittgenstein thought he could account for by means of the picture theory of the proposition.

---

[1] Since the 1950s this matter has loomed large both in philosophical semantics and theoretical linguistics under the heading of 'the creativity of language', and 'explaining' it has become a professional preoccupation. For a critical discussion see G. P. Baker and P. M. S. Hacker, *Language, Sense and Nonsense* Ch. 9.

The idea of analysis Wittgenstein took from Russell. The requirement of determinacy of sense had Fregean roots. Frege demanded of a logically correct language that every proper name be assured a reference and every concept-word be sharply defined. Otherwise there will be well-formed propositions to which the Law of Excluded Middle will not apply. Wittgenstein demanded of every possible language that the sense of its sentences be determinate (any indeterminacy or vagueness must be determinately indeterminate, i.e. the precise range open to the facts must be settled). Hence an apparently vague proposition must be analysable into a disjunction of possibilities. What follows from a proposition is determined by its sense; but in that case it must be wholly settled in advance of experience precisely what does follow. 'We might demand definiteness in this way too:', he wrote (*NB*, p. 64), 'if a proposition is to make sense then the syntactical employment of each of its parts must be settled in advance.—It is, e.g., not possible *only subsequently to come upon* the fact that a proposition follows from it. But, e.g. what propositions follow from a proposition must be completely settled before that proposition can have a sense!' The conjunction of these conceptions of analysis and determinacy of sense seemed to point definitively to the idea of mutually independent elementary propositions as the final product of analysis. For all entailments seemed to be consequences of inner complexity. Such elementary propositions would be composed of simple names combined in accord with rules of logical syntax. The meanings of simple names are simple sempiternal objects constituting the 'substance' of the world. The logico-syntactical co-ordination of these names in a proposition represents the concatenation of objects into a state of affairs which may or may not obtain. The picture theory of meaning has as its foundation an account of the nature of the elementary proposition thus conceived.

Wittgenstein presents his account of the nature of propositional representation as an application of a perfectly general explanation of any kind of representation. Any picture, model, or representation represents what it represents in virtue of being isomorphic with it. A model[2] must be composite, i.e. it must consist of a multiplicity of

[2] The German *Bild* means both picture and model, and in this brief discussion I have brought the latter association to the forefront. It points in two very different directions, namely the idea of a model (as in the Paris law court) which gave Wittgenstein the original idea, and the mathematicians' concept of a model. In 1931 Wittgenstein said, 'I have inherited this concept of a picture from two sides: first from a drawn picture (*Bild*), second from the model (*Bild*) of a mathematician, which already is a general concept.

elements which stand for elements of the situation which it represents. A model must have both form and structure. The structure of a model is the conventionally determined way in which the elements of the model are arranged in order for it to be a model. The possibility of structure Wittgenstein called 'pictorial form' (e.g. the 3-dimensionality of a diorama). Different kinds of models in different 'media' will have different 'representational forms' (e.g. models, pictures, musical scores). Different representations of the same state of affairs with different representational forms will share the same logical form, i.e. identical multiplicity and conventionally determined possibilities of arrangement. Whatever has a pictorial form also has logical form. Any representation shares *with what it represents* its logico-pictorial form. The elements of a model are connected with elements of the situation it represents by the 'pictorial relationship' (an issue we shall return to in section 3). For a model to represent the situation it does represent, the structure of the model, i.e. the fact that its elements are arranged as they are, must represent a corresponding possible arrangement of objects in the represented situation. Model and modelled are, in this sense, isomorphic. What, in a model, represents is not the complex of objects of which it consists, but the *fact* that they are arranged as they are. Only a fact can represent a situation. A model is true if things are in reality as it represents them as being. To know whether it is true or false, however, it must be compared with reality, i.e. verified in experience. One cannot, merely by looking at a model, discern whether things are actually thus or not. The model only determines that things either are so or are not so, and in that sense, only a logical space, not a place.

Three corollaries flow from this general conception of representation which dovetail neatly with Wittgenstein's antecedent views on the impossibility of a theory of types and the ineffability of internal relations. First, no model can be true *a priori*. Secondly, there must be an internal relation between a model and whatever it represents, which consists in logico-pictorial isomorphism. Thirdly, no model can represent its own internal relation to what it models (or, indeed, any other internal relation). For if a model could represent its own pictorial form, then it could lack that pictorial form. But since its pictorial form is an internal feature of a model, it is essential to its identity *as* a model *of* whatever it represents.

For a mathematician talks of picturing (*Abbildung*) where a painter would no longer use this expression'. (*WWK*, p. 185.)

Propositional representation must share the essential features of representation in general, viz. the *logical* features of a picture or model. A proposition must be composite, composed of function and argument (not an assemblage of names but an articulation of names). Its elements stand for the elements of the situation it depicts. It must have a form (the combinatorial possibilities of its elements in accord with rules of logical syntax) and a structure, i.e. a determinate relation between its elements. The structure of the proposition must be isomorphic with the logical structure of what it represents. The configuration of objects in the situation it represents will then correspond (given the 'method of projection') to the configuration of simple signs in the propositional-sign. What represents in the propositional-sign is the fact that its constituent expressions are arranged as they are, given the conventional rules of syntax and given an 'interpretation' of the constituent names. A proposition is essentially bipolar. Truth consists in an agreement between proposition and fact, but to know whether a proposition is true or not, one must compare it with the world, verify it.

Of course, ordinary propositions are not like this. They contain complex concept-words, names of complexes, vagueness, and hence hidden generality, etc. It is rather the elementary proposition, the final product of analysis, that satisfies these conditions. Ordinary propositions, with all their logical complexity are built up out of elementary propositions by means of truth-functional combination. The elementary proposition is a logical picture of an elementary state of affairs. It is composed of simple unanalysable names having various logico-syntactical forms. The names have a meaning, namely the simple objects in reality to which they are connected (for which they 'go proxy'). Their logico-syntactical forms mirror the metaphysical forms of the objects they stand for. The proposition, i.e. the propositional sign in its projective relation to the world, represents a state of affairs which may or may not obtain. The possibilities of truth and falsehood of all elementary propositions exhaust the range of all possible worlds.

If the term 'picture theory of the proposition' is to refer to the overall account of propositions in the *Tractatus* then the picture theory must include not only the above claims concerning the pictorial character of the elementary proposition but also Wittgenstein's general account of the form of generation of non-elementary propositions out of elementary ones by means of truth-operations. For if the concept of the elementary proposition is given, so too are the concepts of all possible forms of combining elementary propositions. We noted in the previous chapter that he repudiated the claim that the logical connectives are 'representatives', arguing instead that they are 'operations' and are all reducible to the single operation of successive negation upon sets of propositions.[3]

Fascinating as the details (and obscurities) of the picture theory are, I shall pass most of them by. But a number of general remarks as guides to reflection on the position adopted in the *Tractatus* are worth dwelling on briefly. First, it is important to be clear what are the essential features of the theory. It is a general account of the nature of propositional representation. Its core is the account of the logically independent elementary proposition. Essential to that is the conception of isomorphism between what represents and what is represented. For it is in terms of isomorphism that the possibility of propositions being false but meaningful is explained. There seems to be, as Wittgenstein later phrased it, an essential 'harmony between language and reality'. The proposition depicts a possible state of affairs. If that state of affairs does not obtain, the proposition is false. But even if it is false, it depicts, as it were, how things are *not*. The 'harmony between language and reality' was explained in the picture theory in terms of the idea of simple unanalysable names (logically proper names) which refer to sempiternal objects that concatenate to form facts. The doctrine of isomorphism (with its attendant theses) is an *essential* part of the picture theory. So too is the claim that all genuine propositions are truth-functions of elementary propositions, that all entailments are consequences of inner complexity, that all necessity is to be accounted for in terms of tautologousness, and that there is such a thing as 'the general propositional form'. Hence it is incorrect that one can isolate a logical core of the picture theory of meaning that is independent of logical atomism, let alone a logical core that persists throughout Wittgenstein's later work.[4]

Secondly, it is sometimes said that the picture theory of the proposition incorporates a truth-conditional theory of meaning. This is thoroughly misleading and anachronistic. The *Tractatus* did indeed give a truth-conditional account of the sense of molecular propositions. *Given the sense of the constituent elementary propositions*, the sense of a

[3] For an illuminating explanation, see A. J. P. Kenny, Wittgenstein Ch. 5.
[4] Hence I disagree with A. J. P. Kenny's account of the logical core of the picture theory (op. cit. pp. 62 ff.) and its continuity in Wittgenstein's philosophy (ibid., pp. 227 ff.).

molecular proposition is given by the conditions (the distribution of truth-values among its constituents) under which it comes out true in its truth-table. But an elementary proposition has no *truth-conditions*. Given what 'truth-conditions' means in the *Tractatus*, the very idea that an elementary proposition *could* have truth-conditions is absurd. The sense of an elementary proposition is a function of its constituent expressions (their meanings and forms), and consists in a depiction (in the manner explained by the picture theory) of a certain possible state of affairs. One must beware of reading post-Tarskian developments and shifts in the concept of a truth-condition into the *Tractatus*.[5]

Thirdly, the *Tractatus* is sometimes said to propound a form of Realism.[6] Doubtless many different things might be meant by 'realism'. In epistemology and metaphysics it is often contrasted with idealism. In ontology it is typically contrasted with nominalism. In philosophy of mathematics it is associated with Platonism and contrasted with constructivism. And in semantics it is typically associated with truth-conditional theories of meaning (as that expression is *now* understood) and contrasted with notional theories of meaning associated with conditions of *assertion*. This, it is argued, turns further upon distinguishing two diametrically opposed conceptions of truth and meaning. On a realist truth-conditional theory the meaning of sentences is given by specification of conditions of truth that may well be 'verification-transcendent', i.e. they may be such conditions as are wholly independent of our possible knowledge. For meaning is given by objective conditions in virtue of which a proposition is true, not in terms of evidence by reference to which we know or are entitled to assert it to be true. On an anti-realist conception, meaning must be given in terms which we can effectively *recognize* as establishing truth or falsity. For, it is argued, we have no conception of verification-transcendent truth. Accordingly the meaning of an expression must be given by its *assertion-conditions*. Consequently anti-realism is associated with, though it does not necessitate, reductionism. Further complexity is introduced by distinguishing whether or not an account of the meaning of certain kinds of proposition (viz. the typical reduction classes such as material object propositions, propositions about the

[5] For a detailed account of the evolution of truth-conditional semantics and the successive changes in the concept of a truth-condition, see G. P. Baker and P. M. S. Hacker, *Language, Sense and Nonsense*, Ch. 4.

[6] I adopted this view in the first edition of this book and also in 'The rise and fall of the picture theory', in I. Block, ed., *Perspectives on the Philosophy of Wittgenstein*. This now seems to me altogether misleading and unhelpful.

past, other minds, traits, and dispositions) is committed to the applicability (realism) or non-applicability (anti-realism) of the Law of Excluded Middle.[7] Hence reductionism which *is* committed to the Excluded Middle would not, according to this conception of the distinction, count as anti-realism.[8]

The connection between these different concepts of realism is, I suspect, tenuous at best. The issue merits detailed scrutiny, but all that can be done here is to demonstrate how unilluminating it is to try to squeeze the *Tractatus* into this Procrustean bed. Is the *Tractatus* realist or idealist in its metaphysics and epistemology? I shall suggest, in the next chapter, that the obscure remarks on solipsism intimate a certain form of transcendental idealism coupled with empirical realism. So in this respect it evades the classification. It is, incidentally, noteworthy that the logical atomism seems in principle compatible with realism or idealism,[9] and it is perhaps no coincidence that when Wittgenstein returned to philosophy in 1929 his first position, before he had moved far away from the *Tractatus*, was phenomenalist. The ontology of the *Tractatus* was, I shall argue below, certainly realist. Among the 'objects' that constitute the substance of the world are simple unanalysable properties and relations.

The schematic account of mathematics in the *Tractatus*, so far from being realist (Platonist) has distinctively constructivist overtones. For Wittgenstein repudiated logicism and denied both the necessity and possibility of giving mathematics any set-theoretic 'foundations' (*TLP*, 6.031). Moreover he apparently held that the basis of mathematics consists in reiterable operations. Far from holding that mathematical propositions 'have truth-conditions' or are 'true in virtue of a mathematical reality', the *Tractatus* unequivocally declared propositions of pure mathematics to be *pseudo-propositions* (*TLP*, 6.2) which express no thought whatever. They are, strictly and technically speaking, nonsense (unlike tautologies). Nothing whatever is said about the applicability of the Law of Excluded Middle to mathematics (though, as we shall see,

[7] This principle of distinction is inspired by a similar contrast between classical and intuitionistic mathematics. Whether it has any general relevance to broader philosophical issues is highly debatable.

[8] The distinction between realism and anti-realism thus conceived is a leitmotif of M. A. E. Dummett's philosophical writing (see especially 'Realism', 'The Reality of the Past' *et al.* in his *Truth and Other Enigmas* (Duckworth, London 1978)). This red herring has led packs of philosophers (myself included) off the scent of Wittgenstein's trail.

[9] What of the sempiternality of simples? That depends on the idealist's account of properties on the one hand and time on the other.

in the 1930s, when Wittgenstein was allegedly in his *anti-realist* phase, he insisted precisely on its applicability).

As far as what is now called 'semantics' is concerned, for reasons explained above, the *Tractatus* cannot be said to have a truth-conditional theory of meaning in its own terms. Nor can it be said to have a truth-conditional account of meaning in *our* terms, if that idea implies that the meaning (sense) of an elementary proposition is given by a T-sentence of the kind now familiar from the work of Tarski (viz. '"*p*" is true iff *p*'). The author of the *Tractatus* would have ruled that out as nonsense (and would not have altered that verdict in later years either (see p. 324 ff.).)

Was the *Tractatus* reductionist? Possibly, but the issue is obscure. For *all* significant propositions result from truth-operations upon elementary propositions that are to be directly verified by comparison with reality. But what precisely are the elementary propositions, what their epistemic status is, and how truth-operations on them will yield propositions about other times or other minds remains a mystery. Was the conception of truth 'verification-transcendent'? The matter seems shrouded in clouds. The elementary proposition is known to be true by being compared directly with (verified by) reality. There is no suggestion that there might be some elementary propositions which we can understand, but which we cannot in principle verify. All propositions are constructed from, and some involve infinite arrays of, elementary propositions. Can we 'compare' an infinite number of elementary propositions with reality? (Is this like traversing 'an infinite number of spaces' at a pace?) We are not told. It is, no doubt, no coincidence that in 1929/30 Wittgenstein treated generalizations as *hypotheses*, i.e. as not completely verifiable. But then also, not as genuine propositions! It is also noteworthy that only minor modification seemed necessary to the general account of meaning in the *Tractatus* to transform it into a form of verificationism, as is evident from Waismann's 'Theses' (*WWK*, Appendix B, esp. pp. 243 ff.), written as an exposition of Wittgenstein's ideas in the *Tractatus* supplemented by Wittgenstein's further modifications to (what seemed to Waismann and the Vienna Circle) a basically intact structure. Members of the Vienna Circle did not conceive of themselves or of Wittgenstein (see Chapter V) as overthrowing the *Tractatus* account of the meaning of molecular propositions in terms of truth-conditions when they insisted that the meaning of a proposition is its method of verification. This seemed merely to be clarifying a good empiricist tenet in restricting what a proposition can meaningfully say to what can, in principle, be an object of (and so established in) experience. So here again, the *Tractatus* evades the unhelpful dichotomy of realism and anti-realism. Of course, as regards the applicability of the Law of Excluded Middle, the *Tractatus* obviously was committed to bipolarity, *a fortiori* bivalency for anything it recognized as a genuine proposition. But what this meant was that anything to which the Excluded Middle does not apply is not, in this sense, a genuine proposition at all. (And that is why even the later Wittgenstein cannot be caught on either prong of this fork.)

In short, characterizing the *Tractatus* as 'realist' is, save in the case of the contrast with 'nominalist', thoroughly unilluminating. The realist/anti-realist contrast (or contrasts) is a strait-jacket which distorts the shape of the *Tractatus*, obscures its thrust and misidentifies its salient preoccupations and achievements. In Chapter XI I shall briefly show that characterizing Wittgenstein's later philosophy as anti-realist is equally misguided.

2. *The Metaphysics of the* Tractatus

We have, in the discussion thus far, spoken glibly of sempiternal simple objects that are the meanings of simple (logically proper) names, of states of affairs, of facts. We have spoken of totalities of objects, of objects concatenating together, of combinatorial possibilities of objects. It is time to try to shed some light upon these dark corners of the *Tractatus*.

The simple objects are, Wittgenstein thought, the final residue of analysis, the indecomposable elements that are the meanings of the unanalysable names that occur in elementary propositions. There *must* be such things, 'The demand for simple things *is* the demand for definiteness of sense' (*NB.*, p. 63) and again:

It seems that the idea of the SIMPLE is already to be found contained in that of the complex and in the idea of analysis, and in such a way that we come to this idea quite apart from any examples of simple objects, or of propositions which mention them and we realize the existence of the simple object—*a priori*—as a logical necessity. (*NB*, p. 60)

This conviction no doubt partly explains why Wittgenstein failed to probe this conception of an object more thoroughly and why he was by and large undisturbed at his inability to produce examples of such entities. He *knew*, so he thought, that there must be such things. There must be unanalysable objects if language is to be related to the world, and they must be indestructible. For only thus can the need for a firm anchor for language be met. Simple objects, he was later to explain, 'were simply what I could refer to without running the risk of their possible non-existence; i.e. that for which there is neither existence nor non-existence, and that means: what we can speak about *no matter what may be the case*' (*PR*, § 36). They must exist in order that it be possible for us to say something false yet meaningful, in order that we should be able to imagine[10] how things are *not* (*BB*, p. 31).

Wittgenstein's conception of a simple object was, I suspect, an heir to Russell's notion of a *term* in *The Principles of Mathematics*, itself a development of Moore's notion of a concept.[11] A term was 'whatever may be an object of thought, or may occur in any true or false proposition, or can be counted as *one*' (*PrM*, p. 43). Synonyms of 'term' are 'unit', 'individual', and 'entity'. Examples of terms are: a man, a moment, a number, a class, a relation, a chimaera. Terms, Russell argued, have being even if they do not exist. They are immutable and indestructible. He distinguished among terms between things and concepts, the former including points and instants (as well as much else), the latter including attributes. An affinity with Wittgenstein's objects is evident. The Theory of Descriptions thinned out this subsistent jungle considerably. Did it, as many commentators have argued, thin it out, (in Wittgenstein's hands) to the point of eliminating properties and relations? I think the overwhelming evidence is to the contrary.

Objects are constituents (*Bestandteile*) of states of affairs; they combine (*verbinden*) to constitute states of affairs. To do so they must, a priori, contain a range of *possibilities* of combination with other objects. This range constitutes the *internal* properties of an object, its form (*TLP*, 2.01231, 2.0141). Space and time are forms of objects (any 'object' spoken of must be somewhere, somewhen). In the same way, being coloured is a form of *visual* objects (a visible 'object' must have some colour or other (*PT*, 2.0251 f.)). A spatial point is an argument-place, a locus for the coinstantiation of features. Objects are sempiternal and unchanging, only their configuration changes. They combine with one another into changing configurations that constitute existing states of affairs. Objects exist only in configurations (it is of their nature to be combined with other objects). That a certain object is combined with another is an *external* property (contingent feature) of

---

[10] For a similar principle see Descartes, *Meditations* I.
[11] G. E. Moore, 'The Nature of Judgment', *Mind* viii (1899), 176–93.

that object (that it is *possible* for it so to combine is an internal feature). Objects concatenate together like links in a chain, i.e. they do not need a *relation* to cement them together (*TLP*, 2.03).

The metaphor of links in a chain was used by Bradley in the course of arguing against the reality of relations:

> But how the relation can stand to the qualities is... unintelligible. If it is nothing to the qualities, then they are not related at all; and, if so, ... they have ceased to be qualities, and their relation is a non-entity. But if it is to be something to them, then clearly we shall require a *new* connecting relation ... here again we are hurried off into the eddy of a hopeless process, since we are forced to go on finding new relations without end. The links are united by a link, and this bond of union is a link which also has two ends; and these require each a fresh link to connect them with the old. The problem is to find how the relation can stand to its qualities, and this problem is insoluble.[12]

Some commentators have taken Wittgenstein to endorse the non-reality of relations in the form of the contention that relations are not 'objects' and, correspondingly, that no names are names of relations.[13] I think this is wrong. Wittgenstein used the chain metaphor for precisely the opposite purpose to Bradley. He was, I suspect, arguing

---

[12] I should be surprised if Wittgenstein ever read Bradley. But he did read Russell's *Our Knowledge of the External World*, where this passage is quoted critically on p. 7. It is taken from Bradley's *Appearance and Reality* (2nd edn., London, 1897) pp. 32 f. That it is quoted *critically* is, I suspect, a reflection of Wittgenstein's view. The passage from Bradley is alluded to in an early version of Waismann's 'Theses' (see *WWK*, p. 252 n.).

[13] For example, G. E. M. Anscombe, *An Introduction to Wittgenstein's Tractatus* 4th edn. (Hutchinson University Library, London, 1971), Chs. 6–7; I. M. Copi, 'Objects, Properties and Relations in the *Tractatus*', *Mind* lxvii (1958); H. Ishiguro, 'Use and Reference of Names', in P. Winch, ed., *Studies in the Philosophy of Wittgenstein* (Routledge & Kegan Paul, London, 1969), pp. 25 ff., 41 ff. The idea that is typically canvassed is that predicates and relation-names are eliminable in an ideal notation and what represents properties and relations are the spatial relations between names. So '$\phi(x,y)$' could be expressed by 'y' and 'fa' by writing 'a' upside down. So, it is held, function signs are dispensable. This interpretation rests on a serious misreading of *Tractatus* 3.1432 (*infra*). As we shall see below it is precisely properties ('like yellow and hard') and relations that *are* 'designated and expressed by a propositional function' (*WWK*, p. 220), and nowhere does Wittgenstein (in the *Tractatus*) repudiate the functional structure of the proposition or intimate the eliminability of function-signs. The idea that the *discernible* spatial configurations of signs on paper suffice in their multiplicity for all properties and relations is absurd (the Bureau of Standards distinguishes 7500 shades of colours alone). The supposition that the depth analysis of language *must be* expressed in *writing* is equally absurd. For that 'a' stands to be left of 'R' and 'b' to the right represents, in our conventions of script, that aRb; but that 'a' is uttered *before* 'R' and 'b' after represents, in our conventions of speech, that aRb. This misguided conception confuses the representational form of *script* with the logical form of proposition (or thought).

implicitly against Russell who, in *Theory of Knowledge*, argued himself into confusion. 'It may be', Russell wrote,

> that there are complexes in which there is only one term and one predicate, where the predicate occurs as relations occur in other complexes. In that case, predicates will be defined as entities occurring in this manner in complexes containing only one other entity. It is, however, doubtful whether there are such complexes, whereas it seems certain that there is a relation of *predication*; thus predicates may be defined as terms which have the relation of predication to other terms. (*TK*, pp. 80 f.)

He tied himself into similar knots with respect to relational propositions, not by holding, as Bradley did, that relations are in some sense, unreal, but by claiming that relations need relating glue to bind together the relata in the right way, as in xRy and yRx:

> if we are given any relation R, there are two relations, both functions of R, such that, if x and y are terms in a dual complex whose relating relation is R, x will have one of these relations to the complex, while y will have the other. The other complex with the same constituents reverses these relations. Let us call these relations A_R and B_R. Then if we decide to mention first the term which has the relation A_R to the complex, we get one sense of the relation, while if we decide to mention first the other, we get the other sense. Thus the sense of a relation is derived from two different relations which the terms of a dual complex have to the complex. Sense is not in the relation alone, or in the complex alone, but in the relations of the constituents to the complex which constitute 'position' in the complex. But these relations do not essentially put one term *before* the other, as though the relation went *from* one term *to* another; this only appears to be the case owing to the misleading suggestions of the order of words in speech and writing. (*TK*, p. 88).

This, Wittgenstein surely thought, is precisely wrong. The proposition *aRb* is not a name of a complex, but a description of a situation. What symbolizes in it is not the complex of signs '*aRb*', but rather the fact that '*a*' stands in a certain relation to '*b*', namely flanking '*R*' on the left, while '*b*' flanks it on the right (*NB*, p. 105; *TLP*, 3.1432). The linear left–right construction of the written symbolism is a feature of its representational form (Semitic languages employ a right–left construction, and Chinese a vertical one). It is the fact that '*a*' is to the left of '*Rb*' that says that '*a*' is *R*-related to *b*; if '*b*' were to the left of '*R*', as in '*bRa*', that would say that *b* is *R*-related to *a*. '*R*' in '*aRb*' looks like a substantive, but of course it is a relation-name. For it is not '*R*' as such that symbolizes here, but rather *that it occurs between* '*a*' *and* '*b*' (*NB*, p.

105) i.e. only relations in a symbolizing fact can represent relations in reality. So it is not '*a*', '*b*', and '*R*' that are 'indefinables' in this schematic elementary proposition, but '*a*', '*b*', and '*xRy*' (where '*x*' and '*y*' are place-holders (*NB*, p. 98)). '*R*', or more accurately '*xRy*', unlike '*a*' and '*b*', is not a proper name, but a name of a relation, and hence symbolizes in a different way from '*a*' and '*b*', and this is *shown by the symbolism* (*NB*, pp. 108 f.). This idea persists throughout the *Notebooks*, and on 16 May 1915 Wittgenstein wrote emphatically 'Relations and properties, etc. are *objects* too' (*NB*, p. 61). It is also noteworthy that Russell, writing *Our Knowledge of the External World* in 1914 on the rebound from Wittgenstein's damning criticisms of the 1913 manuscript *Theory of Knowledge*, changed his views about relations (which is why, I think, he quotes Bradley as exemplification of an error). 'A complete description of the existing world', he wrote, 'would require not only a catalogue of the things, but also a mention of all their qualities and relations'. He continued:

Now a fact . . . is never simple, but always has two or more constituents. When it simply assigns a quality to a thing, it has only two constituents, the thing and the quality. When it consists of a relation between two things, it has three constituents, the things and the relation. When it consists of a relation between three things, it has four constituents, and so on.[14]

I suggest that the abandonment of the position adopted the previous year occurred as a result of Wittgenstein's criticism. If Wittgenstein was *denying* the reality of relations or denying that relations are constituents of facts or denying that among the simple names that lie at the foundations of language are relation-names, it is altogether improbable that Russell would, in this period, adopt the above view without even *mentioning* this (bizarre) alternative.

I can see nothing in the *Tractatus* to suggest that Wittgenstein changed his mind between writing the 'Notes' and *Notebooks* and composing the finished work.[15] He repeats the central point from the 'Notes' (cf. *TLP*, 3.1432), and insists (*TLP*, 4.122) that just as there are formal concepts (i.e. the syntactic forms of concept-words of various kinds) so too are there formal relations (presumably a precisely parallel notion). Objects (such as two shades of blue) stand in internal relations (e.g. of lighter to darker), and there is no suggestion that they

[14] B. Russell, *Our Knowledge of the External World*, p. 51.
[15] G. E. M. Anscombe suggests this in *An Introduction to Wittgenstein's Tractatus*, p. 109 n.

have *no* external (contingent) relations, or that the latter are not themselves 'objects' in an extended sense of the term (*TLP*, 4.123).

In conversations with Desmond Lee in 1930/31 Wittgenstein is recorded as having explained *Tractatus* 2.01 'An atomic fact is a combination of objects (entities, things)'[16] with the following remark:

> Objects etc. is here used for such things as a colour, a point in visual space etc. ... 'Objects' also include relations; a proposition is not two things connected by a relation. 'Thing' and 'relation' are on the same level. The objects hang as it were in a chain.[17]

This is precisely parallel to Russell's position in *Our Knowledge of the External World*. In the 1937 draft of the *Investigations* Wittgenstein wrote that in the *Tractatus* he had been searching for a hidden unity underlying all propositions, and became a prisoner of certain *forms of expression*. One can, he explained with a pair of examples, replace 'The bottle is blue' by 'The bottle has the property blue', or 'The bottle is to the right of the glass' by 'The bottle stands to the glass in the relation to-the-right-of', and here it *appears* as if every sentence is really a combination of names. For here all words with a 'material' meaning seem to be distributed in a network of purely logical relations. As late as 1 March 1944[18] we find further confirmation of our interpretation. Having copied out *Tractatus* 4.22, 3.21 f., 3.14, 2.03, 2.0272, and 2.01, Wittgenstein commented on what a misuse of language it was to use the expression 'object' (and 'configuration') thus. A configuration can be made up, say, of balls which are spatially related in certain ways. But if one says 'I see three objects' one does not mean: two balls and their spatial relation.[19]

The evidence thus mustered in defence of the claim that the 'objects' of the *Tractatus* included relations has *en passant* made it evident that they also included properties (and spatio-temporal points). It is, of course, true that if one searches for an example of something that will satisfy Wittgenstein's specifications, one will search in vain. As Wittgenstein himself realized in 1929, the specifications are inconsistent, and there can be no such thing as a simple object as conceived in the *Tractatus*. Nevertheless, even if it is impossible to make

---

[16] This is Ogden's translation in the first English edition of 1922.
[17] D. Lee, ed., *Wittgenstein's Lectures, Cambridge 1930–32* (Blackwell, Oxford, 1980), p. 120.
[18] cf. Wittgenstein, MS 127.
[19] See also Wittgenstein, *Philosophical Grammar*, pp. 199 ff.

intelligible Wittgenstein's thought of such an 'object', it is possible to make intelligible that he should have had such a thought.

An (atomic) state of affairs he thought of paradigmatically as the instantiation or coinstantiation of properties and relations at a spatio-temporal point or points in the visual field (*NB*, p. 45).[20] Concatenation like links in a chain is coinstantiation or standing in a certain relation. It requires no metaphysical glue in the form of a 'relating relation', since nothing is required to bind a specific shade of red (for example) to a point in the visual field or to 'connect' an object to a relation. (In his first 1929 notebook he emphasized that there is no relation connecting a colour and a place in which it is 'located', they need no *intermediate* link (*MS* 105, p. 27) but connect up together *immediately* like links in a chain.) Properties, relations, points in space and time must have seemed excellent candidates for the indestructible substance of the world—that which can be referred to 'come what may'. (One cannot *destroy* red, one is inclined to think, only such and such a red complex. Red 'an und für sich' cannot be destroyed (cf. *PI*, §§46, 58).) It is further 'of the nature of' properties to occur only in concatenation and it is an internal feature of, for example, colours that they can concatenate with shapes but not with sounds; or of sounds that they can be louder or softer than other sounds, but not than smells or tastes, etc. Different 'unanalysable', 'simple' determinates of a determinable have the same logical form, Wittgenstein thought (wrongly) at this time, for it seemed that their names are always intersubstitutable *salve significatione*.[21] So the only difference between them is that they differ (*TLP*, 2.0233). Thus a shade of red, for example, seems not to be distinguished from another shade of red (or blue) by any of its internal features,[22] and its external properties are fleeting and inessential.

It will be objected correctly that determinates under a determinable are mutually exclusive. So if '*A*' names a spatio-temporal point, '*A* is red' cannot be an elementary proposition, since it is *not* logically independent. It entails '*A* is not green (yellow, orange, etc.)'. Wittgenstein was, to be sure, aware of this. It showed, he thought, that such a proposition was further analysable, and would show itself to

---

[20] This is particularly evident in Wittgenstein's 1929 paper. 'Some Remarks on Logical Form', *Proceedings of the Aristotelian Society*, suppl. vol. ix. This gives better clues to the *Tractatus*, which are confirmed by the *Nachlass*, than is commonly realized.

[21] But one cannot replace 'black' for 'red' in 'The light turned (flashed) red', nor 'white' for other colour names in the description 'Transparent ξ glass'.

[22] This is incorrect, since they will enjoy distinct internal *relations* to other determinates of the same determinable.

contain the exclusion of the incompatible properties, i.e. colour exclusion must be a matter of *tautology* (and '*A* is red. A is green' must be a logical contradiction). If '*p*' contradicts '*q*', then '*p*' must be analysable into, say, a conjunction e.g. '*r.s.t*', and '*q*' into '*v.w.~t*', so that their incompatibility is transparent. Wittgenstein seems not to have realized that analysing colours into fine shades would get him no closer to the desired atomicity requirement (this is evident *ex post facto* from *PR*, Ch. viii; see below pp. 110 f.). And analysing colour in terms of wavelength of reflected light (as seems intimated by *TLP*, 6.3751) is itself an instance of determinate exclusion, since if a certain lightwave is 621 nanometres long, it follows that it is not also 521 or 421 or 620 nanometres.

Undoubtedly he had not thought the matter through. But that does not mean that he had no idea *at all* what objects might turn out to be (as if, for example, they might turn out to be utterly mysterious 'somethings one knows not what', perhaps even transcending any possible experience). Rather he thought he knew that there *had* to be simple objects as a condition of sense, and he had a *rough* idea what they would be (as it were, the direction in which analysis would proceed).[23] And nothing more seemed necessary at the time. Later, as we shall see, he realized that the notion was *incoherent*; and also that the logical requirement which seemed to demand the existence of sempiternal objects was in fact fully satisfied by the *use of samples* which belong not to *what is represented* but rather to *the means of representation*. It was then that he argued that the questions 'Are objects something thing-like, property-like, or relations?' and 'How many objects are there (are there infinitely many)?' are *meaningless*. For objects, properties, relations, are what are represented, not elements of the method of representation. These remarks are not casual clarifications of the metaphysics of the *Tractatus*, but absolutely crucial moves away from it towards the later conception of the role and function of samples in our method of representation.[24]

---

[23] In 1929, before he had completely abandoned logical atomism, he gave the matter closer (and more radical) thought. Here indeed he argued even more emphatically than in the *Tractatus* that one can have no idea what *elementary propositions will look like*, i.e. what their *forms* will be (not what kind of content they have); that must be *discovered* (cf. RLF, p. 163). Real numbers (to budget for degrees of qualities) will have to appear in them (*WWK*, p. 42), as well as numbers signifying spatial coordinates (RLF, pp. 165 f.). Of course, by this time he had already realized that 'objects' did *not* constitute the substance of reality, and were rather elements of representation (*WWK*, p. 43).

[24] The issue is further discussed below, pp. 113 f. For detailed analysis, see

3. Connecting Language with Reality: the role of the mind

It is by means of 'the naming-relation', the association of a logically proper (simple unanalysable) name with its meaning, viz. an object, that any possible language is unambiguously connected with the world. We noted above Wittgenstein's later remark that names with a 'material meaning' may seem to be distributed in a network of purely logical relations. In the *Notebooks* on 3 May 1915 he wrote that

> Names are necessary for an assertion that *this* thing possesses *that* property and so on.
> They link the propositional form with quite definite objects.
> And if the general description of the world is like a stencil of the world, the names pin it to the world so that the world is wholly covered by it. (*NB*, p. 53.)

What did he conceive to be the nature of the correlation of name and object? How is it to be effected? And given that names have to be explained to us (*TLP*, 4.026), what is an explanation of such an 'indefinable'?

In the 'Notes on Logic' Wittgenstein already remarked that the correlation of name and its meaning is psychological (*NB*, p. 99). Logical syntax is a matter of rules of language. Giving *content* to the forms thus created is not. Definition of definables is a normative matter, the connection of indefinables to their meanings in reality is not. In the *Notebooks* Wittgenstein repeatedly suggested that such correlation must be the result of some mental act of meaning or intending a certain word to signify an object one has in mind. It is an act of will which correlates a name with its meaning (*NB*, pp. 33 f.). The phenomenology and indeed the very idea of naming clearly fascinated him (as it has mesmerized humanity since time immemorial):

> What is the source of the feeling 'I can correlate a name with all that I see, with this landscape, with the dance of motes in the air, with all this; indeed what should we call a name if not this'? (*NB*, p. 53)

In the *Notebooks* the main (though not the only) examples of, or perhaps better, approximations to, simple objects are points or minima sensibilia in the visual field (e.g. *NB*, pp. 3, 45, 50 f., 64 f.). These seemed to provide paradigms of items to which a name could be attached *occurrently* by fiat. (It is perhaps with reference to this that he remarked in the *Investigations*' gloss on the errors of the *Tractatus* that

---

G. P. Baker and P. M. S. Hacker, *Wittgenstein: Understanding and Meaning*, esp. pp. 168 ff.

'we rack our brains over the nature of the *real* sign—It is perhaps the *idea* of the sign? or the idea at the present moment?' (*PI*, §105).)[25] In the discussion of determinacy of sense and of my knowing exactly what I mean Wittgenstein emphasized that I can show exactly what I mean by 'lying on' and thus fix the special *Bedeutung* of the expression on this *occasion* of its use (*NB*, p. 68) by pointing with my finger at the complex or fact (e.g. the watch lying on the table) and saying emphatically 'I mean just THIS' (*NB*, p. 70). It is interesting and significant that the underlying theory of meaning appears static, not dynamic—tailored to deal with the language of a particular person (me) at a given time (now). It is, as it were, a momentary language (but a dynamic shared natural language is not composed of a myriad such fragments). 'Things acquire *Bedeutung*', Wittgenstein noted in a different but relevant context, 'only through their relation to my will' (*NB*, p. 84).

In the *Blue Book* Wittgenstein wrote the following revealing passage, arguably with the misconceptions of his youth in mind:

> It seems that there are *certain definite* mental processes bound up with the working of language, processes through which alone language can function. I mean the processes of understanding and meaning. The signs of our language seem dead without these mental processes; and it might seem that the only function of the signs is to induce such processes, and that these are the things we ought really to be interested in. Thus if you are asked what is the relation between a name and the thing it names, you will be inclined to answer that the relation is a psychological one, and perhaps when you say this you think in particular of the mechanism of association.—We are tempted to think that the action of language consists of two parts; an inorganic part, the handling of signs, and an organic part, which we may call understanding these signs, meaning them, interpreting them, thinking. These latter activities seem to take place in a queer medium, the mind; and the mechanism of the mind the nature of which, it seems, we don't quite understand, can bring about the effects which no material mechanism could. (*BB*, p. 3).

The idea that the skeleton of language only takes on flesh and blood through the mediation of the mind, in particular the will, is implicit in the *Notebooks*. Only in thought do signs become symbols, for 'the method of projection is to think the sense of the proposition' (*TLP*, 3.11). Thinking and language are the same, Wittgenstein remarked

---

[25] In MS 157(a), p. 58, commenting on the perverse philosophical idea of an 'ideal' name, Wittgenstein observed that the ideal name (we think) ought to function in the simplest of simple manners, viz. to this name corresponds *this*, and the *this* to which it corresponds should be completely simple.

(*NB*, p. 82), 'For thinking is a kind of language. For a thought too is, of course, a logical picture of the proposition, and therefore it just is a kind of proposition'. This view, a remote ancestor of much nonsense in contemporary 'cognitive psychology' about 'mental representations' and 'the language of thought', Wittgenstein was later to demolish root and branch. He did, however, cleave to it throughout the period of writing the *Tractatus*. In his letter to Russell from Cassino in 1919 he emphasized that a thought is a fact. It does not consist of words, but of psychical constituents which correspond to words and have the same sort of relation to reality as words. What these constituents are, he wrote, he does not know. What relation these constituents have to the fact they picture by means of their configuration is irrelevant. It is a matter for psychology to discover this (*NB*, pp. 129–30), i.e. to investigate *what* psychic entities fulfil this role and in what *empirical* (external) relations they stand to objects they represent.

'Proposition, language, thought, world, stand in line one behind the other, each equivalent to each' (*PI*, §96), Wittgenstein later commented on the *Tractatus* conception. Picture, model, thought, proposition 'they are all constructed according to a common logical pattern. (Like the two youths in the fairy tale,[26] their two horses, and their lilies. They are all in a certain sense one.)' (*TLP*, 4.014) Thought constituents must, of course, possess the appropriate mathematical multiplicity to depict the facts. Hence they must correspond to the names in a fully analysed language. That such configurations, in thought or language, *actually* represent (and do not merely contain the possibility of representing[27] (*TLP*, 3.13)) is a function of the will, of the metaphysical self, which we shall discuss in the next chapter. It is a mental act (albeit of a transcendental self, not of the self that is studied by psychology) that injects meaning or significance into signs, whether in thought or in language. One might call this conception 'The Doctrine of the Linguistic Soul', for it is the soul that is the fountainhead of language and representation.

Simple signs are thus projected on to objects in reality. These signs, we know, are indefinable. So, if we are to share a common language, 'the meanings of simple signs must be explained to us if we are to understand them' (*TLP*, 4.026). This is done by means of elucidations or clarifications (*Erläuterungen*). 'Elucidations are propositions that

---

[26] The allusion is to Grimm's 'Golden Children'.
[27] A. J. P. Kenny's 'Wittgenstein's early philosophy of mind', in I. Block ed., *Perspectives on the Philosophy of Wittgenstein* is helpful here.

contain the primitive signs. So they can only be understood if the meanings of those signs are already known' (*TLP*, 3.263). This wilfully obscure remark has occasioned extensive exegetical controversy. Opinion has polarized around two extremes. One possibility is that an elucidation is an ostensive definition. On this account the correlation between the names which are elements of the elementary proposition and things in the world, correlations which are 'as it were, the feeler of the picture's elements, with which the picture touches reality' (*TLP*, 2.1515), are established by ostension. (Of course, the term 'ostensive definition' (*hinweisende Definition*) does not occur in the *Tractatus* since it was not yet in use as a technical term.[28]) The other possibility is that an elucidation is a 'full-blown proposition'[29] (i.e. elementary proposition) in which the signs are used to make a true or false statement. On this view it is emphasized that one cannot grasp the meaning of a name independently of its use in propositions. We do not first learn the meaning of a name by hooking it on to an object[30] and then put it together with other words to form a sentence.

Both these views are partly right, partly wrong. Clearly Wittgenstein was *not* saying that before one can understand propositions one must understand the names that occur in them and that in order to understand names one must understand the propositions in which they occur. Equally obviously, elucidations are *propositions*, i.e. bipolar. But it would be exceedingly odd if *every* elementary proposition counted as an *Erläuterung*. For it must have an explanatory function. Wittgenstein was not, I think, suggesting that we just 'pick up' the meanings of simple names from attending to their use in various elementary propositions. Rather, his conception was akin to Russell's in *Principia* *1: 'The primitive ideas are *explained* by means of descriptions intended to point out to the reader what is meant; but the explanations do not

---

[28] 'Ostensive definition' was first coined by W. E. Johnson, *Logic* (Cambridge University Press, Cambridge, 1921), Part I, Ch. VI, §7.

[29] cf. A. J. P. Kenny, 'The Ghost of the Tractatus', in G. Vesey, ed., *Understanding Wittgenstein*, Royal Institute of Philosophy Lectures VII (1972–3), p. 6. H. Ishiguro in her 'Use and Reference of Names', p. 33 argues that elucidations are propositions specifying the internal properties of an object. In one sense this is ruled out absolutely, since there can *be* no such proposition according to the *Tractatus* (it would employ a formal concept as if it were a material one). In a different sense, *every* proposition would then count as an elucidation of its constituents, since *features* of the symbols (i.e. logical form) *show* the internal properties of their meaning.

[30] There is something extraordinarily bizarre about this discussion in the *Tractatus*, unless Wittgenstein was assuming that we *are* all equipped with a fund of logically proper names which we *do* explain to each other.

constitute definitions, because they really involve the ideas they explain.' What sort of propositions could be thought of as fulfilling this explanatory role? I suggest that a *Tractatus* elucidation is a proposition of the form 'This is *A*'. It is, one might say, an ostensive definition 'seen through a glass darkly', misconstrued as a bipolar proposition.

The frequent reference in the pre-*Tractatus* writings to the conative, psychological nature of naming has been noted. This, together with the recurrent emphasis upon indexical expressions, e.g. 'Names are necessary for the assertion that *this* thing possesses *that* property (*NB*, p. 53), 'What seems to be given us *a priori* is the concept? *This*.—Identical with the concept of the *object*' (*NB*, p. 61), 'I mean [by 'lying on'] just THIS (*NB*, p. 70), strongly intimates that it is ostension (though not ostensive *definition*) that binds language to the world. Further speculative support for this contention comes from the *Tractatus*, 2.1511: 'Das Bild ist *so* mit der Wirklichkeit verknupft; es reicht bis zu ihr.' The italicization of '*so*' is a natural way of indicating an ostensive gesture, whether physical or, as it were, 'mental'. The most important evidence in support of this interpretation is *ex post facto*. The first is oblique, for it is derived from Waismann's 'Theses' of 1930. Under the heading of 'Definition', Waismann wrote:

There are two ways of giving a sign meaning: 1. By means of *ostension* [*Aufweisung*]. In this case we explain the use of a word in statements by constructing various propositions by means of that word and each time pointing to the fact in question. In that way we become aware of the meaning of the word. (Ostension really consists in two acts—in an external action, pointing to various facts, and a thought-operation, namely learning what they have in common.) 2. By means of *definition*. In this case the meaning of a sign is explained by means of signs that already have a meaning.

A definition remains within language. Ostension steps outside language and connects signs with reality. A definition can be expressed in language, and ostension cannot. (*WWK*, p. 246)

This is, I think, at least *close* to the conception at work in the *Tractatus*. It is important to note that in a discussion with Waismann in 1932 Wittgenstein said, apropos his new (and abiding) view[31] that ostensive *definition* remains within language, connecting a word with a sample that

In the *Tractatus* logical analysis and ostensive definition were unclear to me. At

---

[31] Published, much to Wittgenstein's annoyance, by Carnap in 'Die physicalische Sprache als Universalsprache der Wissenschaft', *Erkenntnis* 2, 1931, pp. 432–65.

that time I thought that there was 'a connection between language and reality'. (*WWK*, pp. 209 f.)

It was precisely this point that became clear to Wittgenstein when he was writing *Philosophical Remarks* in 1929/30, for §6 is virtually a comment on the view held in the *Tractatus*, making clear the fact that the envisaged elucidations were, in that book, confusedly assigned two essentially *incompatible* roles, viz. as bipolar propositions and as rules (explanations of meaning) i.e. ostensive definitions:

> If I explain the meaning of a word 'A' to someone by pointing to something and saying 'This is A', then this expression may be meant in two different ways. Either it is itself a proposition already, in which case it can only be understood once the meaning of 'A' is known, i.e. I must now leave it to chance whether he takes it as I meant it or not. Or the sentence is a definition. Suppose I have said to someone 'A is ill', but he doesn't know who I mean by 'A', and I now point at a man, saying 'This is A'. Here the expression is a definition, but this can only be understood if he has already gathered what kind of object it is through his understanding of the grammar of the proposition 'A is ill'. But this means that any kind of explanation of a language presupposes a language already ... I cannot use language to get outside language. (*PR*, §6)

The second sentence 'Entweder ist er selber schon ein Satz und kann dann erst verstanden werden, wenn die Bedeutung von *A* bereits bekannt ist' corresponds precisely to the *Tractatus* 3.263 'Sie können also nur verstanden werden, wenn die Bedeutung dieser Zeichen bereits bekannt sind'. The *Tractatus* elucidation was, I think, conceived of in the *form* of the sentence 'This is *A*', a form shared by the bipolar proposition 'This is *A*' and by the ostensive definition (which is a rule, not a bipolar proposition) 'This is *A*'. Such an elucidation was meant to have the bipolarity of a genuine proposition, coupled with the ostensive explanatory role of ostensive definitions. And since Wittgenstein was, as he later said, 'confused about ostensive definition', it was meant to link, or show the link, between language and reality. Repudiation of that idea, and denial that the 'harmony between language and reality' resides in a form of correspondence between proposition and fact, became a leitmotif of Wittgenstein's philosophy in the 1930s.

We have so far said very little about epistemology. The *Tractatus* has little to say on that subject. 'Theory of knowledge is the philosophy of psychology' (*TLP*, 4.1121), Wittgenstein wrote, by which he meant that the analysis of specific epistemic terms (such as 'knowledge' and 'belief') belongs to philosophical psychology, and all else belongs to logic. So there *is* no distinctive domain for epistemology. It is possible that a more explicit guide to Wittgenstein's conception at this stage can be gleaned from a highly *uncharacteristic* passage in Russell's *Theory of Knowledge*:

> It is obvious that much of epistemology is included in psychology. The analysis of experience, the distinctions between sensation, imagination, memory, attention, etc., the nature of belief or judgment, in short all the analytic portion of the subject, in so far as it does not introduce the distinction between truth and falsehood must, I think, be regarded as strictly part of psychology. On the other hand, the distinction between truth and falsehood, which is plainly relevant to theory of *knowledge*, would seem to belong to logic... It would seem, therefore, that it is impossible to assign to the theory of knowledge a province distinct from that of logic and psychology. (*TK*, p. 46)

Be that as it may, one general principle is emphatically affirmed. In so far as post-Cartesian epistemology was conceived as a justification of knowledge claims in the face of sceptical challenges, Wittgenstein's principle does indeed discharge epistemology from the ranks. 'Scepticism' he wrote, 'is *not* irrefutable, but obviously nonsensical, when it tries to raise doubts where no questions can be asked. For doubt can exist only where a question exists, a question only where an answer exists, and an answer only where something *can be said*' (*TLP*, 6.51; *NB*, p. 44). This observation is a riposte to Russell who claimed that 'Universal scepticism, though logically irrefutable, is practically barren'.[32] To show that such overwhelming scepticism is nonsense is to show that it traverses the bounds of sense; and to show *that* is the task of logic. Wittgenstein never wavered in his adherence to this principle.

Equally, in an important sense, he never thought that there was a special branch of philosophy concerned with justifying cognitive claims, showing that we are justified in reasoning inductively, justified in believing that others have experiences, justified in trusting our senses. For if a certain form of justification is established by experience it is of no direct concern to philosophy. If it is a priori it involves internal relations between concepts (e.g. memory and the past, behaviour and psychological states or experiences). But there is, he came to think, no such thing as 'vindicating' internal relations. They themselves are the fixed points around which all else revolves. They can only be described; and description of internal relations between

---

[32] Russell, *Our Knowledge of the External World*, p. 67.

epistemic concepts is not essentially different from description of any other kind of internal relations. It belongs to grammar and is given by grammatical rules, and these have no justification.

What does signal a profound change between the *Tractatus* and Wittgenstein's later philosophy is not a shift in his conception of scepticism nor in his view about the proper domain of epistemology. It is rather his realization that the particular form of anti-psychologism in logic which he took over from Frege was misguided. A principle of purity in logic which severs the concept of meaning from the concept of understanding and allocates the account of the latter to psychology is wholly misguided. The correct characterizations of understanding, thinking, meaning something by one's words are of direct and central relevance to philosophical investigations into the nature of language and representation. The meaning of an expression is not something *correlated* with it by some means which psychology may investigate, let alone by the activities of a transcendental self; the sense of an expression is not something that we *attach* to it by some mental mechanism that is irrelevant to logic. It is its *use*, with understanding, in accord with an accepted explanation of its meaning or sense, against an *essential* background of human life and activity.

IV

EMPIRICAL REALISM AND TRANSCENDENTAL SOLIPSISM

1. *The Self of Solipsism*

The discussion of the metaphysical doctrines of the *Tractatus* would be incomplete without an examination of the oracular remarks in the 5.6's on solipsism and the self. These belong (in Kantian terms) to the 'metaphysics of experience'. The fundamental contention of the section is that there is a sense in which solipsism is true, 'what the solipsist *means* is quite correct; only it cannot be *said*, but makes itself manifest [*es zeigt sich*]' (*TLP*, 5.62). In the sense in which solipsism is true, however, the expression of it coincides with pure realism (*TLP*, 5.64). The obscure argument supporting these claims rests upon two struts. First, it rests upon considerations of the relationship of language, the world, and the self; secondly, upon the analysis of the relations between the concepts of the knowing self, the empirical self, and the metaphysical self. The task of this chapter is to explore these relationships.

First, was Wittgenstein in any sense, a solipsist? If he was, then one must explain how a strictly thought-out solipsism coincides with realism. Secondly, the connections between any solipsistic views in the 5.6's and the rest of the *Tractatus* must be examined to see whether the putative solipsism follows from the account of language and meaning given in the book. These are the immediate purposes of the following discussion. One of the primary means to attain them will consist in a detailed comparison of some of Wittgenstein's doctrines with those of Schopenhauer from whom they are derived.[1] This will not only throw light upon the *Tractatus* but will also serve a more long-term objective. This is to show that the detailed refutation of solipsism and of idealism, which Wittgenstein produced in the 1930s and incorporated, in low key, in the *Investigations*, is directed *inter alia* against views which

[1] Schopenhauer's influence upon Wittgenstein is illuminatingly, if briefly, discussed in P. Gardiner, *Schopenhauer* (Penguin, Harmondsworth, 1963), pp. 275–82.

he himself held as a young man. The Schopenhauerian influence upon Wittgenstein is most prominent in the *Notebooks 1914–16*, where his idealist and solipsist bent is most readily demonstrable. Thus even if the explanations I shall suggest of the *Tractatus* solipsism are incorrect, the latter purpose will be satisfactorily fulfilled if the explanations of the Schopenhauerian sections of the *Notebooks* are correct.

I shall begin the examination of the topic not at section 5.6 where it is broached, but at 5.631 where the analysis of the self commences. Once some light is thrown upon Wittgenstein's doctrines of the soul in the *Tractatus* some leeway can be made against the intractable remarks on solipsism.

Wittgenstein's first point is that there is no such thing as the thinking, representing subject (*denkende, vorstellende, Subjekt*). The argument supporting this contention resembles the standard Humean argument[2] of the non-encounterability of the self in experience. If I wrote a book entitled *The World as I found it* I should mention my body, but the subject, my self, could not be mentioned in the book for I do not find it in the world. Here there is an important difference between Wittgenstein and Hume.[3] For Hume, who *looked for* the self in (introspective) experience, supposed that it at least made *sense* to talk of finding it (indeed, he seems absurdly to have thought that a permanent perception would fit the bill). But Wittgenstein, like Kant, held that the 'non-encounterability of the self' in introspection is an essential, not a contingent feature of experience.[4] Similar points are made in the *Notebooks*. On 4 August 1916 we find him querying 'Isn't the representing subject in the last resort mere superstition?' (*NB*, p. 80). A week later he remarks 'The I is not an object. I objectively confront every object. But not the I. So there really is a way in which there can and must be mention of the I in a *non-psychological sense* in philosophy' (*NB*, p. 80). Two months later he repeats the same points in a slightly altered terminology. The illusory non-existent subject is called the 'knowing subject' (*erkennendes Subjekt*). It is important to bear in mind that the Humean argument of non-encounterability was directed against the Cartesian conception of the self as a *res cogitans*.

---

[2] Hume, *A Treatise of Human Nature*, I.iv.6.
[3] See B. Williams, 'Wittgenstein and Idealism', in G. Vesey, ed., *Understanding Wittgenstein*, pp. 77 f. One can search only for that which it makes sense to find.
[4] Later he would view it as nonsense, resting upon misconstrual of the grammar of the first-person pronoun.

The similarity of Wittgenstein's argument to that of Hume goes beyond the repudiation of the thinking, knowing, subject as an object of experience located within the world. Section 5.641 points out *en passant* that the subject-matter of psychology is the human soul. Wittgenstein's suggestions for the proper analysis of the human soul bear strong affinities to Hume's constructive analysis of the self. The clues to Wittgenstein's proposal lie in the earlier discussion of propositions about belief as potential counter-examples to the thesis of extensionality (*TLP*, 5.541). The superficial view of the meaning of propositions such as '*A* believes *p*', which Wittgenstein attributes to Russell and Moore, is that *A* stands in the relation of believing to the proposition *p*. Both Moore and Russell had indeed flirted with such a conception at earlier phases in their careers. Moore, in *Some Main Problems of Philosophy*, toyed with the idea that belief was a special act of mind directed towards an objective entity, viz. a proposition.[5] Russell, in his three articles 'Meinong's Theory of Complexes and Assumptions' published in *Mind* xiii (1906), argued similarly that belief was a mental attitude towards a proposition that exists whether or not it is believed. Wittgenstein brushes this dual relation theory of judgement aside: it *looks as if* the proposition *p* stood in some relation to the object (soul, mind) *A* (and so it looks as if one proposition occurs within another, viz. '*p*' in '*A* believes that *p*', without being a base for a truth-operation, contrary to the thesis of extensionality). But this is confused (as Moore and Russell had, for various reasons, realized by 1910).

It is clear, Wittgenstein insists, that '*A* believes that *p*' (or '*A* says, or thinks, that *p*') are of the form ' "*p*" says *p*' and this does not involve a correlation of a fact with an object, but rather the correlation of facts by means of the correlation of their objects (*TLP*, 5.542). This analysis satisfies the requirement on any analysis of judgement, namely that it be impossible for a judgement to be a piece of nonsense. Russell's theory, he adds, does not satisfy this requirement (*TLP*, 5.5422). Here Wittgenstein is referring to Russell's *later* multiple-relation theory of judgement that occurs in his 1910 paper 'On the Nature of Truth and Falsehood'[6] and is repeated in the 1913 manuscript *Theory of*

---

[5] He also tied himself in knots, arguing in Chapter 3 that propositions are among the things that exist in the universe, and in Chapter 14 that there are no such things.

[6] B. Russell, 'On the Nature of Truth and Falsehood', in *Philosophical Essays* (Longman, London, 1910), pp. 170 ff. The issue is discussed in detail in D. F. Pears, *Bertrand Russell and the British Tradition in Philosophy* (Fontana, London, and Glasgow, 1967), Chs. XII–XIII, and in his paper 'The Relation between Wittgenstein's Picture

Knowledge. The essentials of the theory are expressed in the following paragraph:

> judgment is not a dual relation of the mind to a single objective, but a multiple relation of the mind to the various other terms with which the judgment is concerned. Thus if I judge that *A* loves *B*, that is not a relation of me to '*A*'s love for *B*', but a relation between me and *A* and love and *B*. If it were a relation of me to '*A*'s love for *B*' it would be impossible unless there were such a thing as '*A*'s love for *B*', i.e. unless *A* loved *B*, i.e. unless the judgment were true; but in fact false judgments are possible. When the judgment is taken as a relation between me and *A* and love and *B*, the mere fact that the judgment occurs does not involve any relation between its objects *A* and love and *B*; thus the possibility of false judgments is fully allowed for.[7]

Wittgenstein's central (but not only) objection was that Russell had purchased the possibility of false judgement at the price of allowing nonsensical judgements. Nothing in Russell's theory ensured the preservation of logical form between the elements of the judgement. But a correct theory of judgement must make it impossible for one to judge that 'this table penholders the book' (*NB*, p. 96).[8] This objection, Russell said, paralysed him, leading to the recantation in 'The Philosophy of Logical Atomism',[9] although it was not until even later that Russell was prepared to dispense with the self as an element in the final analysis of '*A* judges that *p*'.

The form of '*A* believes that *p*', Wittgenstein argued, is ' "*p*" says *p*', which does not correlate a fact with an object, but correlates two facts by correlating their objects. This analysis is subsequently said to show that the so-called 'soul' is composite and hence not really a soul. This gives a clue to the interpretation. Facts are always composites of objects, and only composite things (although not 'complexes', which are not facts at all) can 'say' something, for the possibility of saying depends upon the existence of an articulated structure whose elements can be correlated with what is said by means of projection. Only a fact

---

Theory of Propositions and Russell's Theories of Judgment', in C. G. Luckhardt, ed., *Wittgenstein, Sources and Perspectives* (Cornell University Press, Ithaca, New York, 1979), pp. 190–214.

[7] Russell, 'On the Nature of Truth and Falsehood', p. 180.

[8] Wittgenstein's first objection to Russell's theory of judgement is in his letter of June 1913 (*NB*, p. 121). It is developed in 'Notes on Logic' (*NB*, p. 96), but does not reach final formulation until the 'Notes Dictated to Moore' (*NB*, p. 118), where the self is eliminated from the analysans.

[9] B. Russell, 'The Philosophy of Logical Atomism', repr. in *Logic and Knowledge*, ed. R. C. Marsh (Allen & Unwin, London, 1956), p. 226.

can represent a state of affairs. '*A* believes *p*' involves the correlation of two facts in the same way as the proposition '*p*' says that *p* in virtue of the correlation of the elements of the proposition-constituting fact with the objects configured in the fact that *p* (if it is a fact). The obscure relation between the mind and the uncoordinated terms of the judgement in Russell's theory is here replaced with the (hardly less obscure) method of projection correlating elements of thought or utterance with objects. It should now be clear why the analysis was thought to show the complexity of the 'soul'. The apparent unitary subject *A* which seemed related to an object, viz. a proposition, is a multiplicity of elements some of which are structured into a fact that pictures the fact or possible fact that *p*. The 'unitary subject' recedes into the 'metaphysical self' (*infra*) leaving behind a *composite* empirical self.

We have already mentioned Wittgenstein's remark in the *Notebooks* that thinking, even though non-verbal, is a kind of language (*NB*, p. 82) and his letter to Russell of 19 August 1919 in which he wrote:

'... But a *Gedanke* is a *Tatsache*: what are its constituents and components, and what is their relation to those of the pictured *Tatsache*?' I don't know *what* the constituents of a thought are but I know *that* it must have such constituents which correspond to the words of Language. Again the kind of relation of the constituents of the thought and of the pictured fact is irrelevant. It would be a matter of psychology to find out .... [A *Gedanke* consists] of psychical constituents that have the same sort of relation to reality as words. What those constituents are I don't know. (*NB*, pp. 129–30.)

The mind or self *A* is not an object, but a complex array of psychical elements. '*A* believes *p*' is allegedly analysable in such a way that the existence of the psychical constituents which correspond to the constituents of the possible fact that *p* is specified. These psychical constituents are related in some contingent way to whatever other facts or configurations of elements constitute the empirical self *A*. *A*'s belief consists of these psychical elements of a manifold being correlated with objects constituting a fact, together perhaps with some kind of 'colouring'. For, to be sure, the differences between distinct propositional attitudes are not captured by the suggested analysis. These differences were, in Wittgenstein's view, a matter for psychology not logic. From the logical point of view the only important points to establish are that '*A* believes *p*' is—appearance not withstanding—not a counter-example to the thesis of extensionality, and that it has the same logical multiplicity as p.[10]

It thus emerges that Wittgenstein was willing to adopt a neo-Humean analysis of the empirical self. There is no empirical soul-substance thinking thoughts, there are only thoughts. The self of psychology is a manifold, a series of experiences, a bundle of perceptions in perpetual flux. However, the claim in 5.5421 that this analysis of propositions about belief shows that 'there is no such thing as the soul—the subject, etc.—as it is conceived in the superficial psychology of the present day' is, when juxtaposed with 5.641, misleading. For 5.641 refers to the human soul as the legitimate subject-matter for empirical psychology. Yet 5.5421 says that 'a composite soul would no longer be a soul', and the analysis does show the soul to be composite. The claim should be interpreted thus: the soul conceived of as a unitary simple subject encounterable in private experience and constituting the meaning (*Bedeutung*) of 'A' in 'A believes that p' does not exist. But conceived of as a manifold, it is the legitimate subject-matter of psychology. All that empirical psychology needs to say about the psyche can be said. Philosophy has no concern with this. But nevertheless philosophy must discuss the I in a non-psychological sense. The reason given for this in the *Notebooks* is that the I is not an object I confront. In the *Tractatus* the obscure reason given is that 'the world is my world'

The philosophy which is concerned with the self is not the envisaged philosophy of analysis of the post-*Tractatus* era but the nonsensical philosophy of the *Tractatus* itself. The self with which philosophy is concerned is not the human being, or the human body, or the soul which is the concern of psychology. It is rather the metaphysical self (*TLP*, 5.641). We are introduced to this concept immediately after the thinking self has been dismissed as illusory. In 5.632 Wittgenstein wrote 'The subject does not belong to the world: rather, it is a limit of the world.' The subject here referred to is not, of course, the thinking subject, but the metaphysical subject. This is clear from the following section 5.633, and confirmed by the source of the remark in the *Notebooks* (*NB*, p. 79). The metaphysical subject is the bearer of good and evil. Why is it not part of the world? Wittgenstein merely hinted at

---

[10] Whether according to the *Tractatus* 'A believes that p' makes sense (is well-formed) or is rather a pseudo-proposition is very unclear. Anscombe, in her *Introduction to Wittgenstein's Tractatus*, pp. 87 ff. argues for the former possibility. Kenny, in his 'Wittgenstein's Early Philosophy of Mind', pp. 144 ff., for the latter.

an argument by way of analogy. The metaphysical subject is related to the world as the eye is related to the visual field. Nothing in the visual field entitles one to infer that it is seen by an eye. The eye of the visual field (not of course the physical eye, but what Wittgenstein later called 'the geometrical eye' (*NFL*, pp. 297, 299)) is the source of the visual field, not a constituent of it.

The point is not that I always notice the position from which I see what I see, but that 'I also always find myself at a particular point of my visual space, so my visual space has as it were a shape' (*NB*, p. 86). Section 5.634 hints at the shreds of an argument that faintly echoes Kant's 'the "I think" ' that must be capable of accompanying all my representations. No part of our experiences is a priori. Whatever we see could be otherwise. But, by implication, that our experience belongs to us and could not belong to another is a priori. It could not happen that we should need to employ some principle of differentiation to distinguish within the flow of experience those experiences that belong to us from those that belong to others. The 'owner of experience in general', the possessor of all the experience *I* can ever encounter, is the metaphysical subject.[11]

How is this to be interpreted? The received interpretation is that Wittgenstein was in effect dismissing the notion of a metaphysical self. Black[12] argues that Wittgenstein entertains the idea of a transcendental ego and eventually rejects it. The Cartesian ego, he claims, is not part of experience but the limit of experience. But since this way of speaking is nonsense, there is no sense in talking of a metaphysical subject. Hence consistent solipsism leads to realism, and he who intends to be a solipsist can be brought to see that there is nothing he really intends to say. Considerable light can be thrown upon the issue by a brief comparison of Wittgenstein and Schopenhauer. Schopenhauer[13]

---

[11] David Pears, in 'Wittgenstein's Treatment of Solipsism in the *Tractatus*', in his *Questions in Philosophy of Mind* (Duckworth, London, 1975), pp. 281 ff. points out that the above paraphrase equivocates between taking 'experience' phenomenalistically (as referring to sense data, etc.) and taking it realistically (as experience of public objects). This is correct, but if it is correct that the solipsism Wittgenstein was concerned with is *transcendental* then arguably Wittgenstein would not have thought of himself as forced to choose between these alternatives. What is experienced would be conceived, in Kantian terms, to be phenomenally real but transcendentally ideal.

[12] M. Black, *A Companion to Wittgenstein's Tractatus*, pp. 308 f. See for similar views G. Pitcher, *The Philosophy of Wittgenstein*, pp. 144 ff.

[13] Schopenhauer, *The World as Will and Representation*, ii.198 f. trans. E. F. J. Payne (Dover, New York, 1966); subsequent references in the text—abbreviated as *WWR*—will be to this two-volume translation.

accepted Kant's masterly refutation of the Cartesian doctrine of the soul as a unitary thinking substance. Kant's diagnosis was that Descartes confused the unity of apperception with the perception of a unitary subject. This rejection of the thinking, knowing, representing self as a constituent of the world did not, however, prevent Schopenhauer from a quasi-reification of the transcendental ego to constitute the foundation of his particular version of transcendental idealism. The transcendental self, he claimed, is 'as an indivisible point' (*WWR*, ii.278). Though it is simple, like the *res cogitans*, it is not a substance (ibid.). The metaphysical subject and its object, i.e. the world as representation, 'limit each other immediately' (*WWR*, i.5). The transcendental ego is a presupposition of the existence of the world (ibid.): the knowing subject thus conceived lies outside space and time which are merely the forms of its sensible intuition. As the source of the forms and categories of experience, it is 'a presupposition of all experience' (*WWR*, ii.15). It is the 'supporter of the world, the universal condition of all that appears' (*WWR*, i.5). The self is 'the eye (which) sees everything except itself' (*WWR*, ii.491), the ego is the 'centre of all existence' (*WWR*, ii.486).

Wittgenstein's metaphors are identical with Schopenhauer's. There can be little doubt that the last of the three extant notebooks was written while Wittgenstein was re-reading Schopenhauer. To be sure, he is only mentioned once by name: 'It would be possible to say (à la Schopenhauer): It is not the world of Idea that is either good or evil; but the willing subject' (*NB*, p. 79). Immediately following this remark another Schopenhauerian thought is entered: 'the subject is not part of the world but a presupposition of its existence'. Schopenhauer's transcendental subject limits the world as idea. Wittgenstein's metaphysical subject is a 'limit of the world'. Schopenhauer compared the I to the 'dark point in consciousness, just as on the retina the precise point of entry of the optic nerve is blind ... the eye sees everything except itself'. This metaphor first appears in Wittgenstein's 'Notes on Logic' of September 1913, without any overt reference to the self and without any Schopenhauerian overtones:

The comparison of language and reality is like that of a retinal image and visual image: to the blind spot nothing in the visual image seems to correspond, and thereby the boundaries of the blind spot determine the visual image—just as true negations of atomic propositions determine reality. (*NB*, p. 95.)

As we shall see below, this original employment of the metaphor to illuminate the relation of language and reality, seen in the light of its subsequent use, is important. In the 1916 notebook the eye metaphor is used to illustrate the relation between subject and experience. On 11 June 1916 Wittgenstein wrote 'I am placed in it [the world] like my eye in its visual field' (*NB*, p. 73). The metaphor recurs repeatedly in subsequent remarks (e.g. on 4 August 1916, 12 August 1916, 20 October 1916—*NB*, pp. 80, 86) in obvious Schopenhauerian contexts. It reappears, as we have seen, in the *Tractatus*, 5.633–5.634. Finally, even Schopenhauer's reference to the self as the centre of all existence reappears in the *Notebooks* 'If the will did not exist, neither would there be that centre of the world, which we call the I . . .' (*NB*, p. 80).

These Schopenhauerian influences provide us with important evidence for interpreting Wittgenstein's remarks on the self. First, the argument of non-encounterability of a Cartesian self appears in both Kant and Schopenhauer as part of the refutation of the rationalist doctrine of the soul. Given the Schopenhauerian influence upon Wittgenstein it is plausible to take its reappearance in the *Tractatus*, 5.631 to be directed at the same target, as we have already conjectured. Secondly, the common view that the metaphysical self is identical with the illusory thinking self and hence is not countenanced by Wittgenstein can be conclusively rejected. In the first place, the non-encounterability argument is effective in demolishing a naïve conception of a thinking soul-substance but is wholly ineffective in dismissing the conception of a metaphysical self, since the latter is not alleged to be part of the world, but its limit, not a constituent of the world, but a presupposition of its existence as idea. In the second place, the parallels with Schopenhauer run sufficiently deep to make it a plausible conjecture, in the absence of countervailing evidence, that Schopenhauer's distinction between the illusory Cartesian self and the transcendental self was adopted by Wittgenstein. In the third place, the enigmatic claims that the self is a presupposition of the existence of the world and that it is the centre of the world do not suggest its illusoriness. Finally, the existence of the metaphysical self as a non-empirical object is required by Wittgenstein's doctrines of the will and of good and evil.

Wittgenstein had little to say about ethics in the *Tractatus*. Ethics, in his view, is transcendental. It belongs to those things that cannot be put into words, the mystical. The will is the bearer of value, but as such, not being a phenomenon in the world, cannot be spoken of. Value does not lie in the world, for all that is within the world is contingent. Hence the good or bad exercise of the will cannot alter what is in the world but can alter only the limits of the world by making it, as it were, wax or wane as a whole. Since Wittgenstein did not believe that good and evil are illusory, he could hardly have believed that the ethical will which is the bearer of good and evil is illusory. The ethical will, like the metaphysical self, lies 'at the limits of the world' indeed it is identical with the metaphysical subject. This is evident from the *Notebooks*. The entry for 2 August 1916 reads as follows:

> Good and evil only enter through the *subject*. And the subject is not part of the world, but a boundary of the world . . .

As the subject is not part of the world but a presupposition of its existence, so good and evil are predicates of the subject, not properties in the world (*NB*, p. 79)

Three days later he repeats that the thinking subject is illusory, but continues, 'the willing subject exists. If the will did not exist, neither would there be that centre of the world, which we call the I, and which is the bearer of ethics' (*NB*, p. 80).

The discussion thus far sets some preliminary order into the remarks about the self. Most importantly, it implies that we should take the notion of the metaphysical self seriously. For the moment our main interpretative key is the Schopenhauerian discussion of the *Notebooks*. It should be borne in mind that the concept of a metaphysical self is introduced in the sections 5.631–5.634 as comment upon 5.63 'I am my world. (The microcosm.)' This remark follows the claim in 5.621 that 'The world and life are one', which was a gloss upon the explanation of how much truth there is in solipsism. This suggests that the notion of the metaphysical self may provide the key to understanding Wittgenstein's remarks about solipsism, and that the transcendental idealist context from which the notion is derived may be pertinent to our investigation. Bearing these conclusions in mind one can now return to Wittgenstein's discussion of solipsism.

2. *'I am my World'*

The sense in which philosophy can (*TLP*, 5.641) and must (*NB*, p. 80) talk about the self is with reference to the metaphysical self. What brings the metaphysical self into philosophy is the fact that 'The world is my world' (*TLP*, 5.641). That the world is my world is, according to the *Tractatus*, what the solipsist means, but it cannot be said, it can only show itself. The only explanation of the obscure remark identifying my world and the world, in the *Tractatus*, is the identification of the world and life, and of the self and its world. Neither remarks are, as they stand, perspicuous.

In the *Tractatus* Wittgenstein tells us that the key to the problem how much truth there is in solipsism is to be found in the contention that 'We cannot think what we cannot think; so what we cannot think we cannot *say* either.' The bounds of sense cannot coherently be thought (since that would involve using formal concepts as if they were material ones, and constructing pseudo-propositions in thought that are not bipolar). *A fortiori* they cannot be described in language. It is important to note that this apparent truism of the inexpressibility of the unthinkable appears in the *Notebooks* in a Schopenhauerian context. The entry for 12 October 1916 (*NB*, p. 84) claims that a stone, the body of a beast, the body of a man, and my body all stand on the same level. This contention is arguably directed against Schopenhauer's view that my body stands on a different level from other objects in as much as my direct knowledge of my intentional actions gives me an awareness of my body not merely as idea or representation but also as will (*WWR*, i.103 ff). The idea that one part of the world be closer to me than another as Schopenhauer suggests is, Wittgenstein later remarks, intolerable (*NB*, p. 88)[14] The discussion on 12 October 1916 in the notebook concludes with the remark 'It is true: Man *is* the microcosm: I am my world.' The next entry three days later is 'What one cannot think, thereof one can also not speak'. This makes it plausible to conjecture that this is the key to solipsism precisely because the solipsist's doctrines, though in some sense true, are inexpressible. Those doctrines are the identification of the world with life, of life with the self, of the self with its world, and thus of the world with the world of the self.

Further confirmation of this conjecture comes from the *Notebooks*. For there the key to how much truth there is in solipsism is not held to be the inexpressibility of the unthinkable, but the fact that 'There really is only one world soul, which I for preference call *my* soul and as which alone I conceive what I call the soul of others.' This 'soul' or 'self' is, of course, not L.W., any more than the 'I' of Descartes' 'I think, therefore I am' is R.D. Rather, the soul thus conceived is stripped of all particularity. One might express one's solipsistic

[14] See also *NB*, p. 82.

thought here, Wittgenstein much later explained, by saying 'I am the vessel of life' (*BB*, p. 65). This key to the truth of solipsism (which is remarked upon in the second notebook on 23 May 1915 (*NB*, p. 49)) follows the claim that, '*The limits of my language* stand for the limits of my world.' This remark suggests a linguistic rather than a metaphysical route to solipsism. We shall explore this possibility below. The entry following the 'key to solipsism' is that it is possible for me to write a book 'The world I found', which, like the key statement itself, intimates the epistemological and metaphysical route to solipsism which is the concern of the third notebook. This array of evidence gives support to the suggestion already mooted that the clue to Wittgenstein's concern with solipsism lies in the notion of the metaphysical self as derived from Schopenhauer's transcendental idealism. It is to this that we shall now turn.

Section 5.621 of the *Tractatus*—'The world and life are one'—originally appeared in the third notebook on 11 June 1916 as one of the items Wittgenstein claimed to know about God and the purpose of life:

I know that this world exists.
That I am placed in it like my eye in its visual field.
That something about it is problematic, which we call its meaning.
That this meaning does not lie in it but outside it.
That life is the world. (*NB*, pp. 72–3)

The thought gets its final formulation 'The World and Life are one' on 24 July 1916, together with the beginning of an explanation. Physiological life, Wittgenstein explains, is of course not 'life' in the sense in which the world and life are identical. Nor, for that matter is psychological life. Life, he repeats, is the world. On 1 August 1916 Wittgenstein remarks 'Only from the consciousness of the *uniqueness of my life* arises religion—science—and art' (*NB*, p. 79). On the following day he adds 'And this consciousness is life itself.' Thus the world is identified with life, life is identified with consciousness and consciousness in general with the solitary self of solipsism. It is not surprising that the subsequent comment in the notebook is 'Can there be any ethics if there is no living being but myself?', and even less surprising that he remarks 'I am conscious of the complete unclarity of all these sentences.'

Confirmation for the solipsistic interpretation of these passages can be found in Wittgenstein's 'Notes for Lectures on "Private Experience" and "Sense Data" ', written between 1934 and 1936. These lecture notes were written long after Wittgenstein's repudiation of any form of solipsism. Indeed much of the discussion in them is concerned with uncovering the deep errors of the solipsist. On p. 296 Wittgenstein's 'younger self', if one may so refer to the antagonist of the internal dialogue, objects to his critic:

> But aren't you neglecting something—the experience or whatever you might call it—? Almost *the world* behind the mere words?

In the course of the lengthy reply of Wittgenstein's 'wiser self' to the solipsist's case he says:

> It seems that I neglect life. But not life physiologically understood but life as consciousness. And consciousness not physiologically understood, or understood from the outside, but consciousness as the very essence of experience, the appearance of the world, the world. (NFL, p. 297)

It is, I think, not coincidental that the mature Wittgenstein should phrase his solipsist objector's contentions in words highly reminiscent of his own notes of 1916.

The extent of Wittgenstein's preoccupation with solipsism is further revealed by a series of remarks on 2 September 1916. For the moment the significant ones are as follows:

> What has history to do with me? Mine is the first and only world!
> I want to report how *I* found the world.
> What others in the world have told me about the world is a very small and incidental part of my experience of the world.
> *I* have to judge the world, to measure things. (*NB*, p. 82)

The I that thus confronts the world is, he clarifies in the following entry, the metaphysical self, not the human being, nor the body, nor the empirical self, all of which belong to the world and are on one level. A month later we find Wittgenstein entering a remark couched in pure Schopenhauerian jargon—'As my idea is the world, in the same way my will is the world-will' (*NB*, p. 85).

The remark at 5.63 in the *Tractatus*—'I am my world. (The microcosm.)'—originates in the *Notebooks*' entry for 12 October 1916—'It is true: Man *is* the microcosm.' The identification of the individual consciousness with the microcosm, and the microcosm with the macrocosm, is a central Schopenhauerian thesis. The salient doctrine in Schopenhauer's metaphysics is that of the dual nature of the world as will and idea or representation (*Vorstellung*). As representation the world is relative to the transcendental knowing subject who imposes upon it its forms of representation, space and time, and the principle of sufficient reason. Independently of these forms of representation, the world is pure will, which is the noumenal reality with which we are acquainted through our knowledge of our own actions. Thus man himself mirrors the duality of the world:

> Everyone finds himself to be this will, in which the inner nature of the world consists, and he also finds himself to be the knowing subject, whose representation is the whole world; and this world has existence only in reference to the knowing subject's consciousness as its necessary supporter. Thus everyone in this twofold regard is the whole world itself, the microcosm; he finds its two sides whole and complete within himself. And what he thus recognises as his own inner being also exhausts the inner being of the whole world, of the macrocosm. (*WWR*, i.162)

Schopenhauer admitted that the limitation of one's insight into noumenal reality to one's knowledge of one's own literally embodied will may well incline one to solipsism, or, as he called it, 'theoretical egoism'. Although this theoretical egoism can never be refuted, nevertheless, he claimed, it is really no more than a sceptical solipsism which need not be taken seriously. Despite this repudiation there are very many passages in Schopenhauer that make it difficult to see how he can be so sanguine in dogmatically brushing aside something allegedly irrefutable. In the grip of a misconceived picture, it is very tempting to argue that:

> the whole of nature outside the knowing subject, and so all remaining individuals, exist only in his representation; that he is conscious of them always only as his representation, and so merely indirectly, and as something dependent on his own inner being and existence ...
>
> ... every individual, completely vanishing and reduced to nothing in a boundless world, nevertheless makes himself the centre of the world ... (*WWR*, i.332)

Such passages, and there are many, evidently struck a deeply responsive chord in Wittgenstein.

Schopenhauer's doctrines of man as microcosm bulk large in his discussions of death. 'An understanding of the indestructibility of our true nature', he claims, 'coincides with that of the identity of macrocosm and microcosm' (*WWR*, ii.486). Wittgenstein, like Schopenhauer, has interesting comments on death both in the *Tractatus* and in the *Notebooks 1914–16*. They are darkly mysterious. These remarks will be examined first, and subsequently compared with Schopenhauer's writings, in order to illuminate them and to further our investigation into Wittgenstein's attitude to solipsism.

The remarks on death in the *Tractatus* occur at 6.431–6.4312:

6.431   So too at death the world does not alter, but comes to an end.

6.4311   Death is not an event in life: we do not live to experience death.
If we take eternity to mean not infinite temporal duration but timelessness, then eternal life belongs to those who live in the present. Our life has no end in just the way in which our visual field has no limits.

6.4312   Not only is there no guarantee of the temporal immortality of the human soul, that is to say of its eternal survival after death; but, in any case, this assumption completely fails to accomplish the purpose for which it has always been intended. Or is some riddle solved by my surviving for ever? Is not this eternal life itself as much of a riddle as our present life? The solution of the riddle of life in space and time lies *outside* space and time.
(It is certainly not the solution of any problems of natural science that is required.)

This apocalyptic passage follows the section which we have already examined in which Wittgenstein claimed that the good or bad exercise of the will can only alter the limits of the world not its content; it makes the world as a whole wax and wane. So too at death the contents of the world do not change, one object among the many does not alter. Rather the world as a whole comes to an end. The solution to the riddle lies outside space and time. These are mysterious claims, and are usually dismissed as poetic licence or mystical metaphor. It is, however, worth probing deeper than that.

The claim that death is not an object or mode of experience is readily intelligible even to a hard-headed empiricist. But the suggestion that at death the world ends is puzzling. Considerable illumination is shed by Schopenhauer's doctrines about death and eternal life. Indeed it is only by reference to these that Wittgenstein's remarks can be taken to have a limited degree of intelligibility. We have already seen Schopenhauer's claim that the identity of the microcosm and the macrocosm are essential to understanding the indestructibility of our nature. Part of Schopenhauer's explanation of our indestructibility involves an essential reference to transcendental idealism. The riddles of life, of the existence of the world before our birth and of the continuance of the world after our death, can only be solved with the aid of Kant's doctrine of the transcendental ideality of time (*WWR*, ii.467). For Kant, as Schopenhauer explains, showed that time is the form of all phenomena, but noumena, things as they are in themselves, are 'outside' time. Not only is time the form of empirical appearances, but it is part of the structure of the human mind; time is in us, prior to experience; it lies, in Schopenhauer's words, 'preformed in our apprehension'. The knowing subject which is a presupposition of all experience 'is not in time, for time is only the more direct form of all its representing' (*WWR*, ii.15). Death, Schopenhauer claimed, is the cessation of a temporal phenomenon. But as soon as we abstract time, which is a feature of the constitution of our mind, the notion of an *end* becomes meaningless. If time is transcendentally ideal then from the metaphysical viewpoint it is senseless to speak of life ending with death, or of the world continuing after life has ceased. The conception of eternal life, as commonly understood, is vacuous: it has no experience as its foundation. It does, however, have a negative content, interpreted as a 'timeless existence' (*WWR*, ii.484). It is the present that is truly timeless. Empirically apprehended it is wholly transitory, but it 'manifests itself to the metaphysical glance that sees beyond the forms of empirical perception as that which alone endures, as the *nunc stans* of the scholastics' (*WWR*, i.279).

Wittgenstein's remarks about death are recognizably derived from Schopenhauer. Little sense can be made of his thinking these thoughts without presuming that he saw some deep truth in the Schopenhauerian metaphysical vision and the transcendental ideality of time. Nothing thus far said, however, suggests that it is possible to make sense of *what* he thought.

One final piece of evidence may serve to clinch the interpretation. That what Wittgenstein called 'the mystical' was of supreme importance to him is indubitable. But what he meant thereby is opaque. In the *Tractatus*, 6.45 he wrote:

To view the world *sub specia aeterni* is to view it as a whole—a limited whole. Feeling the world as a limited whole—it is this that is mystical.

It would be rash to try to explain or justify a man's intensely serious and passionate views about the mystical. But one can, with much less audacity, try to trace the development of his thought. In the *Notebooks* on 7 October 1916, Wittgenstein entered one of his few comments on aesthetics:

> The work of art is the object seen *sub specie aeternitatis*; and the good life is the world seen *sub specie aeternitatis*. This is the connection between art and ethics. (*NB*, p. 83).

The alleged connection between aesthetics and ethics is baldly stated in the *Tractatus*, 6.421, in parentheses: 'Ethics and aesthetics are one and the same.' Neither can be spoken of; both are transcendental. There is, however, a further connecting-thread between what Wittgenstein jotted down on aesthetics in the *Notebooks* and the doctrines of the *Tractatus*. Immediately prior to the passage under consideration, at 6.44, he wrote 'It is not *how* things are in the world that is mystical, but *that* it exists.' This thought, in the *Notebooks*, is related to the aesthetic point of view, rather than to the mystical. On 20 October 1916, he remarked: 'Aesthetically, the miracle is that the world exists. That what exists does exist.' Indeed the term 'the mystical' (*das Mystische*) only appears once in the *Notebooks* (p. 51). But we now have two pieces of evidence to associate the aesthetic viewpoint and the mystical one. Further important clues can be discovered in Schopenhauer's aesthetic theory.

Only in the artistic vision, Schopenhauer claims, can one be released from one's bondage to the will. Only aesthetic experience can free the intellect from its servitude to desire and appetite, and emancipate it from the restrictive categories of thought under which we are constrained to view phenomenal experience. Through this emancipation we can come to contemplate, in a will-less freedom, the Platonic Forms or Ideas, and thus achieve a deep comprehension of the inner nature of reality. The artistic temperament and the philosophical one are closely connected in Schopenhauer's view: 'the high calling of these two has its root in the reflectiveness which springs primarily from the distinctness with which they are conscious of the world and of themselves' (*WWR*, ii.382). The phenomenology of aesthetic contemplation is described in some detail by Schopenhauer, and it appears to involve a mysterious transformation of the self. One must rid oneself of the normal categories of thought, cease considering 'the where, the why and the whither of things' and contemplate the 'what'. One must free oneself from the will, from any guidance given by the categorial forms of the principle of sufficient reason, and sink oneself in perceptual experience. One must fill one's whole consciousness with the object of contemplation and lose one's individuality in so doing. One then continues to exist only as pure subject, as unblemished mirror of the object; one stands outside space and time; one becomes a '*pure* will-less, painless, timeless subject of knowledge'. It was this, Schopenhauer claims.

that was in Spinoza's mind when he wrote:
Mens aeterna est, quatenus res sub aeternitatis specie concipit. (*WWR*, i.179)[15]

The reappearance of this striking application of Spinoza's[16] third form of knowledge to the aesthetic vision in Wittgenstein can hardly be coincidental. What is, however, most significant is the correlation of the aesthetic experience thus interpreted with the solipsistic viewpoint. Just as Schopenhauer associated the philosophic and artistic spirit with 'the pure will-less, painless, timeless subject of knowledge' whose consciousness is filled with the object of contemplation, so too Wittgenstein, as we have seen, located the springs of religion, science, and art in the consciousness of the uniqueness of one's life. This consciousness was said to be identical with life itself, i.e. consciousness conceived 'as the very essence of experience, the appearance of the world, the world' (NFL, p. 297). The switch from the aesthetic point of view to the solipsistic one occurs in the course of the continuation of the same entry in the *Notebooks* for 7 October 1916 which we have examined. Having drawn the connection between ethics and aesthetics by reference to a vision of things *sub specie aeternitatis*, Wittgenstein goes on to suggest that the difference between the ordinary way of looking at things and the view *sub specie aeternitatis* is that the former sees things from the midst of them and the latter views them from outside with the whole world as their background. When seen thus, he says, 'the object is seen *together with* space and time instead of *in* space and time', it is seen 'together with the whole logical space'. On the following day, 8 October 1916, the metaphysical, solipsistic application of the fragmentary Schopenhauerian aesthetic doctrines previously discussed is even more striking:

If I have been contemplating the stove, and then am told: but now all you know

---

[15] Schopenhauer's reference is to Spinoza's *Ethics*: 'The mind is eternal in so far as it conceives things under the form of eternity.' (Book V, Prop. XXXI Note.)

[16] This, incidentally, gives some historical justification for Moore's Spinozistic title of the English translation of *Logisch–Philosophische Abhandlung*. See Ogden's letter to Russell, of 5 November 1921, in Russell, *The Autobiography of Bertrand Russell 1914–44* (Allen & Unwin, London, 1968), ii.121.

is the stove, my result does indeed seem trivial. For this represents the matter as if I had studied the stove as one among the many things in the world. But if I was contemplating the stove *it* was my world, and everything else colourless by contrast with it . . .

For it is equally possible to take the bare present image as the worthless momentary picture in the whole temporal world, and as the true world among shadows. (*NB*, p. 83)

With this the large part of the evidence supporting the claim that Wittgenstein adhered to some form of solipsism between 1915 and 1919 which is prominent in the *Notebooks* and *Tractatus* is concluded. The argument has traced a genetic route to this conclusion. Wittgenstein's solipsism was inspired by Schopenhauer's doctrines of transcendental idealism. These he adapted to his own peculiar transcendental form of 'theoretical egoism'. What the solipsist means, and is correct in thinking, is that the world and life are one, that man is the microcosm, that I am my world. These equations have little to do with traditional mysticism and are not descriptions of mystical experiences. Nor are they essentially connected with ethical Stoicism, involving a refusal to identify oneself with part of the world.[17] They express a doctrine which I shall call Transcendental Solipsism. They involve a belief in the transcendental ideality of time[18] (and presumably space), a rather perverse interpretation of the Kantian doctrine of the unity of

---

[17] This is the interpretation given by B. F. McGuinness, 'The Mysticism of the *Tractatus*', *The Philosophical Review*, lxxv (1966), 305-28. McGuinness suggests that realization that the world is my world is an essential part of happiness, that 'I am my world' is a refusal to identify oneself with one part of the world rather than another, and equally with a refusal to identify oneself with the physiological or psychological peculiarities and life of a particular individual. He supports this interpretation primarily by reference to *NB*, p. 82 §7, *NB*, p. 82, §§8 and 9, and *NB*, p. 84 §2, and associates it with traditional mysticism. The last two passages are concerned with combatting Schopenhauer's doctrine of the privileged status of our own bodies in relation to our knowledge of our intentional actions. The first is concerned with identifying the philosophical self with the transcendental subject. These doctrines have little to do with the attribution of importance to parts of the world, or with the happiness of the Stoic attitude.

[18] There is, rather surprisingly, very little about the nature of time in the early writings. That some interpretation can be given to the doctrine that space and time are forms of intuition is intimated in Wittgenstein's 'Notes Dictated to Moore', of Apr. 1914 (*NB*, p. 117). That space and time are relative is suggested in letter No. 25 to Russell, Jan. 1914 (*NB*, p. 129). The views already examined on death, the significance of life, and the solution of its riddle, as well as the conception of the aesthetic or mystical vision, commit Wittgenstein to some form of the doctrine of the ideality of time.

apperception together with the acceptance of Schopenhauer's quasi-reification of the unity of consciousness, and other related and obscure theories about ethics, the will, aesthetics, and religion. Wittgenstein's originality in the matter lies in his attempt to dovetail these doctrines into the sophisticated account of representation with which most of the *Tractatus* is concerned. Unlike Kant and Schopenhauer, Wittgenstein thought that his transcendental idealist doctrines, though profoundly important, are literally inexpressible. Although what the solipsist means is correct, it cannot be said; it shows itself. It is to this aspect of the doctrine that we must now turn, and try to trace the faint linguistic route to solipsism which converges with the transcendental idealist route.

3. 'The limits of language means the limits of my world'

We have seen in the previous chapter that the account of 'projection' of names with logico-syntactical form which Wittgenstein propounded in the *Tractatus* is strongly egocentric on the one hand, and concerned with a 'momentary' language on the other. Anything which I can understand as language must have a content which is assigned to it by my projecting names with appropriate form on to reality. 'Things acquire "*Bedeutung*" only in relation to my will' is not only an ethical principle, but a semantic one. Propositional signs are merely 'inscriptions'; only in relation to *my will* do they constitute symbols. The metaphysical route to solipsism involves trying to grasp consciousness 'from the inside'. The linguistic route tries to grasp language from the inside. From this point of view language is *my* language. In order for propositional signs to have sense I have to think the method of projection. What I cannot project is not language. Without the accompaniment of my consciousness language is nothing but a husk. '*I* have to judge the world, to measure things' (*NB*, p. 82), and the measure of the world is the proposition whose sense *I* think.

This thin linguistic route to solipsism, i.e. the identification of language with my language, is paralleled by a linguistic route to the metaphysical self. For the self which thinks the method of projection cannot, so it might seem, be captured by the language it creates. This 'metalinguistic soul' is, as it were, the blind spot upon the retinal image to which nothing in the visual image corresponds. The boundaries of the blind spot determine the visual image (*NB*, p. 95; see above p. 88). Without it the comparison of language and reality is impossible. A

Empirical Realism and Transcendental Solipsism 101

similar suggestion is explored in a paper by Wiggins.[19] One might argue (fallaciously, Wiggins suggests) that a mind M which is aware of a fact $\langle x.y.z. \rangle$ and knows the truth of the proposition describing it, must in some way assume a structure which mirrors $\langle x.y.z. \rangle$ by means of an array of psychical elements $\langle t.u.v. \rangle$ with a matching multiplicity of elements analogously concatenated by a given method of projection. A mind M, so runs the argument Wiggins demolishes, could not within itself both represent a state-description S, and represent itself M within such a state-description S, knowing both the state-description and its own state. For there, it seems, lies an infinite regress—just as a map of a city cannot include a depiction of the map of the city which stands in the High Street.

The evidence for this linguistic route is slim to say the least. It is, however, the only way of linking the discussion of the philosophical self, and of death and immortality with the rest of the book. It is common to view the *Tractatus* as a complete and wholly integrated work, and hence to think that the so-called 'mystical' parts of the book are 'a culmination of the work reflecting back on everything that went before'.[20] This is, I think, at best misleading, at worst erroneous. It is true that these sections of the *Tractatus* are connected with what went before, although the connection is tenuous. It is also true that they were of great importance to Wittgenstein. It is not obvious, however, that they follow from the earlier sections of the book. The connections can be seen to be a little tighter by reference to two further considerations. The first concerns the doctrine of the manifestation of the inexpressible but correct solipsism.

The 5.6's open with the equation of the limits of *my* language with the limits of my world. The following remark equates the limits of *the* world with the limits of logic. This is explained by reference to the claim that logic cannot anticipate the contents of the world. This explanation concludes with the thesis of the inexpressibility of the unthinkable which, section 5.62 claims, gives the key to the problem of how far solipsism is true. The answer is that what the solipsist means is correct only it cannot be said; it shows itself. What the solipsist means is that *the* world is *my* world. This inexpressible truth shows itself in

---

[19] D. Wiggins, 'Freedom, Knowledge, Belief and Causality', in *Knowledge and Necessity*, Royal Institute of Philosophy Lectures, 3 (1968–9), ed. G. N. A. Vesey (Macmillan, 1970), pp. 150–1.
[20] E. Zemach, 'Wittgenstein's Philosophy of the Mystical', in *Essays on Wittgenstein's Tractatus*, ed. I. M. Copi and R. W. Beard, p. 359.

the fact that 'the limits of *language* (of that language which alone I understand) means the limits of *my* world' ('die Grenzen der Sprache (der Sprache die allein ich verstehe) die Grenzen meiner Welt bedeuten') (*TLP*, 5.62).[21]

That the limits of my language are identical with the limits of my world is more or less intelligible by reference to the claims that logic is prior to every experience (*TLP*, 5.552), and that the content of propositions is given by *my* experience, by *my* injecting content into the forms that mirror the nature of the world. For only 'objects' *I* experience can *I* correlate with names of my language. And only what I thus project is what I can view as language, i.e. as facts standing in a representative relationship. That the limits of logic are the limits of the world seems merely to reiterate the claim that logic is limited to the non-contingent. It is prior to the question 'How?', not prior to the question 'What?'. How the substance of the world is arranged is an *a posteriori* matter. That the world has a substance is not. The limits of logic are the forms of the world (its possibilities), but what belongs to its content is a matter for the application of logic, i.e. experience and its analysis. Logic cannot anticipate experience. It cannot overstep its limits to tell us which of all possible words this is, just as experience—the world—cannot tell us what must be thus or otherwise. That the world is my world, that the world and life are one, that I am my world, are all expressions of the dark, inexpressible doctrines of transcendental solipsism already examined. For the putative insight that 'the world is my world' is not a contingent truth that could be otherwise. The self whose representation the world is, is not one among others. That experience in general, the only experience that I encounter is mine—is not something which could be otherwise. 'Whatever we can describe at all could be other than it is' (*TLP*, 5.634), hence this non-contingent ownership is indescribable. Moreover the solipsistic doctrines involve an essential reference to the metaphysical self. But the metaphysical self is neither an object that constitutes the reference of a name in fully analysed language nor is it a composite structure consisting of such objects. Hence 'the self of solipsism shrinks to a point without extension' about which nothing can meaningfully be said. But language mirrors the necessities which limit

---

[21] The heated controversy over the correct translation of this passage has now been settled by reference to Wittgenstein's corrections to Ramsey's copy of the first edition of the *Tractatus*. 'Allein', it is now clear, refers to 'Sprache' and not to 'Ich'. See C. Lewy, 'A Note on the Text of the *Tractatus*', *Mind*, lxxvi (1967) 419.

reality in its structure. That the world is my world manifests itself in the identity of the limits of language—which is my language—and the limits of the world—which is my world. Or so it seemed to the author of the *Tractatus*.

This leads us to the final solipsistic doctrine of the *Tractatus*. 'Solipsism, when its implications are followed out strictly, coincides with pure realism. The self of solipsism shrinks to a point without extension and there remains the reality coordinated with it' (*TLP*, 5.64). Wittgenstein's doctrines have of course followed out the implications of solipsism. How do they show that solipsism, paradoxically, coincides with pure realism? The analysis of propositions about other minds will not mention the metaphysical self, or a Cartesian *res cogitans*. It is plausible to think that such propositions will be analysed in some way or other in terms of names referring to elements of my experience.[22] Hence if epistemological realism is, roughly speaking, the commonsense view of the world expressed in propositions such as '*A* has toothache', 'The tree is shedding its leaves', then transcendental solipsism does not deny that such propositions are sometimes true. Nor indeed does it claim that 'I am the only person who exists' is true. What it claims is that the analysis of such propositions into elementary propositions is to be carried out in a certain way. The truth of solipsism will manifest itself in the fact that the analysis of 'I have toothache' will differ in important ways from the analysis of '*A* has toothache' (where *A* is not myself). The former will involve reference to the experience of toothache. The latter will refer only to the behaviour which others manifest when they are said to have toothache. But even in the analysis of 'I have toothache' the metaphysical self, the self of solipsism, will not appear. It will be the constant form of all experience, presumably represented in the ideal notation by the variable or variables taking names of unanalysable elements of experience or perhaps names of objects in general as values.

Thus everything the realist wishes to say can be said; and nothing

---

[22] This is suggested by much of the material already analysed. Further support is to be found in 'Some Remarks on Logical Form'. An interesting debate on Wittgenstein's solipsism arose out of S. Stebbing's lecture 'Logical Positivism and Analysis', *Proceedings of the British Academy*, xix (1933), 53–88, and was pursued by R. B. Braithwaite, J. O. Wisdom, M. Cornforth, and S. Stebbing in *Analysis*, i (1933). Of course by that time Wittgenstein had changed his position radically, hence his irate letter to *Mind* in response to Braithwaite's paper in *University Studies, Cambridge 1933* (see *Mind*, xlii (1933) 415 f.).

the transcendental solipsist wishes to say can be spoken of. There will be no practical disagreement between them, nor will they quarrel over the truth-values of propositions of ordinary language. But the analysis of such propositions will manifest the transcendental truths that cannot be said. Wittgenstein's doctrine in the *Tractatus* is best described as Empirical Realism and Transcendental Solipsism.

4. *Later Years*

If we turn to Wittgenstein's writings from 1929 onwards we do, of course, find great changes. Certainly he 'cut out the transcendental twaddle' (*transcendentales Geschwätz*).[23] But there is much evidence in what he wrote that there remained interesting continuities through the change. Both differences and similarities will concern us in the following chapters. For the moment, there are two points which are worthy of attention. The first concerns mention of further *ex post facto* evidence for the transcendental solipsist interpretation which has thus far been propounded. The second is an ethical digression.

G. E. Moore, in his notes taken at Wittgenstein's lectures in 1930–3, relates that in the lectures of 1932–3, Wittgenstein said that he himself had often been tempted to say that all that is real and certain is the experience of the present moment. Anyone who is at all tempted to believe that idealism or solipsism are true, he continued, knows the temptation to say that the only reality is my present experience. Given our previous discussion it is now plausible to suppose that Wittgenstein himself was not only tempted, but succumbed. The thought that *this* moment alone has true reality is recognizably connected with the *Notebooks*' contention that it is possible to conceive of the 'bare present image' as the 'true world among the shadows'. It is also related to Schopenhauer's claim that 'the *present* alone is the form of all life' (*WWR*, i.278). It is therefore not coincidental that in his many later arguments against solipsism and idealism he should formulate his adversary's case in terms, metaphors, and similes highly reminiscent of his own youthful thoughts. We have already seen an element of this correlation in the 'Notes for Lectures'. It is not a solitary one. Wittgenstein repeatedly associated the phenomenology of the solipsistic frame of mind with staring (see e.g. *BB*, p. 66; NFL, p. 309; *PI*, §398). Similarly the Schopenhauerian reference to the self as 'the centre of

---

[23] The phrase is Wittgenstein's, though used in a different context in which it is unclear to what he is referring. It was written in a letter to Engelmann in 1918. See *LLW*, pp. 10 f.

the world', which Wittgenstein used to state his case in the *Notebooks*, reappears in the extensive criticism of the solipsist in the 'Notes for Lectures', p. 299. 'But I am in a favoured position', remarks Wittgenstein's adversary, 'I am the centre of the world.' As we shall see in the following chapters, many of his most famous discussions in his later work are directed against his earlier beliefs and some of their consequences which he only subsequently discerned.

I have suggested that the primary inspiration of the so-called 'mystical' sections of the *Tractatus* lies outside the book. To be sure, some aspects of the transcendental theses dovetail into the conception of meaning with the added advantage of emerging from this union as inexpressible. This does not, of course, imply any belittling of the significance of these doctrines for Wittgenstein. On the contrary, the fact that the two strands of thought could be interwoven thus may well have struck Wittgenstein as partial confirmation of each. For there is no doubt that when he compiled the *Tractatus*, it was the very fact that the philosophy of logic which he propounded drew the limits of language at the boundary of all that is 'higher'—ethics, aesthetics, and religion, as well as philosophy itself and the attendant doctrines of transcendental.solipsism—which seemed the main achievement of the book. In a letter to Ludwig von Ficker written apparently in October 1919, Wittgenstein wrote:

The book's point is an ethical one. I once meant to include in the preface a sentence which is not in fact there now but which I will write out for you here, because it will perhaps be a key to the work for you. What I meant to write, then, was this: My work consists of two parts: the one presented here plus all that I have *not* written. And it is precisely this second part that is the important one. My book draws limits to the sphere of the ethical from the inside as it were, and I am convinced that this is the ONLY *rigorous* way of drawing those limits. In short, I believe that where *many* others today are just *gassing*, I have managed in my book to put everything firmly into place by being silent about it ... I would recommend you to read the *preface* and the *conclusion*, because they contain the most direct expression of the point of the book.[24]

It is of course the preface and conclusion that emphasize the importance of setting limits to thought. Moreover the passages just prior to the concluding comment emphasize the inexpressibility of the 'higher'. Despite this avowal it must be remembered that the argument in support of the ineffability of ethics is tenuous to say the least. It

---

[24] Quoted in the Editor's Appendix to *LLW*, pp. 143–4.

hangs on nothing more than the non-contingency of the ethical, a point asserted rather than argued. But logically necessary truths are expressible by the senseless propositions of logic. Categorial necessities are reflected in the formation-rules of language, but cannot be expressed in language. Any attempt to express them involves the use of formal concepts and hence the violation of rules of logical syntax. But ethical pseudo-propositions are not tautologies or contradictions, and certainly it is not obvious that ethical predicates are formal concepts. If they were, then it would be clear why putative ethical propositions are pseudo-propositions. But equally, if they were, they would incorporate variables taking a range of objects of a given category as their values. But if ethical predicates are formal concepts, what are their correlative 'material' concepts, i.e. the substitution instances of such variables? No clue is given us as to what these might be.

In 1929 Wittgenstein overthrew his earlier philosophical views on meaning and representation. With the collapse of the logical independence of elementary propositions, the bulk of the doctrines of meaning in the *Tractatus* went down like a row of dominoes. With them went the peculiar form of solipsism and the implicit transcendentalism that seemingly accompanied and supported it. It is, however, of interest that, in 1929–30 at any rate, the conception of ethics was retained. In the *Tractatus* the ethical views received slender support from the logic and metaphysics. In the transitional period the same doctrines appear to be completely free-floating. The evidence for this is to be found in Waismann's notes of conversations with Wittgenstein, and in Wittgenstein's lecture on ethics[25] given at Cambridge within the period covered by Waismann's notes.

The identity of ethics and aesthetics is reaffirmed (p. 4); that ethics is transcendental is not restated in the same words. It is, Wittgenstein now says, supernatural. The doctrine that the world consists only of facts, and that value does not exist within the world, is quite explicitly stated. If an omniscient man were to write all he knew in a book, Wittgenstein suggests, that book would contain a complete description of the world. But it would contain no judgement about ethics. A corollary of this view is, as previously, radical non-naturalism. Nothing in a world-description would even imply an ethical judgement, for no statement of fact can ever be or imply a judgement of value (p. 6). The ineffability thesis of the *Tractatus* is likewise affirmed. Our words can

[25] Published in *The Philosophical Review*, lxxiv (1965), 3–12; page references in the text are to this volume.

only express facts, not the supernatural. If the essence of the ethical could be explained by means of a theory, then the ethical would be valueless (*WWK*, pp. 116 f.). The attempt to express ethical judgements cannot but yield literal nonsense. It is of their essence that they should do so. For the attempt to state the ethical is to try to 'go beyond the world' and hence beyond significant language. The thought or experience of ethical value, Wittgenstein stresses, can, paradoxically, be conveyed by similes, although even the similes are literal nonsense. Wittgenstein picks upon three experiences which enable him, he says, to fix his mind upon what he means by ethical or absolute value. The first is wonder and amazement at the existence of the world.[26] The second is the experience of feeling absolutely safe,[27] and the last is the experience of guilt. The first is, of course, identical with what in the *Notebooks* he called 'the aesthetic miracle', and in the *Tractatus* 'the mystical'. The second phenomenon, of feeling absolutely safe, is probably related to the meditations in the *Notebooks* upon making oneself 'independent of the world' (*NB*, p. 73; 11 June 1916 etc.). The descriptions of the first two experiences (he does not dwell upon the third) are nonsensical because it does not make sense to wonder at the existence of the world for, he claims, it is unimaginable that it should not exist. One can wonder at so-and-so being the case only if so-and-so could not be the case. Similarly it is nonsense to speak of being 'safe whatever happens'. These are only more or less futile attempts to express the inexpressible. They are manifestations of the deep tendency of the human mind to run up against the limits of language:

... all those conclusions of ours which profess to lead us beyond the field of possible experience are deceptive and without foundation; it likewise teaches us this further lesson, that human reason has a natural tendency to transgress these limits, and that transcendental ideas are just as natural to it as the categories are to [the] understanding ... [28]

The Kantian idea echoes in Wittgenstein, but what in eighteenth-century Königsberg led to an a priori critical rationalist ethics, produced in the twentieth century a romantic ethics of the ineffable.

---

[26] This experience seems much the same as that described by Schopenhauer as the origin of philosophy in general—namely 'a wonder or astonishment about the world and our own existence',—a view derived ultimately from Plato (see *WWR*, ii.170 f).

[27] It is interesting to compare this with Lichtenberg's 'Amintor's Morning Devotion' repr. and trs. in J. P. Stern, *Lichtenberg, a doctrine of scattered occasions* (Thames and Hudson, London, 1963), pp. 325 ff.

[28] Kant, *Critique of Pure Reason*, A 642, B 670.

V
DISINTEGRATION AND RECONSTRUCTION

1. *The Colour-Exclusion Problem*

The philosophy expounded in the *Tractatus* seemed to Wittgenstein to contain at least the blueprint for the solution or dissolution of all the problems of philosophy. Between the completion of the work in 1918 and 1929, Wittgenstein abandoned philosophical research. His task subsequent to his return to philosophy in 1929 involved the pursuit of two general aims. The critical and destructive task concerned the dismantling of most of the *Tractatus* philosophy, and a detailed probing into the faults inherent in the *Tractatus* picture of language. The positive and constructive object was to rebuild an equally comprehensive set of answers to a similar array of philosophical problems. This chapter is concerned first with the disintegration of the *Tractatus* philosophy, and secondly with the general direction of the reconstruction in the 1930s.

With the qualifications implicit or explicit in the last two chapters, the *Tractatus* is a well-integrated philosophy. It is thus plausible to suppose that one could begin dismantling the structure from more than one point. For Wittgenstein himself, however, the weakness became exposed at what might appear a matter of detail, namely the mutual exclusion of determinates of a determinable. The colour-exclusion problem was introduced in the *Tractatus*, 6.3751 to exemplify the contention that all necessity is logical necessity. Appearances notwithstanding, the impossibility of the simultaneous presence of two colours at the same place is not a synthetic a priori truth, but a logical truth. The claim that 'A is red and A is blue' is contradictory (where 'A' refers to a point in the visual field at a given time) implies, in the *Tractatus* system, that the two conjuncts are not elementary propositions and that 'red' and 'blue' are not names of simples. For elementary propositions are logically independent, hence their conjunction cannot be contradictory. The programme implicit in 6.3751 was to show that when '*A* is red' is fully analysed into its constituents, its truth will perspicuously entail that *A* is not blue. 'If statements of degree were analysable—as I used to think', Wittgenstein explained later (RLF, pp. 168 f.) 'we could explain this contradiction by saying that the colour *R* contains all degrees of *R* and none of *B* and that the colour *B* contains all degrees of *B* and none of *R*.'

Wittgenstein's first extensive post-*Tractatus* piece of philosophical writing that survives is MS 105, begun on 2 February 1929. This is the first of the later manuscript notebooks begun immediately upon his return to Cambridge. The central theme of his reflections is the logical analysis of the structure of the visual field. By pp. 36 ff. he had already realized that colour incompatibility meant the non-independence of the elementary proposition as earlier conceived. 'A is red & A is blue' he now saw is not a simple logical *contradiction*, to be revealed as such by *analysis*, but a *nonsense*. 'Some Remarks on Logical Form' tackled the issue head-on. In it he stated clearly the inadequacy of the solution suggested in the *Tractatus*. For the suggested solution merely pushed the problem back one stage. The original idea was to analyse degrees of a quality into a logical product of single statements of quantity together with a supplementary clause—'and nothing else'. While this will show that '*A* is red' entails '*A* is not blue', it re-introduces the same problem. For either the degrees of brightness into which '*A* is red' is analysable are identical, in which case the logical product will not yield anything other than the specific degree, just as the logical product '*A* is 20 °C. & *A* is 20 °C.' does not yield '*A* is 40°C.', or they are not identical. But if they are not identical then one degree again excludes the other—which was the original problem at the colour level. Two obvious solutions remain;[1] either one modifies the logical syntax of the *Tractatus*, or else one abandons the notion of simples as the correlates of logically proper names and as the foundations of language. In 'Remarks on Logical Form', Wittgenstein opted for the first alternative. The option involved two independent moves. The first was the suggestion that real numbers must enter into elementary propositions in order that the irreducible propositions attributing degrees of quality (whether colour, pitch, length, temperature or whatever) have the same logical multiplicity as the quality they attribute. The second and crucial move involved modifying the rules for logical connectives. Mutual exclusion of statements of degree of a quality could not be shown to be

[1] See E. B. Allaire, '"Tractatus" 6.3751', repr. in *Essays on Wittgenstein's Tractatus*, ed. I. M. Copi and R. W. Beard, p. 192.

a consequence of the logical product of constituents of the analysans, so it might seem plausible to try to show that the conjunction of incompatible determinates is ill-formed. Wittgenstein's suggestion amounts to claiming that logical connectives are not topic-neutral, and that the rules for the connectives given in the *Tractatus* were incomplete. The use of the connectives is to be given by truth-tables specific to kinds of propositions or 'propositional systems' (*Satzsysteme*) exemplified by propositions predicating various determinates of the same determinable. Thus for the conjunction of two propositions expressing possession of degrees of one quality, FF, TF, and FT are well-formed, but TT must be ruled out as ill-formed; it is a nonsensical construction which must be excluded from a perfect notation. Thus '*A* is red' does not *contradict* '*A* is blue', for elementary propositions cannot contradict each other; they *exclude* each other (RLF, p. 168). What is the extra-linguistic status of this exclusion? That which corresponds in reality to a proposition containing spatio-temporal co-ordinates in its argument place and taking a name of a colour as function name, *leaves room* for only one entity, e.g. red, at a given place and time, not two, e.g. red and blue. There is no room for two, in the same sense, Wittgenstein stressed, in which we say that there is room for only one person in a chair (RLF, p. 169).[2] The mutual exclusion of incompatible determinates will be represented in a proper notation by the modification of the rules for the logical connectives in the context of connecting two such propositions. The syntactical rules of a perfect notation will prohibit combinations such as '*A* is red and *A* is blue' (RLF, p. 171). But the final formulation of such rules must await the ultimate *a posteriori* analysis of the phenomena in question.

Wittgenstein rapidly became dissatisfied with this patching-up. The thought that the structure of elementary propositions is, in some sense, an *a posteriori* matter yet to be discovered by logical analysis was indeed part of the *Tractatus* vision, although Wittgenstein was subsequently to condemn it as dogmatism (*WWK*, p. 182). But the idea that the rules for the logical connectives must await *a posteriori* researches makes nonsense of the *Tractatus* spirit. In the *Philosophical Remarks*, Ch. VIII, Wittgenstein returned to the subject in a long piece of sustained

---

[2] Russell too had argued that colours, like matter, 'possess impenetrability, so that no two colours can be in the same place at the same time', although they are distinguished from matter in virtue of the same colour being capable of being in many places at once (*Principles of Mathematics*, §440, p. 467).

argument. A proposition *p* attributing a degree of quality to an object, e.g. '*A* is 5*R*', is either elementary or compound. If *p* is compound then it must be a conjunction of elementary propositions each attributing a 'quantity' of *R* to *A*, conjunctively implying *A*'s possession of 5*R*. But this is not possible. For the conjunction of five identical elementary propositions '*A* is 1*R*' will not imply *p*, but only '*A* is 1*R*'. On the other hand, if *p* is analysable into '*A* is 1*R* & *A* is 2*R* . . . & *A* is 5*R*', then first, what is meant by the co-presence of these degrees—how are they to be distinguished? Is one, as it were, superimposed upon the other, rendering it invisible? That is surely absurd. Secondly, '*A* is 5*R*' is the very proposition we were called upon to analyse. Thirdly, these various degrees again mutually exclude each other, they cannot be co-present. Finally, the suggested analysis of *p* is in terms of a conjunction of five alleged constituent degrees of *R*. It also requires, as Wittgenstein suggested in 'Remarks on Logical Form', a supplementary clause specifying that this is all the *R* present. But this, he now argued, is nonsense. For the logical 'and' is a sign of conjunction not of addition. One cannot analyse '*A* is 3 metres long' into '*A* is 2 metres long and *A* is also one metre long'. If it makes no sense to speak of adding further degrees of *R* by conjunction, it makes no sense to lay down that no further *R* can be added.

If *p* is an elementary proposition then the sum of constituent degrees of *R* is internal to *p*. One might conceive of them in terms of the *Tractatus* metaphysics as 'objects which in some way line up together like links in a chain' (*PR*, §80). Even so, '*A* is 5*R*' and '*A* is 6*R*' must be logically related to each other even though they are elementary. '*A* is *nR*' may mean 'only *n*' or 'also *n*'. It makes no difference from the point of view of saving the independence doctrine. If it means 'only *n*' then any other degree or quantity is logically excluded. If it means 'also *n*' then every degree or quantity less than *n* is logically implied.

Wittgenstein concluded that elementary propositions are not logically independent. There seem to be non-truth-functional logical relations (*PR*, §76). Elementary propositions belong to systems of propositions such that although two elementary propositions from different systems or dimensions are logically independent, two such propositions from one and the same dimension are not. Wittgenstein still thought, as he had in 'Remarks on Logical Form', that the rules for the logical connectives are incomplete and must be adapted for different combinations of kinds of elementary propositions, but we do not wait for 'the logical analysis of the phenomena themselves' to complete them. The proper simile for a proposition is not a picture or ruler with a mere yes or no answer (*TLP*, 2.15121 f.); but a ruler with multiple gradations is analogous to a system of propositions which are syntactically interrelated. We compare the whole ruler, i.e. the whole propositional system, with reality, and determining one single point upon it—e.g. 'this is scarlet'—simultaneously determines all other points upon it, e.g. 'this is red, this is not green, not blue, not yellow, etc.' In the *Tractatus* conception of the elementary proposition there had been no determination of the value of a 'co-ordinate', i.e. a determinate of a determinable, but, Wittgenstein rightly says, his remark that a coloured body lies in a colour space (*TLP*, 2.0131) should have brought him to see this.

There is no doubt that Wittgenstein did not long think that the *Tractatus* system was worth refurbishing. With the collapse of the earlier account of the elementary proposition the other struts supporting this austerely beautiful edifice crumbled, bringing most of the structure down in ruins. For a short time he seems to have thought that an account of the logical relations of a proposition in terms of a propositional system would be possible. In the *Philosophical Remarks* Wittgenstein stressed that one task of philosophy is to describe the grammatical conventions which govern the determinate–determinable relations for different determinables. The chapter headings of our philosophical grammar, he wrote (*PR*, §3), will be 'Colour', 'Tone', 'Number', but these terms, like the formal concepts of the *Tractatus*, will not appear in the text. That red is a colour is shown by the fact that 'red' is a substitution-instance of the variable 'colour'. He appears to have thought both that one could reduce all empirical predicates to determinates, and that the *Tractatus* distinction between showing and saying could be preserved more or less intact. But it rapidly became evident that with the discovery of the insolubility of the colour-exclusion problem in the terms set by the *Tractatus* and the corresponding non-independence of elementary propositions a whole host of further doctrines propounded in the *Tractatus* must be called into question. Indeed he did not adhere for long to the view that one should bend one's efforts to the elucidation of propositional systems conceived on the above pattern. In the *Philosophical Grammar*, the notion has almost disappeared, and in the *Blue Book* it has quite sunk from sight.

2. *Dismantling the* Tractatus

First, it became clear that the *Tractatus* conception of a simple sempiternal object was part of a metaphysical mythology. Logic had seemed to demand simple objects to ensure that the last propositional product of analysis should not lack a truth-value. Nor should the fact that it has a *sense* be dependent upon any *contingent facts*. 'What I once called "objects", simples, were simply what I could refer to without running the risk of their possible non-existence: i.e. that for which there is neither existence nor non-existence, and that means: what we can speak about *no matter what may be the case*' (*PR*, p. 72). They were further necessary, it seemed, to ensure determinacy of sense, i.e. to guarantee that all implications are settled in advance of experience. But these requirements are satisfied by the existence of, and the patterns of use of, *samples in our method of representation*. One might indeed say that the *Tractatus* object was in fact a sample that defines an expression, seen through a distorting glass darkly. 'If you call the colour green[3] an object', Wittgenstein wrote (*PG*, p. 209), 'you must be saying that it is an object that occurs in the symbolism.' One might go on to say, he explained, that otherwise the sense of the symbolism, indeed its very existence as a symbolism, would not be guaranteed. But this should not mislead one. It does not imply that green is an object, let alone that it is a sempiternal simple object, but only that the word 'green' is explained by reference to green samples which we pick out by ostension. The colour green is neither simple nor complex, for we have stipulated no criteria for simplicity or complexity of colour and hence have not determined what would *count* as a complex colour (though we could do so). But, when philosophizing, we are prone to confuse the absence of any criteria of complexity for the presence of criteria of simplicity. Words which are defined by reference to samples, e.g. colour-words, sound-words, taste- and smell-words, many measures (lengths and weights in common use) would indeed have no meaning if all possible samples by reference to which they might correctly be explained did not exist.[4] But this does not derogate from the independence of logic.

[3] Of course, in the *Tractatus* it would not have been the colour green but rather an 'unanalysable' shade of green. But that refinement as he now realized, is quite pointless.

[4] Of course, particular samples are typically destructible without undermining the practice of employing the word they serve to define. Many expressions are defined by reference to optional samples that vary from occasion to occasion (e.g. samples of red or sweet). Even canonical samples, such as the standard metre bar in Sèvres or the imperial yard bar in Greenwich are replaceable (the latter was destroyed in 1834 and subsequently replaced). For detailed elaboration, see G. P. Baker and P. M. S. Hacker, *Wittgenstein: Understanding and Meaning*, pp. 168 ff.

It must indeed be possible to describe a world in which everything destructible is destroyed (e.g. in which no red things exist, no green things exist, no blue things exist), but it does not follow that *in* such a world, it must be possible to describe what does not thus exist. It is indeed correct that the logical implications of, say, '*A* is one metre long' or '*B* is black' should be settled in advance of experience (e.g. that *A* is not 2 metres long, or that *B* is darker than the whiteboard). But that does not require the existence of sempiternal simples. It is determined by the patterns of our use of defining samples (*infra*, pp. 197 f.).

It was, Wittgenstein later realized, a misuse of the term 'object' to think of the *position* of a thing as an object[5] or to think of the spatial relation between two items as itself an object (*PR*, pp. 302 f.). It was confused to contend, as a logico-metaphysical insight, that objects cannot be described but only named (cf. *TLP*, 3.221). For that claim was, in one sense, true by definition, since 'object' *meant* the referent of an indefinable word, and 'description' in effect *meant* definition, since it was not denied that an object had external properties (*PG*, p. 208). In another sense, it was nonsense, for if 'object' is illegitimately stretched to include properties, then a 'description' of such an object by reference to its *external* properties involves treating the bearer of the property (the surface or place that is coloured, for example) as a property of the property, which is absurd (ibid). This confusion is strikingly clear from re-examination of the claim that 'if two objects have the same logical form, the only distinction between them, apart from their external properties, is that they are different' (*TLP*, 2.0233). This thought is rooted in the confused temptation to answer such a question as 'What is the difference between blue and red?' by saying 'The one is blue and the other is red'. But that is nonsense, and the question itself should be rejected, for it cannot intelligibly be answered on the model of 'What is the difference between surface *A* and surface *B*?', where it *is* possible to reply 'The one is blue and the other is red' (ibid). It can, however, be answered quite differently, viz. blue comes from purple when it gets more bluish, and red comes from purple when it gets more reddish (and this, one might say in the *Tractatus* language, is a description of blue and red in terms of their internal properties; in one sense, these names do have the same 'logical form', viz. they are both colour-words; in another,

---

[5] Wittgenstein, *TS* 220 (the first draft of the *Investigations*) §110.

they do not, since they enjoy different relations with the other colour-words in this propositional system). Once one realizes that the role allocated to 'objects' in the *Tractatus* is in effect filled by samples, it is obvious that the question of whether objects are thing-like, property-like, or are relations is now *senseless*. For one is no longer talking of what is represented, of the ultimate constituents of reality, but rather of elements (instruments) that belong to the method of representation and are used in order to represent how things are in the world (and also to explain the meanings of words defined by reference to such samples). Equally it makes no sense to wonder whether there are infinitely many such 'objects'.

Similar confusions surrounded the concepts of a fact and of a complex in the *Tractatus*. A complex such as [aRb] in ϕ[aRb] is, as was stressed in the *Tractatus*, distinct from a fact (whether the fact that aRb, or that ϕ[aRb]). But a complex is composed of its parts, e.g. a broom is composed of a broomstick and a brush, not of its parts *and* their spatial relation, e.g. the broomstick's *being stuck into* the brush. The parts of a complex are smaller than the whole, hence the properties of a complex and the relations between parts of the complex are not themselves parts of the complex. Facts, however, are not merely distinct from complexes, but they cannot be said to be *composed* of constituents (*Bestandteile*), to be a *combination* of objects (*Verbindung von Gegenständen; aus Gegenständen zusammengesetzt*), or to be a configuration of objects (*Konfiguration der Gegenstände*). The fact that this circle is red (or that I am tired) is not composed of a circle and redness (or myself and tiredness). The fact that the book is on the table is not composed of *the book, the table*, and *the relation of being on* in the appropriate configuration. So to say is to misuse the term 'configuration' as well as 'composed of'. While a complex has a location and can be moved from place to place, a fact is immobile, and indeed has no location. (And, one might add, it was therefore altogether misleading to contend that the world is the totality of facts, for facts have no spatio-temporal location in the world.) It was equally misleading to conceive of propositions as *describing facts*, for that suggests wrongly that facts, like complexes, are spatio-temporal occupants of the world which are, as it were, set over against language, awaiting description. Rather is it that in stating *that a certain fact obtains*, e.g. that a brown, leather-bound copy of the *Tractatus* which weighs so-and-so many ounces is standing on the table, one may describe a 'complex' viz. the book (*PG*, pp. 199 ff.).

The root of these muddles Wittgenstein diagnosed as 'the confusing use of the word "object"', the misuse of 'configuration', 'constituent' and 'composition' and misconceptions about the concept of a fact. Instantiation or coinstantiation of properties at a spatio-temporal point are not forms of combination. That it makes no sense to speak literally of coloured sounds or smells is not a reflection of metaphysical combinatorial possibilities of 'objects', as it were truths of superphysics about colours, smells, and sounds. Rather is it, as we shall see in Chapter VII, a grammatical convention which casts a metaphysical shadow upon the world.

As the metaphysics collapsed so too did the fundamental ideas that informed the picture theory of the proposition. For if 'objects' are not the substance of the world but rather elements of our method of representation, if facts do not have objects as their constituents and are not composed of anything, if indeed facts are not 'in the world' (or anywhere else) as complexes of (genuine) objects are, if properties, relations, times, and places are not objects at all, then the theses of isomorphism, of the great harmony between language and reality must be deeply confused. And so indeed they were. To be sure, Wittgenstein continued to compare propositions with pictures. But the comparison now is with literal pictures, not 'logical pictures'. Understanding a proposition is akin to understanding a picture (*PG*, p. 42); the difference between a fictional and a factual proposition is comparable to the difference between a genre and a historical painting (*PG*, p. 164); one may act in accord with a proposition just as one may act in accord with a picture (*PG*, p. 163). These are important analogies, but they do not indicate adherence to any residue of the picture theory of meaning.

More importantly, Wittgenstein continues to speak of *the pictoriality of the proposition*. It is crucial to grasp what he meant, thereby. An empirical proposition (statement) describes how things are; it may be false, but it states what must be the case *if* it is true. One might say that it contains a 'picture' of the fact that will make it true. Something very similar holds of expectations, wishes, commands or intentions. If I expect that A will come at noon today, I know in advance of A's coming exactly what will fulfil my expectation, namely just *A* (and no one else) precisely *coming* (not some other action) at *12 o'clock* sharp (neither sooner nor later). So my expectation might be said to contain a picture of what will fulfil it. And in similar vein a command seems to contain a picture of what will comply with it, an intention or desire, a picture of what will satisfy it. These are variations upon the same fundamental features of language, viz. the harmony between language and reality, a point Wittgenstein made explicitly apropos intention, wish, and expectation.

> Here we have the old problem, which we would like to express in the following way: 'the thought that p is the case doesn't presuppose that it is the case; yet on the other hand there must be something in the fact that is a presupposition even of having the thought (I can't think something is red, if the colour red does not exist)'. It is the problem of the harmony between world and thought. (*PG*, p. 142.)

Instead of 'harmony between world and thought' or 'language and reality', one might say 'the pictoriality of thought' (*PG*, p. 163) or 'the pictoriality of language'. *This is the name of a problem, not of a solution.* The *Tractatus* had focused specifically upon the philosophical puzzle of how a proposition can be false yet meaningful. The picture theory of meaning gave a complex and non-trivial logico-metaphysical *explanation* of the pictoriality of thought and language in terms of isomorphism between elementary proposition and atomic state of affairs. Agreement between thought and reality was held to be an agreement in form that was explained by reference to the doctrines of logical atomism. The problem or problems of the pictoriality of the proposition are not essentially different from the problems of the pictoriality of expectation, command, intention, or desire. Here too one may puzzle how it is possible that I can now expect an event, know exactly *what* I expect, when it has not even happened yet, and may never occur. How can an expectation thus anticipate the future and contain a picture of it? When I intend to go to London tomorrow, how is it possible that my intention should now portray what I will do in fulfilling that intention?

It was, Wittgenstein realized in the 1930s, altogether misleading to construe the harmony between language and reality as an agreement of form (*PG*, p. 163). 'For what I said really boils down to this: that every projection must have something in common with what is projected no matter what is the method of projection. But that only means that I am here extending the concept of "having in common" and making it equivalent to the general concept of projection.' (Ibid.) It was confused to think that propositions and states of affairs in the world are set over against each other, the one isomorphic with the other. 'Like everything metaphysical the harmony between thought and reality is to be found in the grammar of the language' (*PG*, p. 162; *Z* §55). It is, of course, true that if I expect *A* to come at noon I expect *A* (not *B*) to come (not to stay where he is) at noon (and not at 3.00 p.m.). But that is no mystery, that is just what I said I expected (*BB*, p. 37). There is, to be sure, a connection between an expectation and what fulfils it. That connection is indeed logical or 'internal', for the expectation is internally related to what fulfils it. But this internal relation is not forged by a metaphysical harmony between language and reality, but rather by grammatical, *intra*-linguistic, connections.

What links an expectation and its fulfilment is the explanation of the verbal expression of the expectation on the one hand, and the grammatical or logical connection between the verbal expression of the expectation and the description of what is called its fulfilment on the other. '*It is in language* that it is all done' (*PG*, p. 143). If I expect *A* to come at noon, the verbal expression of my expectation is: 'I expect that *A* will come at noon'. By '*A*' I mean such-and-such a man, by 'come' I mean doing this . . ., by 'noon' I mean midday. So of course *A*'s coming at noon will fulfil my expectation. Far from having to wait upon the future to see what will fulfil the expectation, or from having to spin metaphysical myths to *explain* why one does not have to wait upon the future, the characterization of the expectation contains a description of what will fulfil it. The very idea that an order, in some sense, anticipates its execution and an expectation its fulfilment by ordering and expecting precisely that which later happens is confused. For of course it may not happen. All we can say here is that an order (or expectation) anticipates the future by ordering (or expecting) that which later happens *or does not happen*. But that is to say that it does *not* anticipate the future; any more than 'It is raining or it is not raining' describes the weather!

It is correct that the expression of expectation determines in advance what will satisfy it or fail to satisfy it, as the proposition determines in advance what will make it true and what will make it false. But that merely means that the proposition '*p*' determines that *p* must be the case for it to be true. This signifies no metaphysical mysteries concerning the structure of the world, but a grammatical articulation, namely that 'the proposition that *p*' for most purposes has the same sense as 'the proposition which the fact that *p* makes true'. Similarly the pictoriality of intention, expectation, and command is fully clarified by specification of intra-grammatical connections. 'The statement that the wish for it to be the case that *p* is satisfied by the event *p*, merely enunciates a rule for signs: (the wish for it to be the case that *p*) = (the wish that is satisfied by the event p)' (*PG*, p. 161 f.). The pictoriality of the proposition is not to be explained by the picture theory of meaning, nor by any residue that might be called 'the logical core of the picture theory', but by a sober description of the relevant uses and rules for the use of the language with which we are familiar, e.g. the inter-substitutability of the above pairs of expressions. The agreement between proposition and state of affairs, the correspondence between true proposition and fact are not theoretical discoveries about the relations between language and reality, but grammatical trivialities.[6]

As the picture theory of meaning collapsed, so too did the corresponding picture theory of *thought*. In the *Tractatus* Wittgenstein had realized that there is an internal relation between propositional attitudes and what satisfies them (what makes a belief true, a desire fulfilled, an intention executed). He had tried to explain this internal relation by a 'picture theory of the mind', holding, as we saw in Chapter IV, that to think (believe, expect, wish, want, etc.) that p is to be in a certain psychological *state*. That state must incorporate the thought that p, and that is possible only if it consists of psychic constituents arranged in a structure (a fact) that is isomorphic (given an appropriate method of projection) with the state of affairs that p. For, it seemed, it is only thus that it is possible to think, believe, expect, wish, or want what is *not* the case. The harmony between thought and reality seemed forged by psychic structures ('the language of thought' as some cognitive psychologists today would have it). But this, it became evident, was confused on many counts. As we have seen, expectation and its fulfilment, belief and what makes it true, desire and its satisfaction *make contact in grammar*. These internal relations are not bound together by a shadowy mental intermediary. They are not bound together *by* anything; but these internal relations *reflect* the grammatical (normative) connections between the verbal *expression* of a 'propositional attitude' and the *description* of its satisfaction. Indeed thinking, believing, wanting, wishing are not typically *states* of mind at all and it makes no sense to conceive of them as composed of psychic constituents in configuration. For the later Wittgenstein the philosophical account of the nature of thinking, understanding, meaning something,

---

[6] The Correspondence Theory of Truth is a metaphysical mountain made out of a grammatical molehill. In repudiating it one must beware not to deny the undeniable, namely that a proposition is true if it corresponds to the facts. For that is a grammatical truth, a rule of grammar licensing us in certain contexts to replace 'a true proposition' by 'a proposition that corresponds to the facts'.

intending, moved from the periphery of his philosophical investigations into the centre. Far from the mind 'creating language' by injecting meaning into logico-syntactical forms (through the activities of the metaphysical will), it is the use of language which 'creates the mind'. For our talk of 'the structure of the mind' is no more than a reflection of the structure of, i.e. the logical relations between, the expressions of the language we use in talking about the mind.

3 *The Brouwer Lecture*

On 10 March 1928, L. E. J. Brouwer, the founder of mathematical intuitionism, came to Vienna to give a lecture entitled 'Mathematics, Science and Language'.[7] Wittgenstein attended this lecture together with Feigl and Waismann. Feigl reports that Wittgenstein came away from it in a state of great excitement and intellectual ferment. In Feigl's view, 'that evening marked the return of Wittgenstein to strong philosophical interests and activities'.[8] In the first edition of this book I discussed Brouwer's lecture under the section-heading 'A New Inspiration' and very tentatively conjectured that the parallelisms between some of the features of Wittgenstein's later philosophy might have their source in inspiration derived from Brouwer. I am now very sceptical about that conjecture, and in the absence of further evidence I should repudiate it. I wrote originally that until more biographical material comes to light it will be difficult to evaluate the extent of the immediate impact of Brouwer's lecture. I still subscribe to that view. But it now seems to me improbable that Brouwer's ideas provided Wittgenstein with a fresh inspiration. His excitement after the lecture may just as well have been a reaction to Brouwer's *misconceptions*, for while Wittgenstein might have been sympathetic to some features of Brouwer's constructivism and some aspects of its Kantian and Schopenhauerian inspiration, he would, even in 1928, have found much to quarrel with.

Wittgenstein was highly self-conscious about the sources of his inspiration. But he did not, in the above cited note (p. 4 n.) in his notebook of 1931, mention Brouwer, whom he had heard only three years earlier. Nor have I found any similar acknowledgement or awareness of Brouwerian influences upon his philosophy of mathematics or logic elsewhere in the *Nachlass*. The only philosophico-mathematical

---

[7] L. E. J. Brouwer, 'Mathematik, Wissenschaft und Sprache', *Monatshefte für Mathematik und Physik*, xxxvi (1929), 153–64.
[8] See G. Pitcher, *The Philosophy of Wittgenstein*, p. 8 n., in which Feigl is quoted.

inspiration he acknowledged is Spengler.⁹ Wittgenstein was indeed interested in intuitionism in mathematics, and he did occasionally mention Brouwer and some of his views quite explicitly. But he viewed intuitionism as an aberration, a perversion in mathematics that stands in need of philosophical therapy, not as a source of inspiration in philosophy of mathematics, let alone as involving an insight that can be generalized to the whole domain of philosophical logic and philosophy of language. I shall list some of his explicit disagreements with intuitionism below. Of course, these later disagreements do not *demonstrate* that Wittgenstein was *not* influenced (at least negatively) by the Brouwer lecture. It is still, perhaps, worthwhile delineating the contour lines of the conception of language and mathematics which Brouwer adumbrated in 1928. There are, at any rate, some interesting affinities as well as many marked differences with Wittgenstein's ideas, both in his early philosophy and in his later work.

Unlike most of his other writings, Brouwer's lecture is not confined to the philosophy of mathematics. It is a thumb-nail sketch, couched in a dense obscure Germanic style, of a comprehensive intuitionist philosophy aimed at exploring the nature and limits of thought. Mathematics, science, and language are the main functions of human activity by which order and intelligibility are imposed upon nature. The will to live manifests itself in three ways: (a) in 'mathematical reflection' or 'mathematical attention' (*die mathematische Betrachtung*); (b) in mathematical abstraction; (c) in the imposition of the will by means of sounds. The two fundamental modes of apprehension which the will imposes upon the world are time and causation. It is interesting that the categorial forms Brouwer specified—temporality and the principle of sufficient reason—place him firmly in the Schopenhauerian tradition.¹⁰ However, Brouwer stressed that there is no extraneous justification for these 'phases of mathematical reflection' other than their usefulness in enabling us to master nature. There is

⁹ Cf. MS 125, p. 31. I presume Wittgenstein was alluding to Spengler's discussion of the cultural relativity of mathematics, of the multiplicity of different mathematics in Chapter II of *The Decline of the West*.

¹⁰ It is curious to note Brouwer's strange remarks upon the voluntary character of the imposition of the categories upon phenomenal experience whereby the latter is ordered and 'stabilized'. 'Everyone can satisfy himself', Brouwer wrote, 'that it is possible at will either to sink into a reverie, taking no stand in time and making no separation between self and the external world, or else to affect such a separation by one's own effort, and to evoke the condensation of individual objects in the apprehended world' (op. cit., p. 154). Compare this with Schopenhauer's views on the ideality of time, and with Wittgenstein's comments on the reality of the bare present image (*NB*, p. 83).

no objective causal nexus, causation is merely our means of ordering phenomena, enabling us to distinguish subjective experience from the phenomenal world. The supposition of the hypothetical objective spatio-temporal and phenomenal world is the primary result of mankind's collective reflection. Mathematical abstraction involves abstracting from the temporal succession of experiences (of 'inner sense' as Kant would put it) to the bare notion of difference or 'two-oneness' from which *Urintuition* or 'basic intuition' the whole series of natural numbers, and ultimately all of pure mathematics can be constructed. Moreover, the construction of mathematics is essentially non-linguistic and mental.[11] Mathematics has no foundation in eternal verities, but is a construction which enables man to extend his dominion over nature by making possible theoretical science with its concomitant practical benefits. The essence of natural language on the other hand lies in its being a means of expression or transference of the will (*Willensübertragung*). Its origin in primitive society lies in gestures and cries. In a developed society, more complex systems of communication involving complex grammatical rules of organized language are necessary. Language is through and through a function of the social activity of man. Non-communicative uses of language (e.g. recording of memories in solitude) are parasitic upon its social uses but mathematical reflection and its mental constructions are independent of language.

Certainty and exactness, Brouwer claimed, are not to be found in language or in the linguistic expression of mathematics. Misunderstandings in discourse and mistakes in recollection (e.g. of confusing one mathematical entity with another) can never in principle be altogether eliminated. The formalist endeavour to construct a metalanguage in which certainty and clarity are completely ensured is futile. It is an illusion resting upon thoughtless faith in classical logic. The laws of classical logic are the specific forms of inference resulting from a language constructed by mathematical reflection upon finite groups. For while mathematics is independent of logic, logic does depend upon mathematics. The application of logical principles, the Excluded

---

[11] In 'Volition, Knowledge, Language' (1933), trans. and repr. in his *Collected Works*, Vol. 1, ed. A. Heyting (North Holland, Amsterdam, 1975) Brouwer wrote 'the languageless constructions which arise from the self-unfolding of the basic intuition, are exact and true ... Thus for a human mind equipped with an unlimited memory, pure mathematics, practised in solitude and without using linguistic signs, would be exact ...' (p. 443).

Middle, Non-Contradiction, Identity, etc., in ordinary language proved sound—normally, linguistically competent speakers agree in their use of these principles. But this agreement was not the result of the autonomous power of the principles but of two quite different factors: first, in the event of apparently false results in reasoning about the world, an explanation was given by re-formulating the facts in question or attributing the error to fallaciously construed natural laws, and not by modifying the principles of logic. Secondly, the phenomenal world happens to display sufficient constancy to allow the useful application of these principles to it. But this, by implication, is a mere contingency.

Classical thinkers (and formalists), Brouwer explained, are unaware of the exclusive character of the word as a means of expression or 'transference' of the will. Instead they took words to express concepts—abstract entities independent of causal law—and they took logical principles to be descriptions of the a priori connections of these concepts. Just as the application of logic to reality was never *allowed* to falsify logical principles, so too any apparent inconsistencies in logic itself was never *allowed* to throw doubt on the reliability of the logical principles, but was taken to necessitate modification of the axioms which led to inconsistencies. That logical principles had this status of apparent privilege on sufferance and by the grace of human will only became clear, and the errors of the formalists correspondingly highlighted, when mathematicians developed set theory. The principles of classical logic which had been abstracted from reflection upon subsets of a definite finite set, and then accorded independent a priori status, were unthinkingly and unjustifiably applied to the mathematics of infinite sets. But here contradictions arose that could not be swept under the carpet. The remedy to these deep-rooted confusions lies in a wholesale reconstruction of mathematics on intuitionist principles. Those parts of mathematics that can be justified thereby are sanctioned, those that cannot must be relinquished. Logical principles which allow for preservation of significance in constructivist mathematical inference are retained, those which do not must be discarded. Brouwer did not, of course, pursue this daunting programme in his 1928 lecture in Vienna. He exemplified his approach in arguing that not all the logical principles that hold good for mathematics of a definite finite set hold good for the mathematics of infinite sets. In particular the Law of Excluded Middle must be rejected.

Brouwer's whole approach clashes with the main intellectualist tradition of European thought. His anti-rationalist voluntarism is a repudiation of the mainstream of mathematical and philosophical thinking. To someone like Wittgenstein who found in Schopenhauer both inspiration and insight,[12] there is a *prima facie* likelihood that Brouwer's emphasis on the primacy of the will would be of interest and may well have struck a sympathetic chord.

Nevertheless, whether Wittgenstein's excitement was because Brouwer as it were pointed the way forward or because Brouwer had *mangled* important insights that Wittgenstein shared, is debatable. Neither the manuscript notebooks of 1929 nor 'Some Remarks on Logical Form' suggest any sudden transformation or conversion. That Wittgenstein would be sympathetic to a constructivist approach to mathematics is to be expected from the few remarks on the subject in the *Tractatus*, and betokens no sudden awakening in 1929. Brouwer's psychologism would surely have struck Wittgenstein as wholly confused; Brouwer's insistence that mathematics is essentially *languageless* mental construction is not compatible with the *Tractatus* conception that the equations of pure mathematics are in effect substitution rules (*TLP*, 6.23) licensing inferences (*TLP*, 6.211) from one non-mathematical proposition (e.g. 'A has 10 bags of 12 marbles each') to another (viz. 'A has 120 marbles'). Here the inter-substitutability of *expressions* is an essential feature of the mathematical *method* (*TLP*, 6.2341, 6.24) and of the point of, and uses of, the pseudo-propositions of mathematics. Already in the *Tractatus* Wittgenstein had insisted that 'The question whether intuition is needed for the solution of mathematical problems must be given the answer that in this case language itself provides the necessary intuition. The process of *calculating* serves to bring about that intuition. Calculation is not an experiment' (*TLP*, 6.233 f.). Brouwer's contention that the laws of logic are *derivative* from mathematics, dependent upon a mathematical intuition of temporal sequence, Wittgenstein would surely have considered to be as confused as its inverse twin logicism. And Brouwer's claim that the Law of Excluded Middle, which we 'impose' on reality (and is derived from mathematical reflection upon sub-sets of a definite finite set), nevertheless *does not apply* to certain propositions involving, e.g. infinite decimals, would, I think, have

---

[12] Wittgenstein's continued high regard for Schopenhauer is attested to by Carnap, 'Intellectual Autobiography', in *The Philosophy of Rudolf Carnap*, ed. P. Schilpp (Open Court, Illinois, 1963), p. 27.

struck Wittgenstein as involving a failure to apprehend what it is for something *to belong to our form of representation*.[13]

The above remarks may be thought to involve reading too much back into the opaque remarks of the *Tractatus* upon these matters. But equally if we turn to Wittgenstein's later writings on the philosophy of mathematics, it is clear that he then viewed intuitionism as an aberration. It is, he wrote 'an unnecessary shuffle' (*PI*, §213) and in a lecture remarked that 'Intuitionism is all bosh—entirely' (*LFM*, p. 237). First, if the alleged 'basic intuition' is, as Brouwer thought, a psychological process, what can it have to do with mathematics, which is not a branch of psychology and is not about 'mental objects' or indeed any other kind of 'object' (cf. *PG*, p. 322)? Intuitionists have confused a primitive (undefined) element of a calculus of signs (viz. the general form of an integer [o, ξ, ξ + 1] cf. *TLP*, 6.03) with a psychological activity.[14] Secondly, if intuition is an 'inner voice', how do I know how to follow its lead, how do I understand the 'language' it 'speaks'? Not by a further intuition (*PI*, §213)! Thirdly, whether intuition is like an inner voice or like an inner *perception*, how do I know that it is *correct*. If it is claimed that there is no such thing as a false intuition (i.e. if 'intuit', like 'recognize', is a success-verb), how do I know that what I have *is* an intuition? In short, an intuition presupposes

---

[13] It is very striking, from a Wittgensteinian perspective, to read Brouwer's explanation of the 'belief' in the Law of Excluded Middle:

The belief in the universal validity of the principle of excluded Third in Mathematics is considered by the intuitionists as a phenomenon of the history of civilization of the same kind as the former belief in the rationality of π, or in the rotation of the firmament about the earth. The intuitionist tries to explain the long duration of the reign of this dogma by two facts: firstly that within an arbitrarily given domain of mathematical entities the non-contradictority of the principle for a single assertion is easily recognized; secondly that in studying an extensive group of simple every-day phenomena of the exterior world, careful application of the whole of classical logic was never found to lead to error. (D. van Dalen ed., *Brouwer's Cambridge Lectures on Intuitionism* (Cambridge University Press, Cambridge, 1981), p. 7).

This is precisely to treat a law of logic as being on the same level as a law of physics, a proposition *of grammar* (hence a rule) as if it were a description, a part of our form of representation as if it were something represented, and a tautology as if it were a proposition that said something.

[14] Thus Brouwer wrote that intuitionism 'considers the falling apart of moments of life into quantitatively different parts, to be reunited only while remaining separated by time as the fundamental phenomenon of the human intellect, passing by abstracting from its emotional content into the fundamental phenomenon of mathematical thinking, the intuition of the bare two-oneness. This intuition of two-oneness, the basal intuition of mathematics, creates not only the numbers one and two, but also all finite ordinal numbers, inasmuch as one of the elements of the two-oneness may be thought of as a new two-oneness, which process may be repeated infinitely.' (L. E. J. Brouwer, 'Intuitionism and Formalism', repr. in *Collected Works*, Vol. 1, pp. 85 f.)

an independent standard of correctness. Only where one can know by experiment or experience, by proof or by calculation does it make sense to talk of knowing by intuition. Hence, fourthly, all talk of 'basic intuition' is nonsense. The sequence of natural numbers does not rest on reasons, evidence, or any other grounds. But just because of that, there is no room for intuition, for this series does not correspond to some *truth*. It is stipulated (*RFM*, p. 37). It is not a basic intuition that assures us that 13 comes after 12 in the series of natural numbers. This is not something we discover or find out. Rather we so *define* 'natural number' that in that series 13 is the successor of 12.

So far from agreeing with Brouwer that the Law of Excluded Middle is something which we impose upon phenomena *and find to be invalid* in certain kinds of case (e.g. whether there are four consecutive 7s in the expansion of π), Wittgenstein thought Brouwer was utterly confused (*PR*, p. 176):

I need hardly say that where the law of the excluded middle doesn't apply, no other law of logic applies either, because in that case we aren't dealing with propositions of mathematics. (Against Weyl and Brouwer.)

The logical proposition '$p \vee \sim p$' is a tautology, not an observation about the characteristics propositions have been found to have. On the other hand, *that* '$p \vee \sim p$' = *Taut*. partly *defines* what we mean by 'proposition' (*AWL*, p. 140). So the supposition that one might *discover* certain kinds of proposition for which the Law of Excluded Middle does not apply is muddled, conceiving of a law of logic on the model of a law of physics to which one might find exceptions that restrict its scope. But 'true' and 'false' *belong to*, are definitive of, propositionhood (as check is of the chess-king (*PI*, §136)). And the laws of logic are not descriptions of the 'logical behaviour' of 'logical objects'. Hence Wittgenstein argued already in 1929/30:

Brouwer is right when he says that the properties of his pendulum number[15] are incompatible with the law of the excluded middle. But, saying this doesn't reveal a peculiarity of propositions about infinite aggregates. Rather, it is based on the fact that logic presupposes that it cannot be *a priori*—i.e. logically—

---

[15] This term is a translation of 'Pendelzahl' in the 1929 lecture. Elsewhere Brouwer refers to it as an *oscillatory binary shrinking number* (see 'Volition, Knowlege, Language', in Heyting ed., *L. E. J. Brouwer, Collected Works*, Vol. 1). This number 'is neither positive nor negative nor equal to zero, it is neither equal to zero nor different from zero and neither rational nor irrational: nevertheless it is a real number and therefore it clearly illustrates the invalidity of the principium tertii exclusi'. This is precisely what Wittgenstein denied, cf. *WWK*, pp. 72 f.

impossible to tell whether a proposition is true or false. For, if the question of the truth or falsity of a proposition is *a priori* undecidable, the consequence is that the proposition loses its sense and the consequence of this is precisely that the propositions of logic lose their validity for it. (*PR*, p. 210)

The idea of such undecidable propositions is nonsense, Wittgenstein argued, but not because such propositions 'transcend our recognitional capacities'. That suggests that there is, in respect of such propositions, a genuine undecidability relative to us that is contingent upon our 'medical limitations' (as Russell put it).[16] But that is absurd, since what is awry is nether an empirical fact about us, nor an epistemological question of what we can or cannot know ('We will never know what Caesar thought the night before his death'). The issue is a logical or conceptual one. It no more makes *sense* for there to be unprovable propositions of mathematics than for a person to make himself a plan or formulate an intention which he himself cannot understand, or for mankind at large to follow certain rules which are actually unknown to anyone. We cannot understand an 'undecidable proposition of mathematics' because *there is nothing to understand*. For if it is 'undecidable' it is not a proposition.

We cannot *understand* the equation[17] unless we recognize the connection between its two sides.

Undecidability presupposes that there is, so to speak, a subterranean connection between the two sides; that the bridge *cannot* be made with symbols.

A connection between symbols which exists but cannot be represented by symbolic transformations is a thought that cannot be thought. If the connection is there, then it must be possible to see it.

For it *exists* in the same way as the connection between parts of visual space. It isn't a *causal* connection. The transition isn't produced by means of some dark speculation different in kind from what it connects. (Like a dark passage between two sunlit places.) (*PR*, pp. 212 f.)

What Brouwer had 'discovered' was not a kind of proposition for

---

[16] In 'The Limits of Empiricism' (*Proceedings of the Aristotelian Society* xxxvi (1935-6, p. 143) Russell, commenting on Alice Ambrose's articles 'Finitism in Mathematics' (*Mind* xliv (1935)), wrote 'Miss Ambrose says it is *logically* impossible to run through the whole expansion of π. I should have said it was *medically* impossible.' For the illuminating reply, see A. Ambrose 'Finitism and "The Limits of Empiricism"' in her *Essays in Analysis* (Allen & Unwin, London, 1966), pp. 59 ff. Russell conceived of infinity as a property of an extension, but Wittgenstein held it to be a property of a *law*, a law or rule specifying an unlimited possibility of constructing propositions or numbers.

[17] A Brouwerian 'undecidable' equation.

which the Law of Excluded Middle does not hold, but only that in mathematics as elsewhere one can so combine symbols to yield something that *appears* to be a proposition but is not one at all (*AWL*, p. 140).

It is true that intuitionist conceptions of mathematics share with Wittgenstein's conception an emphasis upon proof or construction. But they differ far more profoundly, not only over the matter of the applicability of the Law of Excluded Middle, but more importantly over their conception of what a proof *is* and of *what it is* that is proved by a proof. For Brouwer in particular, what is effected in a mathematical (constructive) proof is a certain *mental construction*. A proof given in symbols describes a construction carried out in the mind. Intuitionist mathematics, according to Brouwer, is inner architecture.[18] For Wittgenstein what is proved is that a certain expression *is* a proposition of mathematics, belongs to a system of *rules of representation*. If anything is constructed at all, it is not mental objects, but grammatical rules. A proof fixes the *sense* of the proved formula and gives it a place in the system of rules for the employment of symbols in empirical reasoning that constitutes mathematics. The gulf that separates these two conceptions could hardly be greater.

4. *Moving off in Fresh Directions*

The conception of language and reality as a pair of isomorphic structures linked, as it were, by the 'linguistic soul' was a kind of metaphysical mythology. Wittgenstein slowly realized this in the period 1929–30. No sudden 'conversion' took place, as is evident from the manuscript volumes and the lecture notes taken by John King and Desmond Lee in 1930. Rather, more and more flaws in the earlier philosophy became revealed and his thought moved simultaneously on many fronts. A detailed account of the shifts would require a lengthy book in its own right. Here I shall merely outline some of the major issues that were re-examined and indicate the trajectory of Wittgenstein's reflections.

In the *Tractatus* he held that every natural language has the 'deep-structure' of a formal calculus. It is a system of symbols the use of which is governed by rules of logical syntax. The content of the calculus of language is given by the mind's projecting names on to simple objects that are their meanings. Once he realized that the only

---

[18] Brouwer, 'Consciousness, Philosophy and Mathematics', repr. in *Collected Works*, Vol. 1, p. 494.

legitimate need which in the *Tractatus* called forth the 'objects' is fully satisfied by samples that belong to the method of representation, he abandoned this conception. A language, he now held, is an *autonomous calculus of signs*. Language is not *connected* with reality at all,[19] since samples are themselves elements of representation. The meaning of an expression is not something in the world (nor yet something in a supersensible world) with which an expression is correlated, let alone for which it goes proxy. It is what is given by an explanation of meaning; and explanations of meaning are given by signs (not only words, but also samples, gestures, exemplifications, pictures). So meaning and explanation remain, so to speak, within language.

It gradually dawned on Wittgenstein that behind the elaborate and sophisticated explanations of the essential nature of language and representation which he had given in the *Tractatus*, and the different accounts which Russell and Frege had elaborated as 'ideal languages' or ideals to which natural languages more or less approximate, lay a mesmerizing pre-philosophical *Urbild* or proto-picture. He found a succinct and impressive unself-conscious characterization of this proto-picture in St Augustine's description of how he thought he had learnt his mother tongue. Already in the *Philosophical Grammar* (or, more accurately, in the 'Big Typescript' (*TS* 213, p. 26)) Wittgenstein noted that 'The way Augustine describes the learning of language can show us the way of looking at language from which the concept of the meaning of words derives' (*PG*, p. 57), i.e. the concept—or better, misconception—of meaning as the correlate of a word. Augustine's picture of language eventually became the overture and to some extent the leitmotif of Wittgenstein's masterpiece, the *Philosophical Investigations*. The elemental picture is of words being *names* of things, the former being somehow *correlated* with the latter (for example by ostension, no matter whether actual physical ostension or a mental surrogate for it, such as concentrating one's attention). Words are combined into sentences, the fundamental role of which is to *describe* how things are. This biplanar[20] preconception of language is not, in general, an explicit

---

[19] This does not mean, absurdly, that we do not refer to, talk about, items in the world when we say that the sun is shining or that it is raining, but only that *grammar* pays no homage to reality, that the 'logic of our language' is not answerable to the nature of the world (*infra*, Chapter VII).

[20] Cf. R. Harris, *The Language Myth* (Duckworth, London, 1981), p. 11 for this felicitous phrasing. Harris illuminatingly traces the history in linguistics of this pernicious conception of language as consisting of 'form' and 'interpretation', the latter involving correlation with reality.

part of anyone's philosophical account or 'theory' of language, but rather an invisible force that moulds the theories of language of almost everyone. Frege took it for granted that significant words stand for kinds of things, unjudgeable-contents as he first called them, later objects, concepts, and other functions of different levels. If a name does not stand for a perceptible or mental entity, nevertheless it obviously contributes to the meaning or judgeable-content signified by the sentence in which it occurs. So, Frege argued, it must stand for something non-mental and non-physical, something ideal or Platonic. Hence, for example, number-words stand, in his view, for special kinds of abstract objects. The imposition of a second tier of correlates, viz. senses, over and above references (in Frege's works of the 1890s) merely serves to render more sophisticated and baroque a conceptual house of cards resting upon a natural, unreflective adherence to Augustine's *Urbild*. Similarly Russell's successive philosophical efforts were stimulated by the realization that not all significant expressions (e.g. definite descriptions) stand for entities, from which he concluded that *upon analysis* logic will show that *au fond* every ultimate unanalysable expression stands for an entity (an object of acquaintance). This ideal of analysis, of course, informed the *Tractatus* (though without any explicit commitment to Russell's preoccupation with acquaintance).[21]

This insight into the pathology of the intellect in its reflections upon the nature of language is of colossal importance. For this powerful *Urbild* accompanies our thoughts about language like original sin. Far from being merely a historical curiosity in the works of, say, Frege, Russell, and the young Wittgenstein, it is ubiquitous in contemporary reflections about language, among both philosophers and linguists.[22] Model theoretic semantics, with its sharp distinction of syntax and interpretation and its very conception of a 'model', stands with misguided confidence upon the quicksands of the 'Augustinian' presuppositions. Truth-conditional theories of meaning in all their variety have perforce planted their standard in these quagmires. For if the key to the concept of meaning is the notion of truth, if the meaning of a sentence is given by its truth-conditions and the meaning of a

[21] For a comprehensive account of the myriad possibilities with which the Augustinian conception of language is pregnant, see Baker and Hacker, *Wittgenstein: Understanding and Meaning*, pp. 33 ff.

[22] For a survey and critical analysis of modern theories of language inspired by these nightmares of Reason, see Baker and Hacker, *Language, Sense and Nonsense*.

Disintegration and Reconstruction 131

word by specification of its contribution to the truth-conditions of any sentence in which it may occur, then *every* sentence (not merely declaratives, but also interrogatives, imperatives, optatives) must *have* truth-conditions, otherwise the theory of meaning will be powerless to explain the meaning of a word (e.g. 'door') in sentences that do not express true or false propositions, e.g. 'Shut the door!', 'Is the door shut?', 'Would that the door were shut'. Hence truth-conditional theorists argue that *every* sentence, *mirabile dictu*, contains a descriptive component, variously called 'a sentence-radical', 'phrastic', 'propositional content' that is truth-value bearing (e.g. 'that the door is shut' or 'the shutting of the door by you'), as well as a force-indicator or sign of semantic mood (e.g. 'It is the case . . .', 'Make it the case . . .', 'Is it the case . . . ?' or 'Yes', 'Please!'). So the *essential* function of every sentence *must* be to *describe* a state of affairs! Here philosophers, mesmerized by the Augustinian picture, cook the account books of language which only critical philosophy should audit.

As he gradually realized the nature of the illusions about meaning to which he had succumbed, Wittgenstein also apprehended that his earlier conception of understanding and his assumption that it was *au fond* a psychological matter were deeply misguided. The meaning of an expression is a correlate of understanding, for it is what we understand (or know) when we understand an expression (and know what it means). Hence a correct grasp of the concept of understanding is essential for a correct grasp of the concept of meaning and vice versa. Understanding a sentence is not a mental state. In particular, it is not a mental state in which thought-constituents are concatenated in a certain way in the mind (as he had perhaps thought when he wrote the *Tractatus*) nor is it a mental 'relating relation' of terms that binds together a complex in the mind, as Russell had argued.[23] It is not a psychological process that accompanies a spoken or written proposition, let alone a wholly mysterious such process that brings one into contact with Platonic *Gedanke* as Frege thought.[24] Understanding is an ability, an ability to use the signs of a language in accord with the rules for their use.[25] A language, Wittgenstein held in 1929/30, is a calculus of signs. To understand a language, he argued, is *to be able to operate* the calculus. The use of signs, he insisted, is strictly speaking a kind of

---

[23] Russell, *Theory of Knowledge*, p. 117.
[24] Frege, *Posthumous Writings*, p. 145.
[25] For a detailed account of Wittgenstein's later conception of understanding, see Baker and Hacker, *Wittgenstein: Understanding and Meaning*, pp. 595 ff.

(not merely analogous to) *calculating* (*WWK*, p. 168). The use of a sign in discourse is an operation in exactly the same sense as writing down the result of a multiplication is carrying out an operation. Hence a correct account of understanding a symbolism requires a correct account of the structure of the calculus of which the symbolism consists.

Of course, this conception itself changed dramatically later in the thirties. The idea that a language is a calculus of signs came to seem far-fetched. The notion of a language as a system of interlocking *Satzsysteme* (propositional systems) was gradually replaced by that of a motley of language-games. A language was fruitfully *comparable* to a calculus, he later thought, but was not one; and ultimately the fruitfulness of the comparison ceased to be very impressive. For the dangers and temptations of the comparison are arguably greater than the illumination. Furthermore, the meaning of, and understanding of, a calculus (of arithmetic or of chess) is itself an instance of the issue that calls for philosophical explanation, viz. the nature of representation, understanding, and thought, not a paradigm by reference to which all others are explicable. This became increasingly obvious as Wittgenstein probed a battery of questions about rule-following behaviour from the mid-1930s to the mid-40s. Then his interest shifted from the 'geometry' of a symbolism (whether a language or a calculus) to its place in human life, its use in human behaviour and discourse. A language is something used in speech or writing, in human *activities* which take place and have significance only against complex contexts of human forms of life and culture.

We noted above that the concept of an elementary proposition was replaced by that of a propositional system to which elementary but non-independent propositions belong. Gradually Wittgenstein realized that such central concepts of the *Tractatus* as language, proposition, number, do not have the uniformity he had originally thought. Not only are there, he now argued, diverse *Satzsysteme*, viz. of colours, tones, sounds, etc. but the very concept of a *Satz* (proposition) is inherently variegated. The various things we *call* 'propositions' are not united by sharing common characteristics (*Merkmale*), but are knit together like overlapping fibres in a rope. Of course, we say that propositions are true or false, as we say that the chess king is the piece one checks. But that gives us no independent handle to grasp in identifying a proposition (or chess king). Truth and falsity, one might say, are only *formally Merkmale* of a proposition, they 'belong' to the concept of a proposition but do not 'fit' it (*PI*, §136). True enough, over a very important range, empirical propositions are bipolar. On the other hand, mathematical propositions are not. And, as he realized towards the end of his life, propositions of our 'world picture', such as 'The world has existed for a long time', are not bipolar either. Within the category of empirical propositions there are deep and important logical differences with ramifying philosophical consequences. Although in the very early 1930s he was inclined to claim that ethical and aesthetic sentences do not express genuine propositions, it is, I think, doubtful whether he would have expressed himself thus later. The concept of a proposition is a *family resemblance concept*. It is linked together by intermediate cases, overlapping similarities which do *not* run through the totality.

Extensive philosophical confusions result from failure to appreciate this inherent complexity and non-uniformity of such crucial categorial concepts. There is no such thing, Wittgenstein realized, as 'the general propositional form'. Projecting the essential features of one type of proposition on to others is bound to lead to confusion. Mathematical propositions may have the same grammatical form as certain kinds of empirical propositions, indeed we attach to them a similar array of epistemic terms (e.g. 'know', 'certain', 'believe', 'conjecture', 'prove'). But they differ deeply in their use. Hence to *know* or be *certain* that $25 \times 25 = 625$ is logically altogether unlike knowing or being certain that John is older than Mary (not in being *more* certain or *better* known—rather in the certainty and knowledge being of a categorially different kind).

Just as there is no such thing as 'the general propositional form' so too there is no such thing as 'the general form of a number'. In the *Tractatus* Wittgenstein clearly repudiated logicism, but he did, it seems, think that all numbers can be constructed from the integers. In 1929 he came to think that mathematics itself consists of different propositional systems, e.g. the system of natural numbers, signed integers, rationals, irrationals, complex, hypercomplex numbers, and transfinite numbers. Each of these systems is complete in itself, he held, and nothing but confusion in philosophy of mathematics comes from projecting features of one system on to another or from thinking that one system contains gaps that are later filled by another. Later he came to argue that the very concept of a number *is* a family resemblance concept.

If the sharp categorial concepts of the *Tractatus* are illusory, if it is a fantasy to think that when the concept of a member of a category is given then so is the concept of the general category, then it must be equally misguided to assume that all forms of inference in different propositional systems are uniform and uniformly reducible to tautological transformation. As we have seen, this is evidently wrong in the case of determinate exclusion. No less misguided was it, he now saw, to think that generality is reducible to logical sum or product. There are many essentially different kinds of generality and correspondingly different kinds of inference (*PG*, pp. 257 ff). 'All primary colours', 'all men in this room', 'all men', 'all cardinal numbers', 'all English sentences' involve essentially different logical features, features which are not captured by the uniform contours of the representation of generality in the predicate calculus, let alone reducible to conjunctions and disjunctions of propositions. Hence Wittgenstein turned in the 1930s to explore the ground afresh.

With these far-reaching changes ramifying through his philosophical conceptions of language, logic, and reality, there rapidly and obviously came a profound shift in his very conception of philosophical method. For *analysis*, revelation of *logical form*, disclosure of hitherto unknown linguistic structures (atomic propositions that essentially contain real numbers), and parts of speech (logically proper names) were evidently part of a mythology of symbolism that he had erected in the *Tractatus*. The changes (as well as continuities) in Wittgenstein's later conception of philosophy will concern us in the next chapter.

5. *The Vienna Circle and Wittgenstein's Principle of Verification*

From the point of view of our concern with Wittgenstein's views on the 'self', self-consciousness, and psychological states or conditions of others, an appreciation of his brief verificationist period is important. His principle of verification is a bridge between the transcendental solipsism of the *Tractatus* and the methodological solipsism of the *Philosophical Remarks* (*infra*, Chapter VIII). Similarly, his conception of the relationship between 'propositions' (sense-data statements) and 'hypotheses' is the ancestor of his conception of the relationship between behavioural criteria and that for which they are criteria (*infra*, Chapter XI).

There can now be no doubt at all that in 1929 Wittgenstein was propounding what later became known as the principle of verification (or, verifiability). If there were any legitimate doubts about this a couple of decades ago, they are fully laid to rest by the publication of the *Remarks*, the conversations with Waismann, the Moore and the Lee/King notes of the 1930 lectures. Indeed, there is every reason to think that the members of the Vienna Circle, who made the principle that the meaning of a proposition is its method of verification notorious, derived it from Wittgenstein. Carnap, reminiscing in later years about the ferment of ideas in the Circle,[26] wrote of 'Wittgenstein's principle of verifiability'. Similarly, Juhos, looking back over forty years to his Viennese youth, referred to 'Wittgenstein's "verification thesis" ',[27] and Victor Kraft, writing a history of the Circle (of which he too had been a member), noted that 'This formula ["The meaning of a proposition is determined by its method of verification"] is due to Wittgenstein, whose "Tractatus logico-philosophicus" has been the starting point for the Vienna Circle's theory of meaning and meaninglessness'.[28]

At first blush this seems baffling, even incredible. The principle of verification is certainly *not* to be found in the *Tractatus*. If it is to be found in Wittgenstein's 1929 writings, it might seem to be only a rough suggestion or hint. This appears to be confirmed by a reported remark Wittgenstein made many years later: 'I used at one time to say that, in order to get clear how a certain sentence is used, it was a good idea to ask oneself the question: How would one try to verify such an assertion? But that's just one way of getting clear about the use of a word or sentence ... Some people have turned this suggestion about asking for the verification into a dogma—as if I'd been advancing a *theory* about meaning.'[29]

The matter can perhaps be clarified by a closer examination of the available texts. The principle of verification first appeared in print, it seems,[30] in Waismann's 'A Logical Analysis of the Concept of

---

[26] R. Carnap, 'Intellectual Autobiography', in R. A. Schilpp, ed., *The Philosophy of Rudolf Carnap* (Open Court, Illinois, 1963), p. 45. In his 1957 addendum to his 1930/31 paper 'The Old and the New Logic', he wrote of ' "The principle of verifiability", first pronounced by Wittgenstein' (repr. in A. J. Ayer, ed., *Logical Positivism* (Free Press, Illinois, 1959), p. 146).

[27] Bela Juhos, 'The Methodological Symmetry of Verification and Falsification', in his *Selected Papers on Epistemology and Physics*, ed. G. Frey (Reidel, Dordrecht, 1976), pp. 134 ff.

[28] V. Kraft, *The Vienna Circle, the origin of neo-positivism—a chapter in the history of recent philosophy* (Greenwood Press, New York, 1969), pp. 31 and 197, n. 29.

[29] D. A. T. Gasking and A. C. Jackson, 'Wittgenstein as teacher' repr. in K. T. Fann, ed., *Ludwig Wittgenstein: the Man and his Philosophy* (Dell Publishing Co., New York, 1967), p. 54.

[30] Cf. J. Passmore, *A Hundred Years of Philosophy* (Penguin Books, Harmondsworth, 1968), p. 368.

Probability' published in *Erkenntnis* I (1930–31), 228–48. He acknowledged, on the opening page, that he was 'using Wittgenstein's ideas'. On the second he explained, 'If there is no way of telling when a proposition is true, then the proposition has no sense whatever; for the sense of a proposition is its method of verification. In fact, whoever utters a proposition must know under what conditions he will call the proposition true or false; if he cannot tell this, then he also does not know what he has said.'[31] This seems to be derived from Waismann's 'Theses', composed first in 1930, a slightly later version of which is printed as Appendix B to *Ludwig Wittgenstein and the Vienna Circle*. This was an attempted epitome of Wittgenstein's philosophy, i.e. the *Tractatus* supplemented by Wittgenstein's new ideas as communicated in meeetings with Waismann and Schlick. In section 6, entitled 'Verification', Waismann wrote,

A person who utters a proposition must know under what conditions the proposition is to be called true or false; if he is not able to specify that, he also does not know what he has said.

To understand a proposition means to know how things stand if the proposition is true.
One can understand it without knowing *whether* it is true.
In order to get an idea of the sense of a proposition, it is necessary to become clear about the procedure leading to the determination of its truth. If one does not know that procedure, one cannot understand the proposition either.
A proposition cannot say more than is established by means of the method of its verification . . .
The sense of a proposition is the way it is verified.
. . .
A proposition that cannot be verified in any way has no sense. (*WWK*, pp. 243ff.)

Through conversations in the weekly meetings of the Circle, and by the circulation of the 'Theses', these novel ideas spread. In 'The Elimination of Metaphysics through Logical Analysis of Language' in *Erkenntnis* II (1931–2), Carnap wrote 'the meaning of a word is determined by its criterion of application (in other words: by the relations of deducibility entered into by its elementary sentence-

---

[31] F. Waismann, 'A Logical Analysis of the Concept of Probability' repr. in translation in his *Philosophical Papers*, ed. B. McGuinness (Reidel, Dordrecht, 1977), p. 5.

form,[32] by its truth-conditions, by the method of its verification)'.[33] The following year Schlick published 'Positivism and Realism' in *Erkenntnis* III (1932–3) in which he wrote, echoing the 'Theses': 'If I am *unable*, in principle, to verify a proposition, that is, if I am absolutely ignorant of how to proceed, of what I must do in order to ascertain its truth or falsity, then obviously I do not know what the proposition actually states ... in so far as I am able to do this I am also able in the same way to state at least in principle the method of verification ... The statement of the conditions under which a proposition is true is *the same* as the statement of its meaning, and not something different.'[34] Later, in 'Meaning and Verification' (first published in *The Philosophical Review* 44 (1936) Schlick wrote:

whenever we ask about a sentence, 'What does it mean?', what we expect is instruction as to the circumstances in which the sentence is to be used; we want a description of the conditions under which the sentence will form a true proposition, and of those which will make it false. The meaning of a word or a combination of words is, in this way, determined by a set of rules which regulate their use and which, following Wittgenstein, we may call the rules of their grammar ...

Stating the meaning of a sentence amounts to stating the rules according to which the sentence is to be used, and this is the same as stating the way in which it can be verified (or falsified). The meaning of a proposition is the method of its verification.[35]

In parentheses he added, 'If the preceding remarks about meaning are as correct as I am convinced they are, this will, to a large measure, be due to conversations with Wittgenstein ... I have reason to suppose that he will agree with the main substance of [this article].'

To the eye befogged with the miasma of the 1970s and 1980s this may well appear a bizarre mélange of the *Tractatus*, logical positivism, and of the *Philosophical Investigations*. If we have been convinced that the *Tractatus* is a paradigm of 'realist (truth-conditional) semantic theory', that verificationism is a paradigm of a different, wholly

---

[32] I.e. for a given word, such as 'stone', its elementary sentence is 'x is a stone' where 'x' holds a place for an expression such as 'This diamond'.
[33] R. Carnap, 'The Elimination of Metaphysics through Logical Analysis of Language', repr. in translation in A. J. Ayer, ed. *Logical Positivism* (Free Press, Illinois, 1959), p. 63.
[34] M. Schlick, 'Positivism and Realism' in Ayer, ed., *Logical Positivism*, p. 87.
[35] M. Schlick, 'Meaning and Verification', repr. in his *Gesammelte Aufsätze* 1926–36 (Georg Olms Verlag, Hildesheim, 1969), p. 340.

incompatible theory of meaning,[36] and that the *Investigations* is a mysterious (and misguided[37]) repudiation of *any* general theory of meaning, then we may find this altogether baffling. How was it possible, one may wonder, for intelligent members of the Circle to have been so confused as to try to synthesize truth-conditional semantics with assertability-conditions semantics as enshrined in verificationism, let alone to have also tried to read verificationism back into *Tractatus* 4.024—'To understand a proposition means to know what is the case if it is true'?

This reaction is misguided, stemming from the inclination to view the past through the distorting spectacles of current preconceptions. *Tractatus* 4.024 is, to be sure, not a statement of the principle of verification, but nor is it a statement of 'truth-conditional semantics'. Members of the Circle evidently saw a smooth continuity between that remark in the *Tractatus* and the principle of verification and, given the demise of logical atomism, they were not foolish to do so. On the contrary, they were encouraged by Wittgenstein's current observations. Nor was there any incongruity (even if there *now* seems to be) in seeing these remarks as wholly consistent with, indeed further elaborations of, the dictum 'the meaning of an expression is its use'. For in the *Tractatus* Wittgenstein had already observed that 'In order to recognize a symbol by its sign we must observe how it is used with a sense' (*TLP*, 3.326),[38] and to observe the different ways different propositions are

---

[36] See, for example, M. A. E. Dummett: 'A verificationist theory of meaning differs radically from the account of meaning as given in terms of truth-conditions implicit in Frege's work and explicit in Wittgenstein's *Tractatus* [sic!]. On a theory of the latter kind, the crucial notions for the theory of meaning are those of truth and falsity: we know the meaning of a sentence when we know what has to be the case for that sentence to be true. A verificationist account takes as central to the theory of meaning the entirely different account of that by which we can recognize a sentence to be conclusively shown to be true or to be conclusively shown to be false: we know the meaning of a sentence when we are able to recognize it as conclusively verified or as conclusively falsified whenever one or the other of these conditions obtains'. ('The Significance of Quine's Indeterminacy Thesis', repr. in his *Truth and other Enigmas* (Duckworth, London, 1978), p. 379.)

[37] See M. A. E. Dummett, 'Can Analytical Philosophy be Systematic and Ought it to be?', in his *Truth and Other Enigmas*.

[38] Of this one might say, as Wittgenstein himself observed, that 'One often makes a remark and only later sees *how* true it is' (*NB*, p. 10). It would, of course, be absurd to suggest that *the* conception of 'meaning as use' was already present in the *Tractatus*. The dictum 'The meaning of an expression is its use' (and variations on that theme) does not signify *one* conception, but is compatible with many utterly different ones (e.g. the *Tractatus* and *Investigations*). Only in the context of an overall picture delineating a network of internal relations between the concepts of language, proposition, name,

compared with reality (verified) is to do just that. The gap between the *Tractatus* and Wittgenstein's verificationism, in *one* sense, is not as great as it might seem. The great gulf lies in the demise of atomism and the metaphysical explanation of the harmony between language and reality, not in any substitution of 'assertability-conditions semantics' for 'truth-conditional semantics', for Wittgenstein espoused neither!

We saw (*supra*, p. 61 ff.) that Wittgenstein never argued that the sense of an elementary proposition is its truth-conditions or is given by specification of its truth-conditions. On his conception of a truth-condition this claim would be literally nonsensical. According to the *Tractatus*, the elementary proposition is essentially bipolar, depicting a possible state of affairs which the world either actualizes or does not. To know whether a proposition is true or false, however, one must verify it, compare it with reality. The proposition is, he thought, like a yardstick to be held against reality for a Yes / No reading (cf. *TLP*, 2.1512 f.). With the collapse of the independence thesis for the elementary proposition and the emergence of the conception of a *Satzsystem*, he adjusted his metaphor. A proposition is indeed like a yardstick held against reality, but the *whole scale* of the yardstick gives a range of interdependent readings, e.g. if A is 1 foot long, then it is not 2 foot long, not 3 foot long, etc. and if A is red, it is not green, not yellow, not orange, and so on.

In 1929 Wittgenstein's interest shifted not only to propositional systems, but also to the method of comparing a proposition to reality. This was natural enough. In the *Tractatus* he had claimed that to understand a proposition means to know what is the case if it is true. To come to know whether it is true, i.e. to compare it with reality, must have seemed an essentially unproblematic matter. All that needs to be done is to perceive whether the objects that are the meanings of names are concatenated as the proposition says they are (and this issue, notoriously, was not thought through). But if, as he thought in late 1929, the world does not consist of facts, if facts do not consist of objects that are meanings, if the meanings of simple names are explained by using samples that belong to the method of representation, then the way we compare the proposition (which contains expressions defined in terms of samples) with reality must be pertinent to its

---

meaning, explanation, understanding, use, truth, etc. does the dictum assume a determinate meaning. What its meaning is is shown by the very different kinds of features of expressions of different types that can legitimately be called 'use', and what counts as a description of use.

meaning. The method of comparing a sample with reality must be internally related to the meaning of the proposition in question. We find these themes explored in the *Philosophical Remarks*, p. 77:

> I should like to say: for any question there is always a corresponding *method* of finding.
> Or you might say, a question *denotes* a method of searching.
>
> You can only search in *a space* [i.e. in visual space for shapes and colours, auditory space for tones, tactile space for textures, etc.]. For only in space do you stand in relation to where you are not.
> To understand the sense of a proposition means to know how the issue of its truth or falsity is to be decided.
> . . .
> You must find the way from where you are to where the issue is decided.
> You cannot search wrongly; you *cannot* look for a visual impression with your sense of touch.
> You cannot compare a picture with reality unless you can set it against it as a yardstick.
> You must be able to fit the proposition on to reality.[39]

Given that the picture *theory* (but not the pictoriality) of the elementary proposition is misguided, then to say that you understand a proposition if you know what is the case if it is true is to say virtually nothing. For 'the proposition that *p*' = 'the proposition that *p* is true'. To be sure, if I understand the proposition that it is raining, then I know that if it is true that it is raining, then it *is* raining (if I understand the proposition that *p*, then I know that if the proposition that *p* is true, then it is the case that *p*)! But if the theses of isomorphism between language and reality are a mythology, then we need a fresh explanation of what it *is* for *p* to be the case, of what *counts* as *p*'s being true, of what *counts* as knowing that *p* is the case. For we can no longer explain what it is for *p* to be the case in terms of a concatenation of the constituent *meanings* in reality. Meanings, *thus understood*, are now 'obsolete' (M, p. 258). Meanings of simple expressions are given by explanations of meaning (hence 'remain within language'), often by reference to samples (which are elements of representation). How the proposition is compared with reality, therefore, is a crucial feature of its meaning ('*A* is red' is compared with the *visual* field, not the auditory field). This is expressed by the claim that the meaning of a proposition is its method

---

[39] 'Auf die Wirklichkeit auflegen können', 'You must be able to lay it alongside reality' would perhaps be better (cf. *TLP*, 2.1512).

of verification, for, it now seemed clear, 'To understand a proposition means to know how the issue of its truth or falsity is to be decided'. Indeed, it is the verification which gives the grammar of the proposition, and so answers the question '*What would it be like for it to be true?*' (*AWL*, p. 20). If the meaning of 'red', for example, were an object, then to know the meaning of 'red' would already be to know how '*A* is red' is to be compared with reality. But if the meaning of 'red' is given by an explanation of meaning, e.g. 'This ↑ [pointing at a sample] is red', then in order to know what '*A* is red' means one must further know how to 'lay it alongside reality', how to verify it.

It is important to note that this new conception does not affect the truth-conditional account of the sense of *molecular* propositions, save in cases of logical relations between propositions within a given propositional system.

> What I at first paid no attention to was that the syntax of logical constants forms only part of a more comprehensive syntax. Thus I can, for example construct the logical product *p.q.* only if *p* and *q* do not determine the same coordinate twice.
>
> But in cases where propositions are independent everything remains valid—the whole theory of inference and so forth. (*WWK*, p. 76).[40]

Wittgenstein communicated his new views to Waismann and Schlick in 1929. On 22 December he expounded his verificationism to them. The sense of a proposition is its verification. He required *complete* or *conclusive* verification: 'If I can never verify the sense of a proposition completely, then I cannot have meant anything by the proposition ... In order to determine the sense of a proposition, I should have to know a very specific procedure for when to count the proposition as verified' (*WWK*, p. 47). Three days later, he elaborated further. Difference of verification indicates a difference in meaning (*WWK*, p. 53). If one lays two propositions alongside reality in a different way, then they have different meanings. From Moore's lecture notes (M. p. 266) and King's notes[41] it is evident that he propounded the same ideas to his Cambridge students in 1930/31.

At this phase in the development of his ideas, Wittgenstein distinguished between three essentially different kinds of structures we call 'propositions'. First, there are 'genuine propositions' that are conclusively verified or falsified by comparison with reality. These are

---

[40] Cf. *WWK*, p. 80; this was precisely what members of the Circle understood.
[41] D. Lee, ed., *Wittgenstein's Lectures, Cambridge 1930–32*, p. 66.

propositions that describe immediate experience, i.e. sense-datum statements. For them, there is no gap between appearance and reality, no distinction between seeming and being. They concern 'primary experience'. Secondly, there are 'hypotheses' (*PR*, pp. 282 ff.). They are not directly and conclusively verifiable by reference to experience. Propositions about objective particulars (as opposed to propositions about one's current experiences), about the past, about other people's states of mind, about laws of nature, are hypotheses. They are not propositions in the same sense as descriptions of immediate experience, but are wholly different kinds of logical structures. They cannot be said to be true or false (*WWK*, p. 101; *PR*, p. 283), or at any rate not in the same sense (*PR*, p. 285). To say that a hypothesis is not conclusively verifiable is not to say that there is a verification of it to which, through human frailty, we can only approximate but never fully achieve. Rather a hypothesis has a different formal relation to reality than that of a verifiable proposition properly speaking (*WWK*, p. 210; *PR*, p. 285). One can conceive of it as a law (or rule) for constructing propositions in the sense in which the equation of a curve gives a law for determining the ordinates if one cuts the curve at different abscissae. Analogously, genuinely verifiable observation statements are cuts through the connected structure of the hypothesis (*WWK*, pp. 100, 159; *PR*, pp. 284 ff.). The relationship between a hypothesis and the 'genuine' propositions that support it is therefore a priori. The proposition which gives support to a hypothesis Wittgenstein called 'a symptom' (*WWK*, p. 159). A hypothesis is a rule for the derivation of symptoms (is 'a law for forming expectations' (*PR*, p. 285)) and a symptom provides confirmation for a hypothesis. The probability of a hypothesis is a measure of how much evidence is needed to make it worthwhile to reject the hypothesis (*PR*, p. 286).[42]

The third kind of proposition Wittgenstein distinguished was the mathematical proposition. Unlike the first two kinds, propositions of mathematics cannot be compared with reality at all and neither agree nor disagree with reality (M. p. 267). At first blush he appears to be applying a global conception of verification to all kinds of proposition: experiential propositions are verified by immediate experience or by symptoms, mathematical propositions by *proof*. So, in general, the meaning of a proposition is given by its verification. This, however, is

[42] For a detailed account of Wittgenstein's conception of hypotheses, see F. Waismann, 'Hypotheses', repr. in his *Philosophical Papers*, ed. B. McGuinness (Reidel, Dordrecht, 1977).

altogether deceptive. He certainly held that the sense of a mathematical proposition is given by its proof. 'A mathematical proposition is related to its proof as the outer surface of a body is to the body itself. We might talk of the body of proof belonging to the proposition. Only on the assumption that there's a body behind the surface, has the proposition any significance for us' (*PR*, p. 192). But far from calling a proof 'a verification' in order to emphasize an affinity or parallelism between experiential propositions and mathematical ones, Wittgenstein's concern was to emphasize the difference. 'How a proposition is verified is what it says. Compare the generality of genuine propositions with generality in arithmetic. It is differently verified and so is of a different kind' (*PR*, p. 200). For what a mathematical proof proves is *a grammatical construction*, a *rule of representation*, not a truth about the world (let alone about a world of mathematical objects). 'Nothing is more fatal to philosophical understanding than the notion of proof and experience as two different but comparable methods of verification' (*PG*, p. 361).[43]

Given that Wittgenstein evidently espoused verificationism in 1929/30, how can his later insistence that he had never advanced verificationism as a theory of meaning, but only as 'one way of getting clear about the use of a word or sentence', be explained? Two points are worth making. First, although in 1929 he propounded verificationism as an essential part of his account of non-molecular propositions, he would not, I think, have seen this as a *theory of meaning*. A clue to this is to be found in Schlick's 'Positivism and Realism': 'It would be quite mistaken to see, somehow, in what we have said a "theory of meaning" (in Anglo-Saxon countries this insight, that the meaning of a proposition is determined wholly and alone by its verification in the given, is often called the "experimental theory of meaning"). What

---

[43] It is noteworthy that over the matter of Wittgenstein's views on the nature of mathematics the members of the Vienna Circle were almost wholly at sea. They were inclined to think that the *Tractatus* had showed that mathematical propositions are tautologies (cf. H. Hahn, 'Logic, Mathematics and Knowledge of Nature', in A. J. Ayer, ed. *Logical Positivism*, p. 159) or that at any rate the difference between tautologies and mathematical propositions was insignificant (cf. Carnap, 'Intellectual Autobiography' p. 47). Even more bizarrely, the Manifesto of the Circle, discussing logicism, formalism, and intuitionism surmised 'that essential features of all three will come close in the course of future development and probably, using the far-reaching ideas of Wittgenstein, will be united in the ultimate solution' (*The Scientific Conception of the World: the Vienna Circle*, p. 13). Wittgenstein, however, was not trying, eclectically, to synthesize these, but rather to repudiate the shared presuppositions of the 'foundations crisis' which gave rise to these confused philosophies of mathematics.

precedes every formulation of a theory cannot itself be a theory.'[44] It is plausible to suppose that this was a point Wittgenstein had been eager to emphasize, for in 'Meaning and Verification',[45] just after acknowledging Wittgenstein as the inspirer of verificationism, Schlick reverts to this caveat:

> This view has been called the 'experimental theory of meaning'; but it certainly is no theory at all, for the term 'Theory' is used for a set of hypotheses about a certain subject-matter, and there are no hypotheses involved in our view, which proposes to be nothing but a simple statement of the way in which meaning is actually assigned to propositions, both in everyday life and in science. There has never been any other way, and it would be a grave error to suppose that we believe we have discovered a new conception of meaning which is contrary to common opinion and which we want to introduce into philosophy.[46]

This conforms with Wittgenstein's warnings against 'dogmatism' made in December 1931 (cf. *WWK*, pp. 182 ff.) to Waismann.

The second point to emphasize is that Wittgenstein's verificationism (in this form) was very short-lived. Section 60 of the 'Big Typescript', which is indeed entitled 'Tell me what you are doing with a proposition, how you verify it, etc. and I will understand it' is already much more cautious. Here we find the formulation of the position that is accepted in the *Philosophical Investigations*', viz. 'Asking whether and how a proposition can be verified is only a particular way of asking "How d'you mean?"'. The answer is a contribution to the grammar of the proposition' (*PI*, §353). It may be that this far less rigid conception of the role of verification in the grammar of certain propositions is what Wittgenstein was alluding to in his remark (*supra* p. 135).

It is evident from Moore's lecture notes that in the 1932/3 lectures Wittgenstein was shifting ground dramatically. What, in 1930, he had conceived as 'genuine propositions', viz. reports of immediate experience that are compared directly with reality, are now seen as something quite different. It *makes no sense* to ask 'How do you know you have toothache?'. These are precisely *not* propositions for which there is a method of verification. The question is extensively discussed in 'Notes for Lectures on "Private Experience" and "Sense Data"'. 'If I say what

---

[44] Schlick 'Positivism and Realism' in Ayer ed., *Logical Positivism*, p. 88.
[45] As noted above, this was published in 1936, by which time Wittgenstein had long since abandoned the form of verificationism that characterizes *Philosophical Remarks*. Schlick was evidently aware of *some* of these changes.
[46] Schlick 'Meaning and Verification' in his *Gesammelte Aufsätze*, p. 340.

it is I see', Wittgenstein queries, 'how do I compare what I say with what I see in order to know whether I say the truth?' (NFL, p. 280.) Here, he concluded, there is no comparing of proposition with reality. From these seeds grew the private language argument and the conception of first-person psychological utterances as avowals. We shall discuss these in later chapters. The notion of 'hypotheses' as conceived in 1929/30 disappeared equally rapidly. The term 'symptom', by the time of the *Blue Book*, was given a quite different use, viz. to signify *inductive* evidence, and the expression 'criterion' inherits *part* of its role as *grammatical grounds* for a certain type of assertion. Propositions such as 'Cambridge won the boat-race' or 'It has been raining' are indeed verified, e.g. by reading the newspaper or seeing whether the pavement is wet. But these are inductive evidence, not grammatically related to the propositions they support.[47] The claim that in giving the verification of a proposition one gives its meaning was too sweeping, for in fact it is 'a rule of thumb' (M. p. 266), since 'verification' means different things, and of some propositions it is senseless to ask for their verification. 'How far is giving the verification of a proposition a grammatical statement about it?', he concluded in 1932/3, 'So far as it is, it can explain the meaning of its terms. In so far as it is a matter of experience, as when one names a symptom, the meaning is not explained' (*AWL*, p. 31.).

[47] Cf. M, p. 266, where Wittgenstein seems to have equivocated a little, hedging his bets. His position is made clearer in the Ambrose notes (*AWL*, pp. 28 ff.), although it is still clearly shaky (e.g. in the distinction between primary and secondary criteria).

VI

WITTGENSTEIN'S LATER CONCEPTION OF PHILOSOPHY

1. *A Kink in the Evolution of Philosophy*
The two conceptions of philosophy in the *Tractatus* bear considerable affinities to Wittgenstein's later conception which evolved from 1929 onwards and found its final and polished expression in the *Philosophical Investigations*. There are also, however, deep differences which lie concealed in his semi-ironical use of similar remarks in both works. His oracular epigrammatical style lends itself to ambiguity. His liking for such masters of irony, paradox, and pun, as Lichtenberg, Kierkegaard, and Kraus should be a warning to the superficial reader. His repetition of *Tractatus* dicta frequently constitutes the re-employment of old bottles to hold new wine. The author of the *Tractatus* had, in the opinion of the author of the *Investigations*, succumbed to many kinds of deep philosophical illusion. On the flyleaf of Schlick's copy of the *Tractatus*, Wittgenstein is reported to have written: 'Jeder dieser Sätze ist der Ausdruck einer Krankheit'. (Each of these sentences is the expression of a disease.)[1] The general conception of philosophy was accordingly distorted on many matters, necessitating reinterpretation and correction. Any attempt to trace out continuity and contrast between the earlier and later work with respect to the conception of philosophy must bear in mind the fact that the axis of reference of the whole investigation has been rotated around a fixed point (*PI*, §108). The need to grasp conceptual structures remains, but they are now conceived *sub specie humanitatis*.

In the course of the lectures in 1930–3 Wittgenstein claimed that philosophy as he was now practising it was not merely a stage in the continuous development of the subject, but a new subject (M, p. 322).

[1] See A. Maslow, *A Study in Wittgenstein's Tractatus* (University of California Press, California, 1961), p. x. But one should also remember that he said that the *Tractatus* was not like a heap of old scrap metal purporting to be a watch, but like a watch that does not tell the right time.

Using a simile reminiscent of Russell's claims about logical analysis, Wittgenstein declared that with the emergence of his new style of philosophizing there was a 'kink' in the evolution of philosophy comparable to that which occurred when Galileo invented dynamics. He repeated the point in the *Blue Book* (*BB*, p. 28). His work, he wrote, is one of the heirs of the subject that used to be called philosophy. The important thing, he claimed in his lectures, was not whether his results were true or false, but that a new method had been found,[2] as had happened when chemistry was developed out of alchemy. As a result of the discovery of this method it is now possible to have not only great philosophers but also skilled ones.

What was this sharp discontinuity that Wittgenstein perceived between past philosophy and his work? Philosophers in the past have uniformly conceived of their subject as a cognitive pursuit. Philosophical investigations, they thought, will yield *philosophical knowledge* expressed in philosophical propositions. Different conceptions of such knowledge flourished. Some writers, from Plato onwards, have thought of philosophy, like mathematics, as being concerned with eternal truths about abstract objects such as justice, knowledge, truth, number. It is not an investigation into the ephemera of this fleeting world of appearances, but is rather an investigation into a sempiternal world of essences and ideal objects. Others, such as Descartes, have conceived of philosophy as a study of the foundations of all the sciences. Its results are the rock upon which the edifice of human knowledge stands, and that edifice is only as secure as its foundations are firm. A third conception, which we have encountered in the above discussion of Russell, conceives of philosophy as continuous with the natural sciences. Its task is to construct theories about the most general features of the universe. A fourth, prominent among the classical British empiricists, thought of the subject as an investigation into the essential nature of the human mind, its mode of acquisition of ideas and its method of operation upon them, which will clarify the extent of the possibility of human knowledge. A fifth, distinctly Kantian

---

[2] The remark requires some minor modification. If there are no 'philosophical propositions' then some obvious strain is generated by talking of the results of philosophical investigation as true or false. (A similar problem arose with respect to the Preface of the *Tractatus* in which he remarked 'the truth of the thoughts that are here set forth seems to me unassailable and definitive'; but strictly speaking pseudo-propositions cannot be said to be true.) The claim that *a* method had been found must also be modified, for he was later to argue that there is no *one* method, but many philosophical methods, cf. *PI*, §133.

conception, conceived of the subject as an investigation into the conditions of the possibility of experience, of perceptual experience yielding knowledge of the empirical world, of moral experience involving knowledge of moral truths, and so on. The task of philosophy was to elaborate synthetic a priori truths which would in effect characterize the bounds of sense.

Despite important affinities with the Kantian view, Wittgenstein broke decisively with these cognitive conceptions of philosophy. He had, after a fashion, already done so in the *Tractatus*. For although it abounds in metaphysical pronouncements, it concludes that these are strictly speaking nonsense. Now he cut himself loose even from the notion of ineffable metaphysics. Accordingly he deepened and enriched his earlier insights into the *sui generis* character of philosophy. There are no philosophical propositions and no philosophical knowledge. Unlike the sciences, philosophy does not aim at the accumulation of fresh knowledge. Its quest is for a certain type of understanding. It is no closer to mathematics than it is to physics, and the philosopher's achievements do not consist in attaining knowledge of eternal truths about ideal realms which he brings back to the denizens of Plato's cave, informing them for the first time what numbers really are or what justice truly requires. Philosophy can give other disciplines no foundations, since it is not concerned with uncovering fundamental true propositions upon which the sciences rest. But the very idea that empirical knowledge, if it is to keep scepticism at bay, must rest upon self-certifying indubitable knowledge derived from an examination of one's own mind is a Cartesian myth. Scepticism must be shown to be *nonsense*, not answered by producing indubitabilia out of philosophical top hats. Similarly the supposition that mathematics *needs* foundations (e.g. in set theory) is an illusion of Reason which philosophy should eradicate. Philosophy is not in competition with psychology and is not concerned with investigating the empirical (or any other) workings of the mind. Though there is an important sense in which philosophy is concerned with the bounds of sense, the characterization of the bounds of sense is not by means of special kinds of truths (synthetic a priori propositions) that describe them. In the *Tractatus* 4.003 Wittgenstein wrote, 'Most of the propositions and questions to be found in philosophical works are not false but nonsensical'. This was not brash arrogance, but a claim about the logical character of attempts to traverse the bounds of sense (including the propositions of the *Tractatus* itself). He continued to think that past philosophies conceived on the pattern of cognitive investigations were nonsensical. But his reasons shifted. He no longer thought of 'categorial' concepts as *metalogical* concepts that cannot legitimately occur in a genuine proposition. His diagnosis changed; past philosophers, who misunderstood the character of philosophical questions and the nature of their resolution, unavoidably cast *norms of representation* in the role of *objects represented*. They conceived of features of the grammar of our method of representation as essential truths about the reality we represent by means of our language. Moreover, they typically distorted those features.

Wittgenstein wrote in the early nineteen-thirties:

A commonsense person, when he reads earlier philosophers thinks—quite rightly—'Sheer nonsense'. When he listens to me, he thinks—rightly again—'Nothing but stale truisms'. That is how the image of philosophy has changed.[3]

The image, in both cases, is potentially misleading. It is true that '*Cogito ergo sum*', '*Esse* is *percipi*', 'The self is a bundle of perceptions' are nonsense. But without further explanation it is unilluminating to be told that. It is also true that to insist that not all words are names or that not all sentences are descriptions is to insist on truisms. But again, without an account of why the product of philosophy seems so trivial, this too is unilluminating. (Philosophers hunt for the map of Treasure Island in order to find the treasure, and they do not realize that the treasure is the map!) As we shall see, Wittgenstein gave an elaborate explanation of the matter.

The conception of philosophy that emerged in the 1930s is intimately related to his earlier view, but also importantly different. The marmoreal metaphysical pronouncements of the *Tractatus* (its *de facto* practice) disappear. Philosophy really is (as he had said (*TLP*, 4.112)) an activity of clarification, although not by analysis as conceived in the *Tractatus*. He was indeed trying to effect a fundamental change in the evolution of the subject, attempting to move it on to new tracks that would take it out of the quagmires of interminable and irresoluble disagreements. He was well aware that what he had to say would be difficult to accept, for it not only overturned the venerable conception

---

[3] Quoted by A. J. P. Kenny from MS 219, p. 6 in his illuminating essay 'Wittgenstein on the nature of Philosophy', p. 57, repr. in his *The Legacy of Wittgenstein* (Blackwell, Oxford, 1984).

of philosophy as a cognitive activity, but also ran contrary to the spirit of twentieth-century civilization.[4]

Cognitive conceptions of philosophy are as old as the subject itself. But, as we have seen, there is a different conception of at least a part of philosophy, which has Leibnizian (and earlier) roots and which has emerged into the light in the last hundred years. According to this conception, the task of philosophy is 'legislative' or 'stipulative'. It should concern itself with devising an ideal language which will, for special purposes, be an improvement over ordinary language. Frege conceived thus of his concept-script which he devised for the purpose of proof-theory in deductive sciences or reconstructions of empirical sciences (e.g. mechanics). Russell thought of the language of *Principia* in a similar way as a logically perfect language. This too Wittgenstein repudiated, but not merely on the grounds he had given in the *Tractatus*. He continued to think that the idea that natural languages might be 'logically defective' was absurd, and the supposition that one might devise a 'better' or 'logically more perfect' language ridiculous. But he now no longer even thought that 'concept-scripts' were perspicuous notations for the presentation of the 'logical syntax' of actual language. The supposition that all possible languages have a common essential form is misguided, since the concept of a language is a family-resemblance concept. The idea that the logical structure of a language can be illuminatingly represented in the forms of a logical calculus is chimerical. For natural languages are very *unlike* logical calculi, and a perspicuous representation of their philosophically puzzling features cannot typically be fruitfully given in the forms of artificial notations. The invention of new calculi may have a point, but there is nothing essentially philosophical about it. It is not one of the purposes of philosophy to engage in such activities (as Carnap did in the 1930s and 1940s). Artificial calculi can contribute nothing to the solution of our philosophical problems. For these lie in our existing methods of representation, in our natural languages. They cannot be resolved by being recast in an alternative form of representation, viz. an artificial calculus. At best the latter are only of use in philosophy as

---

[4] He remarked to Drury, 'My type of thinking is not wanted in this present age. I have to swim so strongly against the tide. Perhaps in a hundred years people will really want what I am writing.' (M. O'C. Drury, 'Some Notes on Conversations with Wittgenstein', in *Acta Philosophica Fennica 28, Essays in Honour of G. H. von Wright*, ed. J. Hintikka (North Holland, Amsterdam, 1976), p. 25.)

objects for comparison in the course of pursuing the real business of philosophy.[5]

2. A Cure for the Sickness of the Understanding

The aims of philosophy are variously stated by Wittgenstein, sometimes in a mildly positive fashion, but more often in a negative vein. Positively, philosophy aims at putting in order our ideas as to what can be said about the world (M, p. 323), it is essentially a rearrangement of something we already know, like arranging books in a library (*BB*, p. 44). The aim of philosophy is to establish an order (not THE order) in our knowledge of the use of language (*PI* §132). It strives after the notions of a sound human understanding (*RFM*, p. 302). The most general and recurrent positive formulation of the task of philosophy is the claim that its purpose is to give us an *Übersicht*, a surview or synoptic view.[6] In the *Investigations* Wittgenstein states unambiguously:

> The concept of a surveyable representation (*übersichtliche Darstellung*) is of fundamental significance for us. It characterizes our form of representation, the way we look at things. (Is this a 'Weltanschauung'?) (*PI*, §122; my translation.)

A surview enables us to grasp the structure of our mode of representation, or whichever segment of it is relevant to a given philosophical problem. The concept of a surview is central to Wittgenstein's later philosophy. It is the heir to the 'correct logical point of view' of the *Tractatus* (*TLP*, 4.1213), an heir importantly

---

[5] But the logical calculi invented over the last hundred years are an immense source of further philosophical confusions, of false idols and ideals. Wittgenstein sapiently observed that '"Mathematical logic" has completely deformed the thinking of mathematicians and of philosophers' (*RFM*, p. 300), an observation that is all the more apt today.

[6] The terms *Übersicht*, *Übersichtlichkeit*, and the related verb *übersehen* have given Wittgenstein's translators much trouble. They have chosen to translate it non-systematically in conformity with the demands of English style, thereby partially obscuring the significance and pervasiveness of the concept in Wittgenstein's work, e.g. 'command a clear view' (*übersehen PI*, §122); 'perspicuous representation' (*übersichtlichen Darstellung PI*, §122); 'synoptic account' (*übersichtliche Darstellung Z*, §273); 'Survey' (*Übersicht Z*, §273); 'synoptic view' (*Übersichtlichkeit Z*, §464); 'perspicuity' (*Übersichtlichkeit RFM*, p. 95); 'capable of being taken in' (*übersehbar RFM*, p. 170). I shall try to avoid this multiplicity of approximate synonyms by employing the archaic term 'surview' and related terms 'to survey', 'surveyable' etc. When quoting Wittgenstein I shall use the translator's version (unless it is misleading for other reasons) together with the relevant German term in parentheses.

different from the parent. While the *Tractatus* had sought to achieve a correct logical point of view by 'geological' means, by delving beneath the appearances of language to uncover its latent structure, Wittgenstein's later philosophy seeks a correct logical point of view by 'topographical' means.

> Consider the geography of a country for which we have no map, or else a map in tiny bits. The difficulty about this is the difficulty with philosophy; there is no synoptic view. Here the country we talk about is language and the geography grammar. We can walk about a country quite well but when forced to make a map we go wrong. (Lectures, Michaelmas 1933)[7]

While the correct logical point of view was to be achieved by logical *analysis* into an ideal (logically perspicuous) notation, a surview is to be obtained by a careful *description* of our ordinary uses of language. The main source of misunderstandings characteristic of philosophy is the difficulty of surveying our use of language (*PI*, §122). Language is the means of representation. Its inner structure, constituted by the rules which determine the use of sentences and their constituents is the form of representation, the web of conceptual connections by means of which we conceive of the world. We obtain a proper surview of our form of representation when we grasp the grammar[8] of language, not merely in the sense in which the ordinary speaker of the language does, but in the sense of being able to survey the interconnections of rules for the use of expressions. When these reticulations are perspicuous, one can achieve a firm understanding of the bounds of sense and see what is awry with philosophical questions and their typical answers. For these characteristically traverse the limits of sense, violate—in subtle ways—the rules for the use of expressions, and hence make no sense.

Our grammar is above all lacking in surveyability (*PR* §1; *PI* §122). Moreover, some segments of our language, e.g. psychological terms, present greater barriers to the achievement of a proper surview than others, e.g. terms in mechanics (*Z*, §113). Grammar is not embodied in a static instantly surveyable medium, but is the structure of our dynamic linguistic practices. Of course, as competent speakers of our native tongue, there is a perfectly straightforward sense in which we know the grammar, the rules for the use of our language. We typically

[7] Reported by A. Ambrose, 'Wittgenstein on Universals', in *Ludwig Wittgenstein, The Man and his Philosophy*, ed. K. T. Fann, p. 336.

[8] For a detailed examination of Wittgenstein's conception of grammar see Chapter VII below.

use expressions correctly, i.e. in accord with the rules for their use. We can, and often do, correct mistakes of others and of our own. We can explain what we mean by the expressions we use, and our explanations of meaning *are* expressions of the rules which we follow in using the term we thus explain. (There is *no* question here of a contrast between 'tacit knowledge' and 'explicit knowledge' that has bedevilled much recent philosophical and linguistic theorizing.) But we typically lack a surview of our use, particularly in respect of those features of language that give rise to philosophical perplexity. We may have mastered perfectly the different and distinctive uses of verbs of perception and verbs of sensation and their corresponding nouns, and nevertheless be unaware of the logically crucial differences between the ways they are used. So we are taken in by psychologists' and philosophers' talk of 'visual sensations' that are allegedly caused by the objects we see; and we take as scientific discovery the claim that colours are in effect sensations caused in the brain or mind by the impact of light-waves of certain wavelengths on the retina. We may be skilful users of numerals and number-words, and employ correctly various arithmetical techniques in our daily transactions, yet be bemused and even taken in when mathematicians and philosophers of mathematics tell us that number-words are names of numbers, that numbers are objects (logical objects, as the logicists argued, or mental objects constructed by the mathematician, as Brouwer thought), that they can be proved to *exist*, that they are objects of 'mathematical experience', even apparently mysterious and wonderful ones such as transfinite cardinals. We (and the mathematician and philosopher are included too) fail to see the differences between the ways in which we use and explain the use of names of objects and number-words. We do not realize the crucial differences between talking of chairs and tables as existing and talking of numbers as existing. So we think we are just dealing with different kinds of objects, which *exist* in exactly the same sense, instead of investigating what is *meant* by saying that a number of a certain type exists. So we are gulled into thinking of mathematical knowledge and mathematical discovery as precisely parallel to empirical knowledge and empirical discovery, only about an a priori realm of bizarre entities. We can be rid of these illusions of Reason only by obtaining a surview of the uses of the expressions involved. The complete surview of all sources of unclarity by means of an account of all the applications, illustrations, conceptions of a segment of language (e.g. the transition from mathematics of the finite to mathematics of the infinite (*Z*,

§273)) will produce an understanding of logical connections which will dissolve confusion.[9]

As will be seen from the latter remark, even the formulation of the survey-giving task of philosophy is given a negative slant. This is altogether natural. For the kind of understanding for which philosophy strives, the attaining of an *Übersicht* of (parts of) our form of representation, has as its corollary the elimination of those *misunderstandings* that give rise to philosophical perplexity. Although we wish to arrive at the notions of a sound human understanding, philosophers need to be cured of many diseases of the understanding before they can do so (*RFM*, p. 302). The order we seek to establish is an order which is necessary to banish philosophical worries. The dominant view of the purpose of philosophy is negative—the elimination of confusion, the disappearance of philosophical problems (*PI*, §133). Philosophy aims to dissolve philosophical problems which arise out of language (*PI*, §90); it is a fight against the fascination exercised by forms of language (*BB*, p. 27; *PI*, §109). It destroys those houses of cards, which always seem interesting, great, and important in philosophy, namely putative insights into the real, the metaphysical structure of the universe, the essence of the world. The importance of philosophizing in the new way lies in disillusionment, in curing philosophical thought of the madness which besets it.

The conception of philosophy as therapeutic is a *leitmotif* of Wittgenstein's later work: 'The philosopher's treatment of a question is like the treatment of an illness' (*PI*, §255). There are different philosophical methods, like different therapies (*PI*, §133). What mathematicians are inclined to say about the reality and objectivity of mathematical 'facts' is itself something for philosophical treatment, not a philosophy of mathematics (*PI*, §254). He often compared his methods of philosophical clarification with psychoanalysis[10] (*PG*, pp. 381 f.: 'Big Typescript', p. 410). Philosophical theories (idealism, realism, solipsism (cf. *PI*, §402)) are *latent* nonsense; it is the task of the philosopher to render such theories *patent* nonsense, to make, as it

---

[9] For a more comprehensive account of Wittgenstein's conception of a survey, as well as of its historical parentage, see Baker and Hacker, *Wittgenstein: Understanding and Meaning*, pp. 531 ff.

[10] He thought that Freud was an important thinker, that he had created not a new science of the mind but a new mythology of the mind. His pseudo-explanations are, Wittgenstein held, brilliant and dangerous. Wittgenstein's critical attitude does not affect the analogy in question, nor do the criticisms of psychoanalysis apply to Wittgenstein's own philosophical techniques.

were, a repressed bit of nonsense into explicit nonsense.[11] In a discussion with Waismann in 1931, Wittgenstein observed:

> As long as there is a possibility of having different opinions and disputing about a question, this indicates that things have not yet been expressed clearly enough. Once a perfectly clear formulation—ultimate clarity—has been reached, there can be no second thoughts or reluctance any more, for these always arise from the feeling that something has now been asserted, and I do not yet know whether I should admit it or not. If, however, you make the grammar clear to yourself, if you proceed by very short steps in such a way that every single step becomes perfectly obvious and natural, no dispute whatsoever can arise. Controversy always arises through leaving out or failing to state clearly certain steps, so that the impression is given that a claim has been made that could be disputed. I once wrote, 'The only correct method of doing philosophy consists in not saying anything and leaving it to another person to make a claim.'[12] That is the method I now adhere to. What the other person is not able to do is to arrange the rules [for the use of expressions] step by step and in the right order so that all questions are solved automatically. (*WWK*, p. 183 f.)

The affinity with the psychotherapist is evident.[13] The task of the philosopher is not to lay down rules of language (*PI*, §124), but to elicit the rules from the minds of the bewildered: 'I simply draw the other person's attention to what he is really doing and refrain from any assertions' (*WWK*, p. 186). The exact anatomy of error in the individual mind is of crucial importance, and its recognition *as* correct by the 'patient' is the first step towards realization that the bounds of sense are being traversed. If one discovers through questioning that someone is using different and conflicting rules for one and the same word (e.g. 'pleasure' in the mouth of the psychological hedonist), then one brings him to see a source of confusion and of illusion. If mathematicians or mathematical-logicians produce a contradiction (as Russell found in Frege's system) it is *not* the task of philosophy to resolve it by means of mathematical or logico-mathematical discoveries. It is rather to make clear, to give us a perspicuous representation of, the *route* to that contradiction. It must make *surveyable* the entanglement of rules that led to it (*PI*, §125). Philosopher and therapist alike aim to

---

[11] Cf. Kenny, 'Wittgenstein on the Nature of Philosophy', p. 40.
[12] An allusion to *TLP*, 6.53.
[13] But the deep differences should not be overlooked either. Psychoanalytic technique rests on an allegedly empirical *theory* of the workings of the mind. Wittgenstein's philosophical techniques do not rest on a *theory* of anything.

give the afflicted *insight* into their own understanding and misunderstanding.

3. *Philosophy, Science, and Description*

It will be remembered that in his earliest *credo* about philosophy, in the 'Notes on Logic', Wittgenstein declared that philosophy was purely descriptive; unlike the natural sciences to which Russell had compared it, it contained no deductions. It was conceived to be the description of logical form. According to the *Tractatus*, philosophy, as practised in the book, had the *de facto* status of a description of the essence of the world, thought, and language, but a *de jure* status of nonsense. The future philosophy, the groundwork of which is laid by the *Tractatus*, was to be purely elucidatory. The only strictly correct method in philosophy is to say nothing except what can be said, i.e. empirical, non-philosophical propositions, and, whenever someone tries to say something metaphysical, to demonstrate to him, by means of analysis, that he has failed to give a meaning to certain signs in his propositions (*TLP*, 6.53). The contention that philosophy is purely descriptive pervades Wittgenstein's later work (e.g. *PG*, §30; *BB*, pp. 18, 125; *PI*, §124, etc.). Philosophy is a description of the workings of language (*PI*, §109). It solves certain non-empirical problems by a quiet weighing of linguistic facts (*Z*, §447). Philosophy is a conceptual investigation (*Z*, §458), it describes our conceptual structures from within. It shows how in philosophy, or in psychology or mathematics, we go wrong by taking our concepts wrong—it does so by turning our attention towards the employment of words (*Z*, §463).

The descriptive status of philosophy was originally contrasted by Wittgenstein with the theoretical status of the sciences. Despite the shift in what was meant by 'philosophy is purely descriptive' the contrast remained firm and the antagonism to the Russellian comparison of philosophy to science was maintained. Scientific investigations are irrelevant to philosophy. The discovery of new facts, the invention of new theories, can contribute nothing to the solution or dissolution of the non-empirical problems of philosophy. 'It was true to say', Wittgenstein remarks, referring to the *Tractatus*, 4.111 'that our considerations could not be scientific ones. It was not of any possible interest to us to find out empirically "that, contrary to our preconceived ideas, it is possible to think such-and-such"—whatever that may mean' (*PI*, §109).

The differences between scientific and philosophical investigations are fundamental. Science constructs *theories* that enable the prediction of events and the *explanation* of natural phenomena by reference to the theories. Frequently the construction of such theories involves *idealization*, as in mechanics. The scientific theories we construct are *testable* in experience, falsifiable or confirmable. A succession of scientific hypotheses may be rejected as erroneous, yet nevertheless be conceived to be successive *approximations* to the truth. The sciences make new *discoveries*, and add to human knowledge about the world both by revealing new objects and properties hitherto unknown and by providing new explanations of hitherto inexplicable phenomena. In this sense science is progressive; it builds 'ever larger and more complicated structures . . . adds one construction to another, moving on and up, as it were, from one stage to the next . . .'.[14]

Advances in science cannot *in principle* resolve philosophical problems, for the sciences either employ, and hence presuppose an understanding of, the very concepts that give rise to philosophical perplexity; or they employ different concepts in which case they bypass what puzzles us (and even cheat us out of our puzzlement) and, in some cases, generate fresh conceptual questions. Likewise no discoveries in mathematics can advance philosophical solutions in the philosophy of mathematics (*PI*, §124). That Gödel's theorem can appear as identifying *the* deep philosophical flaw in the logicist programme for mathematics is merely a measure of the confusion of philosophers and mathematicians about the status of mathematics and mathematical proof, just as, for example, the view that relativity theory provides a decisive *empirical* answer to the controversy between Leibnizians and Newtonians over the substantiality of space and time merely reveals the depth of the misunderstandings involved in an essentially conceptual dispute. Such innovations nevertheless have a great impact upon philosophy, not for the solution of old philosophical problems, but rather as alterations in our form of representation, presenting novel problems calling out for a proper surview. Natural science may indeed investigate the causes of the formation of concepts, but the conceptual investigations of the philosopher are not scientific. It is the task of the psychologist, not the philosopher, to study such causal connections (*PI*, p. 193). Problems in the philosophy of mind

---

[14] Wittgenstein, Preface to *Philosophical Remarks*, in which he thus characterizes the spirit of modern western civilization. In *Culture and Value* (p. 7) an earlier draft of the preface observes that progress is the characteristic *form* of our civilization, and within it clarity is a means subservient to building ever more complicated structures.

concerning, e.g. thought, are not scientific. The oddity about thought which, as we have seen led Wittgenstein in the *Tractatus* tacitly to attribute to it so many miraculous hidden operations, does not stem from lack of causal knowledge. The apparent strangeness of mentality stems from lack of a proper surview of mental concepts. The construction of models of the mind, or 'black boxes' in psychological theory can contribute nothing to the solution of philosophical problems (*BB*, pp. 5 f.). Philosophy is not on a level with natural science, the philosopher is not a citizen of any community of ideas (*Z*, §455).

By contrast with the stratified structure of a theoretical science, Wittgenstein continued to think, philosophy is flat. It is, of course, no part of this claim that there are no consequences within philosophical therapeutics; it may well be claimed that the argument against the possibility of a private language shows any form of idealism to be altogether misguided. But there is no theory, in the scientific sense, in philosophy, nor is there any idealization analogous to that which occurs in physics (*PG*, §36). Philosophy explains nothing (*PG*, §30; *BB*, p. 125; *PI*, §109); it only describes. The notion of explanation at work here is that of deductive-nomological explanation characteristic of the advanced sciences. In a somewhat different way, however, it could be said that philosophy explains, for it is part of Wittgenstein's therapy for philosophical illusion that we be brought to our senses by examining intermediate cases in order that we grasp connections. Revealing conceptual connections, which were not hitherto articulated in a perspicuous surview even though they are an integral part of our linguistic practice, is as legitimate a sense of 'explain' as any. Moreover, not only does Wittgenstein explain, in this loose sense, in order to rid us of illusion. He also explains, in great detail and profundity, the multifarious sources and processes which generate philosophical illusion. Since there are no hypotheses to be confirmed or falsified, no new information is needed. We are concerned with examining the concepts we have, not those we do not have.

The two aspects of the claim that philosophy is purely descriptive, namely its concern with describing linguistic use, and its lack of a stratified structure of a theory, meet in the claim that everything relevant to a philosophical problem lies open to view (*BB*, p. 6). That there is something new to find out is the hallmark of a misguided theory-perverted philosophy. There is nothing new to find in philosophy (*WWK*, pp. 182–3). New, hitherto unknown information is pertinent for science and its methods, but not for philosophy. What is needed in philosophy is simply a rearrangment yielding a surview of what we already know (*PI*, §109; M, p. 323). If anything is hidden, e.g. psychological facts about thought and perception, it is of concern to the scientists, but irrelevant for us, for it can, by token of its concealment, play no part in our rule-governed employment of concepts (*PI*, §153). The psychological mechanisms of belief cannot solve any of the philosophical problems concerning belief (*PG*, §63), for these unknown mechanisms cannot be part of the criteria which justify the claim that *A* believes that *p* and hence constitute part of its sense. The nature of our concepts lies open to view in our linguistic practice. What cannot be seen there cannot be an aspect of the concepts. Meanings are not assigned to words by anything but human will and convention; a word has the meaning we have given it (*BB*, p. 28), and we cannot milk more out of the word than we put into it. Thus a second juncture-point of the dual aspects of the descriptive status of philosophy is Wittgenstein's trenchant opposition to logical analysts, whether atomistic like Russell (and the *Tractatus* programme for future philosophy), or non-atomistic, like Moore. There can be no 'scientific investigation' into what a word *really* means, independently of the meaning given it by the practice of a normal speaker (*BB*, p. 28) and manifest in his use of the word and in the explanations he gives of what he means by it. The idea, which Moore was inclined to adopt, that logical analysis explains to people what they mean when they say something, and whether, indeed, they mean anything at all, is an infernal notion (*WWK*, pp. 129 f.). We do not wait upon philosophy to discover whether our ordinary sentences have any meaning. Such confusion rests upon a misguided analogy between philosophical analysis and chemical or physical analysis, and a deep-rooted misunderstanding of the nature of meaning. Meanings are erroneously conceived as the cash-value of words, like money and the cow one can buy with it; the relation is correctly viewed as analogous to that of money and its use (*PI*, §120).

A corollary of these contrasts between science and philosophy is that in the sense in which there is progress in science, there is and can be none in philosophy. If successive error in science can sometimes be viewed as successive approximations to the truth, successive philosophical accounts of conceptual structures cannot. For there is no approximation to sense via *nonsense*, and 'incorrect' philosophical accounts are not *false* but *nonsensical*. Science establishes theories and explanations of certain phenomena and builds upon these, moving onwards to fresh phenomena and the construction of new theories. But it is not so in philosophy:

> You always hear people say that philosophy makes no progress and that the same philosophical problems which were already preoccupying the Greeks are still troubling us today. But people who say that do not understand the reason why it has to be so. The reason is that our language has remained the same and always introduces us to the same questions. As long as there is a verb 'be' which seems to work like 'eat' and 'drink', as long as there are adjectives like 'identical', 'true', 'false', 'possible'; as long as people speak of the passage of time and of the extent of space, and so on; as long as this happens people will always run up against the same teasing difficulties and will stare at something which no explanation seems able to remove . . . I read '. . . philosophers are no nearer to the meaning of "reality" than Plato got . . .' What an extraordinary thing! How remarkable that Plato could get so far! Or that we have not been able to get any further! Was it because Plato was *so* clever?[15]

Is there any sense in which there can be progress in philosophy? Certainly a clearer grasp of the very nature of philosophy can be achieved. In that sense, I should contend, Wittgenstein advanced philosophy beyond measure. Similarly, a surview of segments of our language can be given. Such a perspicuous representation may illuminate for a given generation and put philosophical qualms to rest. But, as knowledge advances and our culture changes, different paradigms capture our imagination (Darwinism, Marxism, Freudian psychology, mathematical logic, computer science, and artificial intelligence all breed new mythologies). These distort our understanding in new ways. Hence each generation is likely to view numerous philosophical problems from at least a slightly different perspective, captured within the gravitational field of a different source of illusions. And to that extent philosophy will have to go over the ground afresh. Each generation is a special case for treatment. In this sense the task of philosophy, like that of a therapist of the ills of the human mind, is never over (Z §447).

Considerable problems still remain. If one aspect of the doctrine that philosophy is purely descriptive is that philosophy describes our use of language, that it simply tabulates and expresses clearly the rules we have been using (*WWK*, p. 184), then does this not make philosophy an empirical science, and truth in philosophy a matter

[15] Quoted in Kenny, 'Wittgenstein on the Nature of Philosophy', p. 58 from 'The Big Typescript', p. 424.

requiring the final arbitration of brute fact? Does it not require philosophers to emerge from their archairs and indulge in lexicography? May not philosophy be riddled with incorrectly tabulated rules of linguistic use? The questions rest on a misunderstanding. Philosophical problems are conceptual, not empirical. Their answers do not lie in the production of empirical assertions about linguistic use, or in the production of special 'philosophical propositions'. Or, in so far as they do, the 'philosophical propositions' are indisputable and undisguised grammatical truisms. Philosophy is an activity whose primary product is the disappearance of philosophical problems. An essential part of the activity is indeed the eliciting and arrangement of obvious rules of use. But, as we shall see, this does not put philosophy in competition with descriptive grammar. For the linguistic investigation receives its purpose from conceptual problems of philosophy, not from empirical problems in linguistics (*PI*, §109). To be sure, the descriptions are of the rules we actually employ as standards for the correct use of expressions, but their aptness is guaranteed by the fact that they are elicited from the person whose bewilderment is in question. Like the psychoanalyst, all the philosopher does is make the patient aware of what he is doing (*WWK*, p. 186). Of course, the philosophical interest of the problem is in general going to depend upon common linguistic practices constituting a shared form of representation. If someone claims that a combination of words has perfectly good sense for him, while we can discern none, we can only assume that he uses language differently from us, or else that he is talking thoughtlessly (*PR*, §7). If the former is the case then if we wish to carry on we must proceed to elicit his novel use. This process requires skill which needs to be exercised in dialogue, skill in asking the right questions at the right time in order to illuminate the conceptual connections embodied in our linguistic practices. The end-product of the skilful philosophical debate is, according to Wittgenstein, the disappearance of a philosophical problem and the attaining of a surview and hence of that kind of understanding characteristic of philosophy.

4. *Philosophy and Ordinary Language*

In the *Tractatus* Wittgenstein had argued that ordinary language 'is in order as it is'. In the *Investigations* §98 he quotes the *Tractatus* with approval, and then proceeds to criticize the conception in the *Tractatus* of the perfect logical order that is to be found underlying ordinary language. The agreement between the two books over the propriety of ordinary language is in a sense superficial. For the perfect logical order which the *Tractatus* found in ordinary language it found not in the appearances of language but despite them. The perfect order was the hidden essence of language which is only revealed by analysis. The preconceptions of the *Tractatus* forced an ideal upon language. Labouring under the illusion that this ideal must be found in language, the *Tractatus* had sublimed logic, twisted its central concepts of sentence, word, and meaning out of all recognition in order to meet the requirements of a prejudice.

To be sure, ordinary language is in good order. But the goodness of its order lies open to view. We are not striving after an ideal language which a philosophical mythology persuades us lies within ordinary language. We seek a surview over ordinary language. For what should such an ideal language express? The same as that which we express in ordinary language? Then logic must investigate ordinary language and not something else (*PR*, §3; *PI*, §120). For were there something else how should we come to know what it is? Logical analysis is analysis of sentences as they are. To be sure some philosophical misunderstandings can be removed by substituting one form of an expression for another (*PI*, §90). Russell's technique of eliminating definite descriptions is effective in dispelling Meinongian worries. Such a process has the appearance of taking things apart and hence was, with some justice, thought of as analysis. But this led to the illusion that there is a form of language consisting of completely analysed expressions, and thus an ideal of analysed language. Since the process of analysis appeared to be a process of eliminating misunderstandings by making expressions more exact, the success of Russellian techniques led to a further illusion of an ideally exact language. And these ideals were sought not in something we all know which is surveyable by a rearrangement, but in unknown and hidden recesses.

The philosophy of logic talks of sentences and words in a perfectly ordinary sense. One must, in respect of what we understand by 'word' or 'sentence', take the standpoint of normal common sense, Wittgenstein now argued (*PR*, §18), and it is precisely here that the change of conception lies. 'Language', 'word', 'sentence', are not, as the *Tractatus* intimated, super-concepts between which a super-order holds, containing the quintessence of language. They are ordinary words having mundane uses like any other words (*PI*, §108). We are talking in logic of the spatio-temporal phenomenon of language, not of a non-spatial atemporal *Unding*. Our talk of language and its elements is analogous to talking of chess pieces when explaining the rules of chess, and we must avoid the temptation to sublime language into ideal essences. We would not treat the king in chess as an abstract essence, and we should not think of propositions as ideal essences, classes of sentences with equivalent meanings (*PG*, §77; *PI*, §108). The scruples of the author of the *Tractatus*, Wittgenstein claimed, are themselves misunderstandings. Analysis of the Russellian type is not illegitimate as long as it does not bewitch us; so too, constructing ideal languages is not illegitimate. For certain purposes it may serve well (*WWK*, pp. 45 ff.). But four points must be borne in mind: first, we *construct* them; secondly, such languages are not *improvements* over ordinary language designed to replace it, but are relatively handicapped; thirdly, their primary role in philosophy is to function as *objects of comparison* to illuminate what is present in ordinary language; finally, artificial calculi have enormously *misled* philosophers.

The function-theoretic structure of the predicate calculus is not *closer to reality* than the subject–predicate structure of syllogistic. It is just different. And in many respects it is even more misleading, for it fosters the illusion that we have at last penetrated to the real logical form of things, or of thought, or of language. But, like the subject/predicate form, so too the function-theoretic calculi represent vastly diverse things in the same logico-grammatical forms. 'Socrates is a man', 'Socrates is mortal', 'Socrates is dead', 'Socrates is virtuous' are all cast in the same form, as are such propositions as 'Red is a colour', 'Two is even', 'Pleasure is desirable', 'I am 6 foot tall', 'I am tired', 'I understand'. An opaque cloak of function/argument structure is cast over expressions of fundamentally diverse logical character and very different uses. There can be no better seed bed for the growth of philosophical illusions.

Wittgenstein clarified this with a powerful and illuminating simile. Imagine that we have to project differently shaped figures from one plane on to another. We could fix a method of projection, e.g. orthogonal, and map the figures from one plane on to the other. We could readily make inferences from the shape of a figure on plane 2 to the shape of the corresponding figure on plane 1. But suppose that we were to decide that *all* the figures on plane 2 should be circles. So different figures on plane 1 will be mapped on to circles on plane 2 in accord with *different* methods of projection. Here, the fact that a figure on plane 2 is a circle tells one nothing about its corresponding figure on plane 1—its circularity is merely a *norm of projection*. Similarly, the subject/predicate form of syllogistic, *and* Frege's function/argument (concept and object) form are norms of representation that serve as a projection of countless *different* logical forms, fundamentally distinct uses of expressions (*PG*, pp. 204 f.). And, when doing philosophy, we are taken in by the common norm of projection, the form, and are oblivious to what is really significant, the different methods of projection, the different uses of expressions. In the *Lectures on Aesthetics* (p. 2), Wittgenstein remarked, 'If I had to say what is the main mistake made by philosophers of the present generation, including Moore, I would say that when language is looked at, what is looked at is a form of words and not the use made of the form of words'. Things have not changed in this respect in the intervening years.

Philosophy, Wittgenstein wrote in a much misunderstood remark, leaves everything as it is (*PI*, §124). This is a gloss upon the claim that philosophy may not interfere with the actual use of language. It can only describe that use and clarify it in order to resolve philosophical questions. But it cannot 'vindicate' the use of language by giving it 'foundations' any more than it can give mathematics foundations. This prohibition on 'interference' does not mean that Wittgenstein was placing an arbitrary restriction on the introduction of new expressions in philosophy. Doubtless he would have resisted, for more reasons than one, the proliferation of jargon, but he did introduce such terms as 'language-games', 'family-resemblance concepts', 'private language'. Outside philosophy he had no objection in principle to stipulating new uses of expressions, 'such a reform for practical purposes, an improvement in our terminology designed to prevent misunderstandings in practice is perfectly possible' (*PI*, §132). But this is not the case with philosophy, since it is not concerned with misunderstandings that occur *in practice*, but with misunderstandings that occur when 'language is idling'. These reflect not the inappropriateness, let alone the incorrectness of ordinary language as it is, but our lack of a surview of it. And these philosophical confusions that occur in our reflections seep into our science and our thought about ourselves and the world.

Nor was Wittgenstein suggesting, in this remark, that philosophy is impotent, that it has no effect on anything, that it is a mere idle game with words. Far from it. Just because of the back-seepage of philosophical confusion, philosophical investigation is of very great importance and may have far-reaching effects. It is true that philosophy may not interfere with mathematics proper if that means providing solutions to mathematical questions. But it is the task of philosophy to examine critically the prose with which mathematicians surround their mathematics, the interpretations they put upon their 'discoveries'. And that will prune mathematics: 'Philosophical clarity will have the same effect on the growth of mathematics as sunlight has on the growth of potato shoots. (In a dark cellar they grow yards long.)' (*PG*, p. 381). Wittgenstein had no objection to Cantor's new calculus with transfinite cardinals, only to Cantor's interpretation of his invention; for example, to his notion that he had discovered a new and wonderful domain of mathematical entities. In response to Hilbert's remark that no one is going to turn us out of the paradise Cantor has created, Wittgenstein said that he would not dream of trying to drive anyone out of this paradise. He would try to do something different: namely to show that it is not a paradise, but a mirage in a waterless desert. Then one will leave of one's own accord.[16]

Similar considerations apply to the relevance of Wittgenstein's reflections in philosophical psychology for empirical psychology.

> The confusion and barrenness of psychology is not to be explained by calling it a 'young science': its state is not comparable with that of physics, for instance, in its beginnings. (Rather with that of certain branches of mathematics. Set theory.) For in psychology there are experimental methods and *conceptual confusion*. (As in the other case conceptual confusion and methods of proof.) (*PI*, p. 232)

When experimental psychologists 'explain' the fact that it takes longer to recognize pictures of a 3-dimensional object at certain orientations than at others by reference to the generation of mental images which are (they conjecture) rotated at constant angular velocity in mental space, they display the depths of their confusions. What is needed is not more experiments, but conceptual clarification. To imagine a rotating object is not to rotate an imaginary object, and to imagine an object moving at constant velocity is not to move an imagined object at constant velocity. It is, of course, not the task of philosophy to adjudicate the correctness of psychological experiments. But it is its task, here as in the philosophy of mathematics, to audit the account books of *sense*.

5. *The Phenomenology and Sources of Philosophical Illusion*

No philosopher has paid greater attention or displayed greater

[16] See R. Rhees, *Discussions of Wittgenstein* (Routledge & Kegan Paul, London, 1970), p. 46, and *LFM*, p. 103.

sensitivity to the phenomenology of language than Wittgenstein. The way in which we 'feel at home' in a language, the aura and 'soul' of words is not merely of great intrinsic interest, but of considerable philosophical relevance inasmuch as it presents great pitfalls to the understanding bereft of the correct logical point of view. Wittgenstein was equally fascinated by the phenomenology of philosophical illusion itself, which is in part a product of the phenomenology of language use. 'To get clear about philosophical problems', he wrote (*BB*, p. 66), 'it is useful to become conscious of the apparently unimportant details of the particular situation in which we are inclined to make a certain metaphysical assertion.' This injunction holds more broadly than for metaphysical errors alone. Wittgenstein gave an array of examples, most of which are culled from his own youthful philosophical explorations. The solipsist's doctrine that 'Only *this* is really seen' will be examined in detail in Chapter VIII. The temptation to make the remark embodying what Russell called 'solipsism of the moment' arises, Wittgenstein suggested, when we stare at unchanging surroundings. We are considerably less tempted by it when we look around while walking (*BB*, p. 66). It is no coincidence that Wittgenstein's suggestion in the 1916 notebook that it is possible to take the bare present image as the true world among shadows follows a discussion of the visual contemplation of a stove as a world (*NB*, p. 83). A similar phenomenon accompanies the illusion, to which Frege among others succumbed,[17] that there is some sense in which colours are essentially private to each perceiver. To the representative idealist, what initially appears (and in fact is) a commonly accessible element in a public world becomes by some strange trick of the understanding a subjective impression which we detach from the world like a membrane (*PI*, §276). When one assures oneself that one knows how green looks to oneself then one turns one's attention upon something that appears to belong to oneself alone. One, as it were, immerses oneself in a colour impression; and it is easier to produce this aberrant state of mind when one is looking at a bright colour or impressive colour scheme. Related to this is a further deep and pervasive mistake especially pertinent to the private language argument which will be examined in Chapter IX. In the case of one's own sensations, for example, one can tell another what sensation one has without *identifying* that sensation by means of a

---

[17] Frege, *Foundations of Arithmetic*, pp. 36-7; and his review of Husserl's *Philosphie der Arithmetik*, repr. in *Translations from the Philosophical Writings of Gottlob Frege*, ed. P. Geach and M. Black, p. 79.

criterion of identity. It is an easy and natural illusion to take one's confrontation with the sensation itself to provide a criterion of identity. When one contemplates one's own subjective experience the experience itself seems to play a part in one's thought. But what is needed here is a concept and a surview of its use, not an 'object'. In these three kinds of delusion, staring or attending play a prominent role as they do in the confusion of sample and description. It is of course no part of Wittgenstein's claim that all idealists, phenomenalists, or solipsists adopted their doctrines because of such experiences. Nevertheless the experiences are revealing, if only because they show how language can 'go on holiday'.

Wittgenstein gave many examples of the frame of mind of the philosopher transfixed by his own forms of representation. Dissatisfaction with grammar, or, more probably, exasperation at one's inability to achieve a surview of it, often expresses itself in a feeling of the inadequacy of language. One is strongly inclined to feel, as William James did, that one knows, experiences, grasps, the inner complexity and multiplicity of the world and the stream of experiences, but that it is inexpressible in ordinary language. The language we have is too crude to describe the richness and subtlety of experience (*PI*, §436 and §610). One may then hanker after an ideal language, ideally precise and rich. One's longings, however, are a displacement of a desire for an absurdity. The richness one thinks one finds in experience and which one believes cannot be discursively conveyed to another is due merely to the non-transferability of experience, not to the impotence of thought. And the 'non-transferability of experience' is not a matter of fact concerning transportation of mental items, but a matter of grammar concerning what it makes sense to say. The disquietude of philosophical obsession is described by Wittgenstein in connection with the *Tractatus*. Held captive by a picture, a preconception of form, a philosopher thinks that he has grasped an essence. Faced with contradictions he feels both that 'this isn't how it is' and also 'this is how it has to be' (*PI*, §112). So indeed had Wittgenstein himself responded as he struggled to force language and thought into the Procrustean bed he had made for it (*NB*, p. 17). The conflict and dilemma are symptoms of an inadequate understanding of conceptual relations.

The *Tractatus* had produced a mythology of symbolism and psychology. Its errors, however, were neither trivial nor unimportant. Once the illusory impressiveness and uniqueness of language as a mirror of the structure of reality is dispelled, the impressiveness retreats to the illusions themselves (*PI*, §110). The author of the *Tractatus* laboured to reveal that the structure of the world cannot be described but only shown. The author of the *Investigations* bent his efforts to reveal how what seemed to show itself was an optical illusion.

Wittgenstein gave no principles of classification for sources of error in philosophy. Perhaps it is not possible to do so with any fruitfulness; certainly the spirit of Kant's transcendental dialectic and doctrine of method were quite alien to Wittgenstein. Hence the eight-fold classification which follows is merely meant to bring together a representative sample of Wittgenstein's diagnoses, and has no pretensions to completeness or exclusiveness. Wittgenstein located the roots of illusion in (1) analogies in the surface grammar of language, (2) projecting the features of one language-game on to another, (3) the phenomenology of the use of language, (4) pictures or archetypes embedded in language, (5) the model of presentation and solution of problems in the natural sciences, (6) natural cravings and dispositions of reason, (7) projecting grammar on to reality, (8) philosophical mythologies.

(1) Wittgenstein distinguished between the surface grammar and the depth grammar of the use of expressions (*PI*, §664). Although the metaphor is more apt for the *Tractatus* account of language, it is readily applicable to the later conception of language too. The surface grammar of a word is the way it is used in the construction of the sentence, that part of its use that can be taken in by the ear. The surface grammar frequently leads us to misunderstand the use of words. The clothing of our language, Wittgenstein remarked in a phrase reminiscent of the *Tractatus* (*TLP*, 4.002), makes everything look alike. Consequently we are unconscious of the great diversity of language (*PI*, p. 224). The thought is indeed a similar one, but the therapy lies not in analysis that will lay bare the true form (the logical form) of problematic expressions, which is hidden beneath the clothing of our language, but in careful plotting of use and circumstances justifying the use of expressions in order to distinguish what at first glance looked similar. Superficially 'thinking', 'writing', and 'speaking', 'thought', 'script', and 'speech' appear grammatically similar. This is one of the many reasons why we tend to ascribe to thought some of the features of speech and script, e.g. a locality (*BB*, p. 7). Writing and speaking are activities performed by means of hand and larynx; we therefore conceive of thinking as an activity of the mind, forgetting that

the agency of the mind, as its substantiality, is wholly different from that of the hand. Since writing produces inscriptions and speaking produces phonemes, we readily conclude that thoughts are analogous products of thinking, only in an ethereal medium. A similar pervasive source of confusion lies in our hankering for substances. Our concept of a substantive expression is, as its name suggests, constructed on the paradigm of a name of a substance. Consequently it is a natural inclination in us to look for a substance for every substantive. We exacerbate this inclination when we couch our philosophical, conceptual questions in the form of questions about entities, e.g. 'What is length? What is meaning? What is number?' instead of 'What is an explanation of meaning? How are lengths measured? How are numerical expressions used?' Consequently we assume Platonistically the existence of special objects to correspond to substantival expressions for which we can find no ordinary objects. We talk of numbers as ideal objects, obscuring the fact that all that can coherently be meant thereby is that the use of numerical expressions is in certain respects similar to that of signs that stand for objects even though numerals do *not* (*RFM*, pp. 262 f.). Subsequently we construct a metaphysics out of our fairy-tale.

(2) A second great source of confusion (which could be seen as a special case of the first) is our tendency to project the features of one language-game or propositional-system (*Satzsysteme*) on to another. For we find that a *fragment* of one language-game is analogous to a *fragment* of another. Nevertheless the two are not homologous, and our conception is misguided. We say, for example, that it is quite certain that it will rain today, that it is quite certain that $25^2 = 625$, and also that it is quite certain that I have a toothache. We take it for granted that these certainties are, if distinct at all, distinct only in degree (proven mathematical truths are, we think, of the very highest degree of certainty). But the certainty of empirical propositions refutes doubt, it does not exclude it as unintelligible. The certainty of a mathematical proposition is of a different *kind*, not of a different *degree*. It *excludes* doubt. And the 'certainty' of first-person psychological utterances is different again. Similarly, we talk of believing that it will rain tomorrow, that $\aleph_1 > \aleph_0$, that promises ought to be kept, and that the world has existed for a very long time. Believing, in each case, is, we think, the same 'propositional attitude'. It just happens to be directed at different 'objects'. We fail to see that to *believe* a mathematical proposition is radically unlike believing an empirical one (it is more

akin to believing that the chess king is the piece that is checked). We know what it is to believe that it will rain tomorrow and also what it is to believe that it will not rain tomorrow. What is it to believe that a triangle has five sides, that $1086 < 3$ or that $12 \times 12 = 5$? We talk of its being true that horses are larger than donkeys, that red is darker than white, that 25 is greater than 20, that it is true that either p or not-p, and so on. But we do not pause to reflect on the differences in what it *means* to say that it is true that . . . *Proposition* is a family resemblance concept and there are prodigious differences between propositions of different kinds, differences reflected in what it means to say that such and such is true. The truth of a proposition in mathematics is no more akin to the truth of an empirical proposition than a chess queen is akin to a queen.

(3) The perennial temptation to explain the notion of meaning something by an expression in terms of mental acts and processes accompanying overt utterances has its roots, in part at least, in certain phenomenological features of speaking, reading, writing, and hearing. Thus, for example, we feel at home with our native language. Its 'atmosphere' is familiar to us, the sound of a word in speech, its appearance in writing are 'comfortable'. When confronted by gross spelling mistakes, mispronunciations, or nonsense writings such as '&§8≠ §≠?+%', the powerful feeling of abnormality and alienation leads us to assume that a positive feeling of familiarity makes a special contribution to a hypostatized inner process allegedly necessary to reading or hearing with understanding. Similarly we tend to project grammatical differences on to the hypothetical mechanisms of the mind, and to try to account for them in terms of mental acts. In the sentence 'Mr. Scot is not a Scot' (*PI*, p. 176; see for comparison *TLP*, 3.323) the first occurrence of 'Scot' is a proper name, the second is a common name. We can readily induce a feeling that the difference between the identical tokens is attributable to a special mental contribution. For try to mean the first occurrence as a common name, and the second as a proper name! One blinks with effort as one tries to parade the meanings before one's mind thus, and the sense seems to disintegrate. Hence one assumes that the sentence ordinarily means what it does because one parades the meanings readily in the familiar order. This is misguided. None of this charade affects the sense of what one says, the feeling of comfortable familiarity is not a parade of meanings in the mind. It may be true that words, or some words, carry with them a special psychological 'corona'. Philosophers have indeed

tried to account for the meanings of logical connectives in terms of feelings, e.g. of hesitation (for disjunction) or denial (for negation), or if-feelings (for implication). But the identity of the concept is independent of the feelings associated with its employment, the feeling of hesitation is quite independent of disjunction (what feelings accompany 'not both not p and not q'?) and the so-called if-feeling is not a feeling that accompanies the word 'if' and that could be identified as the if-feeling independently of the word (*PI*, pp. 181–3). Wittgenstein was not trying to disparage the experiences we associate with language. In the first place, the 'soul' of language which we experience is intimately connected with our cultural history and essential to the power of language in metaphor and poetry, evocation and association. In the second place, our expressiveness in our use of language is closely related to our different experiences of meaning, although the differences of meaning are not a function of either experiences or expressiveness (*PI*, pp. 175, 214). Most important of all, our obscure conception of experiencing the meaning of a word is a reflection of an absolutely crucial capacity of language-users, namely sensitivity to aspects of the meanings of words (*PI*, p. 214). For without the ability to see one word as holding within it its range of linguistic potentialities, to see it unthinkingly in one context as obviously fulfilling one function, and in another context as obviously fulfilling another, we could not operate with our language as we do.

(4) One of the many different senses given by Wittgenstein to the expression 'picture' is analogous to Bentham's conception of an archetype[18] embedded in language. Bentham argued that our concepts of fictitious entities have associated with them archetypal images drawn from operations of objects in the physical world and applied analogically in the context of the fictitious entity. He suggested that archetypes can be a source both of confusion and illumination. They confuse when they are taken literally,[19] illuminate when the analogy between the archetypal image and the sense of the expression of which it is an archetype is revealed. Wittgenstein argued similarly that our language contains vivid pictures which continually mislead us in

[18] Bentham, *Works*, ed. J. Bowring (Tait, Edinburgh, 1843), viii. 246, 'Essay on Logic', Ch. VII, section 7.
[19] An example of such confusion can be found in the writings of the Scandinavian legal realists, e.g. A. Hägerström or K. Olivecrona, who took the archetype of obligation literally instead of examining its use, and thought that by pointing out that obligations are not occult chains or weights they were dispelling metaphysical illusions rather than knocking down straw men.

philosophy. Certain forms of expression, metaphors, and similes absorbed into our language beguile us, forcing us to think that the facts must conform to the pictures thus embedded in language. The correctness of such pictures qua pictures, is not in dispute; it is rather their application which is. For normally the application is given with the picture (*PI*, §§423–5). But in the philosophically most interesting and baffling cases this is not so. A picture forces itself upon one, but the sense of the relevant expression is obscured. The application, and thus the nature of the conceptual connections determining the sense of the expression, is not given by the picture, and is not easy to survey. Both mathematics and the natural sciences abound in such pictures, for clearly the notion of a *ring* of carbon atoms (*PI*, §422), and the Law of Excluded Middle in set theory (*PI*, §426) are bound up with pictures whose application is extremely unclear. Wittgenstein's favourite examples are drawn from philosophy of mind and psychological language. We hanker to know what is going on in someone's head; we reveal to others what is going on inside us, which we ourselves 'know by introspection'. These pictures seem to point to a particular use, and thus they take us in. The false appearance must be resisted, for although the picture may embody fruitful or essential analogies, may show how our imagination presents a given concept (*OC*, §90), it will mislead us unless we grasp the use of the expression by a surview of its grammar. When we want to know what is going on in someone's head we are effectively asking to know what he is thinking. But the picture of the 'inner' and 'outer' which is embedded in our language obscures the use of psychological language and provides a rich source of illusion. We readily come to think that true knowledge of another's mind could only come about by looking into his head, or better, seeing with his eyes. To avoid this, the picture of 'inner' and 'outer' and the metaphor of revealing what is 'inside' must be clarified. Otherwise we will be prone to hypostatize an inner process from which we *read off* the inner (*NFL*, p. 280). So indeed we succumb when we allow the picture of thought as a process in our head to dominate our conception of the mental. We generate an illusion of an occult process in an enclosed space, we conceive of thinking as an activity of the mind as writing is an activity of the body, and we think of expressing an idea which is before our mind as a process of translation from one medium (of ideas) into another (of words). We thus succumb to pictures of the mental in a way in which we would not dream of doing for physical ones. We do not ask a person who 'has a word on the tip of his tongue' to open his mouth to let us see. But faced with the 'problem of other minds' philosophers have often thought that our claims about the mental states of others were uncertain because the minds of others are *stricto sensu* inaccessible to us. We are deluded by a picture because we lack a survey of the grammar of expressions associated with 'mind' and 'thinking'.

The aethereal and the occult are the analogues, in the natural dialectic of psychological concepts, of the abstract object hypostatized in the dialectic of logic and mathematics. No less typical is the craving to ground potentialities in existing states (*BB*, p. 117). We are strongly inclined to conceive of the ability of an object or machine to act in certain ways as being a peculiar state of the object or machine. Equally human abilities, e.g. to solve a mathematical problem, to enjoy music, etc., are readily conceived as states of mind, hypothetical mental mechanisms which will explain conscious mental or physical phenomena. Thus we speak of unconscious and subconscious mental states as parts of such an explanatory mind model, and find it difficult to resist the Lockean temptation to conceive of memory as a storehouse of ideas, or the Central State Materialist's lure to conceive of all mental phenomena as strange properties of the neural (*BB*, pp. 117 f.; *Z*, §§605–15). But our temptation to conceive of an ability as a state, and so to misconstrue our *concept* of an ability must be resisted.

(5) Russell's misconception of philosophy as sharing with science a general method was natural. The scientist's method of asking questions, not to mention his methods of solving them, have proved so fruitful in the past four centuries that it is altogether intelligible that we should entertain similar ambitions for philosophy and wish to set it upon the sure and certain path of a science. To succumb to the scientific method in philosophy is one of the sources of philosophical confusion. It is easy to think of logic as a 'kind of ultra-physics, the description of the "logical structure" of the world' (*RFM*, p. 40); easy but misguided. The assumption of a shared method of reduction led to the myths of logical atomism; the method of idealization merely serves to avert our attention from our task of achieving a survey of language as it is. The confusion of methods results in the obfuscation of the conceptual nature of philosophical problems, leading to that blurring of boundaries between empirical and grammatical issues characteristic of metaphysics (*BB*, p. 18).

(6) A further source of error lies in certain kinds of natural cravings of reason and intellectual drives which, if uncontrolled by criticsm, lead us into illusion. These have already been remarked upon in some

detail. Our metaphysical urge leads us to fruitless philosophical searches for the essence of things and, like Peer Gynt peeling the onion, we search behind the phenomenon of language for the hidden essence of what is essentially apparent although needing arrangement to yield a perspicuous representation. Wittgenstein quoted Goethe with approval: 'Don't look for anything behind the phenomena; they themselves are the theory.'[20] We generate further illusions by conferring a spurious legitimacy upon our use of words in metaphysics. Like Kant, Wittgenstein saw the illusions of metaphysics as the product of a deep-rooted need to thrust against the limits of language. Related to these tendencies is a craving for generality on the one hand and for clear-cut distinctions upon the other. Frege's determination of concepts by *Merkmale* is intellectually more satisfying than the imprecision and untidiness of family-resemblance relations, and the psychological logicians' account of concept-possession in terms of general abstract ideas gratifies our preference for states over potentialities in explanation. Finally, again analogously to Kant, Wittgenstein drew attention to what can be thought of both as a regulative principle of science, if not as an engrained feature of the understanding, namely to search always for the prior condition of every conditioning element we discover in our explanations of phenomena. But this principle distorts our judgement in philosophy. For one of the main difficulties in philosophy is knowing when to stop, recognizing as a solution what looks as if it is only a preliminary to one (*Z*, §314). We account for our true judgement by reference to the applications of rules. But rules are misinterpretable so we proceed to look for a rule to guide us in applying a rule, and do not rest satisfied until we think we have reached an unconditioned rule which cannot be misapplied, e.g. a mental ostensive definition. We confuse the fact that one *can* go on indefinitely supplying rules of interpretation and translation with the contention that one *must*. And then we search for a necessary terminus. Yet, in fact, explanation of concepts needs to go only so far as is necessary for mastery of the concept. It ends in good judgement, not in a rule that *cannot* be misinterpreted.[21]

---

[20] 'Man suche nichts hinter den Phänomen; sie selbst sind die Lehre', quoted in Wittgenstein, *Remarks on the Philosophy of Psychology*, Vol. 1, §889 (Blackwell, Oxford, 1980), from Goethe's *Maximen und Reflexionen*, ed. Max Hacker (Weimar, 1907), no. 575.

[21] An interesting comparison can be made here with Kant: 'If [logic] sought to give general instructions how we are to subsume under these rules, that is, to distinguish

(7) We tend to project grammar on to reality. This curious kind of displacement has various sources, including our inclination (manifest in the Augustinian picture of language) to conceive of all words as names and all sentences as descriptions. We naturally think of 'Nothing can be red and green all over' as a statement about reality, like 'No animal can run faster than 100 mph'. So too we think that '25 > 21' is a description of the nature of these numbers. We dimly apprehend that we have laid down no criteria for complexity of colours, so we think that colours are 'metaphysically' simple (whereas they are neither simple nor complex). The criterionless application of the first-person pronoun 'I' is projected on to reality to yield the doctrine of the Cartesian ego. Grammatical forms (of natural language and of artificial calculi alike) are conceived to be reflections of the nature of things (or even, in Russell's view, of logical 'objects'). Limitless techniques in grammar (of a natural language or of our number calculus) are systematically confused with 'infinite totalities'.

(8) Captivated by the mesmerizing model of science, misconceiving the nature of philosophical investigation, philosophers erect grandiose theories, realist theories, idealist or transcendental idealist ones, anti-realist theories or naturalist ones. Overwhelmed by the battle cries of rival 'isms', swept along by the banners and slogans, we fail to see that these pseudo-theories are quasi-mythological constructions that do not stand in need of either refutation or confirmation, but of dissolution. We are inclined to take sides, to try to vindicate realism or to lend our weight to the cause of anti-realism, thinking that we are siding with the Greeks or the Trojans in a decidable conflict. So we fail to see that we have merely sided with Zeus against Poseidon, or with Aphrodite against Hera. The correct philosophical task is not to side with one 'theory' against another, but to uncover the common misconceptions that breed these pseudo-theories, to demythologize.

6. *Systematic Philosophy*

The survey of Wittgenstein's later conception of philosophy in this

---

whether something does or does not come under them, that could only be by means of another rule. This in turn, for the very reason that it is a rule, again demands guidance from judgment. And thus it appears that, though understanding is capable of being instructed, and of being equipped with rules, judgment is a peculiar talent which can be practised only, and cannot be taught ... [an error in subsumption under rules] may be due to ... not having received through examples and actual practice, adequate training for this particular act of judgment ... Examples are thus the go-cart of judgment.'
Critique of Pure Reason, A 133–4, B 172–3.

chapter is intended to provide the setting upon which his account of 'self-consciousness' and of judgements about the experiences and states of mind of others may fruitfully be paraded. But before turning to this task it is worth pausing to examine briefly one kind of critical reaction to his views on the nature of philosophy. The surface of Wittgenstein's later work is littered with hints and suggestions of the absurdity of systematic philosophy. One might take his failure to produce more than an album of sketches of a landscape (*PI*, p. ix) to be an indication of the impossibility or senselessness of trying to produce a definitive painting. Some critics have stressed that the claim that philosophy is neither a theory nor a doctrine precludes systematic philosophy.[22] Others have noted correctly that his conception of language and philosophy alike precludes what they conceive to be the foundation of all proper philosophy, namely the elaboration of a philosophical theory of meaning.[23] And this is taken to be altogether incredible. It has been suggested that since, in his view, the purpose of a particular description of grammar is to remove a particular puzzle, and since there is no limit to what can confuse and puzzle us about the uses of expressions and their relationships to other expressions, context of use, and purpose of speakers, therefore there can be no complete description of the grammar of an expression.[24]

Different strands must be carefully separated and different conceptions of systematic philosophizing must be distinguished. The claim that philosophy is not a theory dates back to Wittgenstein's earliest writings on the subject. The intended contrast is not between systematic and unsystematic philosophizing in the sense in which one might thus contrast Kant and Nietzsche, but between science and philosophy. The descriptive status of philosophy did not preclude the systematic enterprise of the *Tractatus*. Although by the time of the *Investigations* Wittgenstein was sharply aware of the motley of language and no longer convinced of a pervasive underlying unity, his emphasis on the motley in no way precludes a methodical description (even if he was little interested in comprehensiveness for its own sake). Similarly the denial that there are any theses or doctrines in philosophy does not mean that a methodical account of a segment of grammar cannot be

[22] e.g. J. J. Thomson, 'Private Languages', in *American Philosophical Quarterly*, i (1964) 31.
[23] M. A. E. Dummett, 'Can Analytical Philosophy be Systematic, and Ought it to be?', repr. in his *Truth and Other Enigmas* (Duckworth, London, 1978).
[24] e.g. N. Malcolm, 'Wittgenstein on the Nature of Mind', in *American Philosophical Quarterly Monograph, No. 4: Studies in the Theory of Knowledge* (1970), p. 29.

given. It amounts rather to an insistence that in an important sense there can be no surprises in grammar, that the rules we follow and employ as standards of correctness cannot be unknown to us (though aspects of them and their mutual relations may never have struck us). Wittgenstein's anti-Fregean remarks concerning the indefinability of certain legitimate concepts in terms of their characteristics in no way imply that a careful account of admittedly vague and imprecise concepts is not possible, but only that it may not complete what is incomplete or make sharp what is vague. For that would falsify the description. It should be borne in mind that Wittgenstein was not satisfied with the 'album of sketches' he produced. Waismann's attempted systematization of Wittgenstein's work of the early to mid-thirties in *The Principles of Linguistic Philosophy* may ultimately fail in its representation of Wittgenstein's thought and in its integration of its diverse elements.[25] But it certainly shows that the *Bemerkungen* style and snippet-box method of composition, whatever their force and charm, are not inevitable corollaries of Wittgenstein's philosophy.

Nothing but superficial interpretation shows the impossibility of a detailed and methodical (and in that sense, systematic) description of segments of grammar. One may find it uninteresting in comparison with the pathology of the understanding which so preoccupied Wittgenstein. And it is indeed true that a great deal of grammatical detail (including most of what is of concern to linguists) is unlikely to be pertinent to specific philosophical questions and confusions. On the other hand, the pathologist of the understanding has no monopoly of interest over the anatomist. Completeness and comprehensiveness (in a fairly loose sense) are intelligible goals for a philosopher to pursue. Wittgenstein's plan for the treatment of psychological concepts (Z, §472) gives some indication of the comprehensive possibilities left open, even though he emphasized that what he strove for was not *exactness* but a surview (Z, §464), not completeness, but rather the method of coping with the typical difficulties that arise.

The latter feature is of great importance. For although a detailed and methodical description of the grammar of, say, 'sensation' can be given, one must not be misled by this possibility. First, there *is* no clear-cut concept of *all* the rules for the use of an expression. For particular misunderstandings are typically (though not always) met by giving rules for the application of rules, and in this sense the rules are

---

[25] Partly because, at this stage, Wittgenstein's ideas were changing so rapidly and extensively.

an open list the length of which, as it were, is context- and purpose-relative. Secondly, one must not be deluded into thinking that a comprehensive description of the grammar of a philosophically problematic expression will definitively resolve all philosophical questions about it. For it is surely correct that we cannot anticipate all sources and forms of conceptual unclarity, all misguided analogies and novel mesmerizing pictures that force themselves upon us and bewilder us. Each misunderstanding is a fresh case for treatment, requiring arrangement and juxtaposition of conceptual articulations peculiar to it. In this sense, as argued above, the task of philosophy never ceases.

The sense in which 'systematic' philosophy is excluded is different. To the extent that philosophers hanker for articulated theories about the nature of the world, the mind, thought, or language, then, if Wittgenstein is right, they are running up against the limits of language (*PI*, §119). The results of such 'systematic' endeavours are 'one or another piece of plain nonsense'. Clarification of concepts, description of conceptual relationships, is not theory construction. The resolution of philosophical problems lies in the description of the grammar of expressions (such as 'mind', 'thinking', 'speaking a language') not in building theories (about the mind, thought or language). There are no theoretical discoveries to be made in philosophy, no predictions to be derived from theories and validated in experience, but only insights to be achieved. Such insights result from the juxtaposition of features (rules for the use) of expressions that lead us to see unnoticed analogies or disanalogies which may be the source of our puzzlement, and the apprehension of which may resolve our problems. These insights and the understanding that they yield, the attainment of a surview of a segment of our conceptual scheme, are the goal of philosophical investigation.

VII

METAPHYSICS AS THE SHADOW OF GRAMMAR

1. *Grammar*

By contrast with the philosophical ideals of the youthful Wittgenstein, the viewpoint of the mature Wittgenstein may well seem tarnished and disillusioned. The dramatic change in his conception of the relation between language and reality, of the structures of language, and of the logical structures of the world, led to a re-allocation of the metaphysical from the domain of ineffability, where it lay protected by a penumbra of necessary silence, to the domain of philosophical illusion, a fit subject for the pathology of the intellect. This seems a picture of philosophy fallen from grace. Our understanding of this transformation can be furthered by exploring Wittgenstein's later conception of grammar and its relation to reality. Although the change runs deep, it is instructive to view it in certain respects as a matter of rotating the axis of the investigation one hundred and eighty degrees around the fixed point of our real need (*PI*, §108). In the *Tractatus* the essence of language or thought provided the insight into the structure of reality. In the *Investigations* the essence of language is still, in a qualified sense, the subject of investigation (PI §92). Moreover it might still be said to be isomorphic with the 'structure of reality' (for the proposition that *p* does indeed correspond to the fact that *p*, if it is true), not because language must mirror the logical form of the universe, but because the apparent 'structure of reality' is merely the shadow cast by grammar.

It is illuminating to juxtapose Wittgenstein's conception of grammar with his earlier conception of logical syntax. According to the *Tractatus* the surface grammars of ordinary languages may differ, but this conceals an underlying uniformity that is made manifest by logical analysis. Analysis will bring to view the essential rules of any possible language in virtue of which a symbolism can represent reality. Logical syntax is a system of rules for the use of signs. These rules are of various kinds. There are rules for the combination of propositions by means of truth-functional operators. Different kinds of rules, viz. definitions of names of complexes, introduce abbreviatory symbols. Yet other rules stipulate combinatorial possibilities for simple signs of various kinds. Non-logical expressions in surface grammar will, on analysis, be shown to include names of complexes, and also expressions which are not genuine names at all, but symbols for formal concepts. In a proper notation these will be represented by variables. All categorial expressions, e.g. 'proposition', 'name', 'concept', 'fact', 'object', 'property', 'colour', 'sound', are of this kind. Logical syntax does not, however, include rules correlating simple names with their meanings. There are no *rules* connecting language with reality. The rules of a language determine a network of logical forms. The content of these forms is fixed by mental correlation, by projecting elements of the network on to objects in the world. It is mental processes of meaning and understanding which inject content into otherwise empty, dead, signs.

It is important to note that many of the rules of logical syntax are hidden from view. They are not evident in the surface grammar of ordinary language in which expressions that are logically utterly different appear deceptively uniform. They are not used, as rules typically are, in everyday pedagogic activities. For they have no role in teaching and explaining how to engage correctly in the practices they allegedly govern. They are not cited in justifying the use of expressions or in criticizing or correcting misuses. These rules have logical consequences that are, in a sense, independent to us. To be sure, we recognize these consequences (for example, the mutual exclusion of determinates of a given determinable), but we are, in advance of the logical analysis which has yet to be carried out, unable to explain them. The correct analysis of our everyday propositions is to be discovered: 'we can only arrive at a correct analysis by, what might be called, the logical investigation of the phenomena themselves, i.e. in a certain sense *a posteriori*, and not by conjecturing about *a priori* possibilities' (RLF, p. 163). Accordingly, we are able to construct languages which can express everything that can be expressed 'without having any idea how each word has meaning or what its meaning is—just as people speak without knowing how the individual sounds are produced' (*TLP*, 4.002). The underlying rules of any possible language are, however, followed by speakers, even though they cannot say what they are or employ them as norms of correctness for the evaluation of the use of expressions. Nevertheless these rules are (indeed *must be*) absolutely determinate, for it is they which, together with the non-normative assignment of meanings to simple names, fix the sense of propositions. And sense must be determinate. The distinction between sense and nonsense was conceived to be independent of context and purpose, laid down once and for all.

Grammar, unlike logical syntax, does not consist of rules which of necessity underlie any possible language. That notion, Wittgenstein came to see, involved a mythology of symbolism. The grammar of a language consists of rules for the use of the expressions of that language, not for recherché expressions (viz. logically proper names) allegedly buried beneath them, let alone rules for any possible language. Wittgenstein talked of the grammar of words, of expressions, of phrases and of sentences or propositions. He also talked of the grammar of states, processes or abilities, the grammar of colour or sensation. This fluctuation between what Carnap called 'the formal mode' and 'the material mode' is not a careless mistake. It would be if it were the case that rules for the use of expressions were always and only given metalinguistically (e.g. 'This colour ↑ is, in English, called "magenta"', or 'The English word "bachelor" means an unmarried man') and if the corresponding sentence in the material mode (e.g. 'This colour ↑ is magenta', or 'A bachelor is an unmarried man') were *not* used to give a rule for the correct use of the relevant expression. But we do ask for the meanings of expressions by using sentences such as 'What is magenta?' or 'What is a bachelor?', i.e. the sentences 'What does the word "magenta" mean?' and 'What is magenta?' or 'What does the word "bachelor" mean?' and 'What is a bachelor?' are typically used in exactly the same way. (The grammar of these interrogative sentences, one might say, runs for a large part, along parallel tracks.) And a correct explanation of the meaning of 'magenta' or 'bachelor' is given by 'This ↑ is magenta' no less than by 'This ↑ is called "magenta"', or by 'A bachelor is an unmarried man' no less than by '"Bachelor" means an unmarried man'.

Rules of grammar are rules for the use of words. But Wittgenstein cites as *grammatical* rules things which no grammarian would. For explanations of meaning are not commonly included in *grammar*, but in lexicography. And such explanations of meaning as ostensive definitions, Russellian paraphrases of definite descriptions, or explanations by examples or exemplification are not included even in lexicography. Moreover, Wittgensten cites as grammatical *rules* things which no one (not merely grammarians) would have thought of as constituting rules. Ostensive definitions of the form 'That ⇡ is F' (pointing at a sample) are, he held, rules. Propositions such as 'Red is a colour' or 'Pain is a sensation' express rules. Arithmetical propositions are rules of the grammar of number words, and propositions of geometry are argued to give the grammar of spatial concepts.

Was Wittgenstein stretching the concept of grammar, or even introducing a different concept of grammar? He firmly denied this. It is true that traditional descriptive grammars are not concerned with those features of a language which are relevant to philosophical investigations. Conversely, philosophical investigations are little concerned with morphology or local features of syntax. But this does not indicate that there are two kinds of grammar (or two different senses of 'grammar'), ordinary grammar and philosophical grammar. It indicates two kinds of interest in rules of a language (*AWL*, p. 31). The philosopher's concern with grammar is guided by the fact that his purpose is the resolution of philosophical problems. These problems arise through subtle misunderstandings and misuses of language, and are clarified and resolved by pointing out the ways in which expressions are misused, illegitimate questions asked, rules of language violated. But these rules are not typically the ones that interest grammarians, being primarily explanations of meaning rather than syntactical rules upon which grammarians tend to focus.

Was Wittgenstein stretching the concept of a rule or rules of grammar? Again, there is no evidence to suggest that he thought so. On the assumption that something counts as a rule of grammar (or as the expression of such a rule) not if it has a certain *form* (e.g. a stipulated form of generality, a specification of a deontic character, characterization of norm-subjects), but rather if it is *used* in a certain way (e.g. as a guide to conduct, as explaining or justifying actions, as defining certain actions, as a standard of correctness) then Wittgenstein's claims are defensible. Ostensive explanations of word-meaning by reference to samples do not have the form we naturally associate with typical rule-formulations. 'This ⇡ is magenta' has the form of an empirical predication characteristic of an assertion, but, Wittgenstein pointed out, in appropriate contexts it has the role of an explanation of meaning and constitutes (together with a sample) a rule for the correct use of 'magenta'. '2+2 = 4' has the form of an assertion, but its function is to license such transformations as '*A* poured 2 pints of water into the bucket and then another 2 pints' into '*A* poured 4 pints of water into the bucket' (but *not* 'So there are 4 pints in the bucket'). It is a rule for the use of numerals or number-words in empirical judgements and in drawing inferences from them. 'Bachelors are unmarried men' looks just like 'Bachelors are unhappy men', but its role is quite different. It says nothing about the facts, but gives a rule for the use of 'bachelor', licensing its substitution for 'unmarried man' in typical contexts. Many of Wittgenstein's claims in this region run counter to traditional thought, but they are to be vindicated by investigating the use of certain expressions. Something expresses a rule if it is used as the expression of a rule, and something is correctly said to be a rule if it has the employment characteristic of rules.

Unlike rules of logical syntax as conceived in the *Tractatus*, rules of grammar are open to view. In a conversation with Waismann in 1931 Wittgenstein clarified the change in his viewpoint:

The wrong conception which I want to object to in this connection is the following, that we can hit upon something that we today cannot yet see, that we can *discover* something wholly new. That is a mistake. The truth of the matter is that we have already got everything, and we have got it actually *present*: we need not wait for anything. We make our moves in the realm of the grammar of our ordinary language, and this grammar is already there. Thus we have already got everything and need not wait for the future. (*WWK*, p. 183)

What Wittgenstein called 'rules of grammar' are perspicuous in the ways in which a language is taught, in explanations of word-meaning that speakers give, in the ways in which they criticize and correct misuses of language, in the justifications they give for using expressions thus or otherwise. 'Hidden rules' are not rules at all, since they cannot be used by speakers as rules, cannot fulfil the role of standards of correctness, guides to conduct, or justifications for employing expressions.

The important change in his conception involved the realization that philosophers typically sublime the notion of explanation of meaning out of all recognition. From Plato onwards philosophers have hankered after a misguided ideal of explanation, accepting as a correct explanation only one which will capture the *essence* of the *explicandum* in a formal definition giving, for example, necessary and sufficient conditions for the application of an expression. But this is a misguided ideal, distorting our concepts and our notion of correct explanation. Not all our concepts are sharply defined, prepared for all conceivable eventualities, and they are none the worse for that. For we do not have to apply them in all conceivable eventualities but only in actual ones. If a rule for the use of an expression provides a standard for its correct use in normal circumstances, then it has fulfilled its function. 'A rule that can be applied in practice is always in order' (*PG* p. 282) (We do not complain that the rules of tennis are defective for not laying down what should be done in the event of violent fluctuations in gravitational force!) Formal definitions can be thrown awry by a change in normality conditions no less than other explanations of word-meaning. (Up to what point is an unmarried man undergoing operations for sexual change still to be called 'a bachelor'?) It is, of course, true that ostensive definitions, explanations by example, paraphrastic explanations, etc. *can* be misunderstood. But formal definitions can be misunderstood too. There is no such thing as an explanation of meaning that is immune to misunderstanding, and no such thing as a rule for the use of an expression that cannot be misapplied.

In reflecting upon our use of language we must attend to what is called an explanation of the meaning of an expression and resist the temptations of a false ideal of explanation. So we should recognize the legitimacy and adequacy of explanations of family-resemblance concepts by a series of examples. 'Giving examples is not an *indirect* means of explaining—in default of a better' (*PI*, §71). Rather 'Examples are decent signs, not rubbish or hocus-pocus' (*PG*, p. 273). Similarly, ostensive definitions are perfectly legitimate and typically adequate explanations of meaning.'[1] An ostensive definition of the number two given by pointing at a pair of nuts is perfectly exact (*PI*, §28). So too explanations of meaning by contextual paraphrase, by contrastive paraphrase or by exemplification are typically correct and adequate. For they fulfil the role of standards of correct use in the practice of using language. 'The sign-post is in order—if, under normal circumstances, it fulfils its purpose' (*PI*, §87).

Rules of logical syntax, as conceived in the *Tractatus*, stopped short of explanations of meaning of indefinables. Connecting language to reality was effected by the mind. But this concept of a connection between language and reality is misguided. Grammar encompasses all rules for the use of words, and *all explanations of meaning*, including

---

[1] It is sometimes thought that when Wittgenstein pointed out that an ostensive definition can be misunderstood (*PI*, §28) he was arguing that it is a defective form of explanation. This is quite wrong. He was showing that it is not a magical or privileged form of explanation which unerringly connects language to reality (lays the foundation of language). Like *all* definitions, it can be misinterpreted and misunderstood.

ostensive definitions, belong to grammar. For to grammar belongs everything that is antecedent to truth; rules of grammar determine sense, and that must be fixed in advance of determining the truth or falsehood of a proposition. Nevertheless, just as the Fregean and *Tractatus* ideal of determinacy of sense is a false, chimerical, ideal, so too the supposition that the distinction between sense and nonsense is absolute and context-independent, a feature of type-sentences rather than of the use of token-sentences in varying contexts and circumstances, is false. 'The words "nonsense" and "sense" get their meaning only in particular cases and may vary from case to case' (*AWL*, p. 21). Compositionalist conceptions of meaning (fostered by Frege and the *Tractatus* and developed by their heirs, e.g. Carnap and later theorists of meaning for natural languages) are deeply misguided. The misconceptions flow, *inter alia*, from the idea that there are, in a language, sharply defined category rules which apply in all contexts. But while I know what 'I feel water with my hand' means, and know what 'a foot underground' means, and do indeed understand the sentence 'I feel water 2 feet underground with my hand' uttered by someone poking his arm down a hole, I do not know what 'I feel water 30 feet underground with my hand' means, when said by someone in similar circumstances. It can be *given* a meaning easily enough, but it does not have one merely in virtue of its composition out of meaningful constituents (cf. *BB*, pp. 9 f.).

2. *The Autonomy of Grammar*

It was part of the *Tractatus* conception of the relation between language and reality that language is connected to reality by the assignment of meanings to the simple unanalysable names which are the final product of the analysis of names of complexes. This connection is effected by the mind's associating each logically proper name with its meaning, i.e. a sempiternal object in reality. When he returned to philosophy in 1929 Wittgenstein repudiated this conception. In the requisite sense, *there is no connection between language and reality*. This *prima facie* puzzling remark was linked with the claim that in the *Tractatus* he had misunderstood the nature of ostensive definition. And that, in turn, was connected with the fact that he had confused the shadow cast upon reality by samples belonging to our method of representation with metaphysical simples constituting the substance of the world.

The claim that there is no connection between language and reality does not mean that in making assertions we are not really or not successfully making statements about things in the world. Nor does it express a commitment to some form of transcendental idealism according to which the mind, in some obscure sense, makes nature. It means, in the first place, that the expressions of a language which philosophers have traditionally thought of as simple indefinables do not have a meaning which is an entity in the world, whether mind-dependent (a 'simple idea' in the mind) or mind-independent (simple properties or relations, such as *red* or *to the left of*). Nor is it correct to say that such expressions are given a meaning by being correlated with objects in the world. For this carries in its wake a deep distortion of the notion of correlation, a misleading use of the notion of an object ('property' and 'relation' would be no better) and a confused contrast between 'in the world' and 'in a language' (or 'in grammar').

It means, in the second place, that the samples, which are employed in certain such explanations of meaning, are best conceived of as belonging to grammar, as constituting part of the system of representation. When we explain what 'magenta' means by pointing at a patch on a table of colour samples and saying 'That ↑ is magenta', we are not saying something *about* the patch, but explaining the meaning of the word. It can illuminatingly be conceived of as giving a substitution-rule: instead of the word 'magenta' we can say 'That ↑ colour' (pointing at the sample). If so, then when we say of the curtains that they are that ↑ colour (pointing at the sample) then we are using an element of our method of representation to say something about the world, namely that the curtains are magenta. Hence an ostensive definition belongs to grammar, is a rule for the use of an expression. And the sample is an instrument of language, something that has a role in explanations of meaning and that can be used (in an assertion) to represent how things are. It belongs to what represents and is not what is represented (to 'language', not to 'the world'). But it is important to bear in mind that whether something is a sample (just as whether something is a sign) is not an intrinsic feature of an object, but a feature of its *use*. There are not two 'realms', language and the world, but there is a crucial distinction between what represents and what is represented. The rules governing what represents are the grammar of a language or symbolism, and samples occur in specification of some of these rules. In this sense they belong to our method of representation.

A third aspect of the claim that there is no connection between language and reality is that the conception of a language as a syntactically determined network of interconnected signs which are given content by means of an interpretation associating each proper name with an object, each monadic predicate with a property, each *n*-adic predicate with a relation, etc. is misguided. This conception, which is a version of the Augustinian picture of meaning, projects the forms of our method of representation on to reality and distorts the concept of meaning by conceiving of the meaning of an expression on the model of correlation. But the meaning of an expression is manifest in its use in accord with explanations of meaning, which are rules for the use of expressions. The rules of grammar do not mirror the forms of 'entities' in reality (objects, properties, relations, etc.), for what philosophers are inclined to think of as 'forms' of things in reality are merely the reflection of grammar. It is not an empirical fact (but a *rule of grammar*) that a table is an object, that red is a colour, or that standing to the left of is a relation. It seems, indeed, to be a metaphysical fact, a necessary truth about the world. That is the typical illusion generated by all metaphysical propositions (*infra*). The apparent 'connection between language and reality' is made by the explanations of word-meaning we give, which belong to grammar. So 'language remains self-contained and autonomous' (*PG*, §55).

The claim that grammar is autonomous is central to Wittgenstein's later philosophy. It involves, *inter alia*, a repudiation of the *Tractatus* doctrine of the ineffable isomorphism between language and reality. We are deeply tempted to think that inasmuch as grammar constitutes our form of representation, the way we see the world, it must surely be features of the world which *justify* us in adopting the grammatical rules we have. Is it not the fact that the world has the structure which it has, independently of our cognition or possibility of cognition, that justifies our concepts? We have a colour system, as we have a number system. Do these systems reside in the nature of colours and numbers or in *our* nature (*Z*, §357)? *Not* in the nature of numbers or colours, Wittgenstein replied emphatically. We are continually inclined to take our grammar as a projection of reality, for we attempt to vindicate it by reference to putative facts about the world. We are prone to claim, for example, that there *really are* only four primary colours, and it is this fact which justifies this aspect of our colour concepts, for they are true to reality. We insist (rightly) that it would be vain to look for a fifth primary colour, and infer (wrongly) that we put the four primary colours together because they are similar, and that we contrast colours with shapes and notes because they are different (*Z*, §331). It is against the concept of this sort of justification, which is analogous to the idea of justifying a proposition by pointing to what makes it true, that the claim that grammar is *arbitrary* is directed (ibid.). The relevant sense in which grammar is arbitrary is also the sense in which grammar is autonomous.

First, what analogy did Wittgenstein see between the futility of trying to justify grammar and trying to justify a proposition by pointing at what makes it true? It is obvious that what justifies must be distinct from what it justifies. One cannot justify the proposition that A is red by pointing at the fact that A is red for two interrelated reasons. First, the fact that A is red is only available to one as a piece of evidence and hence as a ground for a claim, if one knows that A is red. So the supposition that what makes a proposition true is what justifies asserting it presupposes what it is meant to justify. Secondly, there is no such thing as pointing *at* a fact, as opposed to pointing *out* a fact (*PG*, p. 200). But again, to point out the fact that p presupposes that p is the case. The attempt to justify grammar falls foul of similar incoherence:

> I do not call a rule of representation a convention if it can be justified in propositions: propositions describing what is represented and showing that the representation is adequate. Grammatical conventions cannot be justified by describing what is represented. Any such description already presupposes the grammatical rules. That is to say, if anything is to count as nonsense in the grammar which is to be justified, then it cannot at the same time pass for sense in the grammar of the propositions that justify it (etc.). (*PR*, §7)

An example may make this clear. We are inclined to think that our colour grammar which defines the concept of primary colour by a four-term disjunction is correct *because* there really are only four primary colours. But this could only function as a justification *if it made sense* to talk of finding a fifth primary colour. Yet that is precisely what is ruled out by our colour grammar. It is not *false* that there is a fifth primary colour, rather there is no such thing. So a justification of this grammatical rule would have to employ a concept different from our concept of primary colour in order to be able to justify the latter. But then it would not be *our* concept of primary colour that it was justifying. One can no more justify our colour grammar by reference to the facts than one can justify the rule of chess that the king is the piece that gets checked by reference to the essence of the king. One cannot justify the *grammatical proposition* (*infra*) that white is lighter than black by reference to the *nature* of white and black and the relation of being lighter than, for it is not a fact of nature, but a grammatical truth, i.e. a rule of grammar, that white is lighter than black.

One might respond to this by pointing out that the *Tractatus* surely recognized that one cannot *express* the justification of grammar by reference to reality. One cannot *say* that red is a colour, that white is lighter than black, or that there are four primary colours, but this is *shown*, ineffably, by features of empirical propositions. Grammar, or logical syntax, is ineffably justified by reference to the metaphysical structure of the world! But that conception turns, *inter alia*, upon three ideas which Wittgenstein repudiated. First, it depends upon taking concepts such as colour (or primary colour) as having the exclusive role of formal concepts, correctly represented in an ideal notation by variables. But that is misguided (*PI*, §97). We rightly ask what colour the rose is, say that we observe the changing colours of the sunset, remark what a wonderful colourist Lotto was, and tell our children to colour the black and white pictures in their colouring books. Such concepts as colour, sound, smell (and similarly, proposition, fact, word) are not *super-concepts* (ibid.). Secondly, it misconstrues propositions such as 'Red is a colour', 'Black is darker than white', 'Colours are not audible' as illegitimate pseudo-propositions that violate the bounds of sense in an attempt to say what can only be shown. But in fact these are not attempts to say the unsayable, but expressions of grammatical rules (*infra*) in which formal concepts do indeed have an important role. Thirdly, it assumes that we cannot intelligibly envisage alternative grammars, different ways of applying concepts to reality. This is immensely tempting, for it is obviously true that different grammatical rules would determine *different* concepts. It is unthinkable, we rightly say, that something should be red and green all over simultaneously, and we think wrongly that we have here a necessary fact of nature. But in a world in which everything was iridescent and opalescent, shimmering, and 'changing colour' (as we would say) every moment and from every angle of vision, our colour grammar would be useless. Yet inhabitants of such a world might employ an array of verbs, e.g., 'redding', 'greening', 'blueing' in a manner akin to our employment of colour adjectives. They would say of an object that it is redding from here and greening from there, and sometimes that it is redding and greening all over simultaneously. Of course, they would not conceive of colour as we do. Colours, as they employ the expression, would be *activities* not *properties* of objects. Their grammar would not be correct or incorrect, any more than ours is. But it would, in those circumstances, be more *useful* than ours. It would not determine our concept of colour, but a recognizable relative of it. Similarly in a world in which almost all objects had colours lying within the red-orange range, there might be a colour grammar distinguishing six *different* colours within this range and taking the rest, which occur rarely and in small expanses, as one colour (and diverse shades). So yellow, green, blue, violet (as we call them) would all be shades of the *same* colour. Of course, this colour grammar would determine very different criteria for sameness and difference of colour (a sapphire and an emerald would be said to be the same colour). But it would not be *incorrect*. We might find it amazing that they do not notice the differences. But we too do not draw distinctions whenever we notice differences. The differences have to be important to us, given the kinds of creatures we are, the purposes we have, and certain general features of the world we inhabit (cf. *Z*, §380).

Wittgenstein explained the central point concerning the autonomy of grammar thus:

> The thing that's so difficult to understand can be expressed like this. *As long as we remain in the province of the true-false games a change in grammar can only lead us from one such game to another, and never from something true to something false. On the other hand if we go outside the province of these games, we don't any longer call it 'language' and 'grammar', and once again we don't come into contradiction with reality.* (*PG*, §68)

Grammar cannot come into *conflict* with reality, any more than can rules of a game. For grammatical rules determine a 'logical space' (to use the *Tractatus* metaphor) not a place within it. They determine what *makes sense*, not what is true. Against the autonomy of grammar one is inclined to object:

> 'Yes, but has nature nothing to say here? Indeed she has—but she makes herself audible in another way.
> 'You'll surely run up against existence and non-existence somewhere!' But that means against *facts*, not concepts. (*Z*, §364)

Facts of nature do not make concepts *correct* or *true to the facts*. But we apply our grammars, use our languages, against a context of normality conditions consisting of very general regularities of nature. Like a legal system (*Z*, §§129, 350) our concepts can be said to rest upon such normality conditions, not in the sense of being made true or correct by them, but in the sense of having a point only in such contexts. Unless average human beings had the normal capacities for self-control, foresight, recollection, forming intentions and decisions, much of the criminal law concerning intention, recklessness, negligence, etc. would be pointless. Similarly, in the absence of certain kinds of regularity and constancy of specific natural phenomena, the applicability of concepts would be undermined and the point of kinds of concept-laden activities would be lost. Our concepts of weights and measures only have application and point in a world with relatively constant gravitational fields and relatively stable rigid objects (NFL, p. 278 n.). Of course, one could conceive of an activity very similar to our measurement of length with rulers that expanded and contracted very considerably, or even with elastic rulers (*RFM*, p. 38). But one could also imagine circumstances in which nature rendered measurement pointless. This need not stop one going through the motions of weighing and measuring. There is a sense in which one can stay in the saddle however much the facts buck: but that does not mean that a horse will remain beneath the saddle. For whether we would still call the motions one goes through 'weighing and measuring' is another matter (*OC*, §§615–20).

It is, of course, not only the constancy of the physical world which, in this sense, conditions our forms of representation, but also the constancy of our common human nature. Without shared discriminatory capacities we would not have a common vocabulary of perceptual quality expressions which we characteristically explain by reference to samples. Red/green colour-blindness excludes the possibility of mastering the use of the expressions 'red' and 'green', since the colour-blind cannot employ the samples we employ in ostensive definitions that constitute standards for the correct application of these colour names. If, as a matter of fact, there were radical disagreements in *application* of expressions defined by reference to samples, there would no longer be these language-games:

> If people were (suddenly) to stop agreeing with each other in their judgments about tastes—would I still say: At any rate, each one knows what taste he's having?—Wouldn't it then become clear that this is nonsense?
> Confusion of tastes: I say 'This is sweet', someone else 'This is sour' and so on. So someone comes along and says: 'You have none of you any idea what you are talking about. You no longer know at all what you once called a taste.' What would be the sign of our still knowing?
> But might we not play a language-game even in this 'confusion'?—But is it still the earlier one? (*RPP* II, §§347–9)

This stable background of agreement in responses, reactions and judgements is not confined to language-games with perceptual qualities. It applies just as much to mathematics. On the one hand, if written signs were 'unstable', constantly changing from one figure into another, our mathematics would shrink dramatically. If mathematicians constantly disagreed in the results of their calculations, if double-checking always produced different results, if we could never remember what figure we 'carried' in a computation, etc. then there would be no mathematics (*PI*, p. 226). This does not mean that the truth or certainty of mathematics is based on the reliability of ink and paper, of memory and comparison. (Mathematical truth and certainty are based on proof and convention.) Rather, these constitute the framework within which our mathematical activities take place. If that framework were disrupted, the activities would disintegrate. And similarly, our psychological concepts would have no application if human behavioural responses in certain circumstances (e.g. of injury, danger) were not more or less regular and relatively uniform.

Grammar is autonomous in so far as it is not answerable to reality for truth or correctness. It can also be said to be arbitrary or akin to what is arbitrary (*Z*, §358). The arbitrariness of grammar is an aspect of its autonomy. Cookery rules can be said not to be arbitrary. For they are externally, causally, related to the goal of cookery; and the goal of cookery, viz. the production of good-tasting food, is specifiable independently of the rules whereby it is attained. If one follows rules other than the right ones, one will cook badly and produce ill-tasting food. So one can distinguish correct from incorrect cookery rules by reference to the external end of the activity of cooking. Rules of chess, however, are arbitrary. They define the activity of playing chess and cannot be justified as being a means to an external goal of chess (e.g. amusement). If one systematically follows other rules than those of chess, one is not playing chess badly, but playing another game (e.g. losing chess). So the rules of chess cannot be said to be right or wrong as cooking rules can. Rules of grammar are, in this respect, like the rules of chess. They determine the meanings of expressions (constitute the meanings) and are not answerable to any meaning. One cannot intelligibly ask whether the rule '$\sim\sim p = p$' is *the* correct rule for negation as opposed to the rule '$\sim\sim p = \sim p$'. They are different rules determining different concepts, and it would be potentially misleading to say they determine different kinds of *negation* (*RFM*, p. 104), although correct to say that the two concepts overlap.

Different grammatical rules, unlike different cookery rules, are not right or wrong, but rather determine different concepts. 'if you follow grammatical rules other than such and such ones, that does not mean you say something wrong, no, you are speaking of something else' (*PG*, §133)[2]. Rules of grammar are arbitrary in the same sense as the choice of a unit of measurement, i.e. that the choice of unit is not determined as true or false by the lengths of the objects to be measured (ibid.). But it is no coincidence that we do not measure the dimensions of houses in microns or the distances between cities in ells. It would not be *wrong*, but very inconvenient.

The latter point is important to note lest Wittgenstein's argument be distorted. Grammar has a kinship *also* to the non-arbitrary (*Z*, §358). The claim that it is arbitrary does not mean that it is capricious, unimportant, or a matter of individual whim. Nor does it mean that we cannot ever give *reasons* why such-and-such grammatical rules are useful, or that there cannot be reasons why, for rather specialized purposes, we choose to adopt new grammatical structures. Relativity physics employs the expressions 'space' and 'time' differently from the ways in which ordinary speakers do and also from the ways Newtonian physics does. They are used in accord with different grammatical rules and determine different *concepts*. Reasons can be given for this (as for the employment of Riemannian rather than Euclidean geometry), not in terms of truth or correctness ('space really is Riemannian' is as absurd as 'A kilometre really is 1000 metres') but in terms of predictive and explanatory fruitfulness of the theories expressed in that grammar. The grammar, however, is *not* a theory about anything—it determines what makes sense and asserts nothing about the facts.

3. *Grammar and Metaphysics*

'Like everything metaphysical', Wittgenstein wrote in the *Philosophical Grammar* (*PG*, p. 162), 'the harmony between thought and reality is to be found in the grammar of the language.' The irony underlying this enigmatic remark is that it is just as applicable to the philosophy of the *Tractatus* as it is to the *Investigations*, but its significance changes dramatically from one context to the other. The deceptive continuity seems further reinforced by such remarks as '*Essence* is expressed by grammar' (*PI*, §371), and 'Grammar tells us what kind of object a

---

[2] This does not mean that there is no such thing as speaking ungrammatically or senselessly. That depends upon what rules one is or means to be following, which will be manifest in the explanations of meaning one gives when challenged.

thing is' (*PI*, §373). The veil of deception begins to lift, however, when the conventionalism of the later philosophy is revealed. In the *Remarks on the Foundations of Mathematics* Wittgenstein noted in strikingly Fregean terminology: 'it is not the property of an object that is ever "essential", but rather the mark of a concept' (*RFM* p. 64). A few pages later the Fregean terminology reappears, again in the context of a rebuttal of Platonism: 'For what is the characteristic mark of "internal properties"?'; Wittgenstein's response begins ironically from Platonist grounds: 'That they persist always, unalterably, in the whole they constitute; as it were independently of any outside happenings.' And then in two powerful metaphors his new conception is revealed: 'As the construction of a machine on paper does not break when the machine itself succumbs to external forces—or again, I should like to say that they are not subject to wind and weather like physical things; rather are they unassailable, like shadows' (*RFM*, p. 74). For the Platonist metaphysician, a geometrical proof consists in revealing the essential properties of shapes. (The author of the *Tractatus*, like Plato, had conceived of properties as ingredients of a thing (*RFM*, p. 63).[3]) On such a conception a geometrical proof that 'this shape consists of these shapes' is thought of as showing that a given shape has been constructed once and for all, by whoever put the essential properties into things. It is as if God had constructed shapes thus. 'For if the shape is to be a thing consisting of parts, then the pattern-maker who made the shape is he who also made light and dark, colour and hardness' (*RFM*, p. 64). The substance of the world, objects that are unalterable, and subsistent independently of what is the case (*TLP*, 2.024–2.027) had seemed to be not shadows, but the bricks of reality. The scaffolding of logic had appeared to be both as pure as crystal and as hard as or harder than concrete (*PI*, §97). Under the spell of such a vision Łukasiewicz wrote:

> Whenever I am occupied even with the tiniest logistical problem e.g. trying to find the shortest axiom of the implicational calculus, I have the impression that I am confronted with a mighty construction, of indescribable complexity and immeasurable rigidity. This construction has the effect on me of a concrete tangible object, fashioned from the hardest of materials, a hundred times stronger than concrete and steel. I cannot change anything in it; by intense labour I merely find in it ever new details, and attain unshakeable and eternal

---

[3] Cf. L. Wittgenstein, 'Remarks on Frazer's *Golden Bough*', repr. in G. Luckhardt, ed., *Wittgenstein, Sources and Perspectives* (Cornell University Press, Ithaca, NY, 1979), p. 70; cf. also *PG*, Appendices 1–4.

truths. Where and what is this ideal construction? A Catholic philosopher would say: it is in God, it is God's thought.[4]

It is against such conceptions that Wittgenstein wars in his later philosophy. The simile of God the creator is misleading. For were it the case that 'in the beginning was the word' it would (in these matters) not be the word of God, but of human convention. Yet this is not the case, for human conventions are essentially interwoven with human *actions*, rest upon shared human patterns of behaviour, and are employed within a framework of common human reactions and behavioural dispositions. Hence '... write with confidence "In the beginning was the deed." '[5]

Connections which are not causal, but stricter, harder, more rigid, are always connections in grammar (*RFM*, p. 88), laid down in rules for the use of expressions and manifest in our applications of expressions in practice. The unshakeable certainty that seems attached to such connections is simply a reflection of our determination to employ these rules as part of our form of representation (*RFM*, p. 170). The 'hardness of the "logical must" indicates our inability, or our refusal, to depart from a concept' (*RFM*, p. 238). The inexorability of the laws of logic is *our* inexorability in applying them (*RFM*, p. 82). What is logically possible or impossible just is: what makes sense. And what makes sense in a given language is determined by the grammar of the language, by the arbitrary rules for the use of expressions (and their manner of application in practice). Essences are reflections of forms of representation, marks of concepts, and thus made rather than found. We create our forms of representation, prompted by our biological and psychological character, prodded by nature, restrained by society, and urged by our drive to master the world. Essences are a product of convention, not a discovery of reason. All talk of essence is talk of conventions, and what seems to us to be the 'depth' of the essences is the fact the depth of our need for the conventions (*RFM*, p. 65).

Of course, our commitment to a form of expression, especially when it is couched in the material mode, will not only look 'metaphysically necessary', since it seems about *objects* rather than mere *signs*,[6] it will

---

[4] J. Łukasiewicz, quoted and trans. P. Geach, in *A Wittgenstein Workbook*, by C. Coope, P. Geach, T. Potts, and R. White (Blackwell, Oxford, 1970), p. 22.

[5] Quoted in *OC*, §402 from Goethe, *Faust*, Pt. 1.

[6] But in the sense in which 'The sofa is blue' is about the sofa, 'Blue is a colour' is *not* about blue. What is? If anything, then 'The sofa is blue' ('Blue is exemplified by the sofa'!). Cf. *LFM*, pp. 250 f.

also seem a priori true. Putative metaphysical propositions have the form of empirical propositions. Scientists tell us that the ultimate constituents of matter are such-and-such particles; metaphysicians tell us that the ultimate constituents of reality are sense-data. Scientists inform us that no animal can run faster than 80 m.p.h.; metaphysicians inform us that no one can have another person's pains. Scientists discover that Vulcan (the once supposed intra-Mercurian planet) does not exist, metaphysicians discover that material substances do not 'really' exist, or that events do not 'really' exist. Scientists prove the existence of Pluto or Uranus, metaphysicians prove that they exist ('*Cogito, ergo sum*'), God exists, or that the 'external world' exists. Or so it seems.

The illusory subject of metaphysics arises from aping the methods of science. The philosopher asks questions which look like scientific questions, but are not; and misled by the forms of these questions, attempts to reply to them with answers that appear to state facts about the world. This, Wittgenstein claimed, 'leads the philosopher into complete darkness' (*BB*, p. 18). For putative metaphysical questions blur the distinction between factual and conceptual investigations. 'A metaphysical question is always in appearance a factual one, although the problem is a conceptual one' (*RPP* I, §949). Conceptual problems are not usefully characterized in terms of a distinction between analytic and synthetic propositions, and Wittgenstein by and large eschewed this traditional terminology. For such distinctions are typically thought of as applying to type-sentences in virtue of their form and irrespective of their use. On no acceptable account of analyticity are propositions such as 'Nothing can be red and green all over simultaneously' or 'White is lighter than black' analytic. But it would be unilluminating, if not confusing, to classify them as synthetic *a priori* for their role is no different from that of 'Bachelors are unmarried men'. And it is their role which gives them their status as 'necessary propositions'. These sentences express grammatical rules. There is a sharp distinction between using a (token) sentence to express a rule of grammar and using one to state a fact. These distinct uses of sentences are as exclusive as using a rod to measure lengths of objects and measuring the length of the rod. Conceptual investigations are investigations into our measuring rods and their uses, not into what is measured. Conceptual problems are *toto mundo* distinct from factual, scientific, ones, and cannot be resolved by scientific advances, but only by clarification of the use of words.

Metaphysics as the Shadow of Grammar 197

Metaphysical propositions appear to describe the necessary features of the world. They look like super-empirical descriptions of reality. But in fact they are either expressions of grammatical rules for the use of words or nonsense. This claim can be clarified by examining such metaphysical propositions as 'Red is a colour', 'Nothing can be red and green all over', 'White is lighter than black' which we are naturally inclined to think of as stating truths about the world. It is important to note that they have no significant negation. It would only make sense to say that it is *false* that something *can* be red and green all over simultaneously or that white is *darker* than black if we could say what would be the case if it were actually true. But we cannot. Of course, we are inclined to say that it is *unthinkable* that something be red and green all over simultaneously, or that it is *unimaginable* that white be darker than black. And that is correct. But not because of limitations on our cognitive or imaginative powers. Rather, because no sense attaches to the sentences 'A is red all over and also green all over' or 'A is white, B is black and A is darker than B'. Such sentences do not express propositions describing possibilities which happen not to obtain. Nor do they describe impossibilities, for a 'logically impossible state of affairs' is not, as it were, a possibility that is impossible. These sentences are nonsense, for they violate grammatical rules.

The apparently metaphysical propositions 'Nothing can be red and green all over simultaneously', 'White is lighter than black', are expressions of rules for the use of colour names. They license inferences between empirical propositions, e.g. 'A is red all over, so it is not green' or 'A is white, and B is black, so A is lighter than B'. We explain what 'red' means by a sample, and what 'green' means by a *different* sample. An object A is red all over if it *is* the colour of the sample; in which case it would be incorrect, a misuse of 'green', to say that A is green. We explain the expressions 'lighter-than' and 'darker than' by ordered pairs of samples of white and black. This explanation (grammatical rule) is correctly applied if we say of the whiteboard that it is lighter than the blackboard. The licence to infer, in advance of experience, that the *white*board is lighter than the *black*board is given in the form of the proposition 'white is lighter than black', which expresses a grammatical rule (*RFM*, pp. 75 f.).

The negation of 'White is lighter than black' is 'White is not lighter than black'. That, however, is not an expression of a rule for the use of 'white', 'lighter than', and 'black'. It does not determine the meanings of these expressions as we use them. If we were to take it as the expression of a rule, it would be a rule for *different* expressions (homonyms) with *different* meanings—not a rule of our colour grammar but of some other one. (Similarly, 'The king moves three squares at a time' is not a rule of chess but, if a rule, then a rule of a different game determining a different concept of a king in a game.) But taken thus, it would no longer be the negation of 'White is lighter than black'. Yet it is not a false proposition either, for it is altogether unlike '*A* (a white shirt) is darker than *B* (a yellow shirt)' which is a false (empirical) proposition. For we might dye *A* dark blue, and then it would be true that it is darker than *B*. 'White is darker than black' is not a false empirical proposition, but it is not a grammatical truth either. Is it not a false necessary proposition? No—for to say of 'White is lighter than black' that it is a true necessary proposition is just to say that it expresses a norm of representation; but to say of 'White is darker than black' that it is a false necessary proposition is not to say that it expresses a norm of representation which has the further property of being false. It is to say that it does *not* express a norm of representation. But since it does not express a true or false empirical proposition either, it is best dismissed as nonsense. And its apparent negation 'White is lighter than black' is best viewed not as a *truth*, but as a rule. There is *no such thing* as something white being darker than something black, just as there is no such thing as checkmate in draughts.

A similar manœuvre clarifies the use of 'cannot' in metaphysical propositions. 'I can't travel back in time' or 'You can't count through the whole series of cardinal numbers' sound like 'An iron nail can't scratch glass' or 'You can't swim across the Atlantic.' But this is deceptive, for the metaphysical propositions are not about human frailty or 'medical limitations'. They are expressions of conventions for the use of expressions (*BB*, p. 54). The sentence 'An iron nail can't scratch glass' could be rewritten as 'Experience teaches that iron *doesn't* scratch glass', thus getting rid of the 'can't'. It is not experience that teaches, but rather grammar that *stipulates* that there is no such thing as time travel, i.e. travelling backwards in time. One might say that 'can't' here is not the negation of 'can'. 'You can't count through the whole series of cardinal numbers' is like 'There is no goal in an endurance race' (*BB*, p. 54). It is an expression of a grammatical rule which excludes the phrase 'counting through the whole series of cardinal numbers' from use. There is no such thing as counting through the whole series of cardinal numbers, so there is not something we cannot do—there is here nothing *to* do.

Our mystification at the necessitarian character which we discern in metaphysical propositions is an expression of our failure to apprehend their role. We think that necessary propositions are propositions just like empirical ones, but which have the baffling property of being necessary. And we then concoct tales about 'truth in all possible worlds' to try to explain the mystery. So we fail to see that to say that a proposition is necessary is not to say something about the truths that it describes, but rather to say that its role is not to describe truths at all. A 'true' metaphysical proposition is an expression of a norm of representation, and its apparent necessity is not a reflection of the adamantine metaphysical structure of all possible worlds, but of our commitment to employing it *as* a norm of representation. Whenever, in such contexts, we say that something *must* be the case (e.g. when a Newtonian physicist such as Hertz says that an irregular motion of a planet *must* have a cause, if not a visible mass that accounts for it, then an invisible one) we are using a norm of expression (*AWL*, p. 16). The Law of Universal Causation, for example, that so mesmerized Kant, is a norm of representation of Newtonian mechanics, not a synthetic a priori truth about reality (and it is not a norm of representation of quantum mechanics). Necessities in the world are the shadows cast by grammar.

Consider: 'The only correlate in language to an intrinsic necessity is an arbitrary rule. It is the only thing one can milk out of this intrinsic necessity into a proposition'.[7] (PI, §372)

The metaphysician, however, does not propound propositions such as 'Red is a colour', 'Pain is a sensation' or 'I can't have your pains' *as* expressions of grammatical rules. His quarry is the ultimate nature of reality or the metaphysical limits of human knowledge. Hence he makes such further claims as 'Reality consists of sense-data', 'Only the present is real', or 'Only my pain is real'. He claims insights into what really exists which surpass those of the physicist, arguing that material substances don't really exist, or that events don't really exist and should be banished from our 'ontology'. He seems to be in competition with the physicist, using the results of physics to pronounce upon the true character of what is real. For he claims that physics shows that

---

[7] Why 'Consider'? And why is the whole enclosed in quotation marks? Perhaps because there is no such thing as an objective 'intrinsic' necessity.

material objects are not really solid, being composed of particles which fill space so thinly that it is almost empty, or that objects are not really coloured, but merely have powers to produce sensations of colour in us.[8]

These claims look like claims about the character of objects in the world. They have the form of empirical claims, and indeed some of these propositions might be used to make empirical claims, e.g. 'Only my pain is real' might be used to claim that the others are only pretending, 'This tree doesn't exist when no one is looking at it' might mean 'This tree vanishes when nobody sees it' (*BB*, p. 57). This is misleading, for the metaphysician does not mean that he has found out by the ordinary criteria which give words their meaning that other people are pretending to be in pain, that his desk is not really solid and that we should beware of leaning on it, or that the objects in his room are not really coloured but colourless and transparent. It is no use objecting to him by saying 'Oh no, my headache is real too' and 'I really do have a headache, I'm not just pretending', or by pointing out to him that while the glass panes in his windows are colourless and transparent, the furniture in the room is not. For in fact he is using words differently from us, namely without an antithesis (*BB*, p. 46). We may insist that the Airfix models on the table are not solid, but that the table is, or that the desk top is not solid, having a cavity between top and bottom, but that the table top is good solid oak. But the metaphysician insists that *nothing* in the room is solid. We may point out that not everyone in the sick-bay is malingering, but the metaphysician is not concerned with the contrast between being in pain and pretending to be in pain. He insists that it is inconceivable that anyone other than himself is in pain or has real experiences (*AWL*, p. 22). What the metaphysician is actually doing is objecting to our conventions for the use of expressions, rejecting the grammar which gives these expressions their meaning. In the guise of insights into what is real, what actually exists, and what properties things have, the metaphysician is in effect doing no more than recommending a new *form of description*.

It is exceedingly important to notice, however, that the great metaphysicians of the past were not aware that that was what their claims amount to, or, if they were aware of this, then only partially and defectively. Descartes, Locke, and Berkeley are misleadingly charac-

---

[8] Of course, such claims are often made by scientists themselves. Metaphysics is a disease of the intellect that affects not only philosophers.

terized as 'revisionary metaphysicians'.[9] They did not think of their remarkable intellectual constructions as recommendations for a better structure of thought about the world, if that means an alternative grammar, a different method of representation. Rather, they thought of their work as producing a more correct picture of the world, a conception of the world which is true to the facts. And this is precisely where they were deeply confused. For grammar is not responsible to reality. A notation is not true to the facts, rather it is what is asserted by the use of the notation in making empirical statements that is (or is not) true to the facts. Grammar is antecedent to truth and determines only what it makes sense to say.

That the traditional metaphysician is thus confused (hence not, properly speaking, 'revisionary') is evident from two features of typical metaphysical arguments. First, he does *not* clearly see himself as merely objecting to a notation, but thinks of himself as attaining new insights into reality:

> He sees a way of dividing the country different from the one used on the ordinary map. He feels tempted, say, to use the name 'Devonshire' not for the county with its conventional boundary, but for a region differently bounded. He could express this by saying; 'Isn't it absurd to make *this* a county, to draw the boundaries *here*?' But what he says is 'The *real* Devonshire is this'. (*BB*, p. 57)

We could answer him, Wittgenstein pointed out, by saying 'What you want is only a new notation, and by a new notation no facts of geography are changed'. A new notation, a new way of drawing the boundaries can affect, as it were, only the administration of the territory.

Secondly, the metaphysician does *not* consistently go through with the construction of a new notation (*AWL*, p. 23). The solipsist may reject the grammar of 'pain', and say, instead of 'I have toothache' and '*A* has toothache', 'There is toothache' and '*A* is manifesting toothache behaviour'. But he cannot coherently say 'Only *my* toothache is *real*', for 'my toothache' belongs to the same grammatical system as 'your toothache', and 'real toothache' to the same system as 'pretended toothache'. The metaphysician *retains* elements of our existing notation while severing the grammatical connections which give them their sense. It makes sense to say that the table is not solid, for it also makes *sense* to say that it is. But if being composed of nuclei and

---

[9] P. F. Strawson, *Individuals* (Methuen, London, 1959), p. 9.

electrons is what it is *not* to be solid, then nothing around us is solid and the contrast between what is solid and what is not is lost. If it is recommended that we call 'solid' only immensely dense plasma, and that everything else is to be called 'not solid', we can only reply that that is not how we use the words 'solid' and 'not solid', and that there is little to be said for this recommendation. But when the metaphysician (who may be a misguided physicist) tells us that things around us are not really solid, he means to tell us startling news, not merely that chairs and tables do not consist of dense plasma. He misuses the term 'solid', misapplies the atomic picture of matter as consisting of 'thinly filled space', and saws off the very branch upon which the scientist is perched. For the scientist intended to explain the atomic structure of *solid* objects (*BB*, p. 46). Similarly, Descartes, Locke, and their present-day followers tell us that although when we look at a bunch of flowers we have 'ideas of colour', colour sensations, or sense impressions, the flowers are not really coloured at all (as we think them to be) but only have powers to cause such ideas or impressions in us. Yet they do not mean that the flowers are colourless (like the glass in the window pane). They are in effect claiming that it makes no *sense* to attribute colours to objects. But, if so, it also makes no sense to say that flowers are *not* coloured (just as it makes no sense to say that the number two is *not* green, since it is not red or yellow either, nor is it colourless and transparent). Only of what it makes sense to say that it *is* a certain colour does it make sense to *deny* that it is that colour, or to deny that it is coloured at all. The metaphysician's claim, it is evident, violates our rules for the use of colour words, for it is part of our *grammar* of colour that material objects can be coloured, i.e. that it makes sense to say of them that they are red or yellow, and that the alternative to being coloured is being colourless. These are not factual claims, but grammatical propositions. Again, the metaphysician does not consistently go through with the construction of a new notation. He does not eschew the use of colour words as we use them, but restricts them to phrasal contexts such as 'looks red to *A*', 'appears red to *B*', 'has a sensation of red', or worse still 'has a red visual impression'.[10] To this fragment of our grammar of colour, he adds a new concept of red, namely the power in objects to cause sensations, appearances, or impressions of red in us. But the use of 'red' in the

[10] It is noteworthy that some of these philosophical favourites are sorely awry. There is no such thing as a *sensation* of red, let alone a red sensation (if that is construed as akin to 'sensation of pain'), and visual impressions are neither coloured nor colourless.

phrase 'appears red' or 'looks red' is parasitic upon (internally related to) the ordinary use and meaning of colour words. Any attempt to sever that connection requires that the concepts of appearing red, looking red, etc. be defined by private ostensive definition. That, as Wittgenstein showed in the private language argument (see Chapter IX), is an incoherent requirement. Trying to graft the new concept of red upon the fragment of the old grammar of red is like stipulating that pawns should move in accord with the rules for the movement of draughts pieces and thinking that the king, just because it still moves only one square at a time, is still a chess king.

Failure to grasp the fact that different parts of our grammar may be thus interlocked is endemic even among philosophers who eschew traditional metaphysics. Thus Carnap, in his paper 'Empiricism, Semantics and Ontology',[11] saw that while 'internal questions' concerning the existence of dodos, unicorns, or Tasmanian tigers are genuine empirical ones, 'external questions' such as 'Does the material world exist?', or 'Are material objects real?' are not. They are, he thought, no more than questions about what 'language' or grammatical structure we ought to employ. Although we are all brought up to use a material object or 'thing' language, 'we are free to choose to continue using the thing language or not; in the latter case we could restrict ourselves to a language of sense-data and other phenomenal entities'.[12] But the grammar of sense-data (e.g. 'it looks to me as if...', 'it appears to me just like ...') is an offshoot of the grammar of objects and their perceptual properties. One can no more construct a grammar of sense-data that is independent of the grammar of objects that one can abolish the institution of marriage and yet continue to talk (as in our existing idiom) of marrying money. That is to say, if one severs the internal relations between concepts of As and concepts of Bs, and abandons the use of concepts of Bs, one is *not* left with concepts of As, but with something else, which may be mere nonsense or may be given a fresh sense.

Revisionary metaphysics is not something philosophers have ever seriously, consistently, and self-consciously engaged in. Moreover the confusions and unclarities that bred the great metaphysical systems of the past would not be solved or clarified by adopting a different grammar, but only concealed. For a different grammar defines *different*

---

[11] R. Carnap, 'Empiricism, Semantics and Ontology' repr. in his *Meaning and Necessity* (University of Chicago Press, Chicago, 1956), pp. 205 ff.
[12] Ibid., p. 207.

concepts, which cannot make clear existing ones (save by juxtaposition). A different grammar may be useful for specific *practical purposes*, but that is not what metaphysicians typically have in view. It might well be said that Einstein introduced a different grammar and brought about a shift in the grammar of space and time for purposes of relativity physics, abandoning the Newtonian concepts. But it would be misleading to call *this* 'revisionary metaphysics'.

What then of 'descriptive metaphysics'? Is there such a subject, and if so, what is its subject-matter and what is the nature of the truths it hopes to elicit? Strawson[13] characterized it as the endeavour to describe the structure of our thought about the world, aiming to lay bare the most general features of our conceptual scheme, differing from the rest of philosophy (or conceptual analysis) only in its scope or generality. If this means that an investigation into the concepts of a material object or a person, and perhaps also into such concepts as space and time, fact, event, and process, belongs to metaphysics thus construed, whereas investigations of concepts such as colour and sound, perception and sensation, illusion and hallucination do not, there is little to cavil at save the arbitrariness of any dividing line. And one should point out that the boundaries between the more and the less general will be context- and purpose-relative. Such an investigation will result in grammatical propositions, rules for the use of the very general expressions in question. If we are to employ this notion of 'descriptive metaphysics' we should be forewarned of three pitfalls.

First, it is misleading to suggest as Strawson does, that there are *truths* of metaphysics to be discovered or rediscovered.[14] Clarification of our concepts of a material object, a person, of facts, events or properties does not yield truths other than grammatical ones, and they are not *discoveries* but rules for the use of expressions. The point of the activity is the resolution of philosophical puzzles which arise out of unclarity about the employment of these very general expressions, and this is done by clarifying their use.

Secondly, it is misleading to suggest that the philosopher investigating these very general concepts 'must abandon his only sure guide [viz. the actual use of words] when the guide cannot take him as far as he

[13] Strawson, *Individuals*, pp. 9 ff.
[14] Ibid., p. 10. I am not suggesting that it is incorrect to say that it is *true* that, for example, space and time form a unity or that a person is not a body conjoined with a mind, but only pointing out that these 'truths' are akin to 'It is true that the chess queen stands on her own colour' or 'It is true that promises ought to be kept', and altogether unlike 'It is true that iron rusts' or 'It is true that cheetahs run faster than leopards'.

wishes to go'.[15] We might agree with Strawson that 'the structure he seeks does not display itself on the surface of language', but deny that it 'lies submerged'. If anything lies submerged, it is not part of the grammar of these expressions, for what is hidden from sight can fulfil no normative role. But we may concede that the surface forms of grammar are altogether deceptive (e.g. the surface forms of concepts such as *pain* deceptively resemble the forms of concepts of objects: the grammatical appearance of concepts such as *fact* is misleadingly akin to that of *event* or *process*). The antidote to this is not to pursue what is *submerged*, but painstakingly to examine the diverse *uses* of these similar forms. (e.g., events and processes occur or go on somewhere, somewhen, but facts have no spatio-temporal location).

Thirdly, we must beware of thinking that when we are dealing with these very general expressions we have to do with hard, ultimate categorial terms—the rigid, structural elements of our conceptual scheme, the formal concepts (akin to variables) that constitute the scaffolding of any possible language, 'the indispensable core of the conceptual equipment'[16] of any thinking human being. But if there is a *logically* indispensable core, that would be because our *concept* of thinking is internally (grammatically or conceptually) related to the employment of these very general terms. That may be doubted;[17] but, if correct, it would not involve any supra-grammatical insight, only a clarification of what we are and what we are not willing to call 'thinking'. The illusion that 'category' expressions are 'super-expressions' is, as we noted, one that Wittgenstein first succumbed to and later exploded:

We think we are standing on the hard bedrock, deeper than any special methods and language-games. But these extremely general terms have an extremely blurred meaning. They relate in practice to innumerable special cases, but that does not make them any *solider*; no, rather it makes them more fluid. (*RPP* I, §648)

Far from 'thing', 'person', 'event', 'property', 'fact' being the rigid scaffolding of our conceptual scheme, they are soft and flexible, collapsing at the very points on which we wish to hang something when

---

[15] Loc. cit.   [16] Loc. cit.

[17] Similar considerations apply to our concept of a language. Is it so circumscribed that we would deny that a system of signs is a language unless it incorporated verb nominalizations for designating events and sentential nominalizations for facts, or unless it admitted uses of signs *we* would call fact-stating or event-describing? Wittgenstein obviously disputed this (*PI*, §19).

doing philosophy. And then, of course, we attempt to shore them up—and falsify them.

Finally, such a conceptual investigation will *not* produce insights into the nature of the world, but only into the grammar of our descriptions of the world.[18] That is not to diminish its importance, but correctly to locate its importance. Such conceptual clarifications are as important as the deep, ramifying confusions that are endemic not only in philosophy but in the empirical sciences and in human thought in general, confusions that stem from lack of a correct logical point of view and from the difficulty of surveying our grammar. But what we clarify in such investigations is not the empirical landscape before us but our point of view, not what we apprehend but our vision.[19]

4. *A Note on Kant and Wittgenstein*

It has often been remarked that there are affinities between Wittgenstein's philosophy, both early and late, and Kant's. In the first edition of this book I made much of this, and I have continued to make something, although rather less, of it now. Certainly Wittgenstein was sympathetic to Kant's critical method. Lee records a conversation with Wittgenstein in 1931/2 in which Wittgenstein remarked on it:

This is the right sort of approach. Hume, Descartes and others had tried to start with one proposition such as 'Cogito ergo sum' and work from it to others. Kant disagreed and started with what we know to be so and so, and went on to examine the validity of what we suppose we know.[20]

Both philosophers shared a conception of philosophy as concerned with the bounds of sense, even though their conception of what determines the latter differed. Both thought that many propositions of

---

[18] Austin famously claimed: 'When we examine what we should say when, what words we should use in what situations, we are looking again not *merely* at words (or 'meanings' whatever they may be) but also at the realities we use words to talk about: we are using a sharpened awareness of words to sharpen our perception of, though not as final arbiter of, phenomena.' (J. L. Austin, 'A Plea for Excuses', repr. in his *Philosophical Papers*, Clarendon Press, Oxford, 1961, p. 130.) If Wittgenstein is right, then Austin's methodological remark is misguided.

[19] Hence there is no such subject as ontology. If ontology is a study of what really exists, it is science, not philosophy. The questions 'Do dodos (Tasmanian tigers, unicorns) exist?' are intelligible questions, which it is not the business of philosophy to answer. The questions 'Do material objects (events, properties) exist?' are pseudo-questions constructed on the model of genuine questions. The task of philosophy is not to answer them, but to show that they are nonsensical.

[20] Desmond Lee, ed., *Wittgenstein's Lectures, Cambridge, 1930–1932* (Blackwell, Oxford, 1980), pp. 73 f.

traditional metaphysics violate the bounds of sense, misuse concepts, and hence make nonsensical claims. More than any other philosophers, Kant and Wittgenstein were concerned with the nature of philosophy itself and sought to curb its metaphysical pretensions by clarifying its status and circumscribing what one may rationally hope for in philosophical investigation. Both saw philosophical and metaphysical *illusions of reason* as at least a large part of the subject, and the eradication of such illusions as a major goal of their work. And they shared a highly critical attitude towards traditional empiricism and rationalism alike.

Despite these (and other) affinities, the differences in their methods and conclusions are no less marked. I shall be concerned here only with a very narrow range of interlocking issues. First, there is deep and ramifying disagreement between Kant and Kantians on the one hand and Wittgenstein on the other over the intelligibility of the notion of synthetic a priori propositions. Of course, Wittgenstein agreed that arithmetic and geometry are not analytic or *a posteriori*. If being synthetic a priori were the residual alternative, one might be forced to pigeon-hole Wittgenstein's views with Kant's. But that would be quite wrong. A synthetic a priori proposition for Kant was a proposition that was *true* of the empirical world, but could be known in advance of experience. It was conceived of as a *necessary* truth about the phenomenal world, and Kant's object was to show that we could have knowledge of such truths in so far as they are conditions of any possible (conceptualized) experience. What Kant thought of as synthetic a priori truths about the world, Wittgenstein held to be norms of representation. Propositions of arithmetic and geometry are expressions of rules for the description of quantifiable magnitudes of objects and their dimensions, of stuffs and their quantities, of spatial properties and relations. They no more 'hold true' of the world than does the proposition that 1 metre = 100 centimetres. The world does not, of transcendental necessity, *accord* with our arithmetical or geometrical propositions—it neither accords with them nor fails to accord with them. Rather, we *apply* the grammar of number and the grammar of spatial relations to the items we encounter in experience. But the grammar thus applied is neither true nor false, [21] it is only the

---

[21] Surely it is *true* that $2 + 3 = 5$? Indeed it is; that is what is called a true proposition of arithmetic. And we call '$2 + 3 = 6$' a false proposition. But note that truth and falsity here fulfil a quite different role from the role they fulfil in the case of empirical propositions. True and false arithmetical propositions correspond not to mathematical

empirical propositions that we express by the use of that grammar that are true or false. The *inferences* we make in accord with that grammar are what we call valid inferences, but they are not 'true to the facts'. Rather, if the conclusion of such an inference is a proposition which is discovered in experience to be false, we fault the premisses and measurements, not the inference. Kant thought that there is and could be only one geometry—Euclidean, and that it is necessarily true of physical space. Since his times alternative geometries have been produced. It does not follow, as the Vienna Circle thought it did, that pure geometries are uninterpreted calculi and applied geometries are alternative theories of physical space. Rather, as Wittgenstein argued, alternative geometries are alternative *grammars* of space and spatial relations.

Secondly, Kant thought that it is part of the task of philosophy to *prove* things. Thus he argued that

it still remains a scandal to philosophy and to human reason in general that the existence of things outside us (from which we derive the whole material of knowledge, even for our inner sense) must be accepted merely on *faith*, and that if anyone thinks good to doubt their existence, we are unable to counter his doubts by any satisfactory proof.[22]

Wittgenstein thought that the notion of proof in philosophy was obsolete. Empirical sciences can prove the existence of things, e.g. Pluto, or their non-existence, e.g. Vulcan, by amassing empirical evidence. That is not the role of philosophy. Arithmetic and geometry construct proofs for theorems, i.e. prove that certain propositions belong to arithmetic or geometry and are accordingly rules of representation to be incorporated into our system of mathematics. That too is not the task of philosophy. Scepticism is not to be answered by proving that we *do* know what the sceptic doubts, but rather by showing that the sceptical doubts make no sense.

That this is the trajectory of Wittgenstein's thought cannot be gainsaid. He did not, however, follow it through on this specific issue.[23] Hence the following sketch of an argument is intended merely as an indication of possible moves in keeping with the spirit of his thought.

facts, but to *sense* and *nonsense* among empirical propositions (e.g. 'I poured 2 pints into the bucket and then another 3 pints, *so* I poured 6 pints' is nonsense). What we call 'false arithmetical propositions' are best seen as *not being propositions of arithmetic at all*, for they have none of the roles of arithmetical propositions.

[22] Kant, *Critique of Pure Reason*, Preface to the second edition, B xl, note a.
[23] Although *On Certainty* furnishes a wealth of argument that impinges on it.

It makes sense to doubt only where it makes *sense* to know or to be ignorant. But there is no use for the phrase 'A does not know that the world exists', nor is it clear that there is any such thing as attaining knowledge, discovering, or finding out that the world exists. One can have evidence for the existence of dodos or dinosaurs, but not for the existence of the world (or for its non-existence). This grammatical observation is precisely what is not grasped by the Cartesian sceptic or his Kantian antagonist.

Scepticism about the external world rests upon the idea that 'our senses inform us' of things 'outside us', giving us *evidence* for the existence of extra-mental objects. The sceptic draws our attention to the fact that we sometimes err in our perceptual judgements and concludes that the 'evidence of our senses' is unreliable. For if we sometimes err, and there is no intrinsic mark of veridical perceptual evidence, then for all we know, we might always err. Kant thought that we must counter this argument by proving that the external world exists. Wittgenstein's method in philosophy suggests that we counter the argument by showing that it makes no sense to claim that the world exists or to deny that it exists, and hence that the sceptic's challenge is nonsensical (cf. *OC* §§35 ff.). Three points suggest themselves:

(1) First, the sceptic's argument misuses the idiom of 'external' and 'internal'. The world is not 'external', though it is not in the mind either. Of course, I can have the world in mind ('Oh, what a vale of tears it is') or bear it in mind ('Beware of the ways of the world'). But it is true that the world I think about is not a thought. However, that is a grammatical observation, and neither needs, nor can be given a proof.

(2) The sceptic wrongly conceives of our perceptual organs as information transmitters and of our exercise of our perceptual capacities as information processing. (This misconception is still rife in modern empirical psychology and neurophysiology.) But our senses do not *inform* us of anything. Rather, we inform ourselves about objects (our own body and objects outside our body) by the use of our senses. Yet we use our eyes and ears to discern how things are in our vicinity, not to discern something, viz. 'perceptions', that inform us at second-hand how things are.

(3) The sceptic's argument wrongly conflates what might be called the language-games of empirical evidence (e.g. 'The pavements are wet, so it must have been raining') with the language-games of witnessing (e.g. 'I know it is raining because I can hear it'). This is understandable, since the question 'How do you know?' occurs in both. But the

differences are crucial. 'Because the pavements are wet' constitutes my evidence for rain, 'Because I can hear it' does not (and the utterance 'It seems to me just as if I heard some rain on the window pane' is certainly not my evidence for my hearing the rain, let alone for the fact that it is raining). The fact that someone *else* reports perceiving something may be evidence for *me* that things are as he reports perceiving them to be (he is a reliable witness). But my perceiving, my exercise of my perceptual capacity for discerning how things are, does not furnish me with *evidence* that things are as I perceive them to be. My bearing witness to an observed event does not consist in giving my evidence for thinking it happened, but in giving others evidence which consists in my having witnessed the event.

Hence the grounds for Cartesian scepticism are incoherent, and the sceptic's doubts are not to be answered by proving that we know what he claims is doubtful. Rather, his doubts make no sense:

... 'There are physical objects' is nonsense. Is it supposed to be an empirical proposition?

And is *this* an empirical proposition: 'There seem to be physical objects'?

'A is a physical object' is a piece of instruction which we give only to someone who doesn't yet understand either what 'A' means, or what 'physical object' means. Thus it is instruction about the use of words, and 'physical object' is a logical concept. (Like colour, quantity, . . .) And that is why no such proposition as: 'There are physical objects' can be formulated. (*OC*, §§35 f.)[24]

To say that the external world exists, if it means anything, is to say that material objects that are independent of our perceptions of them exist. But to say that material objects are independent of our perceptions of them is a grammatical proposition, a rule for the use of material object names. To say that material objects *exist*, if it means anything, is just to say that material object names have a use in making true or false statements, e.g. that it makes *sense* to say that Pluto exists but Vulcan does not, that dodos and dinosaurs no longer exist and that the Tasmanian tiger probably does not. But *that it makes sense* is not something that could intelligibly be doubted. For it is just to say that there are rules for the correct employment of names of material objects. To 'doubt' these, like doubting the rules of chess, would not betoken admirable caution, but lack of understanding.

Of course, whether particular propositions employing material

---

[24] It is important to note that Wittgenstein adds that this, by itself, is not an adequate reply to the sceptic.

object names are true or false is something to be settled in experience. Here doubts may *sometimes* be legitimate. 'A doubt about existence only works in a language-game' (*OC*, §24), though even then not *every* doubt is intelligible (e.g. doubting whether I have two hands in normal circumstances is not). But doubt about the whole language-game is never intelligible *as a form of doubt*. One might, however, take it as the expression of dissatisfaction with the 'notation', with the whole language-game with material object names. If that, however, is what the sceptic is inchoately driving at, then he must equally renounce the use of 'It seems to me just as if . . .', 'It subjectively appears just like . . .', for these expressions are parts of, refined articulations of the language-game he is repudiating. For the concepts of 'Looking as if . . .', 'seeming to be . . .', 'appearing just like . . .' are parasitic upon the concepts of being thus-and-so. But then he can no longer express his scepticism by saying 'I know how things sensibly seem to me to be, but I can never know how things actually are'.

This move leads naturally to the third and final point of contrast I wish to draw between Kant and Wittgenstein, namely the matter of transcendental argument. Kant's transcendental arguments constitute attempts to derive synthetic a priori propositions which are true descriptions of the phenomenal world (hence synthetic), but which hold necessarily of it and can be known in advance of experience. The primary example of such a synthetic a priori truth is the principle that every event has a cause. The premisses from which Kant endeavours to vindicate such propositions are statements concerning our subjective experiences which express our knowledge of our inner states. In a rather different vein Kant argues that we can infer, from our knowledge of the character of our subjective experiences as possessing a unity (manifest in our ascribing successive experiences to ourselves) and a temporal ordering, that the objects of our experiences are of a certain kind. In particular, we can infer that the objects of our experience are objective existences (though not things-in-themselves) in a unified spatio-temporal world.

Wittgenstein is often thought of as sympathetic to the strategy of a transcendental argument. This is held to be evident in his private language argument, on condition that we read that argument in the spirit of Strawson's *Individuals*.[25] Thus conceived, the argument seeks to show that self-ascripton of experience has, as a condition of its

---

[25] P. F. Strawson, *Individuals*, ch. 3.

intelligibility, the *possibility* of knowledge of others' psychological states on the basis of their behaviour. Put rather differently, the possibility of criterionless self-ascription of experience presupposes the *justifiability* of other-ascription of experience on the basis of behavioural criteria. A slightly different perspective upon the private language argument focuses not upon the correlativity of self- and other-ascription, but upon the necessary publicity of language. Hence, it is said that

> Wittgenstein argues that there can be no knowledge of experience which does not presuppose reference to a public world. I can know my own experience immediately and incorrigibly, but only because I apply to it concepts which gain their sense from public usage. And public usage describes a reality observable to others besides myself.[26]

If this were Wittgenstein's argument, it would indeed bear deep affinities to Kant's transcendental arguments.

We shall see, in Chapters IX and X, that this is *not* a correct account of the private language argument. It is an impressive and persuasive variant of it which depends upon repudiating Wittgenstein's detailed explanation of the character of first-person psychological propositions, of what philosophers call 'self-consciousness' or 'self-awareness' and of what are and what are not descriptions of one's own psychological states. Wittgenstein emphatically denied that 'I can know my own experience immediately and incorrigibly', not because I can know my experience only mediately and corrigibly, but because there is no such thing as 'knowing my experience'. A common premiss of the Cartesian sceptic and of defenders of transcendental arguments is that we *know* of our own psychological states, that such propositions as 'I am in pain', 'It sensibly seems to me just as if I were perceiving such-and-such', 'I seem to remember thus-and-so' are expressions of knowledge. This is precisely what Wittgenstein repudiated. The Strawsonian transcendental argument presupposes that these uses of language involve an *identifying reference* to a *dependent particular*, viz. an experience, the *ascription* of the experience thus identified to a *subject*, viz. oneself, which in turn is *referred to* by the first-person pronoun. This self-ascription, though not resting upon the behavioural criteria which characterize other-ascription, nevertheless has 'an entirely adequate basis'.[27] *All* these claims run contrary to Wittgenstein's arguments (see Chapter X). On his view, they involve

[26] R. Scruton, *Kant* (Oxford University Press, Oxford, 1982), p. 35.
[27] Strawson, *Individuals*, p. 107.

misconceptions of the use of the first-person pronoun, of identifying reference and of ascription of experience. They misapprehend the character of a report or description of one's own experience, construing these on the model of reports or descriptions of experiences of others. And they in effect project *one part* of a unified language-game on to *another part* of that same language-game, as it were projecting the movements of the major pieces in chess on to the pawns.

If this is a correct construal of Wittgenstein's argument, then it is mistaken to take him to be constructing transcendental arguments. For he would deny the shared premiss of the sceptic and Kantian, namely that we *know* our own experiences as expressed in such propositions as 'I am in pain', 'I seem to perceive . . .', 'As I recollect . . .'. But that is the foundation from which transcendental arguments spring. This, however, is not the end of the disagreement, but the beginning. For, as we have seen, Wittgenstein denied that what Kant conceived of as synthetic a priori truths are in fact true descriptions of the world, insisting instead that they are grammatical truths or norms of representation. But there is, in Wittgenstein's view, no such thing as justifying a rule of grammar or deducing a rule of grammar from empirical propositions. (Even if the premisses of a transcendental argument are wrongly taken as descriptions of inner states or knowledge of the character of subjective experience, they could not justify a grammatical proposition.) The principle of universal causation is, he claimed, not a truth about events, but a norm of representation of Newtonian physics. Its apparent necessity is not a reflection of the mind's 'making nature', as Kant's Copernican Revolution suggested, but of conventions of representation for the description of nature. Similarly, if Kant's Transcendental Deduction and Refutation of Idealism are attempts to prove that the external world exists independently of our experience of it or that we can have knowledge of the external world, and if that putative proof rests on our alleged knowledge of our subjective experiences, it is evident that Wittgenstein would not follow that route. For 'knowledge of our subjective experience' expresses a ramifying misconception of the function of first-person psychological propositions, and what is alleged to be proved is either nonsense, or a disguised grammatical proposition that expresses a rule for the use of words.

Nevertheless, even though there is little agreement between Kant and Wittgenstein at the strategic level, they shared a common grand-strategy. Both sought to show that the Cartesian sceptic traverses the bounds of sense. That distinguishes them importantly from empiricists and rationalists alike. The Kantian tries to show this by arguing that a condition for the sceptic to know what he admits to knowing, viz. that things sensibly seem thus-and-so to him, is that he can and typically does know how things, independently of his experiences, are. Wittgenstein took a different route, arguing that the sceptic's doubts make no sense, that his conception of knowledge of subjective experience is incoherent, that his challenge to the justifiability of our cognitive claims misconceives completely their structure and evidential relations,[28] and that the global propositions which he holds to be doubtful are altogether misconstrued.

[28] This is the main theme of *On Certainty*, in which Wittgenstein yet again ploughs up the field of European philosophy.

VIII

THE REFUTATION OF SOLIPSISM

1. *Introduction*

Wittgenstein's claims that a philosophical problem has the form—'I don't know my way about' (*PI*, §123) and that his own purpose in philosophy was 'to show the fly the way out of the flybottle' (*PI*, §309) are notorious. What is less well known is that the archetypal fly in the original flybottle was the solipsist. In the 'Notes for Lectures on "Private Experience" and "Sense Data"', written between 1934 and early 1936, Wittgenstein wrote:

The solipsist flutters and flutters in the flyglass, strikes against the walls, flutters further. How can he be brought to rest? (NFL, p. 300.)

The puzzles surrounding solipsism thus became for Wittgenstein a paradigm of the diseases of the intellect to which philosophers are so prone.[1] The solipsist, like the idealist, is caught in the net of grammar, and by disentangling the knots tied by his futile struggles one can better understand Wittgenstein's conception of philosophy and its methods. His refutation of solipsism comes in three phases. The first stage is to be found in the writings and reports of the transitional period from 1929 to the academic year 1932/3. The *Philosophical Remarks* is particularly important here, but the notes taken by Waismann and Moore are also significant. The second and most revealing phase of his concern with uncovering the errors of solipsism (in particular) and idealism (in general) is between 1933 and 1936. The *Blue Book* and 'Notes for Lectures' contain Wittgenstein's most important arguments in refutation of solipsism. The third and final phase finds its full expression in the *Investigations*, with some additional material in *Zettel*. Here the direct and overt interest in solipsism is diminished, and its place taken by the fully-developed argument

[1] And not only philosophers, e.g. Tolstoy, *Childhood, Boyhood and Youth*, trans. R. Edmonds (Penguin Books, Harmondsworth, 1964), p. 159.

against the possibility of a private language, a brief sketch of which had already appeared in the 'Notes for Lectures'. Although solipsism is only indirectly alluded to, most of the arguments developed in the second phase reappear in highly condensed form in the *Investigations* and *Zettel*. The task of the present chapter is to trace the process whereby Wittgenstein gradually freed himself from metaphysical illusion. I shall first examine the intermediate period between the *Tractatus* and the *Blue Book*, and then show how the elegant and comprehensive refutation of solipsism and idealism emerged in the second, mature phase. The argument against the possibility of a private language will be examined in detail in the following chapter.

Solipsism is the doctrine according to which nothing exists save myself and mental states of myself. Moreover nothing else *could* exist, for we can make no sense of existential claims concerning any other objects unless we construe them as a *façon de parler*. While idealism denies the existence of objective material particulars, but allows for the existence of objective spiritual substances, solipsism presses on rigorously and relentlessly to argue that other minds can enjoy no more privileged a position than bodies. Indeed, taken to its ultimate conclusion the doctrine culminates in what Russell called 'solipsism of the moment'. On this view only the present experiences of myself exist. Neither the past nor the future can be said to be real. Only my immediate present experience 'has reality'. The doctrine has been relatively little discussed in recent years, although both idealism and scepticism concerning the existence of other minds have been extensively debated. But in the inter-war years the topic of solipsism engaged much attention. This may well have been a partial consequence of the enigmatic remarks of the *Tractatus* on the subject.[2] Russell, in an article entitled 'Vagueness'[3] written in 1923 proclaimed that whereas all illegitimate philosophical problems derive from misunderstood symbolism, and all genuine philosophical problems, barring one, are answerable by means of physics, solipsism constitutes the ineradicable

---

[2] C. I. Lewis, in 'Experience and Meaning' (repr. in *Readings in Philosophical Analysis*, ed. H. Feigl and W. Sellars, Appleton-Century-Crofts Inc., New York, 1949, pp. 128–45), p. 131, implies that *TLP*, 5.6's are a source of the positivists' methodological solipsism, but Carnap, in his discussion of his choice of the auto-psychological basis for construction and of his system of methodological solipsism, does not mention the *Tractatus* at all; see R. Carnap, *The Logical Structure of the World*, trans. R. A. George (Routledge & Kegan Paul, London, 1967), §§64–6. There were of course numerous other sources of the doctrine.

[3] B. Russell, 'Vagueness', *Australasian Journal of Philosophy*, (1923), 84–92.

exception. 'If you are willing to believe that nothing exists except what you directly experience,' Russell wrote,[4] 'no other person can prove you wrong, and probably no valid arguments against your view exist.' What is the intractable problem Russell saw? He expressed it thus: 'Is there any valid inference ever from an entity experienced to one inferred?' On this position, Russell declared, he could see no refutation of the solipsist viewpoint.

Russell's position was nevertheless very different in this respect from the Viennese logical positivists. They took Wittgenstein's opaque remarks on solipsism in the *Tractatus* to point in the diametrically opposite direction from scepticism or genuine solipsism. Carnap, in *The Logical Structure of the World*, adopted a thoroughgoing logical empiricism consisting of a marriage of Mach's ontology with Russellian logic under the slogan 'wherever possible, logical constructions are to be substituted for inferred entities'. His programme was to show that all meaningful statements (*Aussage*) could be reduced to primary statements. He chose as his base what he called 'the autopsychological', and endeavoured to show how statements about physical objects, 'the heteropsychological' or other minds, and cultural objects are reducible to statements about bare unowned experiences. Accordingly he named the constructional programme 'methodological solipsism'. Other members of the Vienna Circle, e.g. Schlick and Feigl, though they disagreed with Carnap on some matters of detail, adopted a similar position. The 'egocentric predicament', as they called the puzzles of solipsism, was, so they thought, a piece of metaphysics, relying as it did upon an illegitimate conception of ownership of experience. But it contained within it grains of truth which they put to good use. For, according to their view, statements about the experiences of others as well as statements about other bodies are constructed out of statements describing possible experiences or 'data' which verify them. From 1927 onwards the members of the circle, especially Waismann and Schlick, had Wittgenstein's authority and insight to sustain them in their endeavour. Whether the members of the Circle ever appreciated the Schopenhauerian transcendentalism of the *Tractatus*, 5.6's which is so evident in the *Notebooks* is very doubtful. Both Schlick and Carnap had developed their views on solipsism and the other minds problem prior to their actually meeting Wittgenstein. On the other hand Schlick's paper 'Meaning and Verification'[5] is Wittgensteinian

[4] Russell, ibid., p. 92.
[5] See Feigl and Sellars, op. cit., pp. 146–70.

through and through and acknowledged as such by Schlick. What is clear is that by 1929 the transcendental solipsism of the early period had been replaced in Wittgenstein's mind by a methodological solipsism which, as has been suggested, above, was in a sense already implicit in the *Tractatus*. The transcendentalism dropped away leaving a radical positivist programme.

2. *From Transcendental Solipsism to Methodological Solipsism*

Just as the transition from the picture theory of meaning of the *Tractatus* to the conception of meaning in the *Investigations* passed through an intermediate phase of extreme verificationism, so too Wittgenstein's account of experience passed through an intermediate phase. In the 1929 discussions with Waismann and Schlick, in the *Philosophical Remarks*, and in the Cambridge lectures of 1930–3 Wittgenstein adopted, roughly speaking, a reductionist position on the problem of other minds. In most essential matters his position differed from that of the positivist account of the 'egocentric predicament' given by some of the main members of the Vienna Circle only in matters of detail.

It will be remembered, from the discussion in chapter V above, that Wittgenstein's point of departure in his work in the early 1930s involved distinguishing sharply between genuine propositions, that are conclusively verifiable or falsifiable by comparing them with reality, and hypotheses. The latter are not conclusively verifiable or falsifiable and are not propositions in the same sense. The general form of genuine, conclusively verifiable propositions is 'I have . . .' or 'I feel . . .'. Wittgenstein's primary example was 'toothache' or more generally 'pain'. Propositions such as 'I have pain' or 'I have no pain' are compared with what is actually the case to establish their truth or falsity. 'I have no pain' means, Wittgenstein declared (*PR*, §62), that if I compare the proposition 'I have pain' with reality it is shown to be false. Having pain or having toothache are primary or direct experiences. In these cases, unlike e.g. 'I have a bad tooth', 'I' does not denote a possessor. No physical eye need be involved in seeing, Wittgenstein remarked (M, p. 306) in a turn of phrase reminiscent of the *Tractatus*, 5.633, and similarly no Ego is involved in thinking or having toothache. The Cartesian *res cogitans* is an illusion; as Lichtenberg had pointed out, we should say 'it thinks', like 'it rains', rather than 'I think'. 'I' in the context of primary experience is an eliminable expression (*WWK*, p. 49). Its elimination would of course not be more correct, but would enable one to grasp the logical essentials of the form of representation of facts of personal experience (*PR* §57). The experience of pain, as Hume had noticed, is not that a person—namely I—has something. I can distinguish in a pain an intensity, a location and diverse phenomenal characteristics, but no owner (*PR*, §65). Or rather, it makes no sense to speak of an owner, because it makes no sense to speak of an unowned pain. A matchbox can have an owner, because it can lack one. It makes sense to speak of ownership only where it makes sense to speak of none. Here ownership is transferable. If we thought of pains thus, i.e. as objective particulars, it would be the perception of the pain that would be unpleasant rather than the pain. And this in turn would involve no owner.

While 'I have ...' in 'I have toothache' has no signifying function because it does not delimit a place within a logical space but merely indicates primary experience, the relation between primary experience and a particular physical body is contingent. That the pain which I call mine occurs in this body is a fact learnt by experience. As things are, seeing is universally correlated with physical eyes, but this is a contingent fact, and could be otherwise. Equally pains are uniformly correlated with a specific body in the sense that I do not feel pains in another person's body but only in the body I call 'mine'. But it is readily conceivable that this should be otherwise, that I should suffer toothache which I locate in someone else's mouth, flinch when his tooth is touched, and recover when his abscess is healed (*PR*, §60).

This distinction between the illegitimate sense of logical ownership of experience by an illusory Ego and the causal dependency of experience upon a particular body is no more than an expansion of what remains of the implicit *Tractatus* doctrines once the transcendentalism is removed. The distinction can now be brought to bear upon the solipsist's predicament. The solipsist contends that only his experience is real. 'I can experience only my own experiences' and 'I alone know when I have pains' seem to him to be irrefutable claims illuminating the essence of the world. Upon them he builds his metaphysics. If they are true, it seems, then the concept of experience in general is only intelligible with reference to that which I have. If 'pain' means that which I have when I say truly 'I am in pain', then the supposition that there can be pain which I do not have is unintelligible. The assumption that other persons exist, have experiences, own perceptions, possess affections must be one which transcends all possible experience. It is not that I can know only of my own experiences but can achieve no higher standard than belief with respect to the experiences of others. It is rather that the belief that another ego has, e.g. pain, is unintelligible. If such a belief is unintelligible, so *a fortiori* is any conjecture, for one can conjecture only that which makes sense. The problem is initially set by the sceptic. All words describing personal experience, Wittgenstein later stressed, involve an asymmetry that urges one to say 'I know when I see something just by seeing it, without hearing what I say, or observing the rest of my behaviour, whereas I know *that* he sees, and *what* he sees only by observing his behaviour, i.e. indirectly' (NFL, p. 278). But if indirectly, then not at all. The solipsist is more rigorous and consistent than a weak-kneed sceptic. For how can something be established as good inductive evidence for an inner state if the inner state is not an object of possible experience? And 'how could I ever come by the idea of another's experience if there is no possibility of any evidence for it?' (*BB*, p. 46).

Wittgenstein's analysis in the first phase of his treatment of the predicament took a few steps in roughly the right direction, and then took the wrong turn leading to a position as wrong-headed as the previous transcendentalism. The solipsist's error, he now argued, is to confuse a fact of grammar with a metaphysical necessity. 'I cannot feel your toothache' is a grammatical proposition, not a description of a feature of the world but an explanation of a linguistic convention. 'I cannot feel your toothache' simply means ' "I feel your toothache" is nonsense'. But if so, then:

> In the sense of the phrase 'sense data' in which it is inconceivable that someone else should have them, it cannot, for this very reason, be said that someone else does not have them. And by the same token, it's senseless to say that *I*, as opposed to someone else, *have* them. (*PR*, §61)

How is this 'no-ownership' theory[6] established?

Wittgenstein proceeded by way of a comparison of 'I have toothache' and 'He has toothache'. If the term 'toothache ' in the two sentences is univocal, then it must be possible both to distinguish his toothache from mine, and to establish whether he has the same toothache as I. The solipsist contends that another person could not have the same toothache as he. What is the force of 'could not' here? My toothache and his toothache will be identical, Wittgenstein

[6] P. F. Strawson, *Individuals*, pp. 95 ff.

The Refutation of Solipsism

suggested, if all the properties of my toothache, e.g. intensity, location, and various phenomenal characteristics, are also properties of his. If this can be established, then he and I have the same toothache. It will not help the solipsist to say, 'But for all that, his is his and mine is mine, and surely that is a difference!' For this move transforms the owner of an experience into a property of the experience. But in that case 'I have toothache' says nothing at all, for it is analytic. For 'toothache' here means no more than this cluster of phenomenal features, one of which is 'being had by me'. So, if it is possible to establish identity, he and I can have the same pain. But is it possible? What is meant by 'He has the same toothache as I'? The temptation is to try to explain 'He has . . .', by reference to my knowledge of what is involved in 'I have . . .'. I know what it means for me to have toothache, so when I claim that he has toothache I mean that he has what I previously had. But this only makes sense, Wittgenstein contended, if 'having toothache' involves only contingent ownership, and 'toothache', like 'matchbox' names an objective particular. If so, then it would make sense to think of him having now what I had before, i.e. of toothache, standing first in a relation to me, and then to him. If that were so, then it would make sense for me to be conscious of his toothache, just as I can perceive the purse in his hand which was previously in mine. But these suppositions do not make sense.

Similarly, if it made sense for me to have toothache which I do not feel, then it *would* make sense for him to have toothache which I do not feel (*PR*, §62). But these are not genuine possibilities; our grammar does not permit locutions such as 'I have toothache which I do not feel'. 'He' and 'I' are not both values of the same sentential-function 'X has toothache'. Where we are concerned with primary experience such as toothache, 'I have . . .' and 'I feel . . .' do not differ. The primary is compared directly with reality, it is not possible to 'have it' and not to be 'conscious of it'.

If we take 'toothache' to mean a sensory datum, a primary experience, then toothache could occur in the mouth of another person only in the sense in which it is logically possible to feel toothache in another person's mouth. In our grammar we would not represent this fact by 'I feel his toothache', but by 'I feel toothache in his mouth'. In short, 'toothache' in 'I have toothache', and 'toothache' in 'He has toothache' have different meanings. I verify 'I have toothache' by a direct comparison of the concept of toothache as a datum with reality. The verification does not require the identification of an owner. The 'my' in the solipsist's assertion 'I feel my pains' is a free-running cog, for nothing in the experience of pain justifies the 'my'; the requisite logical multiplicity is missing in the feeling of pain. But when I say '*A* has toothache' the verification is completely different, the identification of *A* enters into the justification of the utterance, and the representation (*Vorstellung*) of pain sensation as a datum is used only in the same way as the concept of flowing is used when one speaks of an electric current flowing (*PR*, §64). But the concept of the flowing of an electric current is not used in the way in which the concept of the flowing of a river is used. The one is verified e.g. by an ammeter, the other by watching the motions of the water upon the river-bed. Analogously, in verifying '*A* has toothache' the concept 'toothache' as a sensory datum is not used.

But if 'toothache' in 'I have toothache' and 'He has toothache' do not mean the same, then do others really have toothache at all? Has the analysis not committed us to claiming that other people never really have what I have, that they do not have real toothache (M, p. 308)? This is to slip back into the solipsist's fallacy. For the investigation has shown such sentences to be nonsensical. If 'not-*p*' has sense then '*p*' must have sense. Hence to say that others have no toothache presupposes that it is meaningful to say that they have toothache (*PR*, §65). But it has been shown that it is nonsense to say that 'another has what I have'. Hence it is nonsense to say that another does not have what I have. What then is meant by the claim that another person has toothache? The claim is, Wittgenstein suggested, not a proposition *stricto sensu*, but a hypothesis. Hence it is confirmed by the verification of its symptoms. We are under the illusion that the two hypotheses (1) that other people have toothache, and (2) that other people behave as I do when I have toothache, but have no toothache, are distinct. But they can be identical in sense if we conceive of them as involving two different *forms* of expression. The first form of expression is our normal one. We do say of others that they have toothache, and we pity a person whom we judge, on the grounds of his behaviour and physical condition, to have toothache. But our philosophical investigation has shown us that 'toothache' is ambiguous. An alternative form of representation would involve using toothache univocally to mean only a datum. In this second form of expression we shall assert the hypothesis that others behave as I do when I have toothache, but of course they (analytically) have no toothache. If we employed this form of expression we would of course talk in tones of pity of people who, as we would say, have no toothache but who behave as we do when we have toothache. For to be sure, the two apparently distinct hypotheses, that others have pains, and that they have none but merely behave as I do when I have them, must be identical in sense if all possible experience which confirms one, confirms the other too. For the meaning of a hypothesis is given by the range of possible experience which confirms it. Since the two hypotheses do have identical confirmatory ranges, they are identical in their meanings.

Wittgenstein's position was indeed that of a 'no-ownership' theorist. He argued that 'I' has two uses, in one of which it is on a level with 'he', as in 'I have a matchbox' or 'I have a bad tooth', and in the second of which it is not on a level with proper names or other personal pronouns, e.g. 'I have toothache', but is eliminable in favour of the form 'there is toothache' (M, pp. 308 ff.). Nevertheless his doctrine, though it suffers from grievous defects, is not open to the criticism which Strawson brought against his reconstructed version of the no-ownership theory. In Strawson's version of the theory, the protagonist contends that while 'All my experiences are had$_1$ by (i.e. causally dependent upon) body B' is contingently true, the apparently necessary truth 'All my experiences are had$_2$ (i.e. owned) by an Ego E' is the product of illusion. For both E and having$_2$ are pseudo-concepts. Strawson correctly pointed out that this contention is incoherent, for the no-ownership theorist utilizes the allegedly illegitimate sense of ownership (having$_2$) in presenting his case for its illegitimacy. In explaining that the ego is illusory he has to state what he takes to be the contingent truth that is the source of the illusion, namely—'All *my* experiences are had$_1$ by B'. But any attempt to eliminate '*my*' from the statement would result in something that is not contingently true: 'The proposition that *all* experiences are causally dependent on the state of a single body B, for example, is just false.'[7] But in Wittgenstein's version of the no-ownership theory, as in Schlick's, the proposition that all primary experiences are had by a single body B, in the mouth of B, is not 'just false' at all. It is just true, although as the emphasis laid upon the possibility of pain occurring in some other body shows, only contingently true. 'Experience teaches us', Schlick wrote, 'that all immediate data depend in some way or other upon those data that constitute what I call "my body".'[8] The primitive experience thus dependent upon B is, Schlick emphasized, absolutely neutral, or, he

[7] Strawson, op. cit., p. 97.
[8] M. Schlick, 'Meaning and Verification', in Feigl and Sellars, op. cit., p. 162.

wrote, quoting Wittgenstein, 'immediate data have no owner'. Thus far, as the above discussion shows, Schlick and Wittgenstein were in accord, and immune to the criticism to which Strawson's reconstruction is susceptible. Primary experience is contingently had$_1$ by me, i.e. B, and 'had$_2$' is a pseudo-concept.

The price paid for this positivist ploy is high. How is communication possible? How can I understand what you mean when you say 'I have pain'? Schlick, in 'Meaning and Verification', did not even touch upon the issue. But Wittgenstein faced it squarely. Both in the Waismann notes (*WWK*, pp. 49 f.) and in the *Philosophical Remarks* (*PR*, §58), Wittgenstein explained his position thus: one can, he suggested, construct many different languages in each of which a particular person is the centre. The centre would, in his language, say 'There is pain', instead of 'I am in pain'. When others are in pain this is expressed by saying 'They behave as Centre behaves when there is pain'. One could indeed imagine an oriental despot forcing everyone to speak the language of which he alone is centre. In such a case someone A other than the despot would express his pain by saying 'A behaves as the centre when there is pain'. Clearly, Wittgenstein argued, such a mono-centred language is intelligible and univocal; moreover such a language can have anyone as centre. Finally, any two such languages are inter-translatable. The proposition in L_1 that there is pain is equivalent to the proposition in L_2 that C_1 behaves as C_2 behaves when there is pain. Our language is in fact composed of as many isomorphic, inter-translatable, mono-centred languages as there are speakers. Wittgenstein added one further point in which the shadow of his previous transcendental solipsism is still evident:

> Now, among all the languages with different people as their centres, each of which I can understand, the one with me as its centre has a privileged status. This language is particular adequate. How am I to express that? That is, how can I rightly represent its special advantage in words? This can't be done. For, if I do it in the language with me as its centre, then the exceptional status of the description of this language in its own terms is nothing very remarkable, and in the terms of another language my language occupies no privileged status whatever.—The privileged status lies in the application, and if I describe this application, the privileged status again doesn't find expression, since the description depends on the language in which it's couched. And now, which description gives just that which I have in mind depends again on the application. (*PR*, §58)

The application of language is the way in which it is laid alongside reality. The special position of every mono-centred language *vis-à-vis* its Centre lies in its being compared directly with primary experience for verification. Since primary experience in any given language L is unique and incomparable, and since different languages differ only in their application, then all that can be expressed about them is their equivalence, and their uniqueness is inexpressible.

There is a great deal wrong with this philosophical account. Wittgenstein's elaborate dialectic, especially in the *Philosophical Investigations*, unravels the knots in the thread of argument with consummate skill. Hence the detailed criticism of this position will be deferred until we come to examine his later critical views on solipsism and private languages, where explicitly or by implication methodological solipsism is shown to be incoherent. But it is worth while making explicit some of the salient commitments of the account. First, it is clear that despite appearances to the contrary there is no such thing as a shared public language. Each speaker possesses his own private language, although these languages are conceived of as intertranslatable. Secondly, the assumption of inter-translatability requires psycho-physical parallelism. For if the proposition in L_1 'There is pain' is to be extensionally equivalent to 'C_1 behaves as C_2 when there is pain' in L_2, there must in general be a uniform correlation between behaviour and primary experience. Thirdly, in ordinary language one never legitimately ascribes a univocal experiential predicate both to oneself and to others. All experiential predicates in normal parlance are ambiguous. Finally, when A says 'I am in pain' (in ordinary language) I cannot, strictly speaking, understand his meaning. Rather I must take his utterance as a sign rather than a symbol, a symptom of 'A is in pain'.

From Moore's notes of Wittgenstein's lectures in 1930–3 it seems that Wittgenstein's initial reason for abandoning his position concerned the nature of what he had called 'genuine propositions'. Descriptions of 'the primary' were conceived as paradigms of propositions in being conclusively and directly verifiable by collation with reality. But in his lectures of 1932–3 he pointed out that phenomenological propositions are not verifiable at all. It makes no sense to ask how 'I have toothache' is verified. 'How do you know that you have toothache?' is a nonsense question. The two standard ploys of those who take the pseudo-question to be a genuine question with a trivial answer are misguided. 'I know I have pain because I feel it' is vacuous because 'I feel pain' and 'I have pain' have the same meaning. 'I know by introspection' is wrong because it erroneously suggests a perceptual model of inner sense. I cannot look and see whether I have pain. From this first insight much of the later grasp of the errors of solipsism and idealism is derived. For in the *Blue Book*, written in 1933–4 Wittgenstein has already substantially consolidated his position. The verificationism has been replaced and the methodological solipsism completely abandoned. Wittgenstein's reformulation of the solipsist's predicament is comprehensive and assured. It is to this that we shall turn first, prior to examining his detailed refutation of solipsism in the post-1933 writings.

3. *The Solipsist's-Predicament: a restatement and second diagnosis*

Solipsism, Idealism, and Realism, Wittgenstein claimed, are all metaphysical theories. Solipsism and Idealism, striving futilely to illuminate the essence of the world, to throw light upon the nature of reality and our experience of it, propound what are in effect grammatical propositions, i.e. *rules* of representation, as if they were revealing essential truths about what is to be represented. Moreover the grammatical propositions they thus deceptively propound are not, by and large, rules of *our* method of representation. Realism conceives of itself as the philosophy of common sense, purporting to defend the beliefs of common sense against the idealist and solipsist onslaught by means of philosophical argument. This common-sense philosopher is, however, as far removed from the common-sense understanding as is the solipsist and idealist (*BB*, p. 48). It is not the task of philosophy, Wittgenstein argued, to defend true or false beliefs or opinions, but to clarify concepts and their internal relations. *A fortiori* it is not its task to defend common-sense beliefs, but to clarify the method of representation in terms of which those beliefs (and others) are expressed. The realist attempts to justify our grammar as if these rules of representation were *truths* about the world. The solipsist and idealist generate a problem. To be sure, they misunderstand it, and the solution they offer is an outgrowth of their misunderstanding. The realist does not solve the problems over which the solipsist and idealist stumble. Not understanding them properly, he disregards them. The solipsist does not understand how another can possibly have experience. The realist's naïve response is to claim that there is no difficulty at all here, since for another to have experience is for him to have what I have when I have experience. This he conceives to be a 'common-sense answer' to the predicament. But common sense is not philosophy, and common-sense philosophy is bad philosophy. The naïve-realist does not even see the point which the solipsist sees, namely that 'inner sense' does not provide us with a criterion of identity which would make it intelligible to ascribe experiences to others. That explanation by means of identity which the realist naïvely suggests cannot work in this way. Genuine common sense, however, cannot resolve philosophical difficulties. Common sense would respond to the solipsist with questions like 'Why do you tell us this if you do not believe that we really hear it?' (*BB*, p. 58) or, like Dr Johnson, would kick a stone to refute idealism (M, p. 311). Common sense is out of its depths when it turns to philosophy. The philosopher's bafflement cannot be resolved by any information which common sense can produce. The restatement of commonsensical views of the world will not relieve the philosopher of his difficulty in uncovering the conceptual articulations which make that view possible (intelligible).

Neither the solipsist nor the idealist maintains that his claims are empirical (M, p. 311). There is no suggestion that they have found out by reference to the common criteria of normal experience that everyone who has said 'I am in pain' was cheating (*BB*, p. 57). The solipsist does not disagree with us about any *practical* matter of fact. He does not say that we are simulating when we complain of pains, and he pities us as much as anyone else (*BB*, p. 59). Nevertheless the solipsist is under the impression that his claims penetrate to the very essence of things in a way in which ours do not. When he claims that a person cannot have someone else's pains he understandably has the impression that his claim, though not causal, and hence not a matter of psychology or physiology, is nevertheless about the nature of pain:

> It seems as though it would be not false but nonsensical to say 'I feel his pains', and as though this were because of the nature of pain, of the person etc. So that the assertion would after all be an assertion about the nature of things.
>
> So we speak perhaps of an asymmetry in our mode of expression and we look on this as a mirror image of the nature of things. (NFL, p. 277)

Once the web of intellectual deception is spun, the solipsist can even find a kind of experiential basis for his metaphysical views. Wittgenstein, harking back to his own younger days, again and again connected the perplexities of solipsism with the phenomenon of staring, e.g.:

> Thus we may be tempted to say 'Only this is really seen' when we stare at unchanging surroundings, whereas we may not at all be tempted to say this when we look about us while walking. (*BB*, p. 66)

In the appropriate frame of mind this confused metaphysician will be driven to say 'This is what is really seen', gesturing not at the material objects of his vision, but at his visual field. Sometimes, Wittgenstein suggested, the most satisfying expression of his point of view seems to be 'when anything is seen (really *seen*), it is always I who see it' (*BB*, p. 61). Not only does staring give one the feeling that reality is, as it were, diaphanous, that the *only* reality is, as Wittgenstein expressed it in the *Philosophical Remarks* (*PR*, §54), the experience of the present moment, it also lies at the root of the feeling that what one means by 'toothache', 'pain', or 'seeing' (NFL, p. 276; *PI*, §293; NFL, pp. 287 f. respectively) is essentially private. The solipsist drives himself into the position of having to say that what gives these words their meaning is something which only he has, and which no one else could conceivably have, hence it is unintelligible to him that others should have experiences. He:

> tries to bring out *the* relation between name and thing named by staring at an object in front of him and repeating a name or even the word 'this' innumerable times. (*PI*, §38)

Staring rigidly, he impresses upon himself that 'at any rate only I have got THIS' (*PI*, §398), 'I *am* in a favoured position. I am the centre of the world' (NFL, p. 299), or 'I am the vessel of life' (*BB*, p. 65), although if these expressions of his doctrine are to satisfy him it is essential not merely that others do not understand him but that it be logically impossible—meaningless—to say that they understand him.

What is amiss here? If the disagreement between our metaphysicians is not indeed about the facts, then the disagreement is about the notation or grammar by means of which the facts are represented. The solipsist is in effect demanding a different form of representation, and objecting that our current notation is inadequate. His claim that only his own present toothache is real toothache amounts to recommending that instead of saying 'So-and-so (the solipsist) has toothache' we should say 'There is real toothache'. Of course, we could do this, though if we did, we should have to find a new way of marking the distinction between real and simulated pain (*BB*, p. 59). The solipsist fails to appreciate two crucial points. First, that nothing can be changed by the new notation (*BB*, p. 57). Secondly, that he is under an illusion if he thinks that the new notation that he is suggesting has a special metaphysical justification lying in the essence of things. In the *Investigations* Wittgenstein clarified his point further:

You have a new conception and interpret it as seeing a new object. You interpret a grammatical movement made by yourself as a quasi-physical phenomenon which you are observing. (Think for example of the question: 'Are sense-data the material of which the universe is made?')

But there is an objection to my saying that you have made a 'grammatical' movement. What you have primarily discovered is a new way of looking at things. As if you had invented a new way of painting: or, again, a new metre, or a new kind of song. (*PI*, §401)

What the solipsist is in effect suggesting is a new form of representation. His fault is twofold. In the first place he believes that grammar is justified by reference to what it depicts. In the second place his suggestion is not self-conscious. Hence he thinks that he has made a discovery about the nature of the world which in some sense contradicts what we take to be the case. Being confusedly dissatisfied with our form of representation of experience and its objects, the solipsist and idealist suggest fragments of an alternative one. But in their confusion they treat the sentences of their novel grammar, e.g. 'There is real toothache', which can only justifiably be said when the solipsist has toothache, as if they belonged to our conventionally accepted grammar. But in our grammar the solipsist's thought is expressed by '*S* (the solipsist) has toothache'. The solipsist (in particular the methodological solipsist) may point to (the representation of) the man's cheek who says he has toothache, and say 'There is no toothache there'. In our grammar this is expressed by his saying 'I have no toothache there' (NFL, p. 308). Nothing changes through change of notation but the style of looking at the world. That is why it is a *fundamental* error to try to refute idealism or solipsism by defending common sense or by 'proving' that realism is 'true'. To do so plays into the hands of the confused metaphysician, perpetuating the merry-go-round of philosophical illusions:

> *this* is what disputes between Idealists, Solipsists and Realists look like. The one party attack the normal form of expression as if they were attacking a statement; the others defend it as if they were stating facts recognised by every reasonable human being. (*PI*, §402)

4. *The Refutation*

Wittgenstein's most important argument against solipsism in particular and idealism in general is his argument against the possibility of a private language. This undermines both solipsism proper, and methodological solipsism, just as it refutes idealism as well as linguistic phenomenalism. However, in the course of his numerous struggles with the problems involved, Wittgenstein elaborated a variety of arguments. The detailed discussion of the private language argument will be deferred for a while, and I shall attempt to gather together Wittgenstein's arguments in refutation of solipsism. Since these arguments come from different periods of his thought a certain, but I hope not undue, amount of artificiality is involved in so doing.

Wittgenstein, as we have already seen, gave various striking formulations of solipsism. Three of these, given in order of increasing atomicity, are as follows. (1) Whenever anything is really seen, it is always I who see it (*BB*, p. 61). (2) The only reality is *my* present experience (M, p. 311). (3) Whenever anything is seen it is *this* which is seen (*BB*, p. 64). Wittgenstein's strategy is to probe each individual element of these formulae to discover weaknesses, and ultimately to show that the employment of that element presupposes for its intelligibility the existence of a set of conditions which the solipsist repudiates. So his use of the element in question is illegitimate. The order in which I shall present his analysis is as follows: first, with what right does the solipsist use the term 'present' in declaring that only his experience of the present moment is real? Secondly, given the solipsist's framework of thought, is he entitled to use the personal pronoun 'I' as he does? Thirdly, when the solipsist says that at any rate he *has this*, what is the nature of the 'having'? Fourthly, and related to the first three points, is his claim that it is *always* he who sees whatever is seen intelligible? Fifthly, when the solipsist speaks of *experience*, be it seeing, toothache or pain, is this, given his fundamental presuppositions, a meaningful term? Sixthly, when the solipsist gestures ostensively towards his sensory field to indicate 'reality', what is he really doing?

(1) *The Temporality Condition*: Wittgenstein's first point is made emphatically in the Waismann notes (*WWK*, p. 107) and in the *Philosophical Remarks*, §54. It is made briefly and with little argument. The proposition 'Only the experience of the present moment is real', Wittgenstein remarked, seems to contain the final consequences of solipsism. Why so? The chain of argument here must be from naïve realism to idealism, from idealism to solipsism, from ordinary solipsism to a no-ownership solipsism of the present moment. But in this formulation of the ultimate conclusion of solipsism, what contrast is being drawn by the solipsist in his use of 'present'? Not that I did not get up this morning, Wittgenstein retorted; nor that what I cannot remember at this moment is unreal. The word 'present' as employed

by the solipsist is redundant; it does not stand in contrast to past and future. Wittgenstein tried to express his thought by means of two of his favourite metaphors. 'Present' in the mouth of the solipsist is not something within a space, as it would be if it made room for past and future, but is itself a space. 'Present' for the solipsist does not designate a point within a system of temporally related events. Indeed the very contention of the solipsist excludes any other possible points within 'temporal space' from being potentially real. Hence the term is redundant, it means nothing.

The second metaphor Wittgenstein used is that of the film projector or magic lantern. He expressed this as follows:

The present we are talking about here is not the frame in the film reel that is in front of the projector's lens at precisely this moment, as opposed to the frames before and after it, which have already been there or are yet to come; but the picture on the screen which would illegitimately be called present, since 'present' would not be used here to distinguish it from past and future. And so it is a meaningless epithet. (*PR*, §54)

This metaphor first appears in his conversations with Waismann in 1929 (*WWK*, p. 50). He used it frequently in the early and mid-thirties to illuminate the confusions of idealism.[9] It makes sense to refer to the film-frame which is in the lens at the moment as 'the present one'. For it has 'neighbours'. There are prior and subsequent frames. But the picture upon the screen can only be thought of as 'the present projected picture' by reference to the serially related frames upon the film-strip on the spool. Independently of the film on the spool, the film on the screen—to mix two metaphors—is not within a space.

It is interesting how close these metaphors stand to one of the masterly rejections of idealism which is an almost equally compressed discussion. This is of course Kant's 'Refutation of Idealism'. The magic lantern analogy in particular seems apt to illustrate Kant's point:

All grounds of determination of my existence which are to be met within me are representations; and as representations themselves require a permanent distinct from them, in relation to which their change, and so my existence in time wherein they change, may be determined.[10]

It is puzzling that Wittgenstein appears to have dropped his attack

---

[9] See M, p. 310; NFL, p. 297, and *BB*, pp. 71 f. where he uses the phrase 'having neighbours' but without the original film metaphor.
[10] Kant, *Critique of Pure Reason*, B xl note a.

upon the temporality condition as part of his refutation of solipsism in his later work.

(2) *The Personal Identity Conditions*: Whenever anything is really seen, the solipsist claims, it is always I who see it. But *who* is the solipsist referring to when he says 'always *I*'? Wittgenstein replies for the solipsist, and he provides a retort:

> I am tempted to say: 'It seems at least a fact of experience that at the source of *the visual field* there is mostly a small man with grey flannel trousers, in fact L.W.'—Someone might answer to this: It is true you almost always wear grey flannel trousers and often look at them. (NFL, p. 298)[11]

Of course the solipsist's 'I' is not intended as a reference to his empirical self. He might, in reply to this rebuttal, say 'Although by the word "I" I don't mean L.W., it will do if the others understand "I" to mean L.W., if just now I am in fact L.W.' (*BB*, p. 64). What then does he mean? He struggles vainly to express what seems to him to be so crucial: 'Surely . . . if I'm to be frank I must say that I have something which nobody has. But who's I?' (NFL, p. 283). The solipsist's difficulty is that nothing within his sensory field provides him with a connection between what is seen (or heard, or felt) and a person. If *this* is what he sees, it is also what is seen *simpliciter*. How can he bring out the connection between the unique self and that which is seen when 'the idea of a person does not enter into what's seen' (M, p. 309). There is no way for the solipsist to express himself except by more and more picturesque and striking (Schopenhauerian) descriptions of his sense of uniqueness: 'But I *am* in a favoured position. I am the centre of the world' (NFL, p. 299). But this favour belongs to the geometrical eye, not the physical eye. The apparent uniqueness is formal; it belongs, as Kant might have put it, to 'consciousness in general'.

The difficulties which give rise to the particular knot into which the solipsist has tied himself with regard to 'I', are one and the same set of difficulties which incline him and sceptics concerning the existence of other minds to say 'We can never know what someone else sees when he looks at something', or 'We can never know whether what someone else calls "blue" is the same as what we call "blue" ' (*BB*, p. 60). To the sceptic this appears to be the limit of the knowable; human cognition can reach thus far and no farther. But what appears to mark out the limits of knowledge in fact, as we have seen, demarcates the bounds of

---

[11] Compare Frege, 'The Thought', in *Philosophical Logic*, ed. P. F. Strawson (OUP, Oxford, 1967), p. 32.

sense. For 'knowing what he sees' in the mouth of the solipsist means 'seeing what he sees',[12] and 'seeing what he sees' means 'doing his seeing for him', i.e. seeing his visual experiences. This is impossible. But its impossibility is not because of the frailty of the human intellect, but because of the unintelligibility of 'seeing another's visual experience'. Even God, in *this* (bogus) sense, cannot see what I see.

One of the roots of the confusion, Wittgenstein argued in the *Blue Book*, lies in the grammar of the word 'I' (*BB*, p. 66). He distinguished between the use of 'I' as object (e.g. I have broken my arm, I have grown six inches, I have a bump on my forehead) and the use of 'I' as subject (e.g. I see so and so, I hear so and so, I try to lift my arm, I think it will rain, I have toothache).[13] The salient feature of the use of 'I' as subject is that it is immune to error through misidentification of the subject. When I say sincerely that I see or hear, think or have toothache, it is not possible that I should have correctly identified (or have a title to predicate) the seeing, hearing, thinking, or toothache, but be mistaken in thinking that it is I who see, hear, think, or have toothache (i.e. be unjustified in predicating it of myself). But that is not because I have correctly identified who is seeing, hearing, thinking, or having toothache. The solipsist is deceived by the fact that we feel that

in the cases in which 'I' is used as subject, we don't use it because we recognise a particular person by his bodily characteristics; and this creates the illusion that we use this word to refer to something bodiless, which, however, has its seat in our body. In fact *this* seems to be the real ego, the one of which it was said, 'Cogito, ergo sum'. (*BB*, p. 69)

He is of course right that saying 'I am in pain' or 'I intend to go' involves no recognition of a person, but he is wrong to jump to the conclusion that the 'I' refers to a *res cogitans*, or indeed to anything else (see below pp. 235 ff., 281 f.).

A comparison with Kant on this matter is illuminating. Kant too noticed the above-mentioned feature. He stressed again and again that transcendental self-consciousness is original, underived, that the personality of the soul cannot be regarded as inferred, that it precedes a priori all one's determinate thought. It is these features that lead to

---

[12] e.g. Hume, 'Suppose we could see clearly into the breast of another, and observe that succession of perception which constitutes his mind...', *Treatise of Human Nature*, I.iv.6.

[13] It is noteworthy that this distinction between the use of 'I' as subject and as object does *not* reappear in later writings.

the Cartesian confusion, which Kant exposed with such skill in the Paralogisms:

> The dialectical illusion in rational psychology arises from the confusion of an idea of reason—the idea of a pure intelligence—with the completely undetermined concept of a thinking being in general. I think myself on behalf of a possible experience, at the same time abstracting from all actual experience, and I conclude therefrom that I can be conscious of my existence even apart from experience and its empirical conditions. In so doing I am confusing the possible *abstraction* from my empirically determined existence with the supposed consciousness of a possible *separate* existence of my thinking self,[14] and I thus come to believe that I have *knowledge* that what is substantial in me is the transcendental subject. But all that I really have in thought is simply the unity of consciousness, on which, as the mere form of knowledge, all determination is based.[15]

The rationalist claim that self-consciousness assures us of our numerical identity through time and hence of our relative permanence (our complete permanence, i.e. immortality, being assured paralogistically through the putative simplicity of the alleged object of self-consciousness) must be combatted. Kant's line of attack in the third paralogism is to show that the evidence upon which the rational psychologist's proof rests, namely the unity of apperception, is perfectly compatible with a multiplicity of numerically distinct but qualitatively identical selves:

> The identity of the consciousness of myself at different times is therefore only a formal condition of my thoughts and their coherence, and in no way proves the numerical identity of my subject. Despite the logical identity of the 'I', such a change may have occurred in it as does not allow of the retention of its identity, and yet we may ascribe to it the same sounding 'I', which in every different state, even in one involving change of the thinking subject, might still retain the thought of the preceding subject and so hand it over to the subsequent subject.[16]

That Wittgenstein had a similar target in mind can be seen from a passage in the 'Notes for Lectures':

> It seems that I can *trace* my identity, quite independent of the identity of my

---

[14] The confusion of what is an abstraction from the empirically determined self with the supposed consciousness of the existence of a *res cogitans* finds its slightly less abstract, but still precise, parallel in Descartes' confusion of the self with the self-*qua*-known-for-certain. See A. J. P. Kenny, *Descartes, A Study of his Philosophy* (Random House, New York, 1968), chap. 4.

[15] Kant, *Critique of Pure Reason*, B 427.   [16] Kant, op. cit., A 363.

body. And the idea is suggested that I trace the identity of something dwelling in my body, the identity of my mind. (NFL, p. 308)

It is interesting to see that Wittgenstein dispels the illusion by much the same means as Kant's *'coup de grâce* to Cartesianism'.[17] For the mirror image of Kant's above-quoted argument is produced in the 'Notes for Lectures' in reply to the question—How am *I* defined?

may I lift my hand to indicate who it is?—Supposing I constantly change and my surrounding does; is there still some continuity, namely, by it being *me* and *my surrounding* that change? (Isn't this similar to thinking that when things in space have changed entirely there's still one thing that remains the same, namely space?) (NFL, p. 300)[18]

The failure of the idealist to meet the personal identity conditions stems, according to Kant, from the confusion of the unity of apperception with the perception of a pure unity. The purity and simplicity of the 'I think' that must be capable of accompanying all my representations is being fallaciously conceived of as the purity and simplicity of a substance which is the object of intuition. A parallel insight can be found in Wittgenstein, although his constructive account of first person, present tense, psychological sentences is wholly different from Kant's. He tried, he said, in 'Notes for Lectures', to bring the whole problem of idealism and solipsism down to our not understanding the function of the word 'I' (NFL, p. 307).

Not only does the first-person pronoun not refer to a Cartesian ego, but further, it is not really a referring expression at all. It functions very differently from expressions that fulfil the role of referring to something, and these differences are important. 'I' is not a proper name, although I would explain who P. M. S. H. is by saying 'I am P. M. S. H'. But that is no identity statement. 'I' does not mean the same as 'The person who is now speaking' for 'The person who is now speaking is the prime-minister' does not mean the same as 'I am the prime-minister'. It is no more the name of a person than 'here' is the name of a place (*PI*, §410). It is not correct to say that 'I' always *refers* to the person who uses it,[19] although it is true that if someone says 'I

---

[17] P. F. Strawson, *The Bounds of Sense* (Methuen, London, 1966), p. 168.
[18] The argument is further elaborated at NFL, p. 308, with the supposition that I change my body every day.
[19] As is argued by S. Shoemaker in 'Self-reference and self-awareness' repr. in his *Identity, Cause and Mind* (Cambridge University Press, Cambridge, 1984), p. 17.

am in pain' others may refer to him in saying 'He is in pain'. For if the rule for the use of 'I' were that it always refers to its user, it would be incorrect to use it unless one knew who its user, i.e. oneself, was. But someone recovering from an accident and suffering from temporary amnesia is not misusing 'I' if he says 'I am in pain', even though he does not know who he is, does not know who it is that is using 'I'. (To know that it is he himself is to know nothing more than he would express by saying 'I said *I* was in pain'; it is not to know who is.) I no more *refer* to or *identify* who is in pain when I say 'I am in pain' than I do when I groan with pain. Though in both cases what I do will enable others to identify who is in pain (*PI*, §404). But note that if, on a dark night, the sentry barks out 'Who goes there?' and I foolishly reply from the shadows 'I do', I have not identified myself. The function of 'I' is *to draw attention to myself*, not to refer to or identify myself. Normally in so doing, circumstances enable *others* to identify me in some way or other. But not, for example, in the above case (unless my voice is recognizable). If I reply to the sentry 'It is P. M. S. H.', then I have identified myself (and if I am N. N., not P. M. S. H., and am engaged in deception, then I have deliberately misidentified myself). Some people do occasionally use their own names in speaking, and it is noteworthy how odd it sounds (e.g., 'Charles de Gaulle has faith in France'). Here indeed one *might* explain to a bemused bystander 'He is referring to himself', and, of course, here too misidentification is possible. But if someone says 'I have faith in France' it would be wrong to say 'He is *referring* to himself' (unless one meant that he *is* France), and not because it is too obvious to be worth saying. 'I' is like 'now' and 'here', not like 'N. N.', 'the ϕer', nor even like 'He' or 'This'.

If referring be compared with shooting an arrow at a circular bull's eye on a wall, which one may hit or miss, then the use of 'I' can be compared to drawing a circular bull around an arrow embedded in the wall. Although the use of the first-person pronoun is thus peculiar and distinctive, its use is systematically interwoven with the use, by oneself and others, of person-referring expressions. And these depend upon a variety of public criteria that are involved in our concept of a person. They include physical appearance, but also characteristic habits, behaviour, and memory. Were this complex array of facts different in certain conceivable ways, our concept of a person and, as a result, of the identity of a person and our notion of personality would undergo fundamental change. Our present concepts would have no grip. Wittgenstein invites us to consider three thought experiments

(*BB*, pp. 61 f.).[20] The first experiment is this: imagine that all human bodies looked identical but different sets of characteristics, always clustered together, were instantiated now in one body, now in another. Under these circumstances it would be possible to assign proper names to bodies, but there would be no more need to do so than there is now need to christen furniture. One might however name the groups of character-traits and say that they change their habitation among the various bodies. The use of these names would correspond *roughly* with our use of proper names. The second experiment is a generalization of the Jekyll and Hyde tale. Imagine that each man's body and character alternate thus regularly. We could christen each man with two names and talk of a pair of persons in his body. We could also construct our form of representation differently. We are not forced in any one direction. The third experiment is equally bizarre. Conceive of a man's memory on even days including only events that have happened to him on even days, and on odd days his memory, with no sense of discontinuity, comprising only events that occurred on odd days. A further variant of the experiment is to conjoin it with the second so that alternating memories combine with alternating appearance and characteristics. In none of these cases does our present concept of a person dictate an answer to questions such as—Are Jekyll and Hyde one person or two? Are two persons inhabiting the body on alternate days, or only one person with two 'memory systems'? What is made clear by the examples is that our ordinary concept of a person is not tailored for normality conditions fundamentally different from our familiar ones. Furthermore, our use of personal pronouns is bound up with the very same background conditions.

Returning now to the solipsist we must press him to reveal what underlying conditions legitimize his use of 'I'. Certainly not his bodily appearance. When he claims that when anything is seen it is always he who sees, it is not necessary that part of his body should be seen. It is not necessary that if his body is seen it should always look the same. The truth of what he says does not seem to be affected even if he has no body, no behavioural characteristics, no memories. But now his use of 'I' is totally free-floating. It does not stand in contrast to 'You' or 'He', and its use by 'others' is meaningless. The solipsist can still express his solipsism by saying 'I am the vessel of life', but it is logically impossible for others to know what 'I' means in this utterance. For it is

[20] For elaboration, see F. Waismann, *The Principles of Linguistic Philosophy*, pp. 213–16.

logically impossible for the solipsist to know what he means by 'I', because the conditions under which the use of 'I' is meaningful are disregarded or denied to obtain by the solipsist. He has, in effect, removed his use of 'I' from the language-games which give it its role.

(3) *The Ownership Condition*: The failure of the solipsist to meet the necessary conditions for the employment of 'I' carries in its wake his failure to meet the requisite conditions of the intelligibility of ownership of experience. In response to the objection that Wittgenstein is neglecting experience—the *world* behind the mere words—Wittgenstein replies:

here solipsism teaches us a lesson: It is that thought which is *on the way* to destroy this error. For if the *world* is idea it isn't any person's idea. (Solipsism stops short of saying this and says that it is my idea.) But then how could I say what the world is if the realm of ideas has no neighbour? What I do comes to defining the word 'world'. (NFL, p. 297)

The argument of the *Blue Book* (*BB*, pp. 53 ff.), repeated in a more condensed form in the *Investigations* (*PI*, §246 ff.), consists of a redevelopment of the arguments of the *Philosophical Remarks*. The diagnosis of the solipsist's error shifts subtly. He confuses *misconstrued* grammatical propositions with empirical ones, and conceives of features of *this* form of representation as metaphysical truths about the world. But whereas in the *Philosophical Remarks* Wittgenstein had argued that toothache is ambiguous, and that 'having' in 'I have toothache' and 'He has toothache' is a different symbol, he now suggested a quite different analysis. When the solipsist claims that he cannot have the same pain as another, and builds his metaphysics upon this base, we must distinguish, as he does not, between talking of sameness of objects (such as chairs) and sameness of experiences (such as pains) or thoughts. In the case of objects we distinguish between qualitative and numerical identity. Two chairs of the same set may be exactly the same, i.e. qualitatively identical, but numerically distinct. And if I buy your chair, then the chair I now have is exactly the same chair as, i.e. numerically identical with, the chair you previously had. Note, however, that we do not draw such a distinction with respect to the *colour* of two chairs. If my chair is *this* shade of brown, and your chair is also this shade of brown, the two chairs are the same colour. It makes no sense to say 'Ah, but they are only qualitatively the same colour!', for that would imply that the brown colour of my chair is *numerically distinct* from the brown colour of yours. And then it would make sense to ask what distinguishes the colour of mine from the colour of yours; and the only answer would be '*This* brown has this chair as its owner, *that* brown has that chair'. But this is to treat the chair as the property of the colour. And so to do is to project upon the concept of colour the grammar of a substantive. This is absurd. Numerically distinct *objects* can have one and the same colour, but the identical colour they severally have is not 'numerically distinct'.[21]

Thoughts and experiences such as pain are, in this respect, akin to colour. If I think that the battle of Hastings was fought in 1066 and if you think that the battle of Hastings was fought in 1066, we both think the same thought. It would be absurd to suggest that because *I* think *my* thought and *you* think *yours*, therefore my thought is only *qualitatively* identical with yours but *numerically* distinct, for that would be to make the thinker of the thought *a property of what is thought*. But the question of *who* thought that *p* is distinct from the question of *what* A (and B) thought. And if both A and B thought that *p*, then they both had the *same* thought. So too with pain. If A and B both have an intense, throbbing headache in the temples, they have the same pain. That A has such a headache now, and B has it in an hour's time does not make B's headache different from A's (but if his headache were dull and continuous, rather than throbbing, it would be different). That is what we *call* 'having the same headache'. *A fortiori*, the 'fact' that A has *his* headache and B has *his* headache, does not differentiate the headaches. For that, as in the case of the colour of the chairs, would render the owner (the sufferer) a property of the pain.

Of course, we are inclined to object that there are surely two headaches, so they must be numerically distinct! But that just means that there are two *people* with a headache, which may be the same. We confuse here the criterion of identity of the pain (viz. its intensity, phenomenal characteristics, location[22]) with the criterion of ownership of pain (the person who gives expression to the pain, who *manifests* pain). And this is precisely what the solipsist does. For 'Nobody else can have my pain' (which is the first step in his argument) does not imply that you and I cannot have the same pain. It is merely a confusing expression of the grammatical proposition (rule) that 'my

---

[21] Cf. N. Malcolm, 'The Privacy of Experience' in his *Thought and Knowledge* (Cornell University Press, Ithaca, 1977), esp. pp. 114 ff. for illumination on this theme.

[22] If I have a pain in my knee and you have a pain in your knee, then we both have a pain in the same place. It does not, of course, follow that our respective knees are in the same place.

pain' = 'the pain I have', coupled with the mistaken idea that two people cannot have the very same pain and therefore that it is impossible for me to have your pain, i.e. the very same pain as you. But this is confused.

Matters are, however, worse than failure to achieve more than a trivial, confusedly expressed, insight. For in the hands of the solipsist 'Nobody else can have my pain' is transformed into a truth of metaphysics, describing the nature of things. But the unique ownership which he purports to find is something of which he can give no account whatever. For the genuine ownership of experiences is determined by the *person* (human being) who gives expression to them in behaviour in certain circumstances. Yet the solipsist's misconstrual of the use of 'I' masks this from his eyes. And his conflation of the question of the criterion of identity of, e.g., pain with the question of the criterion of ownership multiplies confusion.

The source of the confusion which we have identified under this heading ('the ownership condition') lies in the temptation to construe the grammar of the first-person psychological verb on the model of the third-person one and to construe psychological nouns such as 'pain', 'intention', 'feeling' on the model of names of objects. In our exercise of our perceptual faculties, for example, we perceive, are aware of, or are conscious of substances and their properties in the world around us. And we describe what we perceive by ascribing properties to particulars. In describing what we thus perceive we preface our descriptions by 'I see (hear, smell, etc.)' or 'I noticed (caught sight of, glimpsed, etc.)'. And here too, it seems, we attribute properties (seeing, hearing, smelling) to a substance (me). Surely, we are *aware* of seeing, noticing, hearing or listening; we surely are *conscious* of these mental acts or activities! And so we conceive of *self-consciousness* as 'inner sense', in which we note, and report for the benefit of 'outsiders', what is going on *in foro interno*. Then we may further note that we seem to be aware of the instantiation of these 'experiential properties' (seeing, hearing, feeling) independently of the 'substance in which they inhere'. And this in turn induces us to succumb to a temptation which grammar itself encourages,[23] to reify our experiences. This is nowhere more evident than in Hume: 'we have no perfect idea of a substance; but taking it for *something that can exist by itself*, it is

---

[23] See NFL, p. 302: 'In "I have toothache" the expression of pain is brought to the same form as a description "I have five shillings".'

evident every perception is a substance...'[24] As long as we adhere to the perceptual model of introspection, we cannot help treating our experiences as private objects. We consequently generate a multitude of illusions which we enshrine in a metaphysics, including the illusion of unique and inalienable ownership.

(4) *The Continuity Condition*: The solipsist's use of 'I' was intended to refer to a substance. This spiritual substance was subsequently thought of as the only conceivable existing substance. It was the vessel of life, the sole owner of all conceivable experience. Barring solipsism of the present moment, it was thought to possess a traceable identity through time. Hence a corollary of the solipsist's disregard of the circumstances of the language-games in which the personal pronoun has its home and his inability to understand the meaning of 'ownership of experience', is his failure to satisfy the requisite conditions of continuity. The use of 'I' seemed to indicate a continuous substance throughout the duration of experience to which the experience could be ascribed. As he realizes that his use of 'I' is wholly free-floating, he may now find himself attempting to express his solipsism without using 'I'. Instead of saying 'whenever anything is seen, it is always I who see it', he will now say 'whenever anything is seen, always *something is seen*'. What is unique is experience; the world is idea.

(5) *The Experiential Condition*: The solipsist has given a lot of ground. Indeed his position can barely be intelligibly articulated. It is a no-ownership solipsism of the present moment, moreover his position is now identical with the constructional base chosen by the methodological solipsist. All that exists is the experience of the present moment, and this experience is unique, without being owned. Wittgenstein pursued the issue relentlessly. His answer to this part of the solipsist's claim is embodied in his argument against the possibility of a private language. For the moment all I wish to do is to anticipate the discussion of the next chapter.

The solipsist holds that a given experiential predicate can be meaningful even though its ascription to others is inconceivable. Hence his belief is that such terms can be given meaning and explained (subjectively) exclusively by reference to the actual experiences to which they refer. Wittgenstein's contention was that this is not possible. The solipsist is left with nothing but a vacuous mental gesture. The experience itself cannot serve as a paradigm by reference

---

[24] Hume, *Treatise of Human Nature*, I.iv.5.

to which the name of the experience is given sense (NFL, p. 314). If this is correct, then the solipsist has no right to pick out the experience which he is currently experiencing as unique. For if his claims are correct, he can have no concept with which to pick it out.

(6) *The Ostensive Gesture Conditions*: The solipsist's last stand is to attempt a final reinterpretation of his position. Instead of the variously chosen formulae which we have examined and rejected he now reformulates his claims thus:

'whenever anything is seen, it is *this* which is seen', accompanying the word 'this' by a gesture embracing my visual field (but not meaning by 'this' the particular objects which I happen to see at the moment). One might say, 'I am pointing at my visual field as such, not at anything in it'. (*BB*, p. 64)

It is essential to this formulation, Wittgenstein added, that the pointing should be 'visual' (*BB*, p. 71), that I point to things which I see, not to things which I do not. Better still, I should point out 'mentally'. Any other pointing would be irrelevant, indeed meaningless, from the solipsist's point of view. Wittgenstein began his reply to this with two metaphors. The solipsist's gesture is like that of a man travelling in a car who is in a hurry, and to speed things up pushes against the dashboard. The solipsist's pointing does not serve to pick one thing out in contrast with another; consequently it picks out nothing. When it makes sense to say 'I see this' while pointing at what I see, it also makes *sense* to say 'I see this' while pointing behind me at what I do not see. Wittgenstein connected this with his second metaphor. The solipsist robs his pointing gesture of any possible significance 'by inseparably connecting that which points and that to which it points'. It is as if he had constructed a clock, connected the hands to the dial, and expected the clock to tell the time.

The solipsist's pointing gesture, like his 'present moment', his 'I', his 'ownership', has no neighbour. It is not within a space, it is not the actualization of one possibility among others. Wittgenstein compared the error of the solipsist's gesture to that of a man who thinks that saying 'I am here' will make sense under any conditions whatever, and moreover will always be true. But this is to forget that the use of 'here' depends upon a contrast between 'here' and 'there', and that the use of 'there' is interwoven with the use of further expressions which might be employed to clarify where, e.g. next to the clock on the mantelpiece. In short, these expressions presuppose the existence of a public space in which objects are locatable and reidentifiable by reference to their spatial path through time. For 'I am here' to make sense, it must be intended to be—and be capable of—drawing attention to a point in *common space*. If 'here', however, is intended to point to a spot in subjective space, as the solipsist's gesture and 'this' points to his visual field, then 'I am here', Wittgenstein suggested (*BB*, p. 72), amounts to 'Here is here'. The solipsist's gesture is only a pseudo-gesture. If the solipsist however points, not to his 'visual space' but to common space, and says 'This is really seen', we can reply—'We could adopt a notation in which whatever L.W. sees at a given moment is called "Things really seen". But there is no reason to do so.'

Wittgenstein's refutation of solipsism has now been traced through all its stages. It should be noted that it is a 'refutation' not in the sense of showing solipsism to be a *false theory* (for then one might pursue the will o' the wisp of a 'true theory') but in the sense of showing it to be nonsense. I have concentrated upon the two main relevant works of the intermediate phase. But there is no doubt that much the same target is under continual fire in the *Investigations*. There are very many passages which might confirm this, but the most striking is the following, which encapsulates much of the six-stage argument in one paragraph:

'But when I imagine something, or even actually *see* objects, I have *got* something which my neighbour has not.'—I understand you. You want to look about you and say: 'At any rate only I have got THIS.'—What are these words for? They serve no purpose—Can one not add: 'There is here no question of a "seeing"—and therefore none of the "having"—nor of a subject, nor therefore of "I" either.'? Might I not ask: In what sense have you *got* what you are talking about and saying that only you have got it? Do you possess it? You do not even *see* it. Must you not really say that no one has got it? And this too is clear: if as a matter of logic you exclude other people's having something, it loses its sense to say that you have it.

But what is the thing you are speaking of? It is true I said that I knew within myself what you meant. But that meant that I knew how one thinks to conceive this object, to see it, to make one's looking and pointing mean it. I know how one stares ahead and looks about one in this case—and the rest. (*PI*, §398.)

The solipsist claimed that the present moment is unique, that he is privileged, that it is always he who sees, that what he has when he sees is unique, that his seeing is exceptional, that 'this' is incomparable. Each move is illegitimate. The illegitimacy of each move damns not just solipsism, but phenomenalism and indeed any form of idealism. However, when the ostensive gesture and the utterance 'This is seen' *are* genuine, they point to the world. 'The self of solipsism shrinks to a

The Refutation of Solipsism

point without extension and there remains the reality coordinated with it.' When Wittgenstein wrote this in 1916 he meant something very different from what he later thought about solipsism and idealism. But what this *says* is equally appropriate for his later views.

> We shall not cease from exploration
> And the end of all our exploring
> Will be to arrive where we started
> And know the place for the first time.[25]

---

[25] T. S. Eliot, 'Little Gidding', *Four Quartets*, IV, lines 239-43.

IX

PRIVATE LINGUISTS AND PUBLIC SPEAKERS

1. *A Disease of the Intellect*

Wittgenstein's argument against the possibility of a private language is an endeavour to show that a certain conception of the mind, of self-consciousness or self-awareness, of knowledge of other minds and of perceptual experience, is deeply incoherent. The incoherence of this pervasive picture of the mind is co-ordinate with fundamental misconceptions about language, meaning, and understanding. These in turn strikingly exemplify the distorting force of the pre-theoretical assumption that the essential function of words is to name and of sentences to describe.

The private language argument is, if correct, one of the most important philosophical insights achieved in this century. It is a criticism of the conception of the mind which is not merely the dominant one in European philosophy, but is also pervasive in our culture, in psychology, linguistics, and indeed in the reflections of most people who think about the nature of 'self-consciousness' and the mind. For our reflective conception of our awareness of our own thoughts, desires, and emotions, our intentions, delights or perceptions is moulded by the picture of a contrast between what is 'inner' and what is 'outer'. And we quite naturally construe what is 'inner' on the model of what is 'outer'. We can, we think, *inspect* the objects in the world around us, or *introspect* the 'objects' of the 'world' within us. We take the latter on analogy with the former—and it is precisely there that we fall into confusions.

The consequent array of misconceptions of the mind presupposes a distinctive picture of language. For we are inclined to view the primitive indefinable terms of a language as deriving their meaning from our immediate experiences. Terms like 'red' or 'sour', 'pain' or 'joy', 'thought' or 'desire' are, we think, understood by anyone who has had the experience of seeing red or tasting a sour taste, suffering pain or being joyful, thinking or willing, and who has attached those words to the appropriate experiences. In this sense, the 'foundations' of language are conceived to lie in private experience. I know what I mean by 'pain' or by 'red', one wants to say, I mean *this* ↑—and one, as it were, points within. In *various* forms, such a conception of language and meaning pervades the writings of Descartes and the rationalists, of Locke and the empiricists. It is prominent in Russell and a distinctive feature of much of the work of members of the Vienna Circle.[1] It is strikingly evident in Wittgenstein's own *Philosophical Remarks*.

Characteristically, Wittgenstein did not indicate explicitly any personal targets of attack in his discussion. Apart from an implicit reference to Frege,[2] the discussion is altogether ahistorical. Wittgenstein's aim was to diagnose a disease of thought to which many have succumbed. The source of this disease might be said to lie in the grammar of our language and in our natural dispositions of thought. It lies in the grammar of our language inasmuch as first-person present tense psychological sentences have the same *form* as third-person ones, but profoundly different uses. Moreover many psychological propositions are similar in form to material object propositions (e.g. 'I have a toothache'/'I have a tooth'), and this leads us astray. For we project features of one language game on to another quite different one. It comes naturally to us to be impressed by similarities of form, and it is difficult to grasp the crucial significance of differences in use, let alone to describe them correctly. It would be altogether misguided to suppose that this disease of the intellect is a mere historical curiosity which has, by the late twentieth century, like smallpox, been stamped out. On the contrary, it is rife, not only among philosophers but also in the arguments of those who purport to engage in empirical studies of, or simulations of, the mind and the capacities of creatures with minds. It is important to note that the most adamant anti-Cartesians such as central-state materialists or computational functionalists harbour this infection in subtle and not easily detectable forms. There is no magical immunization against this ramifying intellectual syndrome, for it consists of an array of interwoven fallacies and false analogies that are

---

[1] e.g., R. Carnap, *The Logical Structure of the World*; M. Schlick, 'Form and Content, an Introduction to Philosophical Thinking', in *Gesammelte Aufsätze* 1926–1936 (Georg Olms, Hildesheim, 1969).

[2] The phrase 'uns Allen Gegenüberstehendes' in scare-quotes at *PI*, §273 is a quotation from Frege's *Grundgesetze der Arithmetic*, p. xviii, '*etwas Allen gleicherweise Gegenüberstehendes*'.

deeply appealing. Wittgenstein's private language argument offers a cure for this illness—for those who wish to be cured.

In this chapter I shall examine the notion of a private language and Wittgenstein's critical discussion of it. The attendant conception of self-consciousness and of our knowledge of mental states of others will also be scrutinized. Delineation of Wittgenstein's own account of self-consciousness will be deferred until the next chapter.

2. *Following Rules*

The private language argument begins at §243 of the *Philosophical Investigations*.[3] It does, however, build upon previous conceptual clarifications. Hence it is important to locate it correctly within the argumentative strategy of the book. The preceding hundred sections (§§143–242) are concerned with a variety of themes about following rules. Contrary to conceptions of meaning that are informed by the Augustinian picture of language, the meaning of an expression is not an 'entity' correlated with it. The meaning of a name is not its bearer; meanings are not entities in the physical world to which expressions are 'attached' (perhaps by ostension) but nor are they mental entities; they are not abstract entities, e.g. Fregean senses, which we 'attach' to the words of our languages, for meanings are not entities of any kind. The whole venerable tradition that conceived of meanings of words as entities correlated with words on the biplanar model is repudiated by Wittgenstein. It was with this in mind that he said in 1932/33 that 'the idea of meaning is in a way obsolete, except in such phrases as "this means the same as that" or "this has no meaning"' (M, p. 258). The meaning of an expression is what one understands when one understands the expression. It is what is explained by an explanation of meaning. An explanation of meaning provides a standard or rule for the correct use of an expression. For one's use of a word is correct, makes sense, when it accords with an appropriate explanation of meaning. A person's understanding of an expression is manifest in his use of it (i.e. whether he does use it in accord with the correct explanation) and in his giving correct explanations of it on appropriate

---

[3] S. Kripke, in *Wittgenstein on Rules and Private Language: an Elementary Exposition* (Blackwell, Oxford, 1982) contends that the 'real private language argument' lies in §§143–242, indeed that the *conclusion* is already established by §202. For a multitude of reasons this is a complete distortion of the argument and content of Wittgenstein's book. For substantiation of this verdict, see G. P. Baker and P. M. S. Hacker, *Scepticism, Rules and Language* (Blackwell, Oxford, 1984), ch. 1.

occasions. And also, of course, in his responding appropriately to the use of the expression by others.

Understanding a language is knowing what expressions of the language mean. But this is not a matter of acquaintance with 'entities' of any kind. Knowing what 'W' means (like knowing what time it is) is being able to answer the question 'What does "W" mean?' ('What time is it?'). It is further a matter of using expressions in accord with the rules for their use, rules that are given by explanations of meaning. We are, however, strongly inclined to think that the overt activities of giving explanations or of using expressions correctly are consequences, indeed causal consequences, of understanding. This picture is strengthened by noting that we typically understand an expression at a stroke, often grasp an explanation of meaning in a flash. Wittgenstein held that this conception of understanding involved fundamental confusions. It sends us in search of a mythological inner state or process of understanding from which outward activities flow, and we speculate over what it might be, whether it is conscious or unconscious, mental or neural, accessible to the investigations of theoretical linguists or psychologists. It also fosters a mythology of rules. For if understanding a language is an inner state involving 'mental (or perhaps 'neural') representations' of rules, then rules must be conceived as, in some sense, containing their own applications. They must, it seems, be mechanisms which generate what accords with them. Understanding then seems to be an inner state or process in which one 'lays hold of' or 'grasps' a rule for the use of an expression, and the rule (which, like a logical machine, determines what accords with it) guides the mind (or brain) along its predetermined tracks.

Combatting such misconceptions is the task of *Investigations* §§143–242. Understanding is a capacity (or, at least, akin to a capacity), not an act, state or process. Using expressions with understanding, or suddenly understanding something may be accompanied by a variety of mental events or processes, but none are either necessary or sufficient for understanding. We are inclined to think that following a rule must *essentially* be a matter of conscious or unconscious mental activities or neural ongoings. Wittgenstein tried to shake us free from this beguiling conception in a long examination of following phonetic reading rules in §§156–78. We are tempted to think that one follows such rules when one *derives* the copy from the original, or when one 'feels' the influence of the written characters, when the letters 'intimate' the sounds. We follow the rules, it seems, not just when we act in accord with them, but when we do so *because* of the rules; and we then wonder what exactly it is to 'experience the *because*'. These suppositions are confused. Reading is a rule-guided activity, but its essence is not to be found in any accompanying experiences. Being able to read is (tautologically) an ability, not a mental or neural state or reservoir from which overt performances flow. Reading is the exercise of that ability. It is not something defined by inner processes, but rather by the public criteria in the various circumstances that justify saying of someone that he is reading.

However, if the logical difference between mere *accord* with a rule and actually *following* a rule does not consist in what goes on in the mind or brain when one acts in accord with a rule, what is it? This question is resolved in *Investigations* §§185–242 in the course of reconciling two apparently inconsistent elements in Wittgenstein's description of the grammatical articulations between meaning, use, explanation, and understanding. On the one hand, he has argued that the meaning of an expression is its use. On the other, he has insisted that it is given by an explanation of meaning, viz. a rule for its use. But how can such an explanation, e.g. an ostensive definition or a series of examples with a similarity-rider (in the case of family-resemblance concepts), determine the complex use of an expression? For any rule or explanation of meaning can be variously interpreted. So what determines the 'correct interpretation'? What determines a correct application of the rule? This unclarity is reflected in a parallel puzzle about understanding. For given that we often understand the meaning of an expression in a flash, how can the meaning be the use? For the use of an expression is, as it were, spread out over time (*PI*, §138), not something that can be grasped in a flash. And if what is understood is expressed by an explanation, i.e. a rule, how can this rule, which can be differently interpreted, 'contain' in itself the use of the expression or fulfil a role in determining its use and in guiding a speaker in his employment of it?

Wittgenstein's answer to this battery of problems is subtle. Of course rules determine what accords with them (*PI*, §189), but not because they mysteriously 'contain' their own applications. Of course we often understand the meaning of a word in an instant (*PI*, §197), but this is no more mysterious than the fact that in intending to play chess one does not run through all the rules of chess in an instant to ensure that it is *chess* and not some other game one intends to play. The relation between understanding an expression and the pattern of its correct use is *internal* or conceptual. So too is the relation between a rule and what counts as accord with it. We *use* rules as standards of correctness *in practice*. It is not interpretations that mediate between rules and their correct applications; on the contrary, an interpretation typically presupposes the existence of this internal relation and clarifies it to one who does not grasp it (*PI*, §201). Nothing *mediates* between internally related terms. That they are thus related is manifest in our employment of them, in the ways in which we do or would explain or justify our use of an expression, teach or learn how it is to be used, correct and criticize misuses of an expression or misapplications of a rule. The difference between acting in accord with a rule and following a rule does not turn on any mental or neural accompaniments of action but upon the manner in which the agent would explain why he acted as he did, how he would justify doing as he did, what reasons he would give if challenged. The normativity of rule-guided behaviour is not a causal or nomological feature of it.

A rule for the use of an expression and the acts that accord with it are not independent of each other,[4] but two sides of the same coin, two aspects of a *practice* (which may or may not be a social practice), an *activity* of using symbols. There is no such thing as a rule without a technique of application that is manifest in action. It is his technique of using a rule that determines in practice what the rule-follower *calls* 'accord with the rule' or 'breaking the rule'. Hence also understanding a rule and knowing how to apply it, grasping an explanation of meaning and knowing how to use the word explained are not two independent abilities but two facets of one and the same ability.

The phenomenon of language is part of the web of human action and interaction in the world. It presupposes as its stable framework certain pervasive regularities of the physical world and of human nature. Understanding a language is not a mental state but a capacity or array of capacities to employ symbols in accord with rules in a myriad of speech activities. This conception of language as *Praxis*,[5] this emphasis upon the primacy of the deed[6] is a fundamental aspect of

---

[4] The lively debate about rule-scepticism that has flourished in recent years is predicated upon the wholly incoherent assumption that they are, cf. Baker and Hacker, *Scepticism, Rules and Language*, Ch. 2.

[5] It has been widely assumed that when Wittgenstein uses the term 'practice' he uniformly means 'social practice'. This is mistaken, and trivializes his insight. (See footnote 17 below.)

[6] He liked to quote the remark from Goethe's *Faust* 'Im Anfang war die Tat' ('In the beginning was the deed').

Wittgenstein's philosophy the import and consequences of which ramify throughout his later work. But a long tradition in philosophy presupposes not the primacy of action in language use, but the primacy of thought. The dominant patterns of philosophizing about a very wide range of epistemological questions assumes that the 'foundations' of language lie not in action, not in the techniques of rule-application in overt linguistic activities, but in naming one's own sense-impressions (ideas, sense-data) and then using those names to describe how things are, first with oneself, then in the world. For it seems that we can give words a meaning, lay down rules for their use, within the confines of our own minds. The shattering of this illusion is the concern of Wittgenstein's private language argument.

3. *Philosophical Investigations*, §243

Wittgenstein's discussion opens with the following remark:

A human being can encourage himself, give himself orders, obey, blame and punish himself; he can ask himself a question and answer it. We could even imagine human beings who spoke only in a monologue; who accompanied their activities by talking to themselves.—An explorer who watched them and listened to their talk might succeed in translating their language into ours. (This would enable him to predict these people's actions correctly, for he also hears them making resolutions and decisions.)

But could we also imagine a language in which a person could write down or give vocal expression to his inner experiences—his feelings, moods and the rest—for his private use?—Well, can't we do so in our ordinary language?—But that is not what I mean, The individual words of this language are to refer to what can only be known to the person speaking; to his immediate private sensations. So another person cannot understand the language.

The first paragraph links the subsequent discussion of the private language with the prior argument about meaning, understanding, and following rules. The second paragraph is linked with the first by means of the contrast between the imagined soliloquists and the private-language speaker. The soliloquists give vocal expression to their inner experience for their own private use, and their comments can be understood by others—for the explorer translates them. The private language is characterized by its being unintelligible to others. I shall start by examining the problems involved in the first paragraph of the passage.

§243 follows the concluding remarks of the rule-following discussion. These concern the role of agreement in a shared language. If language is to be a means of communication then speakers must not only agree in the definitions of the terms they employ, i.e. in explanations of meaning, but also agree in judgements. This sounds paradoxical, for it might seem to abolish the objectivity of judgement. But it is not so. Rather is it a consequence of the reflections on rules that a common understanding of a rule for the use of an expression is manifest in a common *technique of application*. That you and I both understand the ostensive definition 'This ↑ is red' in the same way is manifest in our calling (by and large) the same things red. 'It is one thing to describe methods of measurement, and another to obtain and state results of measurement. But what we call "measuring" is partly determined by a certain constancy in results of measurement' (*PI*, §242). Nor is it the case that the objectivity of judgement is vitiated by insisting that agreement in definitions *and* agreement in judgements are both requisite for and a criterion of a common understanding of expressions. For human agreement does *not* determine truth or falsehood. 'Grass is green' does not mean 'Most people believe that grass is green'. But widespread ramifying disagreements over judgements (the application of concepts) would betoken disagreements over definitions (explanations), inasmuch as it would signify disagreement over the techniques of application of expressions in accord with those explanations.

The opening paragraph of §243 introduces a soliloquists' language which is designed not for communication but for monologue. Does this not conflict with the previous suggestions? I think not. The soliloquist has a language which is as rule-governed as ours. Even if the soliloquist is quite solitary, his language, though not shared, is sharable. Although there may be no one to agree with him in his judgements, if there were someone, he could agree. The necessity of agreement adumbrated in §§240–2 concerns only what must be possible, not what must be actual. Such agreement must be actual 'if language is to be a means of communication', which, in the case of the soliloquists, it is not. The necessary conditions involved in the existence of a language imply only possible sociality, only the possibility of inter-personal discourse, not its actuality. It is sometimes thought that the point of Wittgenstein's argument is to prove that a language is *essentially* the shared property of a multiplicity of speakers, or that a neonate Crusoe could not use a language since he couldn't (without extra-insular aid) distinguish seeming to follow a rule from following a rule. This is mistaken. Far from suggesting that a language of a socially isolated individual is inconceivable, because language is always a social activity involving rules that only a social institution can provide, Wittgenstein had no objection to following a rule privately (in solitude), but only to following a 'private' rule, i.e. a rule which no one else *could in principle* understand or follow. It is indeed striking that in various manuscripts[7] Wittgenstein discussed Robinson Crusoe, solitary cavemen, and other such isolated people following rules. The upshot of his remarks is that there is no conceptual problem in the idea of following rules in isolation as long as one's behaviour displays a complexity appropriate to rule-following in the context of a persistent (contingently private) normative technique or practice, i.e. as long as the rules are, in principle, shareable, capable of being followed by others. The technique of following a rule, he argued,[8] can indeed be private in the same sense in which I can have a private sewing machine, i.e. no one but I knows about it. But, of course, to be a private sewing machine, it must be a sewing machine, i.e. it must resemble a sewing machine, public or private. And a rule which a Crusoe follows in solitude must satisfy the conditions for being a rule, it must be 'analogous to what is called a "rule" in human dealings' (*RFM*, p. 344). What is ruled out in the private language argument is not the imaginary soliloquist (solitary or in groups) but one whose concepts, rules, and opinions are essentially unsharable rather than contingently unshared. The importance of the soliloquists is both to stand in contrast with the speaker of a putative private language, and to clarify Wittgenstein's intentions. These are *not* to make points about the social nature and genesis of common languages.

The second paragraph of §243 clarifies what Wittgenstein means by a private language. The imaginary soliloquists employ their language for their own private use. In our ordinary language we can write down our feelings, moods, and inner experiences. Neither of these constitutes a private language. Wittgenstein characterizes a private language by reference to three features: (a) the words of the language

[7] Cf. MSS 165, pp. 74, 103 f., 108 ff.; MS 166, pp. 4,7; MS 124, p. 221; MS C5 p. 25. Hence the debate concerning the possibility of Crusoe inventing a language (A. J. Ayer and R. Rhees, 'Can There be a Private Language?', *Proceedings of the Aristotelian Society* supp. vol. xxviii (1954), 63–94) misconstrues his point. Note also that Wittgenstein explicitly countenanced the intelligibility of innate knowledge of a language (*PG*, p. 188; *BB*. pp. 12, 97). This does not affect the private language argument in the slightest. For if we were born able to speak English or German, it would still be unintelligible for us to explain the meaning of words, to others or to ourselves, by private ostensive definition or to purport to follow a rule which was in principle unintelligible to anyone else.

[8] See *MS* 166, p. 7.

are to refer to what can only be known to the speaker, (b) the words of the language are to refer to the speaker's immediate private sensations, (c) another person cannot understand the language. (c) is presented as a conclusion from (a) and (b), and should therefore not be taken as a primary characterization of a private language.

The discussion from §244 to §256 consists largely of a preliminary clarification of (a) and (b) as conceived by the private linguist. (a) specifies the epistemic privacy of the objects to which the words of the private language refer. The objects are private in so far as only the speaker of the language can know what they are and when they are to be found. (b) specifies the privacy of ownership. The objects of the language are 'owned' by the speaker, and could not be owned by any one else. Sensations (*Empfindungen*) are said to be private in both ways—only the person who has the sensations can really know for certain that he has them, and what he has are unsharable and non-transferable. (No one else can have my pain and I cannot have their sympathy![9])

Wittgenstein does not clarify explicitly what he means by sensation; his main example in the ensuing discussion is pain (§§244–6, 250, 253, 257, 281–4, 286–8, 293, 295–6, 300, 302–4, 310–15). This is misleading, and has misled commentators. Could there be a language the expressions of which signified exclusively a Rylean array of aches, twinges, tickles, and itches? And if there could, what philosophical interest would this have? Yet Wittgenstein intimates that *all* the words in the language are to refer to a person's immediate private sensations. Certainly 'pain' is the name of a sensation, but the distinction between perception and sensation is not significant for Wittgenstein's purposes in the private-language argument. It is noteworthy that he refers to objects in the visual field, *conceived in a particular way*, as sensations in a broad sense of the term. He speaks of a 'private sensation of red' (§273), of 'colour impressions' (§276), 'visual impressions' (§277), 'visual sensations' (§312), of the private visual image before the mind's eye in acts of imagination (§280), and in general, of states of mind, mental and inner processes (§§290, 305–6). All these then can be taken to fall under the category of 'immediate private sensation'. Indeed it is noteworthy that in the early occurrences of the notorious diary example (*PI*, §258), the 'inner object' whose occurrence the private linguist is trying to record is the visual experience of red (e.g. NFL, p. 291). Thus while pain is his paradigm, it is experience in

---

[9] Frege, 'The Thought', in Strawson (ed.), op. cit., p. 28.

general and its 'phenomenal contents', conceived of under the spell of a misguided metaphysics, that are his target. This is partially clarified in §§274–9, but it is quite explicit in works which precede the *Investigations*, in particular the *Blue Book* and the 'Notes for Lectures'. When we think about the relation of objects to our experiences of objects, Wittgenstein points out in the *Blue Book* (p. 45), we are immediately beset by a host of philosophical temptations. We are tempted to conceive of two distinct kinds of world, the mental and the physical. The former seems peculiarly gaseous and ethereal. Later we are inclined to view the mental as the only real, knowable world. While we are thinking thus, our grasp of reality begins to slip. It is against such temptations that the private-language argument is directed. One should thus beware of letting the specific example of pain distort one's vision of the point of the argument.

4. *The Private Language*

The almost perfect example of a 'private language' is that described by Locke in his exposition of the elements of our thought and language in Books II and III of *An Essay Concerning Human Understanding*.[10] Therefore I shall use Locke's theory of language as an 'ideal type' to help illustrate the character of the misconceptions Wittgenstein strove to clarify. I am not suggesting for one moment that he had Locke in mind, indeed there is no evidence that he had ever read Locke. But Locke's conception provides a pedagogically useful 'object of comparison'. 'Words', Locke proclaims, 'in their primary or immediate signification, stand for nothing but the ideas in the mind of him that uses them ... nor can anyone apply them as marks, immediately, to anything else but the ideas that he himself hath' (III.ii.2). Similarly, the words of Wittgenstein's imaginary private language refer to the speaker's immediate private sensations. 'I know what the word "toothache" means,' remarks Wittgenstein's adversary (NFL, p. 315), 'it produces one particular image in my mind.' The words of the private language *refer* to elements of one's experience: e.g., pain or the red patch in one's visual field when one looks at a red object. But if that is what they refer to, what is their meaning? Sometimes Wittgenstein's private linguist conceives of the experience itself as providing the

---

[10] Locke, *An Essay Concerning Human Understanding*, ed. A. C. Fraser (1894, republished by Dover Publications Inc., New York, 1959). For some qualifications of this view of Locke's conception see N. Kretzman, 'The Main Thesis of Locke's Semantic Theory', the *Philosophical Review*, lxxvii (1968), 175–96.

concept. '"The experience which I have seems, in a certain sense, to take the place of a description of this experience."—"It is its own description."' (NFL, p. 277). On other occasions, he suggests that a meaningful term is associated with a replica of an element of one's experience, an exemplar which serves as a paradigm for the meaning of the term (NFL, p. 314; *PI*, §272). So just as a colour sample is employed as a part of the expression of a rule (an ostensive definition) for the use of a colour word, so too a mental image or private experience is conceived as a sample involved in the 'private' expression of a 'private' rule which, of course, no one else could understand. Apropos the recognition of an object as falling under a given concept, seeing an object as a so-and-so, Wittgenstein, in setting out his adversary's position, employs a typically Lockean metaphor.

This shape that I see—I want to say—is not simply *a* shape; it is one of the shapes I know, it is a shape marked out in advance. It is one of those shapes of which I already had a pattern in me; and only because it corresponds to such a pattern is it this familiar shape. (I as it were carry a catalogue of such shapes around with me, and the objects portrayed in it *are* the familiar ones.) (*Z*, §209)

The private experience, whether it is the actual experience *S*, or a recollected image of *S* reproduced by the mind, serves as a paradigm to provide the word '*S*' with its meaning:

It is as if when I uttered the word I cast a sidelong glance at the private sensation, as it were in order to say to myself: I know all right what I mean by it. (*PI*, §274)

How is language learnt, and how is the connection between a word and what it names set up? Locke suggests an elaborate process. The first stage is to stock our memory, the storehouse of ideas (II.x.2) with objects. This is done by means of attention and repetition (II.x.3) which fix a private exemplar of each experience type within our minds. It is then the business of memory to 'furnish to the mind those dormant ideas which it has present occasion for' (II.x.8). Once the store of exemplars is established, children:

... begin by degrees to learn the use of signs. And when they have got the skill to apply the organs of speech to the framing of articulate sounds, they begin to make use of words ... These verbal signs they sometimes borrow from others, and sometimes make themselves, as one may observe among the new and unusual names children often give to things in the first use of language. (II.xi.8)

The use of words is to be the 'sensible marks of ideas, and the ideas they stand for are their proper and immediate signification' (III.ii.1). Wittgenstein's private linguist draws a very similar picture of the process. The private linguist *associates* names with sensations and uses the names in giving descriptions. How is this process of association established? One suggestion might be that one pronounces the name while one has the sensation and concentrates upon the sensation (NFL, p. 290). One gives oneself a private ostensive definition of the private object by *attending* to the object, as it were mentally pointing at it, while saying a word to oneself or writing it down—one *impresses* upon oneself the connection between sign and sensation (*PI*, §258) in order to remember the connection correctly in the future. Another suggestion would be that one *undertakes* to use the sign in the future to refer to the exemplar (*PI*, §262). The function of memory for Locke is to provide the filing cabinet for the speaker's exemplars, and to produce the correct exemplar for each word as the speaker has need of it. Thus memory ensures that one uses the same sign for the same idea. Wittgenstein's private linguist envisages a similar procedure. He conceives of a table or dictionary consisting of exemplars and words associated with them. Only unlike ordinary dictionaries, this one exists in the imagination alone, and provides the 'subjective justification' (*PI*, §265) for the use of the word '*S*'. It is, of course, tempting to think that public samples and ostensive definition are just a *means* for producing the *real* samples, viz. mental ones, which are elements of the *real* rules a speaker knows and follows, i.e. private ostensive definitions (cf. *PI*, §73).

In Locke's model of language, words which stand for simple ideas and which are the foundation of language in so far as they provide the basic links between language and its objects are lexically indefinable (II.xx.1). The only way of knowing what they mean is to have the simple ideas they stand for. Consequently, two strange possibilities are conceivable. First, it is possible that:

> by the different structure of our organs it were so ordered, that *the same object should produce in several men's minds different ideas at the same time*; e.g. if the idea that a violet produced in one man's mind by his eyes were the same that a marigold produced in another man's, and *vice versa* ... this could never be known, because one man's mind could not pass into another man's body, to perceive what appearances were produced by those organs. (II.xxxii.15)

Secondly, grammatical propriety in speech is no guarantee that the noises that are uttered are really words. For unless they are 'backed up' by ideas, the noises lack meaning:

> He that hath words of any language, without distinct ideas in his mind to which he applies them does, so far as he uses them in discourse, only make a noise without any sense or signification ... For all such words, however put into discourse, according to the right construction of grammatical rules, or the harmony of well-turned periods, do yet amount to nothing but bare sounds and nothing else. (III.x.26)

Precisely these possibilities occur to Wittgenstein's private linguist. The inverted spectrum problem, which did not greatly bother Locke,[11] is presented by Wittgenstein as one of the unacceptable consequences of the private linguist's thesis (*PI*, §272). The second possibility was likewise envisaged by Wittgenstein:

> Imagine a person whose memory could not retain *what* the word 'pain' meant—so that he constantly called different things by that name—but nevertheless used the word in a way fitting in with the usual symptoms and presuppositions of pain. (*PI*, §271)

For Locke, language has two uses 'the recording our own thoughts' and 'the communicating of our thoughts to others'. Regarding the first use, it matters little, when we discourse with ourselves, which signs we use to stand for which ideas, as long as our use of the signs is consistent, and our memory reliable. But the matter is different in the case of the second use:

> The chief end of language in communication being to be understood, words serve not well for that end, neither in civil nor philosophical discourse, when any word does not excite in the hearer the same idea which it stands for in the mind of the speaker. (III.ix.4)

So if words are to serve their end successfully, the same associative mechanisms between word and exemplar that exist in the speaker's mind must exist in the hearer's mind. But words which stand for simple ideas are, as we have seen, indefinable. Words which stand for complex ideas are definable only in terms of words that stand for simple ones. So the meaning of words that stand for simple ideas must be shared if successful communication is to ensue:

---

[11] He comments thus: 'I am nevertheless very apt to think that the sensible ideas produced by any object in different men's minds, are most commonly very near and undiscernibly alike. For which opinion, I think there might be many reasons offered: but that being besides my present business I shall not trouble my reader with;' (II.xxxii.15).

the only sure way of making known the signification of the name of any simple idea, is *by presenting to his senses that subject which may produce it in his mind*, and make him actually have the idea that word stands for. (III.xi.14)

Once this is secured, men can converse with each other. Locke sums up his picture of the public use of language thus:

[words are] immediately the signs of men's ideas and by that means the instruments whereby men communicate their conceptions, and express to one another those thoughts and imaginations they have within their own breasts; there comes, by constant use, to be such a connection between certain sounds and the ideas they stand for, that the names heard, almost as readily excite certain ideas as if the objects themselves, which are apt to produce them, did actually affect the senses. (III.ii.6)

We have thus a view about the teaching of a language, about the purpose of language and linguistic acts, and about the mechanism of communication. Identical views are to be found in the mouth of Wittgenstein's private linguist or in Wittgenstein's critical comments upon his adversary's position. The idea that the point of inter-personal uses of language is always to let the hearer know what is going on in the mind of the speaker is emphasized by Wittgenstein as being part of the private linguist's model:

we are so much accustomed to communication through language, in conversation, that it looks to us as if the whole point of communication lay in this: someone else grasps the sense of my words—which is something mental: he as it were takes it into his own mind. If he then does something further with it as well, that is no part of the immediate purpose of language. (*PI*, §363)

More emphatic is his earlier remark:

As if the purpose of the proposition were to convey to one person how it is with another: only, so to speak, in his thinking part and not in his stomach. (*PI*, §317)

In the discussion of the possibility of a private language, Wittgenstein does not explore what must apparently be involved in teaching another person the meaning of the terms of one's private language. He makes it clear from the start that such a language is neither teachable, nor intelligible to others. This has misled commentators into thinking that a premiss in Wittgenstein's critical argument is that an untaught language is logically impossible. This is quite mistaken. The fact that we must learn our language is a contingent fact about our constitution. It would be perfectly conceivable that a child genius should invent names for his sensations (*PI*, §257) like Locke's children (II.xi.8) or that we be born with innate knowledge of a language (*PG*, p. 188; *BB*, p. 12). But it is true that the most natural manner in which a philosopher might try to give an account of teaching a language thus (mis)conceived would be the way which Locke describes. Wittgenstein did explore this in detail in 'Notes for Lectures on "Private Experience" and "Sense-Data" '.[12] The issue arises in the context of a discussion of how a private linguist conceives of our teaching a blind man to say of himself that he is blind. Blindness, of course, is not behaviour, for a man can behave like a blind man and not be blind. But it is his overt behaviour which is common knowledge to himself and to us. On the basis of his behaviour we say that he sees nothing. He correlates a certain experience (one might 'think of the picture of blindness as a darkness in the soul or in the head of a blind man' (*PI*, §424)) with his behaviour and concludes that 'being blind' means *this* experience. The underlying notion of the private linguist is that expressions which refer to personal (or private) experience (and the private linguist claims that all descriptive words do so) are taught *indirectly*. Wittgenstein constructs an analogy. Imagine teaching a child colour words, not by exhibiting colour samples, but by using a white sheet of paper, and various differently shaped spectacles with different lenses which make me see the white paper as a different colour. When I look through the circular spectacles I see the white paper as red. When I put the elliptical ones on I see it as green. Wittgenstein now imagines that we teach the child colour concepts thus:

> when I see him putting the circular ones on his nose I say the word 'red', when the elliptical ones 'green', and so forth. This one might call teaching the child the meanings of the colour names in an indirect way, because one could in this case say that I led the child to correlate the word 'red' with something that I didn't see but hoped the child would see if he looked through the circular glasses. And this way is indirect as opposed to the direct way of pointing to a red object etc. (NFL, p. 286)

The indirect way of teaching here, which is contrasted with the direct way, is the exact analogue of Locke's picture of teaching someone the meaning of a term. But in Locke's model *there is no analogue of direct teaching*: all teaching must be indirect 'because one man's mind could not pass into another man's body' (see also *BB*, p. 185). The notion that teaching someone the meaning of a word—and so bringing it

---

[12] The same analogy crops up in *Zettel*, §421.

about that he acquires the concept—involves presenting him with an object and ensuring that he associates the word one utters with the object (or 'representation') it refers to or some surrogate for it appears in a later section of the *Investigations*:

> it seems to us as though in this case the instructor *imparted* the meaning to the pupil—without telling him it directly; but in the end the pupil is brought to the point of giving himself the correct ostensive definition. And this is where our illusion lies. (*PI*, §362)

The same conception of teaching is outlined in *Zettel*:

> When the child behaves in such-and-such a way on particular occasions, I think he's feeling what I feel in such cases; and if it is so then the child associates the word with his feeling and uses the word when the feeling reappears. (*Z*, §545)

With this conception of teaching a common language goes a certain conception of the mechanism of communication. Wittgenstein portrays this strikingly in the course of constructing his imaginary language-games. The language-game in question is the one in which *B* learns to bring a building stone on hearing the word 'Column!' called out. One might imagine the mechanism thus, Wittgenstein suggests:

> In *B*'s mind the word called out brought up an image of a column, say; the training had . . . established this association . . . this case is strictly comparable with that of a mechanism in which a button is pressed and an indicator plate appears. In fact this sort of mechanism can be used instead of that of association. (*BB*, p. 89)

In the *Investigations* an even more felicitous analogy is used. The picture of communication in this language-game (No. 2) and in the classical empiricist conception of language in general is one in which 'Uttering a word is like striking a note on the keyboard of the imagination' (*PI*, §6).

5. *The Epistemology of the Private Linguist*

The opening sections of the private-language argument explore two senses of 'private' — epistemic privacy and privacy of ownership. Something is epistemically private for a person if only he can know it; it is private in the second sense if, in principle, only he can have it. From these two notions of privacy and their relationship to the private linguist's view that the meaning of word is given by acquaintance with an 'object' that constitutes the meaning, stem the salient epistemological doctrines of the private linguist. Three separate doctrines may be distinguished. The first doctrine might be called classical (non-sceptical) empiricist. I know of the occurrence of my own experiences with a certainty and incorrigibility which are unavailable to others who judge me to be having a certain experience. For while I know that I am having experience E because I am having it, because it is, as it were, before my mind's eye, and I cannot fail to identify it correctly, others know that I am experiencing E only from my behaviour. Since my behaviour is only inductively correlated with my experience and since the proposition that I am behaving in the way in which people normally behave when they experience E does not entail that I am experiencing E, the knowledge others have of my inner states lacks the certainty of my own knowledge. I am, as it were, acquainted with my experience from the 'inside', others can only know it from the 'outside' (NFL, p. 279). Of course, the classical empiricist claims to be able to make perfect sense of the judgement that another person is experiencing E. One is simply judging that the other person has the same as one has oneself when one experiences E.

This epistemological doctrine leads readily to what might be called 'weak-kneed scepticism'. Since I have a 'privileged access' to my own experiences, and others must make do with my behaviour, it may seem appropriate to claim that 'only I can know whether I am really in pain; another person can only surmise it' (*PI*, §246), or 'I can only *believe* that someone else is in pain, but I *know* it if I am' (*PI* §303). In my own case, I know 'directly' that I am experiencing E, just by experiencing E (NFL, p. 278). But in the case of others, it is only their behaviour that is available to me, which gives only 'indirect' access to their inner experiences. I cannot know, the sceptic concludes, whether another person is really experiencing E, or merely behaving as I do when I experience E. Hence the most I can achieve with regard to the inner states of others is belief. It may be that 'So-and-so has excellent health, he never had to go to the dentist, never complained about toothache; but as toothache is a private experience, we can't know whether he hasn't had terrible toothache all his life' (NFL, pp. 289–90). It is worth noting that there is little if any disagreement between the supporter of the argument from analogy and the weak-kneed sceptic, except over terminology. They both agree about the conceptual relations involved, and differ only over the denomination of their currency. The sceptic refuses to debase the term 'knowledge' by employing it both for the case of his incorrigible cognitions of his own inner experience, and for his corrigible and apparently dubious conjectures about the inner states of others, even when these conjectures are correct.

The third position is more tough-minded. It is the doctrine of the solipsist. He accepts the common premiss of his two predecessors—namely that he knows of the occurrence of his own experiences. As they do, he too adheres to the doctrine of private ownership of experience. No two people can have the same pain, and the pain that I have could not possibly be owned by someone else. However, unlike them, he is self-conscious about the consequences of the conception of meaning that is implicit in the two doctrines of privacy. In this he is also more consistent and relentless than they in pushing the argument to its ultimate conclusions. He admits (as Locke did):

The essential thing about private experience is really not that each person possesses his own exemplar, but that nobody knows whether other people also have *this* or something else. The assumption would thus be possible—though unverifiable—that one section of mankind had one sensation of red and another section another. (*PI*, §272)

But this disturbing consequence is not the worst that is to come. For if ownership of experiences is private and non-transferable, and if the meaning of a word is the private exemplar of the object, then 'I know what I mean by "toothache", but the other person can't know it' (NFL, p. 276). For now it is obvious that the private language is unintelligible to others. When I see red, and say 'this is red', 'this is the only real case of communication of personal experience because only I know what I really mean by "red"' (NFL, pp. 276 f.). Another person cannot understand what I say, because in order to understand it he would have to have my experiences for which my words stand, or the surrogate exemplars of my experience which I possess. Nor does it help to say that others will after all understand me provided that they have the same as I have when I experience E, for *ex hypothesi* two people can't have the same experience. Ultimately the tough-minded solipsist will castigate the weak-kneed sceptic, for not only is the private language unintelligible to others, but it does not make sense to talk of *believing* as opposed to knowing that others have experiences. The very idea of experiences belonging to another, and *a fortiori* of believing them to belong to another, must, in all consistency, be nonsensical. For 'experience' means something which is uniquely mine. To suppose that there could be other subjects is nonsense, for I alone am the locus of all experience. To believe that others have experience is to make a hypothesis which transcends all possible experience (*BB*, p. 48). And such a hypothesis could not be backed by meaning (cf. *PI*, §302).

6. *Wittgenstein's Criticism of the Private Language*

To speak and understand a language, Wittgenstein argued, is to have an array of capacities to employ signs in accord with rules for their use, applying those rules in a regular technique which manifests the internal relation between a rule and its applications. The private language envisaged tacitly or explicitly by the mainstream tradition of European philosophy is conceived quite differently. Understanding the expressions of a language is thought to be a matter of *associating* expressions with ideas, sense-impressions or other mental 'objects'. Having a concept is thought of not as a capacity which is paradigmatically manifest in mastery of the technique of using an expression in practice, but rather as a matter of an associative propensity. To the extent that philosophers (and others) who adopted such pictures realized dimly that using language is a normative activity, they unreflectively assumed that the rules of a person's language are given expression in a medium accessible only to him. For the 'rules' of a 'private language' thus conceived are in effect private ostensive definitions which are thought to involve pointing 'mentally' at a mental image, sense-impression, or experience, using it as a sample that will subsequently be capable of fulfilling a role in determining correct or incorrect uses of an expression. On this conception, our common languages are in effect constituted of a multitude of private languages that happen, fortunately, to be isomorphic and to have 'qualitatively identical content' (i.e. what you call 'pain' is qualitatively identical with that which I call 'pain', and similarly for other expressions).

Wittgenstein's opening moves are not directed against this latter misconception of a public language. As noted above, he remarks bluntly at the outset that a private language could not be understood by another person and returns only later to the issue of mutual understanding and communication. For in order to understand someone's 'private language' the other person would have to employ as samples for the correct application of expressions the experiences or sensations of the private linguist. But there seems no such thing as having another person's experiences. We might be inclined to think that it would suffice if the other had experiences that are 'just like' those of the private linguist. But in order for A's experiences to be 'just like' B's there must be a criterion of identity, i.e. something must be determined as *counting* as 'having the same sensation as B'. But as long as the concepts of sensation or experience are conceived to be determined by a 'private' rule involving a 'private' sample, this is unintelligible.

The fact that this conception makes a genuine *common* language impossible is, paradoxically, the least of its flaws. For its mesmerizing power lies in the persuasive picture it gives us of our *own* understanding of our language. 'I know what "pain" means or what "thinking" means just by having pains or by thinking'; this seems natural and indisputable.[13] And as long as that picture holds us in thrall, we will be inclined to think that although objections to the transition from a private to a common public language may be problematic, somehow or other a way around them will be found (if not now then later, if not by philosophy then by empirical science). For, after all, no one seriously doubts that we *do* speak a common language. So if a common language is actual, it must certainly be possible!

Wittgenstein's attack is consequently launched at the very heart of the private-linguist's conception, namely at the supposition that he himself understands his 'private' language, that the putative words of this alleged language are at any rate obviously intelligible to himself.[14] The purpose is to show that we have here only the semblance of a language from which all reality has been stripped. For there are here no genuine samples or any real ostension, no real rules or any technique of applying rules, no correctness or uncorrectness, no

---

[13] Cf. Descartes' reply to the sixth set of objections which argue that in order to prove his existence by the *cogito* argument, he must already know what thinking is and what existence is. To this he replied that 'It is indeed true that no one can be sure that he knows or that he exists, unless he knows what thought is and what existence ... [But] it is altogether enough for one to know it by means of that internal cognition which always precedes reflective knowledge'. *Philosophical Works of Descartes*, ed. E. S. Haldane and G. R. T. Ross, Vol. II, p. 241 (Dover, New York, 1955).

[14] In this respect Wittgenstein's strategy resembles Kant's employment of transcendental arguments (but see above pp. 211 ff.) When the sceptic accepts that one knows how one experiences things as being and challenges us to justify our claims about objective reality, Kant argues that a condition of the possibility of the former is precisely that it should provide grounds for the latter. Wittgenstein did *not* follow this argument. But the private-language argument resembles it in attacking the adversary at the seemingly indisputable point, viz. that he understands what *he* means by 'pain', 'sensation', etc. It endeavours to show that a condition of the possibility of his so understanding is that others can share a common understanding with him, and hence that the conception of the private language is incoherent.

meaning or any explanation of meaning, no understanding or anything to understand.

It seems to us, in our reflections upon our experiences and upon our understanding of words, that 'Once you know *what* the word stands for, you understand it, you know its whole use' (*PI*, §264). This thought is a potent component of the Augustinian *Urbild*. In the case of psychological concepts (or, indeed, all experiential concepts, according to the idealist) it is tempting to think that all that is necessary in order to grasp them is to have the experience, idea, or sensation which the concept signifies or refers to. Wittgenstein warns against this:[15]

> Do not believe that you have the concept of colour within you because you look at a coloured object—however you look.
>
> (Any more than you possess the concept of a negative number by having debts.)
>
> 'Red is something specific'—that would have to mean the same as: '*That* is something specific'—said while pointing to something red. But for that to be intelligible, one would have already to mean our *concept* 'red', to mean the use of that sample. (*Z*, §§332–3)

To possess a concept is to have mastered the technique of the use of a word. It is a skill, not an experience.

One might well concede this. But surely, once one has the appropriate experience, all one needs to do is *to name it*. The private linguist capitalizes on this natural thought (*PI*, §257). Wittgenstein stops him short: naming things is something we do in our public languages against a background of certain kinds of context. We presuppose a great deal of stage-setting without which the act of naming makes no sense. We name people, but that is a language-game that presupposes a large variety of conditions about human beings, their appearance, capacities, behaviour, and also conventions concerning the use and significance of such names. We name perceptual qualities by reference to samples, and that too presupposes much about the relative constancy of such qualities, of samples of such qualities, of shared discriminatory capacities without which such a practice would be pointless. To give a name to pain presupposes the existence of the grammar of the word 'pain' just as naming the colour red presupposes the existence of the grammar of colour words (*PI*, §§30 f.). The question we are invited to reflect on is whether such a set exists upon the mental stage.

---

[15] This move too has an analogue in Kant, namely in the principle that intuitions without concepts are blind.

Private Linguists and Public Speakers 267

The private linguist conceives of himself as *associating* the sign '*S*' with a sensation (*PI*, §258). Surely he can keep a diary about the recurrence of a certain sensation, and write '*S*' whenever it occurs? And does this not show that '*S*' is the name of a sensation? Wittgenstein denies that this is, *in the private linguist's story*, intelligible. For 'sensation' is a word in our public language. It can indeed be said to show the post where the word 'pain' *in our public language* is stationed. But if the private linguist is to invoke it, he must justify its use in a way that is intelligible to us all, i.e. in a way that is recognizably part of the familiar use of the word 'sensation'. But in that case he might just as well explain 'pain' likewise, i.e. *not* by reference to a 'private sample' that is in principle unusable by anyone else (*PI*, §261).

One is inclined to think that the use of public samples in ostensive definitions must have a mental analogue. Why cannot a sensation function as a sample for the correct use of a word? Against this beguiling fiction Wittgenstein directs a battery of arguments. There is no such thing as pointing at any sensation in the sense in which I point at a sample in giving an ostensive definition (*PI*, §258). The private linguist may respond that he can concentrate his attention upon his sensation and *that* is a mental analogue of pointing in an ostensive definition. This Wittgenstein denies; it is an idle ceremony that achieves nothing. For a genuine definition has the role of establishing the meaning of a sign by laying down a rule for its use, but concentrating one's attention on a sensation and saying '*S*' does not do this at all.

One may feel that this is too swift. Surely by concentrating my attention I can impress upon myself the connection between the sign and the sensation which is to function as a sample. Not so, Wittgenstein replies; for this process of impressing upon myself the connection must be conceived to mean that I will remember the connection correctly in future. But no criterion of correctness has been laid down yet for such a case (*PI*, §258). The point does *not* concern the fallibility of memory, but is rather that the putative mental ostensive definition was intended to provide a rule for the correct use of '*S*' and now it transpires that in order to do so it presupposes the concept '*S*'. For to remember *correctly* can only be to remember that a certain sensation or mental image *is* an image of *S*.

One may object again: surely a subsequent sensation may *seem* to be *S*, may seem to be the *same* as the sensation one previously associated with '*S*'? This is incorrect. For something can seem to a person to be *S* only if the concept of an *S* has already been determined. And that, in the private linguist's case, is precisely what has not yet been done. To the private linguist's exasperated claim 'Well, I *believe* that this is the sensation *S* again', Wittgenstein responds ironically 'Perhaps you *believe* that you believe it' (*PI*, §260). One is inclined to say that whatever seems right to the private linguist is right; but if there is, in principle, no distinction between seeming right and being right, then there is no such thing as right (*PI*, §258).

The point is subtle and difficult to grasp. For given that we have our common concept of sensation, of course we can remember what yesterday's sensation was like (a sharp stabbing pain beneath the shoulder blade) and can say whether the current sensation is the same. But, Wittgenstein argued, the conceptual articulations that make this possible (intelligible) are severed in the private-linguist's tale. The point is further clarified in the discussion of the table or dictionary in the imagination (*PI*, §265). We have tables of samples (e.g. a paint chart). Could we not have such a table in the imagination which we might use, as we use a dictionary or public table of samples, to justify our application of a word?[16] We could not; for a table or chart is used as a rule; we appeal to it to justify the use of a word. But justification consists in appealing to something *independent*. If I am inclined to call an object 'eau de nil' or, for that matter, to *deny* that it is, I can check my use of the colour word by reference to an independent table. But a table in the memory is not something independent to which to appeal in order to check whether I can remember correctly what '*S*' means; it does *not* serve to distinguish what seems right to me from what is right.

Calling up a mnemonic image of a table of mental samples in order to check whether I am applying '*S*' correctly, i.e. in accord with the rule for its use, *seems* like calling up a mnemonic image of a colour chart or railway timetable. And we can surely do that. But there is a crucial difference. If the private linguist wishes to check whether he is using '*S*' correctly, i.e. whether *he can remember what '*S*' means*, all *he* has to appeal to is his mnemonic table—which is no more than *his remembering what '*S*' means*. If I cannot recollect the time of the last train, I might try to visualize the timetable I saw at the station. And if I succeed, I will have recalled it. But 'to succeed' here means to remember *correctly*, i.e. to remember what was written on the public

[16] Interestingly enough such conceptual fictions as mental dictionaries have, since Wittgenstein's day, become very popular, most markedly in the writings of theoretical linguists.

timetable. In the case of the mental table against which the private linguist wishes to check whether he remembers correctly what '*S*' means, there is no such thing as 'succeeding', for he is checking whether he remembers what '*S*' means against his memory of what '*S*' means, and *there is nothing independent* to which to appeal. This is as if someone were to buy several copies of the same morning paper to assure himself of the truth of one of them (*PI*, §265).

The private linguist may delude himself into thinking that he can surely 'inwardly undertake to use a word in such-and-such a way' (*PI*, §262). Wittgenstein hastens to disillusion him. To invent or introduce a technique of using a word is one thing, to concentrate one's attention upon a feeling while saying 'This is *S*' is another (*PI*, §263). In his notebooks he developed this point (cf. MS 180(a), p. 76). The internal relation between a rule and its applications is expressed by or manifest in the technique of applying the rule in practice. The connection between a word and a rule for its use (e.g. an ostensive definition) is effected in the practice of its application (cf. *PI*, §197). But in the case of the private ostensive definition there is no technique of application, there is no *practice* of applying '*S*', but only the appearance of a practice ('*Schein einer Praxis*').[17]

What we, in our (public) language, call 'sensations' are not defined by reference to 'private objects'. There is no such thing as assigning a meaning to a word by reference to a 'private' sample in this sense. The idea that our language is underpinned by the private-linguist's chimerical mental samples can be made perspicuous by noting its *irrelevance* to our use of, for example, the word 'sensation':

Imagine a person whose memory could not retain *what* the word 'pain' meant—so that he constantly called different things by that name—but nevertheless used the word in a way fitting in with the usual symptoms and presuppositions of pain'—in short he uses it as we all do. Here I should like to say: a wheel that can be turned though nothing else moves with it, is not part of the mechanism. (*PI*, §271)

When we are tempted to invoke a 'private object' to explain what we mean (e.g. by 'seeing an aspect' of a double-aspect figure), or what our understanding of an expression (e.g. 'the aroma of coffee') consists in,

---

[17] Note that when Wittgenstein talks of the pseudo-transition in the mind from the putative rule (the mental ostensive definition) to its application as *a mere appearance of a practice* or *pseudo-practice* he does not mean that it has the appearance of a *social* practice. Rather, it has the appearance of involving a regular technique of application although it does not involve one.

Wittgenstein suggests 'Always get rid of the idea of the private object in this way: assume that it constantly changes, but that you do not notice the change because your memory constantly deceives you' (*PI*, p. 207).

The point is brought to a head as Wittgenstein shifts to consider the private linguists' construal of mutual communication. In the famous beetle-in-the-box example (*PI*, §293) he pursues further the issue of the redundancy of the 'private object'. The private linguist claims that it is only from his own case, his own experience, that he knows what the word 'pain' means. But if so, Wittgenstein replies, he must also say (as indeed Locke does) that others only know what 'pain' means from their own case. The position of a group of people who *do* succeed in communicating with each other is, on the private-linguist's model, analogous to the following: Suppose everyone had a box with something in it. Each person calls the object in his box 'beetle'. No one has access to the contents of others' boxes and each knows what 'beetle' means by looking into his box. Now *if* we suppose that 'beetle' has a use in the language, then the object in the box and its nature are irrelevant. 'If we construe the grammar of the expression of sensation on the model of "object [*Gegenstand*] and name [*Bezeichnung*]"[18] the object drops out of consideration as irrelevant' (*PI*, §293); i.e. on the private-linguist's conception of the relation between a name and the object it refers to, then, *if communication is possible*, the private object allegedly referred to is a piece of idle machinery and plays no part in the mechanism of communication, and conversely *if the private object does play a part*, then communication is impossible. The 'naming relation' as conceived by the private linguist has nothing to do with the explanation of what is involved in knowing the meaning of a word, or in meaning something by a word, or in understanding what someone else means by a word.

It involves a fundamental misunderstanding (*PI*, §314) to think that one can clarify the philosophical problems concerning sensations by studying one's own headache. For one's headaches are phenomena, and what we are studying in philosophy are concepts rather than objects, and hence the use of a word rather than the object to which the word refers (*PI*, §383). Wittgenstein compares the private linguist

---

[18] Anscombe translates '*Bezeichnung*' as 'designation'. But in paragraph 2 of §293 she translates '*So wäre er nicht der der Bezeichnung eines Dings*' as 'If so it would not be used as the name of a thing'. Its recurrence in paragraph 3 '*Gegenstand und Bezeichnung*' should therefore be translated similarly.

to a person who, when he doubts whether another person is in pain, pricks himself with a pin in order to be sure what 'pain' means (not being content with his imagination which only supplies him with a faint copy of the actual pain). When he has a genuine pain, then, he tells himself, it is the possession of *this* by someone else that he is to doubt. This, however, is absurdly wrong. 'It is as if I were told: "Here is a chair. Can you see it clearly?—Good—now translate it into French!"' (Z, §547). In order to doubt whether another person is in pain, what we need is not a pain, but the *concept* pain (Z, §548). The private linguist may still feel baffled. If 'the object drops out of consideration as irrelevant' then does Wittgenstein not commit himself surreptitiously to behaviourism? But surely there is a difference between pain behaviour accompanied by pain and pain behaviour without pain? 'What greater difference could there be?' Wittgenstein concedes. But how can he agree?

... 'yet you again and again reach the conclusion that the sensation itself is a *nothing*'—Not at all. It is not a *something*, but not a *nothing* either! The conclusion was only that a nothing would serve just as well as a something about which nothing could be said. (*PI*, §304).[19]

On the one hand it seems that the private experience ought to serve as a paradigm to provide a term with meaning, and on the other hand it becomes increasingly obvious that it cannot do so.

The 'private experience' is a degenerate construction of our grammar (comparable in a sense to tautology and contradiction). And this grammatical monster now fools us; when we wish to do away with it, it seems as though we denied the existence of an experience, say, toothache. (NFL, p. 314)

The private linguist endeavours to explain what he means by a word. He attempts to explain by a mental gesture at a private object. 'This' gives his words meaning. But nothing can be said about 'this'. And what started out by looking like an explanation turns out to be a delusion (NFL, p. 315).

The moral of the tale is not that there is no such thing as following a rule in private. That would be absurd, since we do so frequently.

---

[19] Note the analogy with Kant's remark: 'appearances might indeed constitute intuition without thought, but not knowledge; and consequently would be for us as good as nothing' (*Critique of Pure Reason*, A 111). Striking though this may be, it is only an analogy. As far as Wittgenstein was concerned any talk here of knowledge was confused for it makes no *sense* to talk of *knowing* that one is in pain, even if one *does* have the concept of pain (see Chapter X).

There is no conceptual barrier to envisaging solitary creatures who follow rules, although it is true that if their rules (and their rule-following behaviour) were complex, we would find it very difficult to understand them without actually interacting with them. Nor is it the case that one cannot follow private rules, i.e. rules no one else happens to know about, for many people do so, e.g. when writing diaries in private codes. Rather, the moral is that there is no such thing as following 'private' rules, i.e. rules which no one else could in principle understand inasmuch as the rules in question *can have no public expression*. Such putative rules are 'private ostensive definitions', which, since there is no such thing as exhibiting 'private samples', are *essentially* incommunicable. The supposition of the intelligibility of a person's following such rules lies at the heart of idealism and solipsism. If Wittgenstein's argument is correct, the deep and ineradicable flaws of these philosophical pictures have at last been definitively brought to light.

7. 'Only I know' and 'Only I have'

The private linguist insists that his experiences are 'private' in two senses, viz. epistemically private and privately owned. The doctrine of epistemic privacy is expressed by the claim that only I can know that I am in pain, others can only surmise it. To this Wittgenstein's reply is that this is partly false and partly nonsense. The claim that others cannot know that I am in pain, or that I cannot know what experiences others are having, is false, if taken in the ordinary sense of 'know'. There are innumerable occasions upon which we pass judgement upon the 'inner states' of others on good grounds, and in which our judgement is true. If the sceptically-minded retort that what is 'inner' is hidden from us, Wittgenstein's riposte is that the future too is hidden from us, but the astronomer calculating an eclipse of the sun does not say that he cannot in principle know when there will be an eclipse, but only surmise it (*PI*, p. 223). Similarly, if I see someone writhing in pain with evident cause, I do not think: all the same his feelings are hidden from me (ibid.). The misconceptions of the 'inner' and 'outer', of what is 'hidden' and how it is 'revealed' are manifestations of deeply misguided pictures of the mind which we shall explore in detail in the next chapter.

The contention that only I can really know that I am in pain, Wittgenstein argued, is nonsense. It makes no *sense* to say 'I doubt whether I am in pain' or 'I have something, I wonder whether it is pain'. The exclusion of the *intelligibility* of doubt does not license certainty, but rather excludes its intelligibility likewise. So the claim that I know that I am in pain in a way and with a degree of *certainty* that is unavailable to others is nonsense. Moreover, it makes sense to say 'I know' only if it also makes sense to say 'I don't know' or 'I doubt' (believe, suspect, found out, learnt). But these make no sense when affixed to 'I am in pain'. So 'I know I am in pain' is either an emphatic way of saying 'I am in pain' or else it is nonsense (*PI*, §246). The sceptic, here as elsewhere, misinterprets the reflections of grammatical rules in the mirror of linguistic practice, mistaking grammatical conventions that determine what it makes sense to say for epistemic possibilities and impossibilities. He takes doubt, in one's own case, to be excluded by certainty—the certainty residing in the immediacy of experience. But it is grammar that excludes doubt here, not experience. His confusions are rooted in profound misconceptions of 'self-consciousness' or 'self-awareness'. We shall try to uproot these in the next chapter.

Is there any truth in the doctrine of epistemic privacy? In the end only a mouse comes forth. The sceptic suggests that I cannot know of the inner states of others. Wittgenstein's answer is that not only *can* we sometimes know the inner states of other people, but that we sometimes rightly say of a person that he is completely transparent to us. *But* it is also true that one human being can be a complete enigma to another (*PI*, p. 223). This is strikingly brought to our attention when visiting an alien culture. Here the grounds for people's actions and (at least some of) the ends they pursue may be wholly opaque to us. Similarly, although we can sometimes know the inner states of others, we may at other times fail to discover what they are. A thought is 'private'—is *de facto* unknown to others—if it is not revealed or manifested. But it is no longer 'private' if it is not kept secret (*PG*, §41; NFL, p. 314; *PI*, p. 222). In neither case is anything a priori opaque or private, nor is there any metaphysical boundary which sets the limits of possible human knowledge at the portals of other minds.

The second sort of privacy upon which the private linguist's confusions turn is the private ownership of experience. The discussion of the previous chapter should make the confusions perspicuous. Another person, the private linguist claims, cannot have my pains. Well, which *are* my pains? What is it that determines the ownership of pain? 'The subject of a pain is the person who gives it expression', Wittgenstein replies (*PI*, §302). But surely, I know that my pains belong to me not by looking to see whether I manifest pain-behaviour, but by feeling them! This is confused. For it is senseless to say that I *know* that *this* pain is mine, unless one means that there is no such thing as having a pain and wondering whose pain it is. And the putative distinction between having a pain and feeling a pain is a distinction without a difference.

The private linguist is inclined to strike himself on the breast and say 'Surely another person can't have THIS pain!' (*PI*, §253). But this is muddled (he is like someone who says 'No other chair can stand where this chair is standing' and thinks he has said something about the metaphysical immobility of chairs). That another person cannot have my pain is confused. It is, of course, true that: My pain = the pain I have. But now, *what* pains do I have? Well, throbbing headaches, nagging toothaches, etc. Thumping oneself and stressing 'this' *wrongly* suggests that *ownership* is a criterion of identity for pains, whereas it is the phenomenal characteristics and location of a pain that determine what pain one has (*supra* p. 239). And, of course, two victims of migraine often have the same pain.

The 'private ownership' of experience is a grammatical illusion. We do say that a boy has his father's gait or build, that he has his mother's smile or sense of humour. No one would claim that he cannot have the very same gait as his father or the very same smile as his mother but only one exactly similar. So too, if we are both breathing noxious fumes and you complain of a splitting headache, and a few minutes later I too get such a headache, I might say 'I've got your headache now'. This just means 'I've got the same headache as you now'.

Nevertheless, the metaphysical claim 'You can't have my pain' or 'You can't feel my headache' is mesmerizing. Is there no truth behind it? Trivially 'my pain' means the same as 'the pain I have' and not 'the pain you have'—but that does not mean that we cannot have the same pain. It is also a truth of grammar that my pain-behaviour is a criterion for *my* being in pain, not for someone else's being in pain. My suffering is manifest in my pain-behaviour, not in yours. There is no such thing as one person manifesting the suffering of another, though he may have the very same pain. One might say 'I can't feel your toothache' meaning thereby that I can't feel toothache in your tooth. Wittgenstein held this to be an empirical truth that could be otherwise (*WWK*, p. 49; *PR*, p. 92), but one might well argue that the idea of feeling pain in another person's body will stretch the concepts of pain-location, of manifestation of pain, and ultimately of a person's body, beyond breaking point. If so, then the 'can't' is grammatical. One might also say 'I can't feel your pain' to mean that when you have a pain, I do not feel a thing, i.e. I do not (normally) have a pain (let alone the same pain) whenever you do. But that is neither a 'metaphysical truth' nor a grammatical proposition; it is an empirical fact which could be otherwise.

At *Investigations* §248, Wittgenstein remarks 'The proposition "Sensations are private" is comparable to: "One plays patience by oneself"'. The comparison is apt. That one plays patience by oneself is not a fact about all hitherto discovered card-playing societies. It is a grammatical proposition to the effect that it makes sense to say '*A* played patience when he was alone' (unlike '*A* played tennis when he was alone') but not '*A* played patience against *B*'. If *A* played a card game with *B*, and *B* won, then it was not *patience*. We might now apply the solipsist's style of thought to the grammatical remark about patience. The solipsist would say 'Only I can play patience' instead of 'One plays patience by oneself'. Wittgenstein remarks ironically 'Does the solipsist also say that only he can play chess?' (NFL, p. 283). A similar sleight of hand occurs in the way the metaphysician construes the grammatical proposition that sensations are private. What looks to him like metaphysical privacy of ownership is a confusion consequent upon projecting a distinction which belongs to one language-game (i.e. the distinction between being identical and being exactly alike but not identical, which belongs to discourse about material objects) onto a different language-game in which it gets no grip (i.e. the language-game with sensations or experiences). A different kind of confusion is evident in the case of 'Only I know . . .'. What looks like epistemic privacy merely excludes the expression of doubt *and* certainty in the case of one's avowals of experience (*PI*, §247). The metaphysics of privacy is a story of shadow-boxing in the dark, a bizarre tale of self-delusion.

X

'A CLOUD OF PHILOSOPHY CONDENSED INTO A DROP OF GRAMMAR'

1. *Can one know that one is in pain?*
To try to outline the limits of the knowable is one of the traditional tasks of epistemology. Some epistemological doctrines concerning the possibility of knowledge seem both intelligible and reasonable. Kant's demand that the employment of the categories be confined to the province of possible experience if knowledge is to be achieved might be taken as an example. But on further scrutiny, what is acceptable in Kant's account is a purely *logical* or *grammatical* point about the conditions of the intelligible employment of the categories, not an independent epistemological point about the limits of knowledge. And this grammatical point is one which Kant himself violated in his insistence that one may have *beliefs* about objects that transcend any possible experience. Other epistemological doctrines seem intelligible without being, by our ordinary canons, reasonable. Thus the various forms of scepticism confine our possible knowledge within limits far more restrictive than we normally entertain. However, when the sceptics' claims are put under pressure they are typically seen to violate an array of conceptual conditions for the correct employment of expressions which are utilized by sceptics in making their epistemological claims. Hence the latter are not, appearances to the contrary, genuinely intelligible. In both cases what seem to be epistemological theses collapse into grammatical insights or confusions.

As we have seen, Wittgenstein claimed that one cannot know that one is having a given experience. One cannot be said to know that one is in pain, that one is thinking a certain thought, or that one intends to act in a certain way. This seems to be an epistemological point, drawing the boundaries of possible knowledge in a manner that is *prima facie* bizarre. For, he insisted, other people can and often do know that someone else is suffering, is thinking such and such thoughts, or is intending to carry out certain projects. But what they

'A Cloud of Philosophy Condensed into a Drop of Grammar' 277

can thus know, the sufferer, thinker, or intending agent cannot himself know. And this seems decidedly odd. To a philosopher familiar with the broad tradition of European philosophy, Wittgenstein seems to be setting his face against what is most obvious. Whether we can 'really know' that others have experiences, whether our knowledge of the past is genuine, whether the sun will rise tomorrow are questions that have been extensively debated over many centuries. But that we know our own states of mind, that we know how things subjectively seem to us to be, is something that no one has ever challenged. And it seems unchallengeable. What is the point of delimiting possible knowledge in this way? Kant drew the boundaries of the knowable in the way he did in order to put an end to the pretensions of dogmatic metaphysics. The sceptic misguidedly draws the boundaries at the limits of knowledge of subjective experience because the alleged gap between knowledge of subjective experience and knowledge of objects does not seem to him to be bridgeable. (But he would not dream of extending his scepticism to subjective experience itself, for that would be tantamount to sawing off the branch upon which he himself is perched.) In both these cases, and many others, the general motivation—whether justifiable or not—seems reasonably clear. But the Wittgensteinian limitation appears puzzling. Viewed from the perspective of traditional epistemology it strikes one as deeply counterintuitive and as lacking any obvious rationale.

If Wittgenstein's account strikes one thus, it is because one is viewing it from the wrong angle. In one sense, his claims are not epistemological claims at all. They are purely grammatical or conceptual. In insisting that I cannot know that I am in pain, but that you often can know that I am in pain, Wittgenstein was not drawing the boundaries of possible knowledge in an eccentric and idiosyncratic manner. For his claim was not that I do *not* know something that others do, that I am unavoidably *ignorant* of things about which others may be well-informed. Rather was he drawing the bounds of sense, delineating the use of epistemic verbs in respect of psychological expressions. His claim was that it makes *no sense* to say 'I know I am in pain', 'I know that I am thinking such-and-such', 'I know that I intend to act thus-and-so' (or, to the extent that it makes sense, not the bogus sense the traditional epistemologist assumes). Hence, of course, his claim was not that I am *ignorant* of something which others may know. On the contrary, it makes as little sense to say 'I do not know whether I am in pain' or 'I am ignorant of my thoughts' as to say 'I know that I am in pain' or 'I know what I am thinking'. His contention was not that we are in fact ignorant of something which we all wrongly take ourselves to know, but rather that philosophers have misconstrued the grammar of psychological and epistemic verbs, misconceived the use of the first-person pronoun, and constructed a false picture of what they call 'self-awareness' or 'self-consciousness'.

The issue as to whether 'I know I am in pain' makes sense or not may seem minor and insignificant. It seems not *obviously* linked with any major philosophical concern. It is *unobviously* linked, however, with the central problems of the 'metaphysics of experience'. As Wittgenstein himself stressed, the question at issue is fundamental to the debates between Realists, Idealists, and Solipsists, debates in which he did not aim to *take sides*, but which he wished to *undermine*. In his later work he associated his non-cognitive account of first-person psychological utterances with the private-language argument. We shall, therefore, explore the relationship between these two. In so doing we shall examine in further detail his analysis of propositions about the experiences of others. His explanation of the logical character of first-person psychological utterances reveals further confusions in the Cartesian conception of the mind, confusions that reach deeply into philosophical reflections which purport to have liberated themselves from the errors of Cartesianism. Hence we shall examine in detail how the natural picture of the 'Inner' and the 'Outer' which we apply in philosophizing about psychology leads us astray. On a different level, Wittgenstein's account is part of his general onslaught upon the philosophical search for foundations. His antagonism to the enterprise of establishing the foundations of mathematics in logic (or, differently, in so-called 'metamathematics') was noted above, as was his trenchant opposition to his own earlier attempts to establish 'foundations of language' in metaphysical simples. One can see his account of first-person psychological utterances as, *inter alia*, a third thrust against foundationalism, directed against the endeavour to provide foundations for empirical knowledge in our knowledge of how things subjectively appear to us to be. The claim that it is correct to say 'I know what you are thinking', and wrong to say 'I know what I am thinking' does indeed condense a whole cloud of philosophy into a drop of grammar (*PI*, p. 222).

2. *Self-consciousness: the overthrow of the Cartesian picture*

The Cartesian picture of self-consciousness or self-awareness neither originates with Descartes nor is it adopted only by those who embrace the doctrines propounded by him. But it was he who articulated this conception with mesmerizing brilliance; hence it may justly be denominated 'Cartesian'. Each person sees, hears, and feels objects in his vicinity, experiences joy or sorrow, suffers pain or grief. He thinks, believes, doubts, or is certain, has purposes and intentions. If we ask someone what he perceives, thinks, or intends, whether he is in pain or is sad, he may tell us. And in telling us how things are with him, he uses such sentences as 'I see red' or 'I have toothache', 'I am thinking of the weather' or 'I intend to go to London', just as in telling us how things are with another he would say 'He sees red (has toothache)' or 'He is thinking (intends to go to London)'. In the latter cases he ascribes experiences (broadly and loosely speaking) to another; so, in the former cases, it seems, he ascribes experiences to himself. Hence, we are inclined to think, he says of the self which is his, that it has certain experiences. This is possible, it appears, because he is self-conscious, aware of the experiences which are the experiences of the self. In telling us how things are with him, he refers by means of the pronoun 'I' to himself, and ascribes experiences of which he is aware to the self thus referred to. The self seems then to be something which has its seat in the body, although it is not identical with the body—it is that of which one is inclined to say '*Sum res cogitans*' (cf. *BB*, p. 69), it is the essence of the person. Awareness or consciousness of the self thus conceived is introspection, a looking into oneself, a form of perception or 'inner sense'. When one introspects one observes that one's self is in a certain state (e.g. that one has a headache) or is engaging in a certain activity (e.g. thinking). One's observations of what goes on in one's self are privileged, the 'inner' is accessible *directly* only *to* the self. Only he who 'has' it, really knows it. I *know*, with *certainty*, how things are with me, others can only guess. For I can perceive what is 'inner' whereas others must judge how things are with me on the basis of my behaviour, i.e., mere externalities. And much that is 'inner' may remain for ever hidden from others. But, of course, I may, and sometimes do, tell them. My utterances of first-person psychological sentences thus seem to be *reports* of how things are with me, *descriptions* of 'inner' events which I observe *in foro interno*.

In every respect this picture is misguided. It correctly notes important grammatical connections and features of first- and third-person psychological utterances, and draws the wrong conclusions from them. It understandably invokes natural metaphors and similes, and misapplies them. It rightly employs an array of ordinary expressions which are used—differently—in different language-games, but it wrongly projects features of their use in one language-game on to a quite·different one in which those features have no place. First, it is true and important that if a person avows that he is having a certain experience or thinking a certain thought, one cannot dispute his word. He may be untruthful, lying to us about what he feels or thinks, but he cannot (with insignificant qualifications) be *mistaken*. If someone sincerely says 'I have toothache', then (*ceteris paribus*) he does have toothache, for his saying this is a criterion for it being so. But the fact that there is no room for mistake is not because the inner eye enjoys perfect vision. It is further true that there is no room for doubt in my own case; but not because the inner stage is so well lit. It is also true that another person can conceal his feelings, dissimulate, pretend, play-act, that often we cannot say what he is thinking or what he intends unless he tells us. But that is not because he is better informed than we. Nor does the fact that all this is possible suggest for one moment that we can never really know what another thinks, feels, or sees. Secondly, it is natural, when moving within the ambit of psychological expressions to talk of what is *inner* and what is *outer* (experience and behaviour). Others know of my experiences from my behaviour, from what I do and say; I do not. But it is quite wrong to construe this metaphor in such a way that suggests that I know of my experiences from the 'inside', by observing them, that I know 'directly' in my own case, but only indirectly in the case of others. And it is equally misguided to think that when I reveal my thoughts or feelings to you, I let you see inside, where hitherto only I saw. Moreover, it is no better to intimate that when I banish all pretence I still do not *really* reveal what is 'inside'. Thirdly, it is certainly true that we talk of observing, describing, and reporting objects in the room, people, and their behaviour. It is also true that there is such a thing as observing our own mental states, describing our experiences, reporting them. But the latter kinds of describing are deeply and importantly different from the former, as different as knowing John is from knowing the alphabet. It is a cardinal error of the Cartesian picture to take avowals of experience as descriptions of experience and to construe descriptions of experience on the model of descriptions of objects of experience.

We shall start dismantling this misbegotten picture by examining the confused notion of 'the self' and the attendant misconstrual of the role of the first-person pronoun. In the 'Notes for Lectures on "Private

Experience" and "Sense Data"' Wittgenstein stated a version of the non-cognitive account of first-person psychological utterances: 'I know that I have toothache' means either nothing or the same as 'I have toothache'. His following comment is noteworthy: 'This, however, is a remark about the use of the word "I", whoever uses it' (NFL, p. 309). The whole problem surrounding first-person, present-tense, psychological sentences boils down, he suggested, to our not understanding the function of 'I' (NFL, p. 307). It is, *inter alia*, the use of 'I' as subject[1] which gives rise to the illusion that first-person psychological utterances are uniformly reports or descriptions ('self-ascriptions of experience') that rest upon direct observation of the states of oneself. No criteria determine my saying that 'I' am in pain (*PI*, §404). The use of 'I' involves no identification of one particular object among others to function as the subject of the psychological predicate, as the '*self*' to which 'experience is ascribed'. When I say that I am in pain, I do not *recognize* a particular person to whom I then ascribe the pain. It is true that *mis*identification or *mis*recognition are ruled out, but *not* by incorrigible identification or recognition, rather by the fact that the first-person pronoun here does not fulfil the role of making any identifying reference at all.

We saw above (p. 235) that Wittgenstein argued that 'I' is not a proper name, not a name of a person; it is not equivalent to a description such as 'The person now speaking', nor is it a demonstrative pronoun (*BB*, 68) for demonstrative pronouns, e.g. 'this', unlike 'I', are subject to referential failure. 'I', when used as subject, does not denote a possessor, nor does it refer to a particular person. One might even claim 'When I say "I am in pain", I do not point to a person who is in pain, since in a certain sense I have no idea *who* is' (*PI*, §404). The issue is not, of course, that I do not know who I am (though that too is possible), but rather that in saying 'I am in pain' I do not say that such-and-such a person is in pain, but 'I am ...'. In using 'I', I do not pick out one person from among a group of people (*BB*, p. 68), just as I do not name someone when I groan with pain. But, of course, others see who is in pain from my groaning (*PI*, §404). Similarly, 'I', *for me*, is not 'a signal calling attention to a place or a person' (NFL, p. 307), although others can identify who is in pain by reference to my utterance. '"I have pain" is no more a statement *about* a particular person than moaning is' (*BB*, p. 67). Hence 'I know *I* am in pain' is

---

[1] See above, p. 233.

nonsense. Similarly, 'it has no sense to ask "how do you know that it is *you* who sees it?" for I don't *know* that it's this person and not another one which sees ...' (NFL, p. 310). One might object that 'Surely you aren't in doubt whether it is you or someone else who is in pain!' But that is nonsense, for it is a logical product one factor of which is 'I don't know whether I am in pain or not', and that is not a significant proposition (*PI*, §408). All that is true is *that there is no such thing* as 'doubting whether one is in pain'.

One might further object that surely, when one groans, 'I am in pain', one wants to draw the attention of others to a particular person. But this is misleading—I want to draw attention to *myself* (*PI*, §405). No identification enters in here—I do not choose the mouth which says 'I am in pain' or groans (NFL, p. 311). Even if it can be claimed that in saying 'I am in pain' I want to distinguish between *myself* and other people, it does not follow that I want to distinguish between the person P. M. S. H. and the person N. N. (*PI*, §406). The Cartesian might concede all this (after all, Descartes did not argue 'I think, therefore Descartes exists'!), and insist that in saying 'I am in pain' he is referring to *himself*, i.e. the self that constitutes his essence, the *res cogitans*. He may go on to contend that the first-person pronoun refers to, is the name of, this entity. And he may further claim that the essence of the self thus construed constitutes the criterion of identity for the use of the name 'I'. This is a dire confusion resting upon misconstrual of reflexive pronouns. One may say that when one says 'I am in pain' one draws attention to oneself, but not that one draws attention to one's self. For 'oneself' here is simply the indirect (*oratio obliqua*) reflexive pronoun which is explained by reference to the use of the *oratio recta* 'I' and cannot serve to explain it.[2] What philosophers (and psychologists) call 'self-consciousness' is not consciousness of a self, an immaterial subject of experience which has its seat in the body. It is rather consciousness that such-and-such holds of oneself[3] (where 'oneself' is the indirect reflexive). Or, more cautiously, it is the capacity

---

[2] Cf. G. E. M. Anscombe, 'The First Person', in *Mind and Language*, ed. S. Guttenplan (Clarendon Press, Oxford, 1975), pp. 45–66; A. J. P. Kenny 'The First Person', repr. in his *The Legacy of Wittgenstein* (Blackwell, Oxford, 1984), pp. 77–87; and N. Malcolm, 'Whether "I" is a Referring Expression' in C. Diamond and J. Teichmain ed., *Intention and Intentionality* (Harvester Press, Sussex, 1979), pp. 15 ff. Note that one cannot invoke the ordinary (direct) reflexive pronoun to explain the use of 'I' either, e.g. to argue that 'I' is a name each of us uses to refer to himself. For one uses 'I' correctly even if one does not know who one is (e.g. in a case of amnesia).

[3] Anscombe, ibid. p. 51.

to give expression in language to one's thoughts and feelings, one's beliefs and purposes.

The caution here is perhaps advised. For even if one can be thus brought to relinquish the idea that self-consciousness is consciousness of a self,[4] the idea that self-consciousness involves *consciousness of experiences*—which one then reports by the use of first-person psychological utterances—is profoundly appealing. Thus Locke argued that 'it is impossible for anyone to perceive without *perceiving* that he does perceive. When we see, hear, smell, taste, feel, meditate or will anything, we know that we do so.'[5] But this picture of 'inner perception' is incoherent. I do not observe or perceive my own experiences or perceivings (NFL, p. 278). Only someone *else* can see that I see, not I. All I can do (and it suffices) is to see. But there is no such thing as my perceiving my seeing. Similarly, I do not perceive my pains. I *have* them. If it made sense for a person to perceive his own experiences, then it would make sense to misperceive them. Then we could understand what it would be for someone to have severe pain but not to have observed it, or for him to seem to himself to perceive great pain but for there to be no pain at all. But this is perspicuously nonsense; these are not possibilities which do not happen to occur, but forms of words that are excluded from language, that have no roles as descriptions of possibilities.

One is tempted to object that this is too short shrift. Surely when we have a toothache and say 'I have toothache' we say what we say *because* we have toothache and *recognize* what we have *as* toothache. 'Inner sense' is not literally perception, but it resembles perception in being a form of consciousness of 'objects', of what is 'given' in experience, which, when it involves recognition, justifies a cognitive claim. But this too is confused. It makes sense to talk of recognition only where there is a distinction between appearance and reality, for only then can we distinguish recognizing correctly and misidentifying. In certain circumstances *you* can recognize whether I am in pain or not, but *I* never can. Where there is a distinction between seeming and being we can say of something 'It is the same *and* he recognized it' or 'It is the same,

---

[4] Of course, there are many other routes to that conclusion, e.g. Kant's, some of which lead from solid ground (viz. denial that introspection involves awareness of 'a self') to quagmires of confusion, e.g. Hume's (viz. that 'the self' is 'a bundle of perceptions').

[5] Locke, *An Essay Concerning Human Understanding*, II. xxvii, 11, quoted by N. Malcolm, 'Consciousness and Causality', in D. M. Armstrong and N. Malcolm, *Consciousness and Causality* (Blackwell, Oxford, 1984), p. 23. I found this the most illuminating essay on this difficult subject.

but he failed to recognize it (or, misidentified it)'. But it makes no sense to say, 'He has toothache but he doesn't recognize it' or 'He has no toothache, but it seems to him that he does'. For his sincere avowal of pain is itself a criterion for his being in pain, and there is no way to drive a wedge between his having the same sensation and his recognizing the sensation as the same. His avowal of pain is a criterion of his 'recognizing' it, and that means that it is impossible to recognize it wrongly, i.e. there is here no such thing as recognition (LSD, pp. 111 f.). The fact is that when I say 'I am in pain' or 'I see red', I do not say it on the ground of inner observation at all, any more than when I groan with pain or when I reach for something I want, I do what I do on the grounds of my observation of my sensation or my desire. I can indeed tell you why I said 'I am in pain' or 'I am frightened' but not on the grounds of 'inner observation' (*PI*, p. 188).

It is important to note here how subtle and nuanced Wittgenstein's account is. He is not arguing that there is no such thing as observing one's own state of mind (*PI*, §586; *RPP* I, §466). But to observe my mental states and report on them is altogether unlike observing the state of material inside a furnace and reporting on it. And psychological utterances such as 'It hurts', 'I have toothache', 'I see . . .', 'I intend . . .' are not reports of observations of mental states. Indeed, they are not *typically* reports at all. A Proust can wonderfully report his observation of his mental states, describe his evolving jealousies and griefs. But most of us are not that self-conscious, not in the philosopher's sense of this expression, but in the sense that we do not usually reflect that much upon our experiences, reactions, motives, and purposes. Indeed, it is misleading (though not wrong) to refer to self-reflective reports of this kind as reports of *observations* of mental states (*RPP* I, §467), for, in an important sense, the reports do *not rest on observation* (*RPP* II, §177). I observe my own mental states not by 'inner sense' or 'inner perception', but by noting, over a period of time, how my feelings, moods, and emotions wax and wane, how my emotional reactions and responses vary from occasion to occasion, by bearing these facts in mind, reflecting upon them, and evaluating them. We shall revert to this theme below, when we examine the application of the concept of *description* to the mental in the first-person case.

4. *The 'Inner' and the 'Outer'*

These various misconceptions of self-consciousness as a kind of perception are *one* source of the compelling picture of the relation between the mental and its behavioural manifestations as that between 'Inner' and 'Outer'. We are prone to think that when we ascribe psychological predicates to others, we have to make do with *indirect* evidence, viz. their behaviour. So our judgements rest perforce upon mere externalities, we know others only 'from the outside'. But in one's own case, it seems, one is *directly* acquainted with states of oneself, one knows them 'from the inside'. Hence it seems that when we say of someone on the basis of what he says and does that he is in pain, is thinking, is sad or joyful, what we speak of lies *behind* his behaviour. It is, we think, typically *hidden*—inside the mind. This picture is a misconstrual of natural metaphors and similes.

It is noteworthy that we do not say of a toothache that it is internal. What, one might wonder if one heard such an expression, would an *external* toothache be like? It is equally striking that we do not say, save when doing philosophy, that pain is *mental*. On the contrary, we speak of *physical* pain; if we talk of mental pain at all, we refer thereby to anguish, grief, and heartache, not to the pain of angina pectoris or toothache. What we do is to *compare* the relation between toothache and behaviour to the relation between what is 'inner' and what is 'outer' (LSD, p. 118), e.g. to the relation between the concealed movement of the clock within its hood and the observed dial and hands. The comparison is natural enough and the grounds for the analogy are obvious. We say of another that he has toothache on the basis of observing his behaviour (something 'external'), but he says 'I have toothache' without observing his own behaviour (cf. NFL, p. 278). We cannot typically guess what someone sunk in reverie is thinking, but he can tell us. We may sometimes doubt whether someone is really in a certain mental state or only pretending, but he cannot be in doubt. Nevertheless this natural analogy is highly misleading, for it conducts us by way of metaphor to metaphysics. 'We must get clear about how the metaphor of revealing (outside and inside) is actually applied by us; otherwise we shall be tempted to look for an inside behind that which in our metaphor is the inside.' (NFL, p. 280.) In the case of the mechanical clock we may wonder what is going on inside when, for example, clockwork figures dance on the outside to an audible tune. Then we can, e.g., open the back and examine the movement. This is what it is to reveal the inner processes in such a case. But what, in the case of the mind, counts as 'revealing'?

If we cannot tell, from observing a person's behaviour, what he sees, feels, or thinks, we may ask him and he can tell us. But to tell me what he sees is not to let me *see* inside him, nor is it to turn his inside out (NFL, p. 279). We must remind ourselves what *counts* here as 'showing me what he sees'. He can point out what he sees, and if I look at it I *will* see what he sees. But to see what he sees is not to 'peer into his soul'. Or he can point at a sample and say 'What I saw was *this* colour'. But this is not an *indirect* way of communicating what colour he saw; this is what is called 'showing someone what colour I saw'. We are, in our metaphysical moments, inclined to deny this, and to think that one person *cannot* see what another sees, cannot 'see the picture before the other person's eye' (NFL, p. 279). For to do that, one would have to *see his seeing*. But this is confused. In one sense I *can* see his seeing, i.e. I can perceive him observing whatever he looks at. But if what is intended is that I cannot *do* his seeing, that is nonsense. Similarly, if someone tells me with all sincerity what it is that he thinks, then I know what he thinks. I do not complain that all he has told me is mere *words*, that the thought is still 'inner'. So too if a person opens his heart to me, I do not say 'His feelings are still concealed in his heart'.

The concealed/revealed contrast only makes literal sense when we are concerned with signs of one category (NFL, p. 280), e.g. what can be concealed from sight is what can also be revealed to sight. But in applying the metaphor of inner and outer to the case of experience and behaviour we cross categories. To say 'His pains (the "inner") are hidden from me' is like saying 'These sounds are hidden from my eyes' (*LW*, §885), not like 'These sights are hidden by the fog'. When someone is seriously injured and writhing with pain, we do not say 'Still, his pain is hidden'—but nor do we say 'He reveals his pain'. To hide one's pain is to suppress one's natural pain behaviour, to clench one's teeth and bear it. And that too can often be seen! But to writhe in pain is not to *reveal* something. On the other hand, if I tell you that throughout the opera I had a dull headache, that might be called 'revealing my pain' or 'revealing that I was in pain'.

The metaphor of 'the hidden' seems particularly apt in the case of thoughts. For often we cannot tell what someone is thinking unless he expresses his thoughts. But 'hidden' here is profoundly misleading. To say that his thoughts are inaccessible to me because they are in his mind amounts to no more than saying that he thinks his thoughts, or that he speaks to himself silently, and that I cannot guess what he thinks. It does not mean that I cannot *perceive* his thoughts because they are in his mind. For he cannot *perceive* his thoughts either, nor does he *know* them—he thinks them (*PI*, pp. 220 f.; *LW* §§975 ff.). And, of course, he can tell us what he thinks. But when he confesses that he was thinking such-and-such, the criteria for the truth of the confession are not the criteria for a true *description* of a process. For the truth of a description of a process is checked by observation of the process, whereas the criteria for the truth of the confession that he thought such-and-such are his truthfulness, his evident sincerity in the circumstances (no winks and sly grins). He does not say that he thought what he thought on the grounds of *observing* his thoughts, rather he gives expression to his thoughts, voices them (*PI*, p. 222). Of course, there *is* such a thing as hiding one's thoughts. But to hide one's thoughts is not merely to think and not to voice one's thoughts. Not to express one's thoughts is not a kind of hiding, although it will often leave others ignorant of one's thoughts and even mislead them (and hence is *comparable* to hiding (*RPP* II, §§586 ff.)). It *seems* like a metaphysical form of hiding, so secure that it is inconceivable that another will find it (for we think of the mind as a place to which only the owner has access). But this is absurd, for on the one hand, he might unwittingly betray his thoughts (so much for metaphysical seclusion), and on the other, if one means that someone else cannot think my thoughts, that is either false or nonsense. It is false if it means that another cannot think the very same thought or that he can never know what I think (even if I tell him!), it is nonsense if it means that another cannot 'do' my thinking. One hides one's thoughts if one writes them down in a diary which one locks away (*LW*, 974), or if one writes them down in a secret code. One may conceal one's thoughts from the children, for example, if one expresses them to one's wife in a language which the children do not know (*RPP* II, §§563 f.). But here what is hidden is perfectly audible, so where is the *mental thing* that is hidden? The idea that the mind is a metaphysical hiding-place is a wrong picture, resting on misconstrual of metaphor and grammar. And to compare thinking to a secret process is as misleading as the comparison of searching for the apt word to the efforts of someone who is trying to make an exact copy of a line which only he can see (*RPP* I, §580).

Associated with the same syndrome of confusions is the inclination to say 'I know directly that I see, but only indirectly that he sees'. This too is a consequence of a misleading analogy (LSD, p. 13), for we compare the case of a person saying 'I am in pain' as opposed to someone saying *of* him on the basis of his behaviour 'He is in pain' with the case of, e.g., knowing that there is a penny in my pocket by feeling it ('directly') as opposed to knowing that there is a penny in your pocket by hearsay ('indirectly'). But this comparison is misguided. It makes sense to say 'I know there is a penny in my pocket because I feel it' for tactile perception is a form of consciousness of objects, a way of informing oneself about objects around one. I can perceive the penny in my pocket by feeling it, or I can peer into my pocket and see it. I may perceive right or I may err (e.g. it is just a flat disc). But one cannot say 'I know (directly) that I have a pain *because* I feel it' for to feel pain *is* to have pain. 'Feel' in 'feel pain' (as in 'feel excited') does not signify a form of perception. It makes no sense to say 'I thought I felt a pain, but I was wrong', or to say 'I had a pain, but I did not feel it'. So 'I know I have pain because I feel it' amounts to saying that I know I have pain because I have it, i.e. because it is true, i.e. because I am not lying (LSD, p. 13). But that just amounts to saying emphatically 'I have pain' (*PI*, §246). We are inclined to think that when I say 'I have pain' I *derive* this description from the pain, from the private sensation, even though, of course, I cannot *show* this private object to anyone (*PI*, §374). Nevertheless, it is this which *justifies* my saying 'I have pain' and hence also 'I know I have pain'. This is confused. We take this picture from the case of ostensively defining a colour word, e.g. 'red' and then saying of some *other* object that it is red (since it is this ↑ colour (pointing at the sample)). But, of course, when I say of a tomato that it is red, I don't 'derive red' from what I see, but, *if at all*, from the sample which functions as a paradigm. But, as the private-language argument shows, there is no such thing as a mental 'private' object that functions as a sample. 'The private experience is to serve as a paradigm, and at the same time admittedly it can't be a paradigm' (NFL, p. 314). I do not derive 'I have pain' from the experience of pain, and 'I have pain' here is no description. I do not 'know directly' that I have pain, for it makes no sense to talk here either of knowledge or ignorance.

Similarly, it is confused to suggest that our knowledge of the states of mind of someone else is somehow imperfect because we can only know of his experiences by observing his behaviour, i.e. indirectly. This is just how we use 'He sees (is angry; is in pain)'. We say 'He sees the so-and-so' when we see his eyes light on it and see his immediate response. There is no *better* ground for saying that he sees nor is there any *more direct* way of seeing that he sees, *even for him*. We could perfectly well say that this is what it *is* to see directly that he sees, and we might contrast it with seeing indirectly that he sees, e.g. seeing his reflection in a mirror, or watching his torch in the dark as it moves with obvious aforethought from one object to another.

Mesmerized by our metaphor, we are prone to think of the mental as lying *behind* the physical. We do indeed sometimes look at someone and say 'I wonder what is going on behind that face' (*LW*, §978). But we must look more closely at the use of this figure of speech. If I do not trust someone, I may say that I don't know what is going on inside him. But if I do trust him, I don't say that I *know* what is going on inside him (*RPP* II, §602), but rather that I know him well, that I know what he thinks about such-and-such for he has told me. We don't *have* to see the 'external' as a façade behind which the mental powers are at work, and when someone talks to us with obvious sincerity we are not even tempted by this picture (*LW*, §978). The idea of the mind as something which one either sees or does not is similar to, and just as misleading as, the idea of the meaning of a word as an object or process accompanying the word. Does it follow that the mind is just an aspect of the body? 'No', Wittgenstein replied, 'I'm not that hard up for categories' (*RPP* II, §690).

Contemporary philosophers, fascinated by science and by neurophysiological discoveries, correctly repudiate the Cartesian conception of the mind as an immaterial substance. But they are prone to conclude, quite wrongly, that the mind must therefore be a material substance, in fact the brain. Hence they embrace a brain/body dualism which is as deeply confused as its Cartesian ancestor. For they persist in thinking that psychology studies the workings of the human mind by observing human behaviour in certain circumstances, i.e. from the outside. But now in the late-twentieth century, it seems, we *do* know what lies *behind* the outside, namely the functioning of the brain. And as neurophysiology proceeds, we are gradually becoming able to see *what is inside*. This is desperately misguided, combining the errors of Cartesianism with the confusions of materialism. Wittgenstein comments subtly upon the source of error.

> Misleading parallel: psychology treats of processes in the psychical sphere, as does physics in the physical.
>
> Seeing, hearing, thinking, feeling, willing, are not the subject of psychology *in the same sense* as that in which the movements of bodies, the phenomena of electricity, etc. are the subjects of physics. You can see this from the fact that the physicist sees, hears, thinks about, and informs us of these phenomena, and the psychologist observes the expressions [*Äusserungen*] (the behaviour) of the subject. (*PI*, §571.)[6]

---

[6] Anscombe's translation has *Äusserungen* as 'external reactions'. This is, I think,

It does not follow that psychology treats only of behaviour, not of the mind (*PI*, p. 179), for what the psychologist records, *inter alia*, are the utterances [Äusserungen] of the subject which are *not* about behaviour but give expression to, or are manifestations of, experiences (*PI*, p. 179). But if we succumb to the 'misleading parallel' we will be prone to think that in studying behaviour the psychologist has to make do with second-best, that he has only indirect evidence for 'processes in the psychical sphere'. And then it would seem that neuro-physiology can give us direct access. Yet if one could observe whatever neural processes accompany my silently talking to myself would my thoughts be less hidden than if I confess them to you? One might say—'Surely, I have to *believe* the confession'; but one might respond 'Is it easier to believe the neural processes?' If my thoughts are obscure, elusive (and allusive) will their accompanying neural correlates be *less* obscure and elusive? If I talk to myself in an unknown language, will the neural events be in English? If my sincerity is in question, *must* the neural ongoings reveal my duplicity or truthfulness? (The brain cannot lie, one might want to say, it is beyond sincerity and insincerity!) Here we are perspicuously led 'to look for an inside behind that which in our metaphor is the inside'. Of course we say such things as 'while speaking to him I did not know what was going on in his head', while saying which we think of his *thought* processes. For we are also inclined to say 'One thinks in one's head (not in one's stomach)'. So, for a moment, we really would like to see into his head. But 'we only mean what elsewhere we should mean by saying: we should like to know what he is thinking' (*PI*, §427). And we do not think *in* our head, although we sometimes 'do arithmetic in our head' (as opposed to doing calculations on paper) i.e. we do 'mental arithmetic', and we often clutch our head when thinking (but we don't do 'mental thinking'). We sometimes think aloud, and at other times think and do not voice our thoughts.

Silent 'internal' speech is not a half hidden phenomenon which is as it were seen through a veil. It is not hidden *at all*, but the concept may easily confuse us, for it runs cheek by jowl with the concept of an 'outward' process, and yet does not coincide with it. (*PI*, p. 220).

The materialist conception of the mind is bedevilled by much the same misleading picture as the Cartesian one, dogged by the same

unhappy. 'Expressions' is not *much* better in this context, but at least avoids the suggestion of 'mere externalities'.

misconceptions of the metaphors of the 'inner' and the 'outer', of the 'concealed' and the 'revealed', of what lies 'behind' the externalities of behaviour. Only it displays a penchant for grey glutinous, as opposed to ethereal, stuff.

4. *Experience and its Natural Expression*

The philosopher's misunderstanding of first-person psychological utterances (and hence of psychological propositions in general) has deeper roots than misconstruals of metaphors. They lie ultimately in the fallacies of the 'private linguist', in the thought that the meaning of psychological predicates is given by the experiences one has ('the given'). I surely know whether I am in pain, one is inclined to argue, because I *have* it. For it seems as if it is the pain I have which *justifies* my saying 'I am in pain'. But the pain I have cannot justify my saying that I am in pain as evidence justifies drawing a conclusion, since a thing is not evidence for itself. So if it justifies my saying 'I am in pain', it can do so only in the sense in which a sample justifies the use of a word, viz. that a sample is indicated in giving a rule for the use of a word and cited in justifying its correct application (e.g. 'I said that the curtains are indigo because they are *this* colour ↑, and this *is* indigo'). But if *my pain* is a sample for the use of 'pain', then it seems that only I can really know that I am in pain, for only I can compare what I *have* with the sample.[7] And from here it is just one further step to complete scepticism about the pains of others, for if one is only justified in saying 'He is in pain' if what he *has* is this ↑ ('pointing' inwardly at my private sample of pain), then I *cannot* ever be really justified, I can only guess that he has what I have when I say 'I am in pain'. But a moment's further reflection takes us into solipsism. For it makes no sense for him to have what I have, and if what I have is what is *called* 'pain', then others cannot have it. And now total confusion reigns.

Enough of this has been disentangled in the previous chapters to indicate part of what is going wrong. Further knots can be untied by grasping different threads. This familiar pattern of reasoning involves noting a superficial analogy between a language-game with samples (e.g. judgements of colour) and psychological utterances. 'The impression of a "private table" [of samples]', Wittgenstein wrote

---

[7] But note here that one wants the pain to be *both* what is described by 'I have pain' and *also* to be a sample for the use of 'pain'. 'The experience which I have seems, in a certain sense, to take the place of a description of this experience. "It is its own description".' (NFL, p. 277).

(*Z*, §552), 'arises through the *absence* of a table and through the similarity of the game to one that is played with a table.' In both cases we say what we say with a certain directness or immediacy. Colour judgements do not typically[8] rest on evidence, one just looks and sees, and that, in one's own case, is not evidence. Similarly, I do not say 'I have toothache' on the basis of evidence. But we note immediately that judgements of colour are corrigible. So we collapse 'That is red' into 'It looks red to me' or 'I seem to see red', i.e. expressions that are 'psychological' ('descriptions of perceptual experience') and which seem as secure and incorrigible as 'I am in pain'.[9] Now one is prone to think that the sample of red (the use of which makes intelligible the utterance 'I know that is red; it is *this* ↑ colour') is itself *mental*. Hence one views 'I see red' and 'I have pain' as standing on the same level.

The movement of thought here is perverse. Instead of noting the deep differences between the language-games with words defined by reference to samples and those in which samples have no role, we collapse the first into the second. We then multiply our own confusions by conceiving of the language-game with 'pain' (or more generally with psychological expressions) on the model of our *misconstrual* of the language-game with samples. We project a misconceived account of the language-game with colour on to our account of the language-game with pain, partly through taking wrongly the resemblance between 'I have pain' and 'I see red'. We do not notice that what corresponds to pain, so to speak, in 'I see red' is not the red that I see, but my *seeing*, the 'visual experience'. So we think that 'pain' is like 'red' in being defined by reference to a sample, but that red is like pain in being 'essentially private'. ('This ↑ is red', we are inclined to say, pointing, as it were, *visually*). We fail to apprehend the absurdity partly because of our inclination to think of *having* as a kind of *perceiving* anyway.

It is indeed true that if psychological concepts were (*per impossibile*) defined by reference to 'private' (mental) samples, then it would make sense to recognize that one has pain, to misidentify one's sensation, to appear to oneself to have a sensation but not to have it, to have it but not to notice it, and so forth. 'If I assume the abrogation of the normal

---

[8] But there are exceptions, e.g. when objects are being irradiated by distorting light. Here one might say 'I know that tomato is red because it looks black, and red things always look black in this light'.

[9] Descartes notoriously treated 'I seem to see . . .' as the expression of a *cogitatio*, an incorrigible 'thought' in his extended use of the term.

language-game with the expression of sensation, I need a criterion of identity for the sensation; and then the possibility of error also exists' (*PI*, §288). Here it *would* make sense to know, believe, or doubt that one was in pain. But this is absurd, for there is no such thing as a 'private' (mental) sample. The language-game with colours *begins* with looking and observing coloured objects. It ends, so to say, with giving descriptions of the objects thus observed. It is explained by reference to samples employed as standards for correct use; and the framework within which alone this shared language-game can be played is the existence of common colour-discriminatory capacities among its participants. It *seems* as if the language-game with 'pain' should begin with the sensation, which I *have* (perceive!), and which I then describe by saying 'I have pain'. But this, Wittgenstein argued, is precisely wrong. I do *not* perceive my pain, and I do not *identify* my sensations, either by an inner criterion or by employing a 'private' sample. I use a given expression, e.g. 'It hurts', 'I have toothache', without grounds and without an object of comparison.[10] 'But this is not the *end* of the language-game; it is the beginning' (*PI*, §290). This beginning is not a *description* of pain, but an expression of pain which provides a criterion for descriptions given by others. The framework for this language-game consists in the shared human disposition to react to injury by groaning or crying out in pain and assuaging the injured limb. For the beginning of such language-games with psychological expressions lies in natural human behaviour in certain circumstances, in our groans of pain, our gasps of surprise, our trying to obtain things we want, our trembling when in danger, and our paroxysms of anger. (But not *all* psychological expressions are like this.)

The child hurts itself, screams or moans, and we teach it to replace its groans by the utterance 'It hurts', or 'I have a pain'. The utterance of pain no more rests on evidence or on introspection than the moan. In such contexts it is no more a report or description of something 'inner' than is crying out with pain. But the utterance, like the groan, is an *expression* or *manifestation* (*Äusserung*) of pain. It is a learnt form of

---

[10] As noted previously when Wittgenstein wrote the *Philosophical Remarks* he thought that psychological utterances were paradigms of propositions that get compared with reality. ' "I have no pain" means: if I compare the proposition "I have a pain" with reality, it turns out false—so I must be in a position to compare the proposition with what is in fact the case' (*PR*, §62). Only later did he come to realize that in the case of what he had called 'the primary', i.e. immediate experience, 'there is no comparing of proposition and reality. (Collating.)' (NFL, p. 294), there are no samples to function as objects of comparison and there is neither knowledge nor ignorance.

pain-behaviour, and there is an internal, conceptual relation between it and pain, for pain-behaviour, whether a groan or an utterance of pain, is a *criterion* for saying of a person that he is in pain. To be sure, the moan and the utterance alike are *behaviour* and pain is *not* behaviour. One can have a toothache and not manifest it in behaviour, and one can moan and say 'I have toothache' without having toothache. Nevertheless, pain and its behavioural manifestations are not independent. One cannot say 'Here is toothache, and here is behaviour—we can put them together in any way we please' (LSD, p. 10). Similarly, I can see and not say so, and I can say I see something when I do not. But one cannot say 'therefore seeing is *one* process and expressing what we see another, and all that they have to do with one another is that they sometimes coincide—they have the same connections as being red and being sweet' (NFL, p. 286). What is true is that pain-behaviour does not entail being in pain, and being in pain is not necessarily manifest. But it would be quite wrong to think that they are therefore *externally* related, that pain-behaviour is merely a symptom (inductive evidence) for pain. For that would presuppose the possibility of independent identification in order to establish an inductive correlation. And that is unintelligible. We should have no use for the word 'pain', and hosts of other psychological expressions, if their application was severed from the criteria of behaviour (NFL, p. 286).

It would be wrong to say that 'I have pain', *whenever* used, has the same logical status as a moan. Its use, one might say, is *rooted* in natural pain-behaviour, but what grows from this differs as the foliage of a tree from its roots. ' "Toothache" is not only a substitute for moaning. But it is *also* that' (LSD, p. 11). 'It hurts, it hurts!' is a cry of pain, but 'I have a dull ache beneath my left upper front molar' is a report of pain (see below). 'I don't have toothache' neither *means* 'I don't moan' nor is it a substitute for not moaning. 'If I break a tooth, I have toothache' is not a conditional moan. But these latter uses are altogether dependent upon the primitive manifestation of toothache and its replacement by an utterance which, like what it partly displaces, is a criterion for having toothache.

Of course, one wants to say that when one has hurt oneself and moans, one doesn't *just* moan. That is true, but to moan is not to say 'I moan', it is to *give expression* to one's pain. To say 'I am in pain' is behaviour likewise, and here too one is inclined to think that one who utters this is not *just* behaving. This may lead us into thinking that in expressing his suffering he is *referring* to something unseen (perhaps even something which only he can 'see'). But an utterance of pain no more *refers* to something unseen than does the groan of pain, it is rather a manifestation of pain. It is equally misleading to say that the moan or cry of pain is *caused* by the pain, for causal relations are external and presuppose the intelligibility of independent identifications. Your touching my injured arm may cause me pain, and I may cry out 'It hurts'. Here we can say that your touching my arm caused me to cry out. But we should not say that the *pain* caused me to cry out, rather—I cried out *with pain*. The pain is not an intermediate object or event between your touching and my crying out, connected to each in a causal chain.

Just as 'pain' in 'I have pain' can only misleadingly be said to *refer* to something, so too it is misleading (but not wrong) to say that 'pain' is the name of something. For then we shall be inclined to construe the use of 'pain' on the model of names of objects ('table') and their properties ('red'). Primitive behaviour is the expression (*Äusserung*) of sensation, and what replaces it, viz. the utterance 'I have pain', is likewise (in central cases) an expression of pain, a piece of pain-behaviour. Hence 'The word "pain" is the name of a sensation' is not like 'The word "red" is the name of a colour'. Rather is it equivalent to ' "I've got a pain" is an expression of sensation' (*RPP* I, §313). What we call 'the name of a sensation (or feeling, emotion, mood)' is as different from the name of an object as the description of a sensation (feeling, emotion, mood) is from the description of an object (cf. LSD, p. 11). We shall examine the latter distinction below.

Confusion can arise out of the claim that pain-behaviour is an *expression* of pain. We explain the use of 'pain' by reference to the pain-behaviour which justifies its application in third-person cases, and by reference to its use, in the first-person case, in an utterance of pain. We say, rightly, that a moan or a cry of pain expresses something. But now, it seems, we cannot say *what* it expresses (we cannot say 'pain', since that is the word we were supposed to be explaining). We cannot *point* at a sample of what the behaviour expresses, and it does not help to say 'It expresses *something*' (something 'inner' about which nothing can be said!). For pain, as we have seen, cannot be said to be such a something, nor yet a nothing either (LSD, p. 45; *PI*, §304). Both 'pain' and 'the expression of pain' are explained by giving their grammar, specifying the rules for their use; and, of course, we do use these words differently, we do differentiate between pain and its expression. One is tempted to say that the expression of pain gets its importance from the experience *behind* it. But that is wrong. One can groan with pain or groan without pain, but that is not as if something lies behind the groan in the first case while there is only a vacuum in the second. One can say, and Wittgenstein does (NFL, p. 293), that 'the language-game with expressions of feelings are based on games with expressions of which we don't say that they may lie'. When the dog howls with pain or the baby screams with ear-ache, we do not say, 'Maybe they are pretending'; one must *learn* to deceive, pretend, dissimulate. So 'it is senseless to say: the expression may always lie'. However, that does not mean that pain really *corresponds* to the expression. Moaning *with* pain is not behaviour PLUS pain (the 'outer' plus 'the inner' that lies behind it) any more than saying something and meaning it is saying it plus some inner process of meaning it (LSD, p. 10). The idea of 'correspondence' belongs to language-games in which one can point and say 'Namely *this* ↑', and the idea of behaviour *plus* pain is derived from games in which there is a genuine inner and outer. The expression of pain gets its importance not from an experience to which it corresponds or which lies behind it, but from the fact that it is a natural, primitive, pre-cultural reaction to circumstances. So too laughter gets its importance through being natural to us, a natural response to circumstances. It is on such foundations that our concepts of sensation, feeling, expecting, hoping, etc. are erected.

One should, however, note that the relation of the first-person psychological utterance to natural behaviour is complex and differs from concept to concept. We have concentrated thus far, as Wittgenstein did, upon the case of pain. But a few different examples may be salutary. Consider the fact that the child, bouncing in its cot trying to reach its teddy bear, learns the primitive use of 'want!' Later it will learn to say 'I want teddy' and then 'You want . . .', 'We wanted . . .' etc. and 'Next Christmas I want another teddy'. The latter expression of desire is, of course, not a replacement of any natural conative behaviour. My dog can want a bone, but it cannot want a bone for next Christmas. Such desires are accessible only to language-users. As the child masters ever fresh linguistic articulations, the trajectory of its will increases. It becomes *possible* for it to want what it *could not* want before. In the case of 'I dreamt that . . .' (used on awakening) the primitive behaviour which dream-avowals replace is by and large already linguistic. The child wakes up crying 'Mummy, Mummy, a tiger is chasing me' and its mother teaches it to say 'I dreamt that . . .' Here, with the exception of waking up and simply crying with fear, the bedrock of the language-game is itself a use of language, albeit a spontaneous unreflective one. Similarly in the case of perception. One can learn to say 'I see red' only after one has mastered 'That is red'. And one learns the special use of 'It seems to me that I see . . .' (which so confuses the Cartesian) only later. In short, Wittgenstein's account of 'pain' is a guideline, not a mechanical paradigm, for the description of the roots of psychological concepts. It is an *indispensable* guide, but each concept needs careful scrutiny in its own right.

5. Avowals and Descriptions

The thickets screening us from the light to which Wittgenstein tried to lead us are dense and the shadows of confusion they cast are long. Surely, one wants to object, first-person psychological utterances are true or false, for someone may lie about his pains, feelings, or thoughts. If one lies, one says falsely what one knows not to be the case. Does this not suffice to show that avowals of experience are true (or false) and known to be such by the speaker? Does it not also follow that when I say, for example, 'I have toothache', and I speak truthfully, then I am giving a *description* of my mental state, a description which I *know* to be true? It does not; but we are readily deceived here by failure to appreciate the diversity of what is called 'a description', by insensitivity to the use of 'true' in such contexts, and by dogmatic preconceptions about the uniformity of explanations of what it is to lie.

'Perhaps this word "describe" tricks us here', Wittgenstein wrote, 'I say "I describe my state of mind" and "I describe my room". You need to call to mind the differences between the language-games' (*PI*, §290). What we call 'descriptions' are instruments for particular uses which vary (cf. *PI*, §24) just as a *drawing* can be very different things for different purposes, not only a picture to hang on the wall, but also a machine-drawing, a cross-section, an elevation with measurements, a groundplan, a map, etc. (*PI*, §291). There is indeed such a thing as a person's giving a description of his state of mind. But, first, such descriptions are only a small *sub-group* of the vast range of our expressions [*Äusserungen*] of experience (RPP I, §693), and secondly, even when such an utterance *is* a description, it is logically altogether *unlike* the description of an object.[11]

---

[11] Hence I take issue with A. J. P. Kenny's claim that 'I am in pain' is a description in a special sense (*Wittgenstein*, pp. 199 f.). It is typically not a description in *any* sense. But if, at the doctor's, I say 'I have been in pain for three days, at first it . . . then I couldn't walk properly . . . now it is even worse', *that* is a description of how things are with me

If we examine our use of first-person psychological utterances in the variety of contexts in which they are appropriate we will find a whole spectrum of cases. At one end, as a cluster of cases, lie exclamations ('I'm so pleased'), cries of pain ('It hurts, it hurts!') sighs of longing ('Oh, I do hope he'll come'), expressions of emotion ('I'm furious with you') or expectation ('I expect you to come'), avowals of thought or belief, expressions of desire ('I want a glass of wine') or preference ('I like claret') and so forth. These are *very* diverse. A cry of pain may be wrenched from me: 'I'm furious with you' *is* (in certain circumstances, said in a certain tone) a flash of anger or *gesture* of anger. 'I want a glass of wine' is often a request ('Wine over here!') as is an expression of preference ('I prefer claret'). 'I don't believe it!' is an exclamation of incredulity, 'I believe you' an assurance, and 'I believe that . . .' may be a confession of faith, a tentative judgement, or merely a polite denial. (But note that these latter examples are not expressions of *experiences*.)

At this end of the spectrum the concept of *description* gets no grip,[12] nor does that of *truth*. Of course, dissimulation and deceit are possible. But it would be as misleading to evaluate such utterances as true or false as it would be to evaluate a groan of pain, a jump of joy, a start of expectation as true or false, although, of course, there too dissimulation and pretence are possible. (Note that *insincerity* does not belong here either; it is at home with confessions, reports, and utterances seemingly intended to inform.) These diverse uses of first-person psychological sentences are no more *assertions about* or *descriptions of* one's own states of mind than are groans, cheers, or smiles. Of course, one can make inferences from the behaviour, whether verbal or non-verbal, to the person's state or condition. But one can do that from someone's saying 'Give me an apple!' and no one would wish to call *that* a description (*RPP* I, §463). These uses of psychological sentences cannot be clarified by asking such questions as 'What does "I am frightened" really mean, what am I referring to when I say it?' (these encourage us to try to 'catch our soul out of the corner of our eye') but only by examining the context and manner of their use (*PI*, p. 188).

Between this diverse array and genuine descriptions of one's own mental states lie hosts of further cases that belong to neither end of this

(or, as a philosopher might put it, of my 'mental state'). And it is true that it is unlike a description of a room or of the state of a room. (See below pp. 301 f.)

[12] If I cry out 'It hurts, it hurts' while writhing on the ground, and someone solicitious asks 'What hurts?' to which I reply 'My leg', am I describing either my leg or my mind?

spectrum. I may report my feelings to you as a piece of information ('I must tell you—I'm frightened'). This would be no cry of fear—one might even say it in a smiling tone of voice (*LW*, §39). I may air my opinions, since I want you to know what I think. But this is not to describe my opinions, although it is not a spontaneous reaction either. I may tell you what I am doing (e.g. 'I'm looking for John') or what I am going to do ('I intend visiting him'). It is true that 'I intend . . .' is not an expression [*Äusserung*] of an *experience*, but also that it is *never* a description either (*RPP* II, §179; *RPP* I, §599). These kinds of case are no more based on observation, 'read off from within', than are the primitive utterances considered above (*RPP* II, §177; *LW*, §23). They are uttered with a certain intention, but not on the basis of inner evidence or introspection. If I simply want to tell someone about my apprehension, my intentions, my opinion, I am not engaging in the *description* of anything (*LW*, §20). Because such sentences are used in informing someone about the speaker, they also have a role in *explaining* one's behaviour. If my hands shake as I light your cigarette while we both await a *viva*, I may say with a wry smile 'I am scared stiff'. We often tell others what we think about something or other. This informs them of our opinions, and may also explain or justify our plans and projects. But to tell you my thoughts is not to *describe* my thoughts, let alone to describe them on the basis of acquaintance, for I am not acquainted with my thoughts, I think them. Acquaintance and description do indeed belong together, for one is acquainted with that of which one can give a correct description (*RPP* I, §572), but to say what I think, to give expression to my thoughts, is not to describe them. If one is tempted to call 'I think that . . .' a description rather than the expression of the speaker's thoughts, one should contrast how one learns to describe something, e.g. a table, with how one learns to 'describe' one's thoughts. In the former case one learns to observe the object of description, to look at it closely, note its features. One learns differences between kinds of table (Pembroke or sofa table; dining or breakfast table; pedestal or gate-leg table) and styles of table (Chippendale, Hepplewhite, Sheraton), as well as different woods. But to learn to express one's thought is to learn *to be articulate*. One judges a description of a table to be *wrong* (e.g. 'a satin-wood Sheraton sofa table') by scrutinizing the object described and seeing whether the description matches the facts (it's not satin-wood but faded mahogany, not a Sheraton style but a Hepplewhite, not a sofa table but a Pembroke table). What is it for a 'description' of a thought to be wrong? How do we *judge* someone's expression of his own thoughts to be *wrong*? To be sure, we cannot scrutinize the thoughts and see whether the 'description' matches them, but then neither can the speaker (thinker) for he does not tell us what he thinks by observing his thoughts either. That conception belongs to the inner/outer picture of the mind which we have learnt to repudiate. And now that we have repudiated it we should not talk of 'cannot', as if there were something that we are *unable* to do; rather should we say 'there is no such thing in this language-game (as there is no such thing as 'check' in draughts); what you are thinking of belongs to a different game'. We judge a person's expression of his thoughts wrong not if he has made a *mistake*, *misidentified* his thought, but if we have reason for thinking him to be *insincere*, if we think he is untruthful ('Why, only yesterday I heard you say . . .') or intends to deceive us.

One is inclined to think that the possibility of insincerity betokens the necessity of knowledge. For if I can lie to you about my thoughts, I *must* know them! To lie is surely to say what one knows to be false with intent to deceive. And people can and do lie about their thoughts, intentions, and sensations. We are misled here by our inclination to impose uniformity upon different language-games ('A queen is a queen! It doesn't matter whether it's chess or draughts!') To lie about my thoughts is to think one thing and say another. To lie about what I feel is not to *know* what I feel and say something else, but rather to feel thus-and-so and to deny that I feel it (or insist that I feel otherwise). One will still want to object: surely when I lie about my thoughts or feelings I *know* or am conscious that I am really thinking or feeling thus-and-so and not as I said? This is wrong, for the very phrase 'to know that I am lying' is misleading. One may find out that one has unintentionally been deceiving someone, but one does not *find out* that one is lying. One does not 'know' that one is lying because an inner voice, a special feeling, tells one (*RPP* I, §779). The inner voice of guilt presupposes the lie and does not 'inform' me of it. What is true is that if I lie I do not just realize *later* that I have lied (though I might, in another case, realize later that I had said something untrue). Of course I *know* later that I have lied, but not because I *knew* earlier, but because I *lied* earlier.[13] What we think of as awareness, consciousness or

---

[13] A parallel misconception arises in the case of memory: surely to remember that p is to know that p now because one knew that p earlier. But if I can remember being in pain then I must, when I was in pain, have known that I was! Here we are mesmerized by uniform *forms* and oblivious to diverse uses and occasions of use. To remember being in pain yesterday is to have been in pain then and not to have forgotten it.

knowledge of lying (in one's own case) belongs to the category of *capacity*, not that of experience let alone that of information (*RPP* I, §735). It belongs together with consciousness of intention (*RPP* I, §731) which is likewise not a form of knowledge but a capacity to say what one purposes.

The expression 'description of a state of mind', Wittgenstein emphasized, characterizes a certain, rather special, language-game (*LW*, §50). If one just hears a psychological expression, e.g. 'I am afraid', one might be able to guess which game is played from the tone of voice, but one will not really know until one is given the context. Then one will see whether the speaker is making fun of his own fear, expressing amazement that he is afraid, reluctantly confessing it, explaining why his hands are shaking, etc. (*LW*, §43). What then is it to describe one's state of mind? A state of mind has *duration*. So a description of one's current state of mind is typically given in the imperfect tense, interwoven with descriptions of my reactions and of what I did. Thus the following examples can, in appropriate contexts, be said to be descriptions: 'I have been afraid of his arrival all day long. Immediately on waking I thought ... Then I considered ... Time and again I looked out of the window ...' (*RPP* II, §156); 'I can't keep my mind on my work today, I keep on thinking of his coming' (*PI*, §585); 'I have been hoping all day that ...' or 'I'm less afraid of him now than I used to be' (*RPP* II, §§722, 728). These are descriptions of my state of mind, informing you how I have been feeling. So too 'I have a throbbing dull pain beneath my left shoulder blade; it gets very painful when I walk but is not so bad when I am resting' is a description of my pain.

Notice the contrast between my description of my state, e.g. of hope, and an expression of hope. If someone remarks 'John said he might pass through Oxford' and I respond 'I do hope he'll come', that is an expression of hope. If someone were to ask 'For how long have you been hoping that?' one could not say, 'For as long as I have been saying so'. Moreover, even if one had an answer (e.g. 'I've been hoping he'll visit Oxford for ages'), it would be irrelevant to the purpose of, and to the characterization of this use of, 'I do hope he'll come' (*Z* §78).

Notice further that the diverse uses may be *blended*. One might say 'I have spent the whole day in fear. The first thing I thought of this morning was ... My thoughts have been in turmoil all day ... Whenever the phone rings my heart jumps, and *now too I am full of anxiety*.' Wittgenstein examined this kind of case too: 'What are we to say about this mixture of report and expression [*Äusserung*]?[14] Well, what should we say other than that here we have the use of the word "fear" in front of us?' (RPP II, §156).

Finally, while my description may be a lie (like my reports) and while, like all descriptions, it may be inaccurate, exaggerated or understated, it would still be altogether misleading to conceive of it as said on the basis of 'observation of the inner'. My description may involve recollection 'I have been desperately anxious all day ... when the phone rang this morning I almost jumped out of my skin ...' and hence may err ('No, dear', my wife may interrupt my narrative, 'you are exaggerating'), but it would be mischaracterized as consisting in retention of *knowledge* acquired *in experience*.

6. Objections and Deflections

Knowledge is connected with doubt and certainty, with learning and finding out, with the possibility of mistake or deception, with grounds and confirmation. These all apply in our use of third-person present tense psychological sentences, but not in the first-person. 'I know that *p*' makes sense only if 'I don't know whether *p*' makes sense. But 'I don't know whether I'm in pain; maybe I am, maybe I'm not' is nonsense. If someone were to say this we should not understand him. We do have *a* use for similar sentences, e.g. 'I don't know what I think about such-and-such', 'I don't know what I want', 'I don't know whether I'll go'. But none of these concern *ignorance*. 'I don't know what I think (want, intend)' does not mean that I think (want, intend) thus-and-so, but I do not know that I do. It means that I haven't yet formulated, crystallized, my thoughts (they are still in a turmoil), haven't yet *decided* what I want or whether I'll go. What I must do is not find out, but make up my mind.

One might object that surely there is a kind of ignorance here. For do not self-conscious creatures such as we know things about our mental states which merely conscious animals do not? My dog may be in pain, want to go out, expect a bone, but it does not *know* these things about itself! But are we not self-conscious creatures, and do we not therefore know how things are with us? This is misleading. What is true is that we *can say* that we are in pain, want such-and-such, expect so-and-so. Endless consequences flow from this linguistic capacity (there are no mute inglorious Prousts in a canine country churchyard),

---

[14] The translators have 'statement' here. That is definitely wrong.

but for all its immense importance, 'I know ...' does not mean merely 'I can say ...' The dog is not ignorant of its pain and I am not cognizant of mine.

One might also object that the connection of knowledge and doubt is satisfied in first-person psychological utterances. For someone who knows something does not doubt it, and to be sure, when I am in pain I do not doubt whether I am. But this is wrong. For knowledge excludes doubt, not the *intelligibility* of doubt. But 'I doubt whether I am in pain' is *senseless*, not false (*PI*, p. 221).[15] Similar considerations apply to mistake. If I say 'It hurts, it hurts', you may chide me with 'Come, come, it's not so bad', but you may not correct me with 'You're wrong, it doesn't hurt at all'. The former is tantamount to 'Don't make a fuss', the latter is either a joke or nonsense. Similarly, I may say 'I want ...' and you may respond 'You don't *really* want ...', but this is not an accusation of error, rather a plea that I should think again.

One may be disturbed by the fact that the type-sentence 'I am in pain' is a base for sentence-forming operators such as 'He thinks (knows, believes, hopes) that ...'. For the result of such an operation seems to express a true or false proposition, and moreover one which I can know. But can I know that he knows that I am in pain, yet not myself know whether I am in pain? One may worry over the fact that 'I was in pain' and 'I will be in pain' can surely be said to express something I know. Yet how can that be, given that they are just transforms of 'I am in pain'? One may note that one can surely know that no one in the room is in pain. But if I am in the room does not this involve my knowing that I am not in pain? These and other similar objections are exemplary cases of being so mesmerized by *forms* of words that one becomes oblivious to their use, of being so taken by patterns of transformation that one forgets to examine the point of employing the resultant sentences. Of course one can say 'I was in awful pain and I knew that you thought I was laying it on'. It does not at all follow that it makes sense to say 'I knew I was in awful pain'. If it did, it would also make sense to ask whether I might not have been mistaken. It makes sense for me to know or believe that A knows that I am in pain, for it makes sense for me not to know it. But it does not follow from my knowing that A knows that I am in pain that it makes

---

[15] One might object that there is after all room for a kind of doubt in connection with one's pain, e.g. 'I'm not quite sure whether this is a *pain* or just an ache'. But this is no more a case of *uncertainty remediable by further evidence* than 'I'm not quite sure whether I'll come'.

any *sense* at all for me to know *or* not to know that I am in pain. The very question posed above, viz. 'If I know that he knows that I am in pain, is it possible that I should not know whether I am in pain?' is absurd. For the point is not that I do *not* know, but that it is *senseless* to say *either* 'I do not know' *or* 'I know'. It is a mistake to suppose that if I know that no one in the room is in pain, then I must know that I am not in pain. If all the others are laughing merrily, and I am not in pain, then I *am* in a position to say that I know that no one in the room is in pain. It does not follow that I know that I am not, for that is nonsense (but, of course, I am not ignorant of whether I am in pain either). To be sure, I can know that *I will be in pain* or remember that *I was in pain*, i.e. these sentences make sense. But the past and future tense transforms are not *used* as the present tense sentence is. The possibility (intelligibility) of prediction and recollection is interwoven with the intelligibility of certainty, doubt, mistake, evidence, and correction. The legitimacy of 'I know that I was in pain' does not show that one can affix 'I know that' to 'I am in pain' to yield a sentence that can be used to make a cognitive claim. The uses and the *consequences* of using the past and future tense transforms are totally different from the use of 'I am in pain' and the consequences that flow from its use. They are, one might say, altogether different kinds of *behaviour* (compare 'Oh God, I'm so thirsty!', its use and our responses to it, with 'Oh God, was I thirsty!).

Nevertheless, far from being dogmatic, Wittgenstein does point out that these contentious sentences 'I know that I . . .' do have, or might have, legitimate uses. But these do not involve making cognitive claims. 'I know I'm in pain' may be used as an emphatic way of saying 'I really am in pain', or it may occur as an exasperated concessive utterance, parallel to 'Yes, of course I am in pain'. 'I know what I want', I may exclaim angrily; but that is not a cognitive claim, it is a demand that you stop plaguing me with your advice. Again, I might say 'I know what I want, but I won't tell you'. This too is not a claim to special *knowledge*, but a report that I have made up my mind (or that I *do* want something) although I am going to keep it to myself. Even the metaphysician's favoured forms 'Only I can know what I shall do', 'Only I know my thoughts', etc. have *a* use, but not that envisaged by philosophers. One might use such sentences to make grammatical points, to characterize certain language-games. It is a grammatical feature of thinking that others have to guess my thoughts if I don't express them, that often they cannot guess them, and also that I *can* express them if I want to (*RPP* I, §565). One might use 'Only I know my thoughts' in certain contexts to allude to these features. But note too that one might also use 'Only I know what I am thinking of' in a game of charades; here it would be a chortle of triumph: 'You can't guess what I have in mind'.

It was remarked at the beginning of this chapter that Wittgenstein's discussion of first-person psychological utterances can be seen as, *inter alia*, a thrust against foundational epistemologies. That the whole Cartesian and empiricist picture of the structure of knowledge is totally misconceived is scintillatingly argued in *On Certainty*. The anatomization of error goes much deeper there than the point which follows from the non-cognitive account of first-person psychological utterances. But it is only with the latter that I am concerned here. The suggestion that our knowledge of the world around us rests upon, is inferred from, or is justified by reference to, our knowledge of how things subjectively seem to us to be is a cardinal thesis of modern philosophy from Descartes to Russell or Ayer and beyond. 'I seem to see ...', 'It sensibly appears to me just as if ...', 'I have a visual experience of ...' are commonly conceived to function as *descriptions* of perceptual experience, as propositions expressing something the speaker *knows*, and, in the hands of the foundationalist, as grounds or evidence justifying or presumptively implying any cognitive claim I might make about objects. This, it should now be evident, is wholly misguided. These utterances are not descriptions of anything, nor are they expressions of something known, let alone of something known with metaphysical certitude. They are not grounds for making perceptual statements of the form 'I see ...', let alone for judgements about what is seen.

These claims might be established simply by bringing the general considerations of this chapter to bear upon these sentences and their uses. Instead of following this route I shall examine a different one, which Wittgenstein traced in *Zettel*. It makes no sense, he argued, to begin to teach someone colour concepts by teaching him when to say 'That looks red'. For that must be said *spontaneously* when he has learnt what 'red' means (Z, §418). Learning what 'red' means is learning, e.g., to call out 'red' on seeing something red, to bring a red thing on demand, to arrange objects according to a colour, and also to explain 'red' by reference to an appropriate sample and to justify one's application of 'red' (if asked) by pointing at the sample. Only when the technique of using the word has been thus mastered can the distinction between being red and appearing red be taught, not because it is a subtle distinction, like that between scarlet and crimson, but because the concept of *seeming* thus-and-so is parasitic upon the concept of *being* thus-and-so. The red visual impression, Wittgenstein emphasized, is a *new concept* (Z, §423). In the language-game with colours, i.e. in discourse about 'the objective', a person does not occur as perceiving subject. Introducing 'It looks to me . . .', 'It looks to you . . .' gives language a *new joint* (but that does not mean that it is now always used! (Z, §425)). This new articulation makes possible a distinction between describing objects and describing observations ('It looked red to him'). To be sure, the description of 'what is subjectively seen' is akin to the description of an object, as marrying money is akin to marrying a spouse, but just for that reason it does *not* function as a description of an object (Z, §435). Moreover the first-person case is unlike the third-person one. 'It looks red to me' is not a description of an observation, but an expression of how it strikes me. I do not tell you how it strikes me by an inward glance at a sense-impression (Z, §426) but by reflection on the 'outward' scrutiny of the object. But it would be absurd to suppose that 'knowing' how things strike me perceptually is the epistemological or metaphysical rock upon which empirical knowledge is erected. For 'It looks thus-and-so to me' is not an expression of something I *know* (nor of something of which I am ignorant), any more than 'It is, as far as I can see, thus-and-so'. Expressions of how things strike me as being do not provide me with *evidence* for whether I see them to be thus-and-so, let alone for whether they are thus-and-so. The *actual* function in discourse of utterances of the form 'It looks . . . to me' is as far removed from laying solid foundations for knowledge as the schoolboy's utterance 'As far as I can make out it's 7256' is from laying the foundations of arithmetic.

The 'drop of grammar' Wittgenstein condensed is immensely concentrated. For many philosophers it is hard to swallow and impossible to digest. But taken at the right time and in correct dosage its impact upon one's vision is dramatic. One's metaphysically induced astigmatism is cured and one can see the conceptual landscape aright for the first time.

XI

CRITERIA, REALISM AND ANTI-REALISM

1. *The Origins of the Idea*

In Chapter V it was noted that in the *Philosophical Remarks*, during Wittgenstein's brief verificationist phase, he distinguished between 'genuine propositions' and 'hypotheses'. Genuine propositions, he argued, are sense-datum statements that are immediately and conclusively verified by reference to current experiences, compared directly with reality for their truth. Hypotheses (e.g. statements about material objects, the past or future, laws of nature) are not propositions in this sense, but quite different kinds of grammatical structures. They are not conclusively verifiable at all, not compared directly with reality for their truth. They are supported by evidence, viz. 'symptoms', although no accumulation of such evidential support will render a hypothesis certain. So it makes no sense to talk of a hypothesis as certain. Symptoms stand to the hypothesis they support as points on a curve to a curve. The symptoms/hypothesis relation is grammatical not empirical (inductive). For that certain symptoms probabilify a hypothesis partially determines the meaning of the hypothesis. Since any set of symptoms falls short of entailing the hypothesis, the evidential support it gives is defeasible. For addition of further genuine propositions to the set of symptoms for a given hypothesis may undermine the plausibility of the hypothesis.

We saw that Wittgenstein rapidly abandoned this conception. He came to think that what he had conceived of as 'genuine propositions' are *not* compared with reality for truth and falsehood. There is no *verification* of 'I have toothache' or 'A looks red to me', and the role of such expressions is not to *describe* how things are. Such 'propositions', far from being known with certainty, cannot be said to be *known* at all. Similarly, propositions such as 'This poppy is red', 'The book is on the table' cannot be said to be hypotheses if that means that they are at best merely probable or that they cannot be conclusively verified. It only makes sense to talk of something's being probable where it also makes sense for it to be certain.

As the symptom/hypothesis relation disappears from Wittgenstein's writings in 1932/33 we find the first occurrences of the term 'criterion'. It crops up initially in contexts in which emphasis is being given to verification. A statement gets its sense, Wittgenstein argued at this stage, from its verification (*AWL*, p. 17). The question 'What is the verification of *p*?' is another way of asking 'How do you know that *p*?' or 'What are the grounds for *p*?'. This bears on the meaning of a proposition, for it shows the relation of the proposition to other propositions. The sense of a proposition such as 'Moore has toothache' is given by the *criteria* for its truth. Criteria, as the term is employed in the 1932/33 lectures, are verifying grounds for a proposition. That a certain proposition is a criterion for another proposition is a matter of convention. It is laid down in grammar, for it is a rule of grammar, not an empirical discovery, that *p* is a criterion for *q*. In fixing such a rule, one partially fixes the meaning of '*q*'. Does specification of the criteria for '*q*' give the meaning of '*q*'?. No, Wittgenstein argued, for while 'I remember that it rained yesterday' is a criterion for its having rained yesterday, 'It rained yesterday' obviously does not mean 'I remember that it rained yesterday' (*AWL*, p. 28). Similarly, although A's clutching his swollen jaw and groaning are criteria for A's having toothache, 'A has toothache' does not mean 'A clutches his jaw and groans'. Rather, specifying the verifying criteria does not *give* the meaning of the proposition but *determines* the meaning, i.e. the use or grammar, of the proposition in question (*AWL*, pp. 28 f.).

In the *Blue Book* dictations of the next academic year (1933/4), Wittgenstein took further steps to clarify his ideas on this logical relationship. Here he contrasted criteria with symptoms (*BB*, pp. 24 f.). In a complete shift of terminology, he now introduced the term 'symptom' to signify empirical evidence. A certain phenomenon, e.g. an inflamed throat, is a symptom of a certain state of affairs, e.g. having angina, if it has been discovered in experience, by inductive correlation, that the phenomenon is correlated with the state of affairs, e.g. that people with inflamed throats have angina. Accordingly, this evidential relationship presupposes independent identification of the relata. A criterion, however, defines or partially defines that for which it is a criterion. The defining criterion of angina is presence of a certain bacillus in the blood—that is what is *called* 'having angina'.

Hence, as before, criteria are determined or fixed by grammatical conventions (*BB*, p. 24). To explain our criterion for someone's having toothache is to give a grammatical explanation about the word 'toothache', i.e. an explanation of what we call 'having toothache'.

Wittgenstein's brief explanation is not altogether clear. On the one hand, in the angina example, he claimed that 'A man has angina if this bacillus is found in him' is a tautology or a loose way of stating the definition of angina. On the other hand, he did not say that 'A man has toothache if he clutches his swollen cheek' is a tautology or a loose way of stating the definition of toothache. In the latter case, presumably, to specify the criteria is not to *give* the meaning of 'toothache', but rather specification of the criteria *determines* the meaning or use of 'A has toothache', in the sense that explaining the criteria for A's having toothache is an explanation of the grounds justifying one in saying 'A has toothache'. What would perhaps be a tautology (in a loose sense) would be the grammatical proposition 'A's clutching his swollen cheek and groaning is a criterion for A's having toothache'.

In the *Blue Book*[1] Wittgenstein emphasized a further point which surfaces again in his later writings, namely that criteria and symptoms fluctuate, especially in science. Doctors use names of diseases without ever deciding which phenomena are to be taken as criteria and which as symptoms (*BB*, p. 25, cf. *PI* §354; *Z*, §438). This need not signify deplorable laxity, for if certain phenomena are always or almost always found to coincide there is no reason to segregate criteria from symptoms in a definitive manner.

In the subsequent writings the expression 'criterion' occurs quite frequently in a wide range of contexts. It is prominent in discussions of psychological expressions. The criteria for being in pain, for meaning or intending, for understanding or misunderstanding, for thinking, believing, remembering, for having a mental image or visual experience are extensively discussed. It is noteworthy that the notion of a criterion is put to work in discussion of powers and abilities, not only inanimate, e.g. whether X fits into Y, but also animate, e.g. whether A can lift a weight, and 'intellectual' abilities, e.g. the criteria for being able to read, multiply, understand. It is, however, important not to overlook other contexts. Wittgenstein talked also of the criteria for the truth of general statements, emphasizing the differences in the criteria for propositions like 'All the points on the square have been painted

---

[1] The point is already made in *MS* 115, pp. 73 f. in 1931.

white', 'All the men in the room have flannel trousers', 'All cardinal numbers are so and so', 'All the colours of the rainbow are from here to here' (*LFM*, p. 270). These are verified in entirely different ways, which is to say that their grammar is different. Similarly, in his mathematical writings he wrote of a proof's defining a new criterion for nothing's having been lost or added, i.e. that a proof defines 'correctly counting together'. The result of an arithmetical operation (e.g. adding 4 to 1) is defined to be the criterion of carrying out this operation. A geometrical proof gives a new meaning to, e.g., 'can be put together', by laying down a new criterion which determines what is to be called 'putting such and such shapes together'. A proof is said to be a criterion for mathematical truth. The number of sides of a plane figure is a criterion for its being a triangle (or rectangle, pentagon, etc.). The criteria for equinumerosity of finite sets is different from the criteria of equinumerosity of infinite sets, hence 'equinumerosity' has a different *meaning* in the two kinds of case.

The diversity of items which are characterized as criteria and as having criteria is great. The relationships between them seem varied and resistant to regimentation. Many of the things which philosophers have said about Wittgenstein's conception of a criterion depend upon selecting a narrow range of his remarks and disregarding others. How much order, and what kind of order, can be discerned in this motley?

2. *Plotting the Contour-lines*

It is evident that Wittgenstein conceived of criteria as being determined by convention, not discovered in experience by inductive correlation. We fix criteria by laying down grammatical rules. Hence the proposition that *p* is a criterion for *q* is a grammatical truth or grammatical proposition which expresses a rule for the use of words. This is the point of contrasting symptoms with criteria. We discover the symptoms of *X* in experience, and such discoveries presuppose an understanding of '*X*' and the possibility of its non-inductive identification. But a criterion for *X* partly determines the meaning of '*X*'. That *p* is a criterion of *q* (where '*q*' is, for example, the proposition that A is in pain, understands something, or is able to φ) is manifest, *inter alia*, in the ways in which we teach someone the use of an expression. We teach someone that, in certain circumstances, when *p* is the case, then it is correct to assert that *q*. Pain-behaviour, in appropriate circumstances, is a criterion for being in pain. If someone cuts, burns, or otherwise injures himself, and screams, assuages his limb, groans, etc. then we say 'He is in pain', 'He has hurt himself'. Of course, 'being in pain' does not *mean* 'behaving in such-and-such a way'. But that such-and-such behaviour justifies one, in these circumstances, in saying that a person is in pain is a feature of the grammar of 'A is in pain'. It determines its correct use and in this sense is a contribution to an explanation of its meaning.

Wittgenstein frequently talked of criteria as *defining* criteria. The presence of a certain bacillus *defines* what it is to have angina (*BB*, p. 24). The criterion for carrying out a certain mathematical operation (e.g. adding two integers) defines what it is to perform that operation by reference to the result of the operation (*RFM*, p. 319). In science we typically make phenomena that allow of exact measurement into the defining criteria for an expression (*Z*, §438).[2] The criteria of identity that we fix for experiences or for shared understanding or for seeing the same *define* what is to be *called* 'having the same pain', 'understanding in the same way', 'seeing the same colour'.

If the criteria for *p*, in this sense, define or partially define what is to be called ... then a change of criteria must involve a change in meaning. And this is precisely what Wittgenstein claims. Mathematical proofs, he notoriously insisted, are concept-forming. They involve laying down new conceptual connections between number concepts. As a result of a proof we have new criteria for sameness of number of quantifiable objects or magnitudes in empirical transactions, new criteria for *this* being the same area as *that*, new criteria and hence new *meaning* for 'these shapes can be put together' (*LFM*, p. 54). Psychoanalysts present conceptual innovations, viz. talk of unconscious thoughts, desires, or motives, in the guise of new discoveries. They are inclined to think that they have found out that contrary to what was hitherto believed, we can have thoughts, desires, and motives that are just like conscious ones, only unconscious. In fact they are introducing new criteria for thinking, wanting, and having motives, hence new *concepts* (*BB*, pp. 22 f., 57 f., 118). A concept is determined by the rules for its use, and a change of rules implies a change in the concept thus determined.[3]

It is an important feature of Wittgenstein's use of 'criteria' that there

---

[2] Wittgenstein sapiently warns that this can lead one into the illusion that the *proper* meaning has been *found*. Much of the contemporary debate about natural kinds manifests precisely this illusion.

[3] But, of course, to the extent that criteria and symptoms fluctuate, the question as to sameness and difference of meaning will be blurred—as blurred as the meaning of the expression in question.

are often *multiple* criteria for a given state of affairs (for the application of a given concept). There are multiple criteria for expecting someone to tea, manifest in many different things one does and says which justify saying '*A* expects *B* to tea' (*BB*, p. 20). In different circumstances we apply different criteria for a person's reading (*PI*, §164). Criteria of understanding are various, for a person manifests his understanding of an expression in the manner in which he applies it (which itself is varied and circumstance dependent), in the manner in which he responds to its use by others, and also in the ways in which he explains it. The criteria for whether someone is convinced of a proposition incorporate both how he says it (viz. the characteristic avowals of conviction, the tone of conviction) *and* what he *does* (*LFM*, p. 205). The criteria for 'fitting', 'being able to', 'understanding' are 'much more complicated than might appear at first sight' (*PI*, §182), both because of their multiplicity and because of their circumstance-dependence (*infra*).

In giving the criteria for p one may be justifying one's claim that p, explaining how one knows that p, giving reasons or grounds for p's being the case or for p's being true. Are criteria correctly called 'evidence'? Wittgenstein sometimes used this expression (*BB*, p. 51; *Z*, §439; *PI*, p. 228). It is, however, potentially misleading, for the concept of evidence is firmly embedded in what one might call 'our language-games with empirical evidence', i.e. with the relationship between 'symptoms' and that for which they are symptoms. If p is evidence for q, then it at least makes sense to identify q independently of p or *any other evidence* for it. (Breadcrumbs, as Austin pointed out, are evidence for bread, but a loaf of bread on the table is not.) Hence too, it makes sense to have evidence for q, no countervailing evidence, yet to wonder or doubt whether q is the case, for the evidence may be slender. In judging that q on the basis of p one is typically inferring from the observed to be unobserved. This web of connections does not obtain in the case of criteria. If someone falls, breaks his leg, and lies on the ground groaning, it would be misleading to claim that this is good evidence for his being in pain. That suggests the possibility of better evidence to clinch matters, the intelligibility of doubt, the conceivability of coming to know that he is in pain in some other way than by reference to what he says and does. This drags in its wake all the misconceptions of the inner/outer conception of the mind which we examined in Chapter X, for it encourages the thought that observers have only 'indirect access' to a person's pain (thoughts, beliefs, intentions, etc.)

whereas he himself has 'direct access'. Similarly, our criteria for saying that A has the ability to ϕ consist in features of A and his actions. To say that the latter are evidence for A's being able to ϕ encourages the idea that his actual ability is something transcendent, perhaps an unobservable structure (e.g. in A's brain) which determines his performances. But this is a confused picture of an ability.

One kind of reaction to these points is to insist that criteria are indeed not evidence at all. There are no *inferences* (either conscious or unconscious) from the satisfaction of criteria to that for which they are criteria, rather the transitions from criteria to that for which they are criteria do not take place within 'the logical space of reasons' at all.[4] It is tempting to suggest that when we perceive that the criteria for A's being in pain are satisfied, we do directly observe the circumstance that A is in pain and not merely something from which it may be inferred. By parity of reasoning, when the criteria for an ability are satisfied, then it is the ability itself that is evident to an observer. To perceive the criteria for someone's having toothache, understanding something, or for being able to do something is *not* for 'the reach of one's experience [to] fall short of that circumstance itself',[5] rather one experiences the very circumstance. The fact that A has toothache, understands, or can ϕ manifests itself to experience.[6] This is partly right and partly wrong. In so far as it constitutes a warning against the inner/outer picture or transcendent/evident one, it is apt. Similarly, it correctly cautions against assimilating criteria to evidence construed on the model of empirical evidence. Nevertheless it is misleading. For A's behaviour is not A's toothache and his performances are not his ability. In observing what A says and does one observes *that A* has toothache, understands, can ϕ, but one does not see or hear his toothache, his understanding, or his ability. There is no such thing as seeing his toothache, unlike seeing his tooth (and hence also, properly speaking, no such thing as *not* seeing it). To see *that A* has toothache is not to see the fact that he has toothache, though it could be said to be a matter of *registering* the fact that he has toothache. A's behaviour is an expression (*Äusserung*) of his pain, his actions are manifestations of his ability, but this is misleadingly phrased as expressions or manifestations of the *circumstance* that he has toothache or of *the fact* that he can calculate. To say that pain-behaviour or acts of ϕing are criteria for pain or for the ability to

---

[4] The suggestion is J. McDowell's, in 'Criteria, Defeasibility and Knowledge', *Proceedings of the British Academy*, lxviii (1982), 477 f.
[5] Ibid., p. 457.   [6] Ibid., p. 474.

φ is not to say that one performs, consciously or unconsciously, an act of inference in judging A to have toothache or to be able to φ. That involves a misconceived idea of inference as a mental act. It is rather to say that one's ground or reasons for so judging are that A behaves thus and so; i.e. if challenged 'How do you know?' or 'Why do you say that?', we would reply 'I saw him writhing on the ground', 'One could hear his screams in the next room', or 'I saw him hit the bull's-eye three times in succession'. It is true that there is no 'gap' between what is observed (pain-behaviour) and what is judged (that A is in pain); it does not follow that what is observed is what is judged, *if* that means that one observes A's pain *as opposed to* observing *that A* is in pain. (Note the equivocation on 'what'!)

In an attempt to emphasize that criteria for p are grounds or reasons for asserting that p, while distancing the notion of a criterion from that of empirical evidence, it has been said that criteria are 'logically necessarily good evidence'[7] or 'non-inductive evidence'. This correctly stresses the fact that criteria are logical, not empirical, fixed by grammar or convention, not discovered in experience. It brings out the fact that criteria are grounds for judgement, answers to the question 'How do you know?' and hence connected, broadly speaking, with verification (though not with 'verificationism'). It is also a way of highlighting the fact that the criteria for p, just like evidence for p, do not entail that p. Nevertheless, the inevitable associations of the term 'evidence', in particular the implication of a 'gap' between evidence and what it is evidence for, have contributed to confusion. For it has suggested that in observing that the criteria for p are satisfied one falls short of observing that p is the case, or that in inferring from the criteria for p to p (e.g. in justifying one's assertion that p by reference to the criteria for the truth of p) one is inferring from the observed to the unobserved, from what is present to view to what is hidden. But even in the case of psychological predicates and attributions of abilities, what is thus justified is not hidden or transcendent. On the contrary, A manifests his anger in appropriate circumstances in his tones of rage and fuming demeanour, and he manifests his ability to φ in φing, shows that he can φ by φing. A's anger (not the 'fact' or 'circumstance' that he is angry) is expressed in his angry behaviour (not hidden behind it) as his amusement is manifest in his chuckle and the twinkle

---

[7] Cf. S. Shoemaker, *Self-knowledge and Self-identity* (Cornell University Press, Ithaca, 1963), p. 4; A. J. P. Kenny, 'Criterion' in P. Edwards, ed., *Encyclopedia of Philosophy* (Macmillan, NY, 1967), Vol. 2, pp. 258–61.

in his eye, and his delight in his joyous exclamations. So too, the artist's skill is manifest in his paintings (and his activity of producing them), not hidden behind the canvas or something concealed from which his deft brush-strokes flow, just as the dancer's abilities are manifest in her pirouettes and graceful movements. Rather than saying that criteria for *p* are non-inductive or logically good evidence for *p*, it would perhaps be more correct (or at least less misleading) to say that a criterion for *p* is a grammatically (logically) determined ground or reason for the truth of *p*. It is a decisive ground?[8] Is it defeasible? Or can it be both?

Criteria for *q* verify that *q* is the case. If the criteria for *q* are *satisfied*, i.e. if *p* is the case *in these circumstances*, then it is certain that *q*. If someone touches a red-hot poker and screams, hugs his burned hand, etc., then it is certain that he has hurt himself. 'I can be as *certain* of someone else's sensations as of any fact' (*PI*, p. 224). We could perhaps imagine *different* circumstances in which this behaviour would be compatible with the person's not being in pain, but it does not follow that in these circumstances there could be any intelligible doubt. ' "But, if you are *certain*, isn't it that you are shutting your eyes in face of doubt?"—"They are shut." ' (ibid.)[9] Doubt, in such circumstances, would betoken a failure of understanding, lack of mastery of the concept of pain, not admirable caution. Wittgenstein equates the criteria for seeing with *proofs* that someone sees (*RPP* I, §506). Again, to say of someone who moves around the room confidently in daylight, obviously using his eyes, or of someone who reads a passage aloud from a book in certain circumstances, that it is only probable that they see would be unintelligible. Similarly with respect to abilities. If someone conducts a normal conversation with us in English, or plays a game of chess, there is no question but that he

---

[8] As argued by N. Malcolm, 'Wittgenstein's *Philosophical Investigations*', repr. in G. Pitcher, *Wittgenstein* (Doubleday, New York, 1966), pp. 83 ff. and J. Canfield, *Wittgenstein, Language and World* (University of Massachusetts Press, Amherst, 1981), who gives a painstaking survey of the notion of a criterion. Whether criteria are decisive grounds is commonly equated with the question of whether satisfaction of the criteria confers certainty.

[9] But note *RPP* I, §137: 'Am I really always in some uncertainty whether someone is really angry, sad, glad etc. etc.? No. Anymore than whether I have a notebook in front of me and a pen in my hand, or whether this book will fall if I let go of it, or whether I have made a miscalculation when I say 25 × 25 = 625. The following, however, is true: I can't give criteria which put the presence of the sensation beyond doubt; that is to say, there are no such criteria.' The sequel suggests that what Wittgenstein has in mind is that *in certain circumstances* one might have doubts (e.g. over sincerity, pretence) which no behaviour on the person's behalf will remove.

understands English and can play chess. If someone were to say that understanding or being able to play chess are inner processes, hidden from view behind their overt manifestations, we should contradict him. Understanding and abilities are not inner processes at all, although they are not behaviour either. We should remind the person 'of the *criteria* which would prove his capacity to us' (*RPP* I, §302).

This might suggest that if p is a criterion for q, then p entails q. But that would be wrong, at least if made as a *general* claim.[10] Someone may manifest pain-behaviour, yet be pretending. A lucky beginner might successfully φ, yet lack the ability to φ. Criteria are here *circumstance-dependent*, and it is this which gives a point to the claim that such criteria are *defeasible*. If p entails q, then if p is the case, q is the case come what may, independently of circumstances. But if p is a criterion for q, it is so only in certain circumstances. Weeping and wailing, in certain circumstances are criteria for being in pain, in other circumstances they are criteria for grief; change the circumstances again and they are criteria for acting pain or grief.

> Pain-behaviour and the behaviour of sorrow.—These can only be described along with their external occasions. (If a child's mother leaves it alone it may cry because it is sad; if it falls down, from pain.) Behaviour and kind of occasion belong together. (*Z*, §492)

Could one not eliminate this troublesome talk of criteria by conjoining the proposition p which is a criterion for q together with whatever propositions describe the circumstances in which p is satisfied *as* a criterion so that this conjunction will entail q? Wittgenstein thought not, for at least two reasons. First, in connection with psychological verbs, he wrote:

> One learns the word 'think', i.e. its use, under certain circumstances, which, however, one does not learn to describe.
> But I *can teach* a person the use of the word! For a description of those circumstances is not needed for that.
> I just teach him the word *under particular circumstances*.
> We learn to say it perhaps only of human beings; we learn to assert or deny it of them. The question 'Do fishes think?' does not exist among our applications of language, *it is not raised*. (What can be more natural than such a set-up, such a use of language?)

---

[10] In some of Wittgenstein's mathematical examples it is at any rate not *obvious* that what he calls a criterion falls short of entailment or at least, of necessary conditions. Similar considerations apply to the angina example.

'No one thought of *that* case'—we may say. Indeed, I cannot enumerate the conditions under which the word 'to think' is to be used—but if a circumstance makes the use doubtful, I can say so, and also *how* the situation is deviant from the usual ones. (Z, §§114 ff.)

Our mastery of psychological verbs is manifest in our using them, on the basis of their defining criteria in certain circumstances. It is further manifest in how we explain and teach the use of such words. But a correct explanation of what the expressions mean does *not* require a description of the circumstances in which they are to be used. Our explanations of the use of the verb 'to think' do *not*, as a result of failure to describe these circumstances, fall short of what it 'really' means. On the other hand, our explanations are incomplete (and our understanding defective) if we do not say (or cannot discriminate) in what circumstances the expression is *not* to be applied. 'He's not in pain, he's just acting the role' is an explanation (in appropriate circumstances) which is as much a contribution to the grammar of 'pain' as to that of 'acting'. 'He's not really thinking, but just pretending not to hear what we are saying' is a proposition which we may use to teach someone when to *withhold* the judgement that the putative *penseur* is cogitating. The meaning of 'to think' does not outstrip our explanations. On the contrary, it is giving these kinds of humdrum explanations that constitute a criterion for whether somone does understand what 'to think' means.

Secondly, there is no reason for thinking, and every reason for denying, that there *is* a definitely circumscribable list of circumstances such that if they obtain and the person behaves thus-and-so, then he *must* be thinking (in pain, amused or delighted) no matter what else is the case. (Of course, it doesn't follow that if in *these* circumstances, he behaves *thus*, it is anything other than certain that he is thinking, in pain, etc.) Equally, there is no reason for believing that there is a sharply circumscribable list of defeating conditions that could be enumerated, so that we could add the negation of those conditions to the first list to ensure an entailment. *Inter alia*, these defeating conditions are not themselves indefeasible! So to think is to be in the grip of a false picture of our concepts, of our understanding, and of our uses of language.

In this sense, the claim that the satisfaction of the criteria p confers certainty, proves, or is decisive for the truth of q is compatible with the claim that the criteria are defeasible. The assertion that q on the grounds that p is the case implies that the criteria p are not *defeated*, not that they are *indefeasible* and so amount to entailment. To say that the criteria for q are satisfied is not to say that despite having logically adequate grounds for q, nevertheless, for all one knows, q may *not* be the case.[11] On the contrary, it is to say that one *does* know that q, that relative to all one knows, q *is* the case. The claim that criteria are defeasible does not mean that there is any reason for holding that in *these* circumstances they are defeated. It is rather to deny that the criteria p for the truth of q entail that q, and further to point out that were the circumstances different in certain ways, then p would not give criterial support for q. But this circumstance-dependence does not mean that p does not render it certain that q in *these* circumstances. Screaming as one bangs one's knee in the kitchen is a criterion for having hurt oneself; but if all this were taking place on a proscenium stage before an audience, then (*ceteris paribus*), it would not be.

3. *Further Complications*

Although Wittgenstein employed the expression 'criterion' fairly frequently in his later writings, especially in connection with psychological verbs and verbs of powers and abilities, it is not a pivotal notion in a novel theory of meaning. For Wittgenstein was not involved in any enterprise that could rightly be called the construction of a theory of meaning. Moreover, he did not claim that all concepts have criteria, that the only form of explanation of meaning consists in elaborating criteria for the use of an expression, let alone that every legitimately employed sentence is uttered on the basis of criteria.

It is evident, as we have seen in previous chapters, that he denied that first-person psychological sentences are used on the basis of criteria. I can tell you where my pain is and what sort of pain it is (sharp and intermittent), but in so doing I employ no criteria. I may report my thoughts and feelings, avow my intentions, and give my reasons or motives, but it makes no sense to suppose that my word is so reliable because I have inner criteria, accessible only to me, on the basis of which I can say with confidence that I think this, desire that, intend to act thus, or am acting for such-and-such a reason.

It is equally obvious that Wittgenstein held ostensive definitions to be perfectly legitimate and typically adequate explanations of the meanings of words (which is not to say that they do not need stage-

---

[11] Cf. McDowell, op. cit., pp. 457 f.; when lawyers explain that the concept of a legally valid contract is defeasible they do *not* mean that one can never know for certain whether something is a valid contract.

setting). He frequently used, as examples, the ostensive explanations of colour-names by reference to paradigmatic samples. Such an ostensive explanation functions as a rule for the use of the word explained, but it does not give a *criterion* for its use. I say that this flower (that chair, this patch on the wall) is red. What criteria do I use? None. I look and see. I may justify my application of 'red' to this flower by pointing at a sample and saying 'This ↑ colour is red, and the flower *is* this ↑ colour'. But this is not, in the requisite sense, a *ground* for saying that the flower is red, but rather an explanation of what it is to be red (namely, to be this ↑ colour). I am not pointing out justifying grounds, but reiterating the rule for the use of 'red' and insisting that I am applying it correctly. I could just as well bluntly say 'I know what "red" means' (cf. *PI* §§380 f.). If this is correct (and correctly captures Wittgenstein's thought), then there are innumerable mundane judgements that are *not* asserted on the basis of, and are not justified by reference to, criterial grounds. 'The water is cold', 'The pudding is sweet', 'That was a loud noise', 'The cloth feels rough', 'There is a dank smell in here' give but a small sample of such propositions.

Wittgenstein certainly thought that the range of expressions that can legitimately be explained by ostensive definition and by explanations akin to ostensive definition (e.g. explanations of verbs by exemplification) was very wide, much wider than the range of traditional 'indefinables'. It is far from obvious that he would have claimed in all such cases that the applications of expressions thus explained rest on criteria. 'There are three books on the table' (i.e. this ↑ many—pointing at a triplet), 'A is thumping on the table' (i.e. doing *this*), 'I am sitting down', 'He went north' (i.e. in that ↑ direction) are arguably a tiny sample of a further vast range of propositions that are asserted with right, but without criterial justification. We explain what they mean and manifest understanding of them without citing criteria for their application.

Innumerable propositions are asserted without *grounds*; but, equally, many propositions are asserted on the basis of evidential grounds which are *not* defining grounds but symptoms. Vast ranges of scientific knowledge rest on inductive, not criterial, grounds. Such inductive evidence justifies empirical assertions of this kind, but does *not* define or determine the meaning of what it thus supports (e.g. that it will rain tomorrow, that in the last ice-age the glaciers reached as far as the Thames, that the planets move on elliptical orbits, that the laws of gasses, electro-magnetism, optics, or gravity are such-and-such). The bulk of our knowledge of history rests on testimony, written documents, archaeological remains, etc., and while these are not typically *inductive* evidence, they are not criteria either. We know, for example, that Brutus killed Caesar, but our grounds for claiming this are not grounds that determine the *meaning* of 'Brutus killed Caesar'. In both kinds of case indefinitely many propositions may justifiably be asserted, and we may claim to know them to be true, but not on criterial grounds. Their 'assertion conditions' in this sense do not determine their meaning. (We know perfectly well, for example, what 'Richard ordered the murder of the young Princes' *means*, but we do not have, and probably never will have, adequate grounds for denying or affirming it.[12])

We have noted that Wittgenstein thought that many concepts are defined neither ostensively nor by necessary and sufficient conditions, but rather by a range of examples plus a similarity rider. He called these 'family-resemblance concepts'. Here too it may be doubted whether he would have held that the judgement that such-and-such is a game (or a number, or a proposition) rests on criteria or is logically akin in respect of grounds for assertion to '*A* had toothache' or '*A* can read'. Although he talked of scientific concepts manifesting a fluctuation between symptoms and criteria, it is unclear what the scope of 'scientific concepts' is supposed to be. There has been some discussion among commentators about criteria for something's being a lemon, but there is no textual licence for thinking that he held such humdrum concepts as 'lemon', 'flower', 'tree', 'cat', 'dog' to be explained or taught by reference to criteria or to be applied on the basis of criteria. One may move either way, emphasizing the affinities between these and concepts which he clearly thought had criteria, or stressing the differences (which are considerable). But whichever way one moves, one is moving beyond Wittgenstein and evolving one's own concept of a criterion and of criterially defined expressions, not expounding his.

A different complication stems not from Wittgenstein's omission but from commission. In *Investigations* §354 he wrote:

The fluctuation in grammar between criteria and symptoms makes it look as if there were nothing at all but symptoms. We say, for example: 'Experience teaches that there is rain when the barometer falls, but it also teaches that there is rain when we have certain sensations of wet and cold, or such-and-such visual impressions.' In defence of this one says that these sense-impressions

[12] But it does not follow that it is neither true nor false! Of course, we can specify what would constitute adequate forensic evidence.

can deceive us. But here one fails to reflect that the fact that the false appearance is precisely one of rain is founded on a definition.

It is clear that Wittgenstein is not endorsing what 'we say'. But it is unclear what is meant to be a criterion for what, and also unclear what definition is the foundation of the false appearance's being of rain. Is Wittgenstein claiming that the assertion that it is raining rests on the criterion that it looks to me just as if it is raining? This seems incoherent, at least if the criteria for p determine (or are contributions to) the grammar of p. For the meaning of 'It is raining' is surely presupposed by 'It looks to me as if it is raining', and we explain what 'It is raining' means by pointing and saying 'That's rain'. Similarly, as he argued explicitly (Z, §§418 ff.), 'That looks red to me' is *not* a criterion for A's being red, but rather presupposes the explanation of 'red' by ostension. If anything, the definitional connection goes the other way, i.e. one learns spontaneously to say 'It looks red to me' or 'It looks to me as if it is raining' *after* one has learnt to say 'That's red' or 'It's raining' without any *grounds*. We say of *another* person 'It looks red to him' or 'It looks to him as if it is raining' when he responds appropriately to red objects (or inappropriately to white ones!) or to rain in his vicinity, and *also* when he avows that things strike him thus (whether or not they are so).

Visual appearances (thus understood) are *not* grammatical grounds for judgements about how things are, and utterances of the form 'It looks to me just as if . . .' or 'It looks . . . to me' do not have the role of citing grounds that justify the speaker's claiming to know that things are thus-and-so. To hold the contrary would commit one to two claims that surely run contrary to Wittgenstein's later thought. First, it would mean that statements about objects derive their meaning from (or are explained and justified by reference to) expressions of perceptual impressions. This would make 'the private' logically and epistemologically prior to the public, as well as totally misconstruing the actual role of 'It looks to me . . .'. Secondly, it would imply that the meaning of 'It looks F to me' must be explained independently of F, viz. by private ostensive definition. On the other hand, it could well be argued that the concept of 'having a visual impression of rain' is defined by reference to the concept of rain, and also that its raining and A's seeing it constitute criteria for ascribing the visual impression of rain to A. Hence too, A's utterance 'It's raining' or his avowal 'It looks to me as if it is raining' constitutes a criterion for saying that it looks thus to him (that he has 'visual impressions' of rain), irrespective of whether it is raining. In this sense one may agree 'that the fact that the false appearance is precisely one of rain is founded on a definition'. It also follows that the proposition 'When people have visual impressions of rain then typically (but not always) it is raining' is not something taught by experience, i.e. it is not an inductive correlation. The fact that 'these sense impressions can deceive us' does *not* show that it is. But it does not show that sense-impressions of rain are criteria for its raining either, any more than 'It looks red to me' is my justifying ground or criterion for saying 'It's red'.

It is not easy to see how §354 can be reconciled with Wittgenstein's denial that 'It looks red' is a ground for 'It is red', and his insistence in his later writings that looking thus-and-so presupposes and does not determine the concept of its being thus-and-so. §354 dates from 1931 (MS 115, p. 73). Its context is a defence of the claim that verification, i.e. an answer to the question 'How can one know?' is a contribution to the grammar of a proposition. 'What is a chair?' and 'What does a chair look like?' are not independent questions, he insisted. How does one know that it is raining? We see, feel, the rain. We explain the word 'rain' by reference to these experiences. They are criteria for its raining, since 'What is rain?' and 'What does rain look like?' are logically related questions. Whether a phenomenon is a symptom of rain is a matter of inductive correlation, but what is a criterion for rain is a matter of our determination or definition.

Certainly we say 'It's raining' when we see and feel rain, when it looks thus ↑ (pointing at the rain). But it is, I think, wrong to suggest that the *concept* of rain presupposes and is taught by reference to the *concept* of its looking as if it is raining or of its feeling as if it is raining. One may answer the question 'How do you know it's raining?' by saying 'I can see it'. But the concept of rain cannot be said to be *defined* by reference to the concept of seeing, or having sense-impressions of, rain. We teach someone to say 'It's raining' when it is raining and he sees or feels it (and can be said to have visual or tactile impressions of rain). But it is far from obvious that this justifies the claim that visio-tactile impressions of rain are criteria for (and determine the meaning of) rain.

4. *Red Herrings: realism and anti-realism*

In the discussion of criteria in the first edition of this book I suggested that Wittgenstein's conception of a criterion was the linchpin of a novel theory of meaning based not on the notion of a truth-condition but on that of assertion-conditions. Following suggestions made by M. A. E. Dummett,[13] I supposed the *Tractatus* to be expounding a 'realist' semantics and the *Investigations* and *Remarks on the Foundations of Mathematics* to be defending an 'anti-realist' semantics. The concept of a criterion, especially as employed in the discussion of psychological predicates, seemed to fit this picture. Indeed, it appeared to enrich and make more plausible the idea of an anti-realist theory of meaning precisely because it involved a logical relation which, unlike entailment, was defeasible. It seemed, among other things, to save this version of 'anti-realism' from the implausibilities of verificationist reductionism. These misbegotten seeds have sprouted many a weed over the past fifteen years. It should by now be evident that such a conception is misguided. It involves a serious misinterpretation of Wittgenstein's conception of a criterion. Moreover the suggestion that Wittgenstein was, in his later writings, propounding a form of anti-realism is even more fatal to understanding his thoughts than characterizing the *Tractatus* as 'realist' is to its interpretation. It distorts his conception of meaning and understanding, misinterprets his philosophy of mind, and grossly misrepresents his philosophy of mathematics. Of course, it does not follow that he was defending a form of 'realism' either. In order to see matters aright we must jettison this unfortunate pair of pigeon-holes altogether.

Anti-realism, as this term of art is currently employed, is associated with the following theses or principles. (1) It repudiates the idea that the meaning of a sentence is given by its truth-conditions independently of whether these lie within our 'recognitional capacities'. Instead, it suggests that the meaning of a sentence is given by the conditions (which we can recognize as obtaining) which justify asserting it. (2) It denies the intelligibility of 'verification-transcendent' truth as espoused by 'realism'. It holds that we can make no sense of attributing truth to a proposition which we cannot recognize to be true. The anti-realist conception of truth is firmly linked to such conditions as we have the capacity for recognizing as obtaining. (3) Accordingly anti-realism abandons the principle of bivalence, for there may be statements, empirical or mathematical, for which we lack the requisite recognitional capacities. ('*A* was brave' said of someone now dead who was never in a dangerous situation is held to exemplify one such statement, 'There are four consecutive 7s in the expansion of π' another.) (4) Anti-

[13] M. A. E. Dummett, *Truth and other Enigmas*, preface and essays, 1, 11, 21 (Duckworth, London, 1978).

realism is associated with, indeed is a generalization of, intuitionism in mathematics. The anti-realist, like the intuitionist, repudiates the notion of transcendent truth, and replaces it by verification or assertion-conditions, as the intuitionist replaces it by proof (or, it is held, by our capacity for the recognition of proof). (5) As befits its name, anti-realism is linked with various forms of denial of the objectivity of truth of various kinds of statement. Realism, it is argued, conceives of truth as determined 'objectively' by how things are in the world (or 'in mathematics') independently of our capacity to recognize whether they are thus or not. Anti-realism insists that, with respect to certain kinds of statement at least, there is no objective 'fact of the matter', independent of our recognition or capacity for recognition, that determines such objective truth, that there is nothing in reality 'in virtue of which' our statements are true independently of our capacity to recognize them to be so. (6) Finally, anti-realism is associated with reductionism in so far as bivalence for statements of the reduction-class is repudiated.

It may well be wondered how Wittgenstein's philosophy got drawn (by myself and others) into this maelstrom of philosophical theorizing of questionable intelligibility.[14] The only answer I can offer is: through anachronistic misreading, through selection of a handful of remarks taken out of context, through persistent misinterpretation, and through a disposition to try to squeeze Wittgenstein's thought into preprepared pigeon-holes that represent only our own misconceptions.

I argued in Chapter III that it was erroneous to identify the *Tractatus* as propounding realism in its account of meaning. It is true that it cleaved not merely to bivalence but even to bipolarity as definitive of propositions with sense. And it held that the meaning of a molecular proposition is given by its truth-conditions (i.e. 'The expression of agreement and disagreement with the truth-possibilities of elementary propositions expresses the truth-conditions of a proposition' (*TLP*, 4.431)). But this explanation *presupposes* the meanings of the constituent elementary propositions, and an elementary proposition can no more have truth-conditions than it can be a tautology or contradiction. If we switch, anachronistically, to the post-Tarskian conception of a truth-condition as given by a sentence of the form ' "p"

---

[14] A detailed analysis of the incoherences of anti-realism is a task for another occasion. The primary objective of the ensuing discussion is to demonstrate the inappropriateness of the realist/anti-realist dichotomy in characterizing Wittgenstein's philosophy.

is true if and only if *p*', it is equally evident that that is ruled out by the *Tractatus* as nonsense. It is altogether unclear whether the *Tractatus* held that the truth of propositions can or cannot be 'verification-transcendent', since it is silent on the matter. With respect to mathematical propositions, far from embracing realism, it showed some sympathy with constructivism and none at all with logicism or Platonism. In its metaphysics and epistemology it arguably adhered to a transcendental idealist (solipsist) view which cannot be said to be either ordinary realism or empirical idealism. Only in respect of the traditional opposition of realism and nominalism can the *Tractatus* be said to be clearly and unequivocally realist.

Did Wittgenstein change his views on these matters? He certainly abandoned his conception of the elementary proposition as independent, as a logical picture, as consisting of logically proper names whose meanings were simple objects, and as representing a state of affairs in virtue of isomorphism. But he did not alter his conception of tautology and contradiction, nor is there any suggestion that he had second thoughts about explaining the meaning of molecular propositions by reference to their truth-conditions (e.g. '$p \supset q$' by 'TTFT (p,q)')—given the meanings of '*p*' and '*q*'. Since he never thought that the meaning of an elementary proposition is given by its truth-conditions, he can hardly be described as abandoning that view in his later work.

Nevertheless, he said enough on the matter to make it clear that he would have considered truth-conditional theories of meaning of the kind currently propounded incoherent *ab initio*, not merely because he would have thought the very idea of a *theory* of meaning an aberration (which he would) nor merely because that conception rests on a misguided picture of a language as a calculus of meaning rules (which he definitively undermined). These two important points involve complex ramifications which I shall not discuss here;[15] fortunately, it is not necessary for present purposes. For Wittgenstein clearly thought that the front-runner in truth-conditional theories of meaning falls at the first fence. On contemporary accounts, the truth-conditions of a non-molecular *sentence* are supposed to be given by a so-called T-sentence ' "*p*" is true if and only if *p*'. In Wittgenstein's view, for reasons that are independent of the considerations prominent in the *Tractatus*, this is either nonsense or vacuous. He spelled this out strikingly (long before current intoxication with the heady brew of truth-theories) in the *Philosophical Grammar*:

[15] But see G. P. Baker and P. M. S. Hacker, *Wittgenstein: Understanding and Meaning*.

So is it correct to write ' "*p*" is true', ' "*p*" is false'; mustn't it be '*p* is true' (or false)? The ink mark is after all not *true*; in the way in which it's black and curved.

Does ' "*p*" is true' state anything about the sign '*p*' then? 'Yes, it says that "*p*" agrees with reality.' Instead of a sentence of our word language consider a drawing that can be compared with reality according to exact projection-rules. This surely must show as clearly as possible what ' "p" is true' states about the picture '*p*'. The proposition ' "*p*" is true' can thus be compared with the proposition 'this object is as long as this metre rule' and '*p*' to the proposition 'this object is one metre long'. But the comparison is incorrect, because 'this metre rule' is a description, whereas 'metre rule' is the determination of a concept. On the other hand in ' "*p*" is true' the ruler enters immediately into the proposition. '*p*' represents here simply the length and not the metre rule. For the representing drawing is also not 'true' except in accordance with a particular method of projection which makes the ruler a purely geometrical appendage of the measured line.

It can also be put thus: The proposition ' "*p*" is true' can only be understood if one understands the grammar of the sign '*p*' as a propositional sign; not if '*p*' is simply the name of the shape of a particular ink mark. In the end one can say that the quotation marks in the sentence ' "*p*" is true' are simply superfluous. (*PG*, pp. 123 f.)

Hence the desired metalinguistic ascent is either nonsense, or collapses into the trivial (though correct) observation that '*p* is true iff *p*', or more accurately, that 'It is true that *p* iff *p*'.

Further reasons can be given to support this verdict, and it is worth a brief digression[16] to clarify the fundamental incoherence. Even if we waive Wittgenstein's qualms about attributing truth to sentences (which we should not[17]), the canonical form ' "*p*" is true iff *p*' does not intelligibly specify *conditions* which the *sentence* '*p*' must meet in order to be true. Contrast this with the concept of a truth-condition for a molecular

---

[16] For further elaboration, see G. P. Baker and P. M. S. Hacker, *Language, Sense and Nonsense*, Ch. 5.

[17] Very briefly, truth and falsehood apply to what is asserted, said, or stated; but what one asserts, says, or states (as opposed to what one utters) is not a *sentence*. What is true or false is also what is believed or disbelieved, proved or refuted, well-supported or disconfirmed, but we do not believe (disbelieve, prove, refute, support, or disconfirm) sentences, only what is expressed by their use. What is true or false is what is certain or doubtful, convincing or implausible, credible or incredible, conjectured or discredited. But these are not properties of sentences at all, or not in the same sense (an incredible sentence might be one written in letters a mile high, a doubtful sentence would be one of questionable grammaticality). In a different but related (temporal) use of 'true', one may hope that one's wishes may come true and that one's worst fears will not. But one does not wish or fear sentences (or propositions for that matter). And so on through a vast web of concepts which do not include sentences. For more detail, loc. cit.

proposition in the *Tractatus*, according to which the proposition that $p \supset q$ is true on the condition that p is true and q is true, or that p is false and q is false, or that p is false and q is true. But snow's being white is not a *condition* which the *sentence* 'Snow is white' could intelligibly be required to satisfy, any more than the sentence could satisfy the condition that there is no life on Mars. This (atomic) sentence might (cumbersomely) be said to have grammaticality conditions, or legibility conditions, but not truth-conditions.

Something can be said to be a condition for something else only if it satisfies requirements of relevance, independent ascertainability,[18] and non-circularity. A condition for a will to be valid is that *it* be duly witnessed, not that something *else* irrelevant to the will be witnessed. A condition for A to obey B's order to ϕ is that A understand the order, but not that A ϕs—that is not a *condition* for obedience, it is obedience itself (given satisfaction of the conditions of obedience). The suggestion that ' "p" is true iff p' states a truth-condition for 'p' satisfies none of these requirements.

Incomprehension may lead one to compare ' "p" is true iff p' with 'McInroe will win if the court is hard'. This is foolish, since the latter but not the former satisfies the independent-ascertainability requirement, the non-circularity requirement and the relevance requirement (the court at Wimbledon, not at Timbuctoo, let alone at the Inns of Court, must be hard). It would be jejune to suggest that this account of the concept of a condition turns on mentioning (rather than using) the expression signifying what is said to be conditional, and to propose as a counter-example 'Reagan will ϕ on condition that Gorbachev ψs'. What is mentioned in the canonical formula is a *sentence*, since the misguided truth-conditional theorist insists that he is spelling out conditions for the truth *of a sentence*. But it is noteworthy that dropping the 'superfluous quotation marks', as Wittgenstein put it, to yield 'It is true that p iff p' will not produce a truth-*condition* for p either, since p's being the case is not a *condition* for the truth of (the proposition that) p.

The contemporary concept of a truth-condition is a philosophical and metaphysical misconception resulting from a distorted view of a pair of grammatical propositions: first, 'It is true that p' = 'p' and secondly, 'The proposition that p' = 'The proposition made true by the fact that p' (*PG*, p. 161). The latter triviality is *not* a statement of the relation between language and the world or an expression of the

---

[18] i.e. it must be possible to establish that the condition is satisfied independently of whether what it is a condition for occurs or obtains.

metaphysics of 'realism' according to which what is true is true 'in virtue of' objective facts-in-the-world. On the contrary, it points at the source of the confused thought that there is any such thing to be said *or denied*.[19]

Wittgenstein clearly denied the intelligibility of the canonical form of explanation of meaning favoured by truth-condition theorists. Does it follow that he embraced anti-realism or assertion-conditions semantics? Not at all. He did indeed hold that the question of how a proposition can be verified is one particular way of asking 'How do you mean?', and that the answer is a contribution to the grammar of the proposition (*PI*, §353). But that does not make him a verificationist, let alone an anti-realist. For while I verify that *this* is red by looking, that *this* is cold by touching it, that *this* is fragrant by smelling (and these remarks are contributions to the grammar of these propositions), the meaning of such sentences is not given by something called 'verification conditions', but by explanations of meaning involving ostensive definitions employing samples. Of avowals it makes *no sense* to ask 'How do you know?' (and that fact too makes a contribution to their grammar), but it does not follow that 'I have toothache', 'I intend to go to London', 'I dreamt of a white Christmas' are meaningless. Mathematical propositions are meaningful, and their meaning is given by their proof, but proof is *not* a kind of verification. Wittgenstein did argue that criteria or grounds of assertion of third-person psychological propositions are grammatical features of their use which determine (but do not give) their meanings. But as we have noted, it was not part of this argument that all propositions are asserted on the basis of criteria. In those cases where he explicitly denied any criterial grounds, he did *not* suggest that understanding 'consists' in a 'recognitional capacity'. On the contrary, he repudiated this suggestion as incoherent (*PI*, §§377 ff; MS 180(a), pp. 52 ff.).

The meaning of an expression, on Wittgenstein's view, is not given by specification of something called its 'truth-conditions', or by

---

[19] Undoubtedly part of the confusion stems from the incantation 'if a proposition is true then there is something in the world in virtue of which it is true'. This is the source of endless confusion, cf. B. Rundle, *Grammar in Philosophy* (Oxford University Press, Oxford, 1979), §§39–43 for illuminating clarification.

It might be argued that talking of truth-*conditions* is but a harmless *extension* of our ordinary concept of a condition. Whether that is so depends, of course, on what one does with it. That it is anything but harmless in the hands of philosophers constructing truth-conditional theories of meaning is argued in G. P. Baker and P. M. S. Hacker, *Language, Sense and Nonsense*, Chs. 5–6.

specifying 'its contribution to the truth-conditions of any sentence in which it may occur'.[20] Nor is the meaning of an expression given by specification of something called its 'assertion conditions'. It is given by explanations of meaning, and these do not belong to any *theory*. Rather are they grammatical rules, rules for the correct use of expressions. They are not rules of a meaning calculus tacitly known or yet to be discovered, but humdrum explanations by the use of which we teach and explain, justify and criticize, correct mistakes and clarify ambiguities in our uses of words. They are very varied: in some cases expressions are explained by citing criteria for their application, in others by giving a *Merkmal*-definition, in some cases an ostensive explanation may be given, in others a series of examples; for certain purposes a paraphrase will fulfil the role of an explanation, for others a contrastive paraphrase; in some instances an exemplification will be in order, in others a gesture.

All this, however, can only appear in the right light when one has attained a greater clarity about the concepts of understanding, meaning, and thinking. For it will then become clear what can lead us (and did lead me) to think that if anyone utters a sentence and *means* or *understands* it he is operating a calculus according to definite rules. (*PI*, §81)

Such clarity, alas, has not yet been attained by contemporaries embarked upon the quest for the Grail of a theory of meaning for a natural language.

Did Wittgenstein repudiate the intelligibility of verification transcendent truth? It is not easy to see what this means. If it means that there are many propositions which we understand but do not know to be true and never will, then surely only folly would lead one to deny that platitude. Indefinitely many propositions about the past, present, and future fall into that category, and there is no hint in any of Wittgenstein's post-1931 writings to suggest that he thought otherwise. Two issues can be separated. First, are there different 'concepts of truth' in Wittgenstein's writings? Secondly, what is the source of the idea of animus towards 'verification transcendence' that is attributed to Wittgenstein in his later writings?

Did the *Tractatus* propound a 'realist conception of truth' and the

---

[20] Among other flaws, this conception forces the benighted theorist of meaning into arguing that *every* sentence includes a truth-value bearing component, viz. a sentence-radical, which expresses a sense, and a force-indicating component. This too Wittgenstein held to be nonsense (cf. *PI* §§22 f.).

Investigations an 'anti-realist' one? It is doubtful whether the question makes sense. But it is certain that Wittgenstein's conception of truth, i.e. of what is meant by 'true' did not change. He never thought that 'true' is a theoretical term[21] or a metalinguistic predicate. In the *Tractatus* he invented a notation (the T/F notation) which eliminated negation, disjunction, conjunction, and implication altogether. Later he insisted, perfectly consistently, that the converse move is equally legitimate, viz. instead of 'p is true' we can restrict ourselves to 'p', and instead of 'p is false' to 'not-p', i.e. instead of *truth* and *falsity* we can use *proposition* and *negation* (*AWL*, p. 106). He did not envisage such absurdities as a 'theory of truth', nor would he have countenanced the bizarre idea that philosophical puzzles about truth, meaning, and explanation of meaning might be resolved by inventing a 'different concept of truth'. For if it is a different concept, it is not the concept that is the source of our philosophical unclarities about *truth*, and the latter cannot be unravelled by introducing a new concept. (If there is a knot in *this* piece of string, it won't be disentangled by being given a rubber band!)

The association of anti-realism with an animus towards verification-transcendent statements stems from generalizing the mathematical intuitionists' account of mathematical propositions. The intuitionists reject the realists' (Platonists') conception of mathematical propositions as being true or false independently of our possession of, 'our capacity for recognizing',[22] a proof for them. Proof is the sole means in mathematics for establishing a statement as true. Generalizing this notion, contemporary anti-realism opts for *verification* as the pivotal notion in the account of meaning, understanding, and truth. The condition for a statement's being verified, unlike the condition for its truth on the 'realist' conception, is one which we must be credited with the capacity for effectively recognizing when it obtains. But just as intuitionists reject the general validity of the Law of Excluded Middle for certain classes of mathematical statements, so the anti-realist

---

[21] It might be suggested that in the hands of meaning theorists it is. If one thinks that their activities make sense, that there could be such a thing as a *theory* of meaning, then that might be so. Their use of 'true' might stand to the ordinary one as Newton's use of 'force' stands to the ordinary one. But then they would not be engaged in philosophy, nor would they be clarifying what it is for a proposition or belief to be true, what the relation is between the truth of empirical propositions and the truth of mathematical ones. For our philosophical problems concern *our* concepts of truth, belief, thought, proposition, etc., not some other concepts belonging to a pseudo-science.

[22] It is by no means clear that this phrase means anything. An 'unsurveyable proof' is not a proof.

rejects it for certain classes (e.g. the reduction classes) of empirical propositions.

This idea finds no echo in Wittgenstein. As we noted in Chapter V, he had little sympathy with intuitionism, and his conception of the relation between a mathematical proposition and its proof differed radically from theirs. Goldbach's conjecture, or statements about Brouwer's pendulum number are mischaracterized as arithmetical propositions that transcend our powers of recognition. Indeed, any talk here of 'powers of recognition' is out of place since we are not dealing with an epistemological issue but a logical or grammatical one, and an improvement in our recognitional powers is irrelevant (see pp. 127 f.) It is misleading (not wrong) to conceive of a mathematical proof as establishing the *truth* of a mathematical proposition. Rather it is the proof which gives *meaning* to a mathematical proposition, it establishes it *as* a proposition of mathematics. A 'mathematical conjecture' is not a proposition of mathematics in search of a truth-value, but a sign in search of a use. It has *no sense*, for it is the proof that gives it its grammar. Mathematical propositions are rules of representation, and a proof establishes a proposition as a new rule (not a discovered truth or an 'invented' one) by incorporating it into the body of mathematical propositions. Far from generalizing the relationship of a mathematical proposition and its proof to an empirical proposition and its verification, Wittgenstein (as we have seen) emphasized their difference. 'Nothing is more fatal to philosophical understanding than the notion of proof and experience as two different but comparable methods of verification' (*PG*, p. 361). For a proof establishes *a grammatical rule* (i.e. a proposition of mathematics) which is then employed to distinguish what makes sense from what does not in empirical reasoning about magnitudes, shapes, numerical and spatial relations. But experience establishes a truth, namely that things are thus-and-so in the world.

It is also obvious that Wittgenstein's remarks on the Law of Excluded Middle have been distorted out of all recognition by the anti-realists' Procrustean efforts. A mathematical proposition that 'transcends our recognitional capacities' is not a mathematical proposition which is neither true nor false, but a nonsense (see p. 127). The utterance 'There are four consecutive 7s in the expansion of π' does not express a proposition.

If a logic is made up in which the law of excluded middle does not hold, there is no reason for calling the substituted expressions propositions. Brouwer has actually discovered something which it is misleading to call a proposition. He has not discovered a proposition, but something having the appearance of a proposition. (*AWL*, p. 140)

Applying the Law of Excluded Middle to so-called 'undecideable propositions' in mathematics gives us a *picture* ('Either there are four 7s or there are not, there is no third possibility') which is altogether misleading (*PI*, §352). But what this shows is not that there are propositions to which the Law of Excluded Middle does not apply, but rather that there are verbal constructions which look like propositions but which are not. To say of an infinite series that it does (or that it does not) contain a certain pattern makes sense only under quite specific conditions, namely when it is in the *rule* for the series (*RFM*, p. 269), as is the case with regular recurring series. The Law of Excluded Middle, expressed in the form '$p \vee \sim p$' is an empty tautology (given that 'p' makes sense!); the principle that $p \vee \sim p$ = Taut is a rule that partly defines what a proposition is. Far from repudiating this, Wittgenstein held that anyone who did so (save in the case of a few relatively trivial kinds of exception (see *RPP* I, §§269 ff.)) was confused to the point of not understanding what logic is.[23]

Anti-realism is argued to be committed to denying the objectivity of certain kinds of truth. The intuitive idea of objectivity is explained by reference to the distinction between being true and being judged to be true. Wittgenstein is held to have repudiated that distinction in two primary connected areas, viz. mathematical propositions and statements about rule-following. It would be a lengthy task to explain and justify the riposte that such attribution rests on misunderstanding. Here a few pointers must suffice. Wittgenstein did *not* deny the objectivity of mathematics *if that means* that he thought that '$2 \times 2 = 4$' means the same as 'Human beings believe that $2 \times 2 = 4$'. These propositions have *entirely* different uses, the former being a mathematical proposition and so the expression of a rule of representation, the latter being (if intelligible) an empirical proposition to the effect that human beings have *arrived* at the mathematical proposition (*PI*, p. 226). Far from denying the objectivity of mathematics, Wittgenstein was concerned to clarify what it means to insist upon it, for typically those who do so are deeply enmeshed in misleading *pictures* of objectivity:

---

[23] 'To say that the law of excluded middle does not hold for propositions about infinite classes is like saying "In this stratum of atmosphere Boyle's law does not hold"' (*AWL*, p. 140). That makes sense in *physics*, but not in logic or mathematics.

what a mathematician is inclined to say about the objectivity and reality of mathematical facts, is not a philosophy of mathematics, but something for philosophical *treatment*. (*PI*, §254)

This applies to the intuitionist no less than to the Platonist (or his heir, the realist). To be sure mathematical propositions can be said to be certain, indeed 'objectively' certain. The question to be clarified is: what does it mean to say that? Mathematical propositions are rules, and their certainty is established by proofs. For a proof puts the mathematical proposition 'in the archives', allocates it a role in our method of representation. The mathematical proposition is not a *description* of an objective domain of numbers, nor is it a *description* of a subjective domain of mental constructions. It gives the grammar of number-words. The proof confers certainty upon it, not by proving its *truth*, but by incorporating it—by a network of grammatical relations— into the body of mathematics. Once proven all doubt is *excluded* (not *refuted*)

The mathematical proposition has, as it were, officially been given the stamp of incontestability. I.e.: 'Dispute about other things; *this* is immovable—it is a hinge on which your dispute can turn.' (*OC*, §655)

Here, as everywhere else, Wittgenstein was not siding with one philosophical theory (anti-realism, intuitionism) as opposed to another (realism, Platonism), but diagnosing the intellectual diseases that inform both.

Equally misconceived is the suggestion that Wittgenstein's discussion of following a rule was intended to show that there is no objective fact of correctly following or incorrectly following the rule. It is argued that nothing stated in the relevant rule, nothing in a person's previous behaviour and nothing that goes on in his mind determines 'objectively' whether, in writing '1002, 1004' after '1000' he is following the rule '+2' which he was requested to follow. Only the assent of the community to which he belongs, only the fact that most people in such circumstances act thus, justifies us in saying that the rule '+2' was applied correctly.[24] And this is held to be a form of anti-realism or denial of objectivity 'realistically' conceived. But again, this altogether

---

[24] This is the interpretation Kripke gives of Wittgenstein's discussion (S. Kripke, 'Wittgenstein on Rules and Private Language'). The flaws in his account of Wittgenstein are exposed in G. P. Baker and P. M. S. Hacker, *Scepticism, Rules and Language*, Ch. 1, and the incoherence of the sceptical problem and the sceptical solution offered is laid bare in subsequent chapters.

misinterprets Wittgenstein's argument. The rule and nothing but the rule determines what it is correct to do at the 500th step (*PI*, §§189 f.). For the rule and what accords with it are internally, grammatically related, just as an expectation and what fulfils it, a desire and what satisfies it, a command and what complies with it. Doubts about internal relations betoken confusion, and attempts to cement such internal relations by subjectivist glue (viz. community assent constituting assertibility-conditions for '*A* has followed the rule') make no more sense than trying to glue one side of a coin to the other side of the same coin. Far from making out a case for a denial of objectivity and for denying that a rule determines what accords with it (as a proposition determines what makes it true, and an expectation what fulfils it), Wittgenstein was concerned to expose *misconceptions* of this internal relation which generate mythologies of symbolism (viz. of rules as 'logical machines' generating consequences independently of their use). It is ironic as well as sad that upon Wittgenstein's exposure of these misconceptions, anti-realists have erected fresh and yet greater houses of cards.

A final observation or two. It should barely be necessary to stress that Wittgenstein (after 1931) had as little sympathy with reductionism (concerning objects, others' mental states, the past) as he had with the attempts to reveal the *foundations* of arithmetic, knowledge, or morality. He denied the *intelligibility* (not the *truth*) of behaviourism, as of idealism or phenomenalism. Secondly, while he did, in his later work, deny the ineffable realism of the *Tractatus* (in the only legitimate sense in which it can be said to be realist) this was not to embrace nominalism, but (as always) to clarify what it means to say that, e.g. red *exists* (cf. *PI*, §§55 ff.). Finally, participants in the current disputes about realism and anti-realism make much of the claim that casting (or more accurately, miscasting) as many philosophical problems as possible in the framework of 'realism' and 'anti-realism' has far-reaching metaphysical implications. The achievement of this re-arrangement is held to be that it shows that the theory of meaning underlies metaphysics.[25] This contention alone should have sufficed to show that something is deeply awry with presenting Wittgenstein in this setting. For he thought that the very idea of a theory of meaning is an

---

[25] Dummett writes 'the whole point of my approach to these problems has been to show that the theory of meaning underlies metaphysics. If I have made any worthwhile contribution to philosophy, I think it must lie in having raised this issue in these terms' (*Truth and Other Enigmas*, preface p. xl).

absurdity, and adamantly denied that he was propounding one. Furthermore, he thought that metaphysics was *at best* disguised grammatical trivialities, and more commonly simply nonsense. Any suggestion that Wittgenstein's philosophical clarifications have metaphysical consequences is a sure sign that they have been misconstrued.

> Where does our investigation get its importance from, since it seems only to destroy everything interesting, that is, all that is great and important? (As it were all the buildings, leaving behind only bits of stone and rubble.) What we are destroying is nothing but houses of cards, and we are clearing up the ground of language on which they stand.
> The results of philosophy are the uncovering of one or another piece of plain nonsense and of bumps that the understanding has got by running its head up against the limits of language. These bumps make us see the value of the discovery. (*PI*, §§118 f.)

INDEX

ability, 173, 309, 312, 313, 314 ff.
agreement, 191 f., 251 f.
Allaire, E., 109 n.
Ambrose, A., 127 n., 152 n.
analogy, argument from, 262
analysis, *see* logical analysis
Anscombe, G. E. M., 67 n., 69 n., 86 n., 270 n., 282 n.
antipsychologism, 29, 80
anti-realism, 62 ff., 322 ff.
assertion-conditions, 62, 138, 320, 329
assertion-sign, 31 f.
association, 257, 261, 267
Augustine, 129
Augustine's picture of language, 129 ff., 175, 187, 247, 266
Äusserung (*see also* avowal) 289 f., 291 ff., 297 ff., 313
Austin, J. L., 206 n., 312
avowal, 280, 284, 297 ff., 328
Ayer, A. J., 253 n., 305

basic intuition (*Urintuition*), 122, 126
Begriffsschrift, *see* concept-script
belief, 83 ff., 119, 159, 169 f., 298
Bentham, J., 171
Berkeley, G., 50, 200
bipolarity, 32, 52, 56 f., 60, 65, 133, 139, 324
bivalence, 8, 32, 65, 323, 324
Black, M., 25, 26, 87
Boltzmann, L., 2, 4 f.
Boole, G., 46 n.
Bradley, F. H., 67, 68, 69
Braithwaite, R. B., 103 n.
Brouwer, L. E. J., 120 ff., 153, 331

Canfield, J., 315 n.
Cantor, G., 165
Carnap, R., 53, 54 f., 77 n., 124 n., 135, 136 f., 143 n., 150, 181, 185, 203, 216, 217, 246 n.
categories (categorial concepts), 33, 133 f., 149, 185, 205

central state materialism, 173, 246
certainty, 122, 133, 169, 195, 273, 308, 315, 317 f.
chess, 163, 188, 192, 198, 203, 213, 249
cogito, 91, 233, 282
colour, 21, 69, 70, 71, 114, 186, 187 ff., 197, 202 f., 238 f., 292 f., 305 f., 319
exclusion, 71 f., 108 ff., 196, 197
common sense, 226 f.
complex, 30, 38 n., 68, 115
concealing/revealing, 280, 285, 286 f., 314
concept-script, 6, 16, 22, 24, 29 f., 150
connecting language with reality, 73 ff., 129, 184, 185 ff.
constructivism, 62, 63, 120, 123, 124, 325
conventionalism, 50 ff., 194 f.
Copi, I., 67 n.
correct logical point of view, 22, 151 f.
correspondence theory of truth, 119
criteria, 306 ff.
Crusoe, Robinson, 252 f.

Darwin, C., 14 f., 160
death, 94 ff.
defeasibility, 307, 316 ff.
Descartes, R., 10, 50, 88, 91, 147, 200, 202, 206, 234 n., 246, 265 n., 279, 282, 292 n., 305
description, 114, 115, 129, 131, 280, 281, 287, 293, 297 ff.
theory of, 8, 10, 16, 30, 66
desire, 119, 296, 298
determinacy of sense, 58, 65, 113, 185
determinate/determinable, 71, 108 ff.
direct/indirect, 260, 280, 285 ff., 312 f.
doubt, 210 f., 271, 272 f., 282, 303, 315
Drury, M. O'C., 150 n.
Duhem, P. M. M., 2
Dummett, M. A. E., 63 n., 138 n., 176 n., 323, 334 n.

Einstein, A., 204
Eliot, T. S., 244

elucidation (*TLP*, 3.263), 75 f.
Engelmann, P., 104 n.
epistemic privacy, 254, 261, 272 f.
Erdmann, B., 50
essence, 21, 24, 174, 193 ff.
ethics, 89 f., 97, 98, 105 ff., 133
evidence, 209 f., 291, 292, 312 ff.
Excluded Middle, law of, 32, 46, 58, 63, 65, 122 f., 124, 125 n., 126 ff., 172, 330 ff.
expectation, 116, 117, 118, 119
experience, self-ascription of, 212, 279, 281
   primary, 219, 221, 224, 225
explanation of meaning, 78, 129, 140 f., 153, 180, 181 f., 183, 184 f., 186, 187, 247, 249, 309, 317, 318 f., 329

fact, 18, 19 f., 33 f., 56 f., 59, 60, 61, 69, 70, 83, 84 f., 115, 116, 118 f.
family resemblance, 52, 132 f., 150, 170, 174, 177, 184, 320
Feigl, H., 120, 217
Ficker, L. von, 105
first person pronoun, 82 n., 218 f., 223, 232 f., 235 ff., 241, 279, 281 ff.
first person psychological utterances, 278 ff., 291 ff., 318
first/third person asymmetry, 220, 246, 279, 302, 306
formal concept, 20, 21, 33, 39, 69, 106, 189, 205
formal property, 20, 39
formal relations, 37 n., 69
formal statement, 25, 26
formalism (in mathematics), 122 f.
foundationalism, 148, 164, 246, 257, 278, 305 f., 321 f.
Frege, G., 1, 4 n., 5 ff., 11, 17, 22, 28 ff., 56, 57, 58, 80, 129, 130, 131, 138 n., 150, 155, 164, 166, 174, 185, 194, 232 n., 246, 247, 254 n.
Freud, S., 154 n., 160

Galileo, G., 15, 147
Gardiner, P., 81 n.
Gasking, D. A. T., 135 n.
geometry, 193, 208
Gödel, K., 157
Goethe, J. W., 174, 250 n.
Goldbach's conjecture, 331
grammar, 129 n., 149, 152, 168 f., 176 ff., 228 f.
   alternative grammars, 189 f., 203 f., 222 f., 228 f.
   arbitrariness of, 188 ff., 192 f.
   autonomy of, 185 ff., 201
   justification of, 188 f., 229
   and metaphysics, 193 ff.
   rule of, 78, 116, 118 f., 125 n., 128, 179 ff., 186, 187, 188, 189, 195, 197, 198 f., 207 f., 275, 308, 329, 331
   surface, 168, 180, 205
grammatical form, 8, 10, 22, 29
grammatical proposition, 198, 204, 213, 220, 226, 304, 310
Grimm brothers, 75 n.

Hägerström, A., 171 n.
Hahn, H., 53, 143 n.
harmony between language and reality, 60, 116 f., 193 f.
harmony between thought and reality, 117, 119
Harris, R., 129 n.
Hertz, H., 2 ff., 13, 15, 17, 199
Hesse, M., 3 n.
Hilbert, D., 50, 165
Hobbes, T., 50
human nature, constancy of, 191 f.
Hume, D., 82 f., 206, 219, 233 n., 240 f., 283 n.
hypothesis, 64, 142, 145, 218, 222 f., 307

'I', *see* first person pronoun
I, the, 82, 86, 91, 93, 232
ideal language, 6, 10, 11, 16 f., 29 f., 129, 150, 162, 163, 167
idealism, 63, 104, 213, 216, 226 f., 229, 231, 235, 278
identity, numerical/qualitative, 238 f.
inference, 31, 32, 47 f., 134, 197, 208, 313 f.
innate knowledge of a language, 253 n., 260
Inner/Outer, 172, 245, 272, 278, 279, 280, 284 ff., 300, 312, 313
Inner sense, 122, 226, 240, 279, 283, 284
intention, 116 f., 277, 299
internal property, 19, 39, 66, 114
internal relation, 17, 47, 48, 59, 69, 71 n., 79 f., 118, 119, 203, 250, 269, 334
interpreting, 249, 250
intuitionism (in mathematics), 121 ff., 324, 330
inverted spectrum, 257 f., 263

Index

Ishiguro, H., 67 n., 76 n.
isomorphism, 58 ff., 116, 117, 140

Jackson, A. C., 135 n.
James, W., 167
Johnson, S., 227
Johnson, W. E., 76 n.
judgement,
  dual relation theory of, 83
  multiple relation theory of, 83 ff.
Juhos, B., 135

Kant, I., 10, 22 f., 50, 82, 87, 88, 96, 99, 100, 107, 122, 147 f., 168, 174, 176, 199, 206 ff., 231, 232, 233 ff., 265 n., 266 n., 271 n., 277, 278, 283 n., 302 ff.
Kenny, A. J. P., 61 n., 75 n., 76 n., 86 n., 149 n., 155 n., 160 n., 234 n., 282 n., 297 n., 314 n.
Kierkegaard, S., 146
King, J., 128, 135, 141
Kirchhoff, G. R., 4
knowledge, limits of, 232 f., 276 f.
knowledge of subjective experience, 212 f., 262, 272 ff., 276 ff.
Kraft, V., 135
Kraus, K., 4 n., 146
Kretzman, N., 255 n.
Kripke, S., 247 n., 333 n.

language, as a calculus, 128 f., 131, 132, 150, 325
  limits of, 23, 100 ff., 105 ff.
language-game, 132, 211
laws of thought, 5, 44 f., 49
Lee, D., 128, 135, 206
Leibniz, G., 150, 157
Lewis, C. I., 216 n.
Lewy, C., 102 n.
Lichtenberg, G. C., 18, 107 n., 146, 218
links in a chain, 67, 70, 71
Locke, J., 173, 200, 202, 246, 255 ff., 263, 270, 283
logic,
  as axiomatic science, 10, 42 ff., 48 f.
  laws of, 11, 42 ff., 122, 123, 124, 125 n., 126, 195
  proof in, 46, 49, 52
  propositions of, 10, 14, 18, 25, 34, 38 f., 41 f., 44 f., 46 f., 49, 50, 51, 52 f.
logical analysis, 8, 9, 10, 20, 24, 30, 58, 65, 109, 111, 130, 134, 152, 159, 162, 163, 179 f.
logical connectives, 35, 40 f., 109 f., 111, 171
logical constants, 10, 11, 34 ff., 37, 39, 40 n., 42
logical experience, 36 f., 39
logical form, 8, 9, 10, 13, 14, 36 f., 38, 39, 59, 60, 114, 163, 164
logical objects, 32, 34 ff., 37, 38, 39, 40
logical syntax, 18, 19, 20, 25, 33, 58, 60, 73, 179 ff., 184, 189
logicism, 5 f., 7, 8, 63, 133, 325
Loos, A., 4 n.
Łukasiewicz, J., 194
lying, 280, 300 f.

McDowell, J., 313 n., 318 n.
McGuinness, B., 99 n.
Mach, E., 2, 4, 217
Malcolm, N., 176 n., 239 n., 282 n., 283 n., 315 n.
Maslow, A., 146 n.
mathematics, 63, 121 ff., 133, 142 f., 153, 164 f., 192, 208, 332
  proof in, 128, 142 f., 310, 311, 328, 330, 331, 333
  propositions of, 63, 124, 127, 128, 133, 142 f., 169, 170, 207, 328, 331, 332 f.
Maxwell, J. C., 3, 4
meaning (see also picture theory of, truth-conditional theory of), 74, 129, 130 f., 132, 136 f., 138, 139, 140 f., 143 f., 159, 170 f., 181, 187, 247, 249, 308, 310, 311
Meinong, A., 83, 162
memory, 256, 257, 258, 267, 268 f., 270, 300 n.
metaphysics, 14, 22, 23, 24, 51, 52, 53 f., 116, 117 f., 148, 174, 193 ff., 238, 240, 334 f.
  descriptive, 204 ff.
  revisionary, 201 ff.
mind, Cartesian conception of, 278 ff., 289 ff.
mistake, 280, 300, 303
Moore, G. E., 66, 83, 98 n., 104, 135, 141, 144, 159, 164, 215, 225
mystical, the, 96 ff., 105

naive-realist, 226 f.
names, logically proper, 20, 33, 57, 60, 73, 74 n.

name-relation, 74, 228
naming, 73, 77, 114, 266 f.
negation, 40 f., 42, 53
of necessary propositions, 197 f., 275
Neurath, O., 53
Newton, I., 157, 199, 204
Nietzsche, F., 176
nonsense, 18 f., 25 ff., 185
no-ownership theory, 220 ff.

objects (in the *Tractatus*), 19 f., 21, 33, 39, 65 f., 69 ff., 113 ff.
objectivity, 252, 324, 332 ff.
observing, 280, 281, 284, 285, 287
Olivecrona, K., 171 n.
ontology, 7, 206 n.
ordinary language, 7, 10 f., 15 f., 17, 22, 29, 161 ff., 167
ostensive definition, 76 ff., 129, 181, 182, 184, 186, 252, 269, 288, 319, 328
private, 257, 261, 264 f., 267, 269, 272
ownership of experience, 87, 89, 102, 167, 217, 219, 220 ff., 238 ff., 272 ff.
private, 254, 261, 263, 272 ff.

pain, 218, 219, 220 ff., 227 f., 233, 236, 239 f., 254, 262 f., 264, 265, 266 f., 270 f., 272 ff., 276 ff., 286, 288, 291, 292, 293 ff., 303 f., 310, 313, 314, 316, 317
Pap, A., 53 n.
Passmore, J., 135 n.
Pears, D., 83 n., 87 n.
Peirce, C. S., 46 n.
pendulum number, 126 f.
personal identity, 232 ff., 236 f.
philosophy, 12 ff., 146 ff.
pictoriality of the proposition, 116 ff.
picture theory of meaning, 56 ff., 116 ff.
Pitcher, G., 120 n.
Plato, 107 n., 147, 148, 183, 194
Platonism, 50, 52, 53, 62, 63, 130, 168, 194, 325, 330
Poincaré, H., 2, 50
Post, E. L., 46 n.
practice, 250, 253, 269
pretending, 296, 317
private language, 212, 224, 225, 245 ff.
projecting grammar onto reality, 175, 187
property, 71, 114
proposition, 31 ff., 52, 57, 60, 112, 116, 118 f., 126, 127, 132 f., 136 f., 139 f., 141 ff., 169 f.

as abstract object, 29 n., 32
comparison of proposition with reality, 139, 140, 141, 145, 221, 293 n.
elementary, 30, 48, 51, 52 f., 58, 60, 61 f., 64, 71 f., 109 ff., 139, 324, 325
undecideable, 127, 332
propositional form, general, 51 f., 133
propositional representation, 58 ff.
propositional system (*Satzsystem*), 110 ff., 132, 133, 139, 141, 168
psycho-analysis, 154 f., 161, 311

Ramsey, F. P., 16 n., 25 n., 26, 102 n.
realism, 62 ff., 103, 137, 226, 229, 278, 322 ff.
recognition, 283, 284
recognitional capacity, 127, 323, 328, 331
relations, 67 ff.
report, 279, 284, 299
representation,
form of, 59, 67 n., 150, 151, 167, 187, 195, 200, 222 f., 228 f.
method of, 72, 113, 115, 149, 186
norm of, 149, 198, 199, 207, 213
res cogitans, 82, 103, 218, 233, 279, 282
Rhees, R., 165 n.
rules, 174, 177 f., 248 ff., 253, 329
accord with, 249 f., 334
following, 132, 249 f., 253, 271 f., 333 f.
hidden, 180, 183
of inference, 47, 48
use of, 180 f., 182, 183
Rundle, B., 328 n.
Russell, B., 1, 2, 4 n., 8 ff., 13, 14, 15, 16, 17, 19, 22, 25, 28 ff., 50, 58, 66, 67 n., 68, 69, 70, 76, 79, 83 ff., 110 n., 127, 129, 130, 131, 146, 150, 155, 156, 159, 162, 166, 173, 175, 216 f., 246, 305

samples, 72, 113 ff., 139 f., 167, 185, 186, 191, 197, 256, 266, 268, 291, 292 f., 305, 319, 328
private, 256, 263, 264 f., 267, 271, 291, 292
Satzsystem, *see* propositional system
saying/showing, 18 ff., 25, 106, 168
scepticism, 79, 148, 208 ff., 213 f., 220, 232, 262, 276, 277, 291
Schlick, M., 54, 136, 137, 141, 143, 144, 146, 217, 218, 223 f., 246 n.
Schopenhauer, A., 2, 4 n., 81, 82, 87 f.,

Index

89, 91, 92, 93 ff., 104, 107 n., 121, 124, 232
Schröder, E., 46 n.
scientific method, 13 f., 156 f., 159, 173
Scruton, R., 212
self, 84, 85, 86, 89, 279, 280 ff.
   Cartesian conception of, 82, 88, 89
   Humean conception of, 82, 86
   metaphysical, 2, 85, 86 f., 88, 89, 90, 92, 102, 103
   of solipsism, 81 ff., 102, 103
   transcendental, 89
self-consciousness (self-awareness), 212, 234, 240, 262, 273, 278 ff., 284 ff.
self-evidence, 10, 42 ff.
self-reference, 235 f., 281 ff.
sensations (*see also* pain), 166 f., 254, 257, 267, 268, 269, 270, 284, 292 f., 295
sense, bounds of, 91, 148, 152, 155, 213 f., 276, 277
sense/force distinction, 31 n., 131, 329 n.
senselessness, 18 f., 45 f., 47
Shoemaker, S., 235 n., 314 n.
sincerity/insincerity, 286, 287, 290, 298, 300
solipsism, 81 ff., 166, 167, 201, 215 ff., 263, 278, 291
   methodological, 216 n., 217, 218 ff., 229, 241
soul, 83, 84, 86, 89, 91
Spengler, O., 4 n., 120
Spinoza, B., 98
Sraffa, P., 4 n.
Stebbing, S., 103 n.
Strawson, P. F., 201 n., 204 f., 211 f., 223, 235 n.
symptom, 142, 145, 222, 225, 294, 307, 308 f., 310, 311 n., 312, 319, 320
synthetic a priori, 22, 148, 196, 207 f., 211

Tarski, A., 64, 324
tautology, 45 ff., 49, 50 f., 54, 55
technique, 250, 252, 253, 266, 269, 305

Thomson, J. J., 176 n.
thought (thinking), 74 f., 91, 105, 172, 205, 239, 273, 277, 286 f., 290, 299 f., 302, 316, 317
Tolstoy, L., 215 n.
transcendental arguments, 211 ff., 265 n.
transcendental idealism, 63, 87 n., 92, 95, 96, 99, 100, 186
transcendental solipsism, 99, 102, 103, 104, 219, 224
truth (falsehood), 32, 52 f., 59, 60, 126, 132, 136, 140, 207 n., 324, 326 ff., 329 f.
truth condition, 47, 48, 62, 64, 130 f., 138 n., 139, 324, 325, 326 ff.
truth conditional theory of meaning, 61 f., 64, 130 f., 137 f., 325

Übersicht, 151 ff., 157, 159, 160, 164, 206
understanding, 29, 74, 80, 116, 131, 132, 136, 139 ff., 247, 248 f., 250, 264, 266, 312
unity of apperception, 88, 99 f., 234 f.
use, 138, 152 f., 164, 168 f., 172, 187, 205, 248, 249

value, 89 f., 106 f.
verification, 64, 134 ff., 218, 221 ff., 225, 307, 308, 310, 314, 328, 331
verification-transcendent, 62, 64, 323, 324, 325, 329
Vienna Circle, 53 ff., 64, 134 ff., 208, 217, 218, 246

Waismann, F., 64, 77, 106, 120, 135, 136, 141, 144, 155, 177, 183, 215 n., 218, 230, 231, 237 n.
Weininger, O., 4 n.
Wiggins, D., 101
will, 89 f., 94, 97 f., 121, 124
Williams, B., 82 n.
Wright, G. H. von, 1

Zemach, E., 101 n.

www.ingramcontent.com/pod-product-compliance
Ingram Content Group UK Ltd.
Pitfield, Milton Keynes, MK11 3LW, UK
UKHW041915140426
5217IPUK00013B/158